Constructing the U.S. Rapprochement with China, 1961–1974
From "Red Menace" to "Tacit Ally"

With Nixon's historic reconciliation with China in 1972, Sino-American relations were restored, and China moved from being regarded as America's most implacable enemy to being a friend and tacit ally. Existing accounts of the rapprochement focus on the shifting balance of power between the United States, China, and the Soviet Union, but in this book Goh argues that they cannot adequately explain the timing and policy choices related to Washington's decisions for reconciliation with Beijing. Instead, she applies a more historically sensitive approach that privileges contending official American constructions of China's identity and character. This book demonstrates that ideas of reconciliation with China were already being propagated and debated within official circles in the United States during the 1960s. It traces the related policy discourse and imagery, examining their continuities and evolution into the early 1970s and the ways in which they facilitated Nixon's new policy. Furthermore, the book analyzes the implementation of the policy of rapprochement and demonstrates how the two sides constructed the basis for the new relationship based on friendly mutual images, shared interests, and common enemies. It reveals how, beginning in 1973, Nixon and Kissinger pursued the policy of supporting China as a "tacit ally" against the Soviet Union.

Evelyn Goh is Assistant Professor at the Institute of Defence and Strategic Studies, Nanyang Technological University, Singapore. She graduated with first-class honors in geography from Oxford University and also obtained an M.Phil. in environment and development from Cambridge University. In 2001, she completed a doctorate in international relations at Nuffield College, Oxford. Dr. Goh has been a Visiting Fellow at the East-West Center in Washington, D.C., where she received the 2004 Southeast Asian Fellowship. Her main research interests lie in the areas of U.S. foreign policy, U.S.–China relations, and Asia-Pacific security and international relations. She has published on the diplomatic history of U.S.–China relations, U.S. strategy in the Asia-Pacific region, the implications of 9/11 on U.S. power, and environmental security.

Constructing the U.S. Rapprochement with China, 1961–1974

From "Red Menace" to "Tacit Ally"

EVELYN GOH

Nanyang Technological University

CAMBRIDGE
UNIVERSITY PRESS

CAMBRIDGE UNIVERSITY PRESS
Cambridge, New York, Melbourne, Madrid, Cape Town, Singapore, São Paulo, Delhi

Cambridge University Press
The Edinburgh Building, Cambridge CB2 8RU, UK

Published in the United States of America by Cambridge University Press, New York

www.cambridge.org
Information on this title: www.cambridge.org/9780521108621

First published 2005
This digitally printed version 2009

A catalogue record for this publication is available from the British Library

Library of Congress Cataloguing in Publication data

Goh, Evelyn.
Constructing the U.S. rapprochement with China, 1961–1974 : from "red menace" to
"tacit ally" / Evelyn Goh.
    p.   cm.
Includes bibliographical references and index.
ISBN 0-521-83986-6
1. United States – Foreign relations – China.   2. China – Foreign relations – United
States.   3. United States – Foreign relations – 1961–1963.   4. United States – Foreign
relations – 1963–1969.   5. United States – Foreign relations – 1969–1974.   I. Title.
E183.8.C5G625   2004
327.73051´09´046–dc22   2004045808

ISBN 978-0-521-83986-0 hardback
ISBN 978-0-521-10862-1 paperback

Contents

Contents

Foreword

This book is important for three main reasons. First, it enhances our understanding of one of the most important bilateral relationships of our era. Sino-American relations have moved in regular cycles between periods of hostility and somewhat grudging coexistence since the establishment of the People's Republic of China in 1949. Most of the rest of the world has been affected by the changing state of those relations: they have had a major impact on regional security, on great power alignments, and on the central norms of the global system that involve matters of war and peace. In the early twenty-first century, we have arrived at a point where the relationship is perceived to have stabilized. For some, it warrants the description that it is the best it has ever been, or at least the best since President Nixon's landmark visit to China in 1972. Dr. Goh's study offers an opportunity to reflect on that comparison, usefully reminding us of some of the factors that contribute to a continuing fragility in those bilateral ties. Above all, her work helps us to understand what has made it possible for negative U.S. images of China to be transformed into descriptions of the country that are positive enough to permit bilateral cooperation in the three major domains of security, economics, and culture.

Second, the study is particularly valuable because of its approach. In the past, the relationship between these two countries has almost entirely been examined through a realist lens, with shifts in the balance of power regarded as the key to explaining how periods of conflict have given way to eras of cooperation. Dr. Goh's book, however, shows that there were several options available to U.S. administrations as they struggled to make sense of the opportunities provided by the Sino-Soviet split. Instead of relying on balance-of-power logic, she takes the ideas that underpinned

U.S. arguments for reconciliation with China seriously and shows how debates about the nature of the Chinese state and its capabilities provided openings for significant adjustments in the direction of U.S. policy. The study therefore tells us a great deal about the process of policy change, about how new pathways can be laid to assist in the reversal of previously deeply entrenched policy stances.

By drawing with great skill on the archival material that has steadily been declassified in the United States over the last decade or so, Dr. Goh demonstrates convincingly how China's identity was redefined over the course of several U.S. administrations. Her interpretive approach underscores the point that sensitivity to the historical record can productively be married with international relations concepts – in this instance, particularly with the conceptual insights that come from constructivism. This has allowed her to offer an illuminating and strikingly new interpretation of this bilateral relationship, and to present it in such a way as to appeal to a wider audience than would otherwise have been the case. Certainly, she can be credited with encouraging beneficial interdisciplinary dialogue.

Finally, I come to the author herself. I first met Dr. Goh when she became an M.Phil. student in international relations at the University of Oxford. As she moved into research for her D.Phil., I had the privilege and pleasure of working with a capable and promising student and of watching her fulfill her potential as a scholar worthy of joining the academy. Evelyn was one of the most stimulating and rewarding of the students whom I have supervised – independent of spirit, tenacious in following through her arguments, and always setting herself the highest of standards. This book is based on her earlier doctoral research, but it represents a significant deepening of that earlier treatment of the Sino-American relationship, rounding out the discussion of the Chinese side and reflecting with a new maturity on the wider significance of those bilateral encounters. It is her first book, but it will certainly not be the last in what I am sure will be a long and distinguished academic career.

Rosemary Foot
Professor of International Relations
St. Antony's College
University of Oxford
December 2003

Acknowledgments

I have nurtured this first book under a wealth of instruction, exchange, and encouragement from a large number of teachers, colleagues, and friends. Most of this book was written during my graduate studies, when the International Relations department at Oxford furnished an eclectic and stimulating intellectual environment, for which I am especially grateful. At Oxford, Rosemary Foot has been my most consistent mentor and friend, one who unstintingly brought to bear her meticulous and rigorous scholarship in guiding this project. Khong Yuen Foong helped to nurture my interest in American foreign policy, and my turning to U.S.-China relations was in response to one of his early suggestions. I must also thank the staffs of the Rhodes House, Vere Harmsworth, and Nuffield College Libraries for their assistance. In Washington, I am indebted to William Burr of the National Security Archive for his generous help in obtaining and sharing some vital documents. At the National Archives in College Park, I wish to thank John Taylor and Ed Barnes, as well as Pat Anderson and Bill Joyner of the Nixon Presidential Materials Staff. Susan Naulty at the Nixon Library and Mike Parrish at the LBJ Library were particularly helpful. The other part of my fieldwork consisted of interviews with various ex-officials in the United States, of whom Richard Solomon and Winston Lord were especially generous with their time. In the course of my research, Glynis Baleham, Andrew Dodds, Anne Dow, Mohamed Kourouma, Nicole Lindstrom, Thomas Mark, Schanett Riller, Stefan Röthlisberger, and Nancy Tucker helped me to obtain information, accommodation, books, and documentary material. As my collaborator in an ongoing related project, Gavan Duffy has brought valuable new insights to the Kissinger–Mao dialogues by the application of linguistic theory. In the course of presenting portions of this work in various settings, I have also received useful comments and help from Karma Nabulsi, Frank Costigliola, Jeffrey Engel, Alastair Iain Johnston, and David Sylvan. Joey Long and Ang Cheng Guan read portions of the manuscript and, along with two anonymous readers who scrutinized the whole manuscript, provided critical suggestions for its improvement. I am also grateful to Lewis Bateman and Sarah Gentile of Cambridge University Press for their efforts to bring this book to print. The culpability for any errors and misrepresentations, of course, remains mine alone. Funding for this project came from various sources. My graduate study was supported by a Nuffield College Funded Studentship and a British Overseas Research Student Award, while my fieldwork was supported by grants from the Cyril Foster, Goodhart, and Mellon Funds in Oxford; a British Federation of Women Graduates Research Award; and a research grant from the Institute of Defence and Strategic Studies in Singapore. This last institution has, moreover, since February 2002 provided me with a working environment that has been most conducive to research and writing. Finally, the long process of writing this book would have been an arduous struggle if not for my friends Michelle Chew, Adrian Lim, Marco Pagnozzi, Elaine Tan, Misa Tanaka, Kamakshya Trivedi, Alyson Tyler, and Margaret and Malcolm Yee. Above all, I owe special gratitude to Robert McGeorge and also to my family, who have stood as pillars of support over the years.

NOTE ON TRANSLITERATION

Chinese names and places are rendered throughout the text in the Pinyin system of transliteration, except where they occur in different form in quotations, or where familiar names might be confused if altered.

Abbreviations

ACA	Office of Asian Communist Affairs, Bureau of East Asian and Pacific Affairs, Department of State
AFP	*American Foreign Policy: Current Documents*
CCP	Chinese Communist Party
CFPF	Central Foreign Policy Files
ChiCom	Chinese Communists
ChiNat	Chinese Nationalists
CIA	Central Intelligence Agency
CKS	Chiang Kai Shek
ConGen	Consulate General
DoD	Department of Defense
DoS	Department of State
DSB	*Department of State Bulletin*
EA	Bureau of East Asian and Pacific Affairs, Department of State (from November 1966)
FE	Bureau of Far Eastern Affairs, Department of State (1949–October 1966)
FRUS	*Foreign Relations of the United States*
GLF	Great Leap Forward
GRC	Government of the Republic of China
HAK	Henry A. Kissinger
HK	Hong Kong
INR	Bureau of Intelligence and Research, Department of State
JCS	Joint Chiefs of Staff
JFK	John Fitzgerald Kennedy
LBJ	Lyndon Baines Johnson
NA	National Archives
NA-PR	National Archives Pacific Region

NIE	National Intelligence Estimate
NPM	Nixon Presidential Materials
NSA	National Security Archives
NSC	National Security Council
NSSM	National Security Study Memorandum
NYT	*New York Times*
PPP	*Public Papers of the Presidents*
PRC	People's Republic of China
PRCLO	People's Republic of China Liaison Office
RN	Richard Nixon
RNL	Richard Nixon Library
ROC	Republic of China
SNF	Subject-Numeric Files
SNIE	Special National Intelligence Estimate
SoS	Secretary of State
S/P	Policy Planning Staff
UN	United Nations
UNGA	United Nations General Assembly
USLO	United States Liaison Office (Beijing)
WH	White House
WP	*Washington Post*

Constructing the U.S. Rapprochement with China, 1961–1974

From "Red Menace" to "Tacit Ally"

I

Introduction

Discourses of Reconciliation

Your handshake came over the vastest ocean in the world – twenty-five years of no communication.
> Chinese Prime Minister Zhou Enlai to President Richard Nixon, Beijing, 21 February 1972

It was the week that changed the world.
> Nixon, Shanghai, 27 February 1972

President Richard Nixon's historic visit to the People's Republic of China in February 1972 marked a Sino-American rapprochement and the beginning of the route to normalization of relations. This came more than twenty years after mainland China was "lost" to the communists and, less than a year later in 1950, attacked American-led United Nations forces in Korea. Thereafter, a key tenet of U.S. Cold War strategy was to "contain" Communist China by means of bilateral alliances and military bases in East Asia, and to isolate it by severing trade, travel, and diplomatic contacts and refusing to recognize the communist regime. The next twenty years were characterized by American opposition to UN membership for mainland China, three crises in the Taiwan Straits, offensive rhetoric, threats of nuclear attack, and the fighting of a proxy war in Vietnam. In ending this hostile estrangement in 1972, Nixon thus executed a dramatic reversal of U.S. China policy. The U.S.–China rapprochement was the most significant strategic shift of the Cold War prior to 1989, more so than the Sino-Soviet split. As Nixon and his National Security Adviser Henry Kissinger claimed, the rapprochement "changed the world" by transforming a Cold War international system made up of two opposing ideological blocs into a tripolar one in which great-power foreign policy was conducted on the basis of "national interest" and power balancing.

This reversal of policy, while dramatic, is not generally considered difficult to explain.[1] The U.S.–China rapprochement is understood as the result of the operation of the realist logic of balance-of-power.[2] Washington and Beijing were brought together by a shifting balance of power, which saw the former's military superiority reduced in relation to Moscow, and the latter no longer an ally but a significantly weaker adversary facing a possible war with the Soviet Union.

The Sino-Soviet relationship was characterized from the start by ideological tension, which developed as the two states competed for leadership in the international communist movement.[3] This conflict was evident not only in the fierce disagreements about issues such as the communist revolutionary struggle and relations with the United States, but also in Moscow's declining support for its ally.[4] By the late 1960s, the conflict had developed military dimensions, with troop build-ups on the Sino-Soviet border. The Chinese decision for rapprochement with the United States was motivated by two sets of reasons. First, at the national security level, Beijing needed the U.S. opening to deter a Soviet attack. China's strategic position in relation to its militarily superior neighbor worsened

---

[1] The best accounts of the rapprochement are found in Harry Harding, *A Fragile Relationship: The United States and China since 1972* (Washington, DC, 1992), pp. 35–40; Robert Ross, *Negotiating Cooperation: The United States and China, 1969–1989* (Stanford, 1995), pp. 1–54; John Garver, *China's Decision for Rapprochement with the United States, 1968–1971* (Boulder, 1982); and William Bundy, *A Tangled Web: The Making of Foreign Policy in the Nixon Presidency* (New York, 1998). A detailed but journalistic account based on new documents and interviews is provided by Patrick Tyler, *A Great Wall: Six Presidents and China* (New York, 1999), pp. 45–180. For a succinct recent account of the Chinese decision based on new documents, see Chen Jian, *Mao's China and the Cold War* (Chapel Hill, 2001), Chapter 9.

[2] Realist and neo-realist schools of thought perceive the international system to be anarchical, causing states to be preoccupied with ways to enhance their relative military power in order to secure themselves against threats from other states, including forging alliances to balance against another powerful state. See Hans Morgenthau, *Politics among Nations: The Struggle for Power and Peace* (New York, 1949); Kenneth Waltz, *Theory of International Relations* (Reading, 1979); and Stephen Walt, *The Origins of Alliances* (Ithaca, 1987).

[3] See Steven Goldstein, "Nationalism and Internationalism: Sino-Soviet Relations," in Thomas Robinson and David Shambaugh, eds., *Chinese Foreign Policy: Theory and Practice* (Oxford, 1994).

[4] Moscow's qualified military support for Beijing had been evident as early as the 1950s, when, anxious to avoid a conflict with the United States, it tried to dampen Chinese bellicosity during the Taiwan Straits crises. See Gordon Chang, *Friends and Enemies: The United States, China and the Soviet Union, 1948–1972* (Stanford, 1990), pp. 187–8, 199–200.

dramatically in 1968, when Soviet forces invaded Czechoslovakia and the Kremlin used the Brezhnev Doctrine to justify its use of force to defend socialism in neighboring communist states. Soviet escalation of border clashes in 1969 and hints of an attack on Chinese nuclear installations convinced Beijing that Moscow harbored imperialist intentions toward a China weakened by the Cultural Revolution.[5] Second, at the international level, Beijing wanted to preempt a superpower collusion intended to contain China in the context of the developing Soviet-American détente. At the same time, China's strategic position vis-à-vis the United States was also changing: the 1969 Nixon Doctrine portended a relative American withdrawal from the region after Vietnam, which would reduce the scope of immediate Sino-American conflict. This rendered the United States a potential ally with whom China could cooperate as a balance against the primary Soviet threat.[6] This Chinese maneuver reflected the flexible alliances of classic realist politics; indeed, China is recognized as one of the most explicitly and consistently *realpolitik* of regimes.[7]

The American desire for rapprochement can similarly be placed within a realist framework. The late 1960s saw the United States in a weakening position vis-à-vis its superpower rival: the Vietnam conflict had sapped American military, political, economic, and psychological strength, allowing relative Soviet ascendance, notably in the form of a closing of the "missile gap." China's weakness was an opportunity for the United States to turn the Sino-Soviet split to its advantage by enlisting China in an implicitly anti-Soviet alignment. The United States was already seeking détente with the Soviet Union, and rapprochement with China supplemented this overall strategy of reducing tensions. At the same time, it was thought that the prospect of closer relations between the United States and China would alarm the Soviets into quickening the détente process. Washington also hoped that China would put pressure on Hanoi to negotiate peace with the United States, or if not, that the rapprochement itself would raise doubts in Hanoi about the reliability of its Chinese ally and predispose the former to negotiating a settlement.[8]

[5] Garver, *China's Decision for Rapprochement*, Chapter 2; Lowell Dittmer, *Sino-Soviet Normalization and Its International Implications, 1945–1990* (Seattle, 1992), pp. 188–91.
[6] Garver, *China's Decision for Rapprochement*, Chapter 1; J. D. Armstrong, *Revolutionary Diplomacy: Chinese Foreign Policy and the United Front Doctrine* (Berkeley, 1977).
[7] Alastair Johnston, "Cultural Realism and Strategy in Maoist China," in Peter Katzenstein, ed., *The Culture of National Security: Norms and Identity in World Politics* (New York, 1996).
[8] Henry Kissinger, *White House Years* (Boston, 1979), pp. 685, 182, 190; Harding, *A Fragile Relationship*, pp. 35–40.

Thus, the rapprochement was brought about by strategic developments and shrewd leaders skilled in *realpolitik*: since, in the realist model, a key aim of states is to prevent the rise of a potential hegemon in the international system, Washington and Beijing lay aside their mutual antagonism in order to cooperate in curbing the rising power of Moscow. However, this account is conceptually problematic because it implies that structural changes automatically induce appropriate, rational responses from states. This leads to two key shortcomings.

First, the account lacks historical context. This stems in part from the fact that until recently, the key primary sources were Nixon, who took office in 1969, and Kissinger, who had a personal academic penchant for *realpolitik*.[9] Yet even if one accepts the primacy of the realist explanation, there remains the question of why reconciliation did not happen earlier. The strategic implications of the Sino-Soviet split became publicly apparent in 1962, when their ideological quarrel moved into the realm of interstate relations.[10] Why did the balance-of-power response from Washington and Beijing take so long? What other factors were involved in determining the timing and the nature of rapprochement?

The 1960s is sometimes regarded as a decade during which China policy was moribund because U.S. officials remained locked into a rigid Cold War ideology.[11] Yet during the 1960s, the informed public was already pushing for a relaxation of the policy of isolating China. There were two distinct sets of public arguments for conciliatory moves toward China. The first – issuing from religious groups, "old China hands," "Chinese friendship" groups, scholars, and others of a liberal-humanist persuasion – was moralistic, arguing for reconciliation in order to reverse an unjust U.S. policy. The second set of arguments stemmed from the mass public's worry about the Chinese threat to American security interests. The hope here was that rapprochement would help to reduce tensions with China and limit American commitments in Southeast Asia.

---

[9] For a trenchant analysis of Kissinger's *realpolitik* convictions in theory and practice, see Stanley Hoffman, *Primacy or World Order: American Foreign Policy since the Cold War* (New York, 1978), Chapter 2.

[10] In 1960, Moscow withdrew its technicians, suspended all agreements for scientific and technical cooperation, and radically reduced trade with China. By 1962, it had closed all its China consulates. Their reactions to each other's major foreign adventures in 1962 – the Chinese openly criticized the Soviet handling of the Cuban crisis, while the Soviets covertly offered help to India in the Sino-Indian war – portended the death of their alliance.

[11] Kissinger was the most dismissive – see his *White House Years*, p. 685.

This trend became increasingly marked as the 1960s wore on and the public sense of "Vietnam fatigue" heightened.[12]

There were similar trends within policy-making bodies. Rosemary Foot has described the arguments among some midlevel American officials that the dangers of dealing with China had diminished because it had been weakened by the Sino-Soviet split and by the failure of its ambitious economic programs. A second argument was based on the continuing need to limit Chinese power. Given China's huge standing army and growing nuclear capability, international arms control regimes would require Chinese participation if they were to be effective. The third argument stemmed from the realization that Washington's policy of isolating China was being seriously challenged in the international arena.[13] How did these other ideas of reconciliation with China relate to Nixon's rapprochement? If there were significant changes in China policy thinking prior to 1969, how can we account for the timing of the rapprochement, occurring as it did only during Nixon's first term and not before?

The second main shortcoming of orthodox accounts of the rapprochement is that they have been occupied with explaining *why* but not *how* reconciliation was achieved. Insufficient attention has been paid to the policy-making and policy advocacy processes, which can offer important insights that will aid in setting the context for and facilitating understanding of the "why" questions.[14] While memoir accounts of the rapprochement incorporate the role of agency, they do not deal systematically with how ideas affect the policy-making process. The most significant puzzle of the time is how the rapprochement could have happened. The existing

[12] Leonard Kusnitz, *Public Opinion and Foreign Policy: America's China Policy, 1949–1979* (Westport, 1984), pp. 115–17; A. Doak Barnett, *Communist China and Asia: Challenge to American Policy* (Oxford, 1960); Akira Iriye, ed., *U.S. Policy Toward China: Testimony Taken from the Senate Foreign Relations Committee Hearings 1966* (Boston, 1968).

[13] Rosemary Foot, *The Practice of Power: US Relations with China since 1949* (Oxford, 1995), pp. 207–18, 32–46. See also Arthur Waldron, "From Nonexistent to Almost Normal: US-China Relations in the 1960s," in Diane Kunz, ed., *The Diplomacy of the Crucial Decade: American Foreign Policy during the 1960s* (New York, 1994); Rosemary Foot, "Redefinitions: The Domestic Context and America's China Policy in the 1960s," in Robert Ross and Jiang Changbin, eds., *Re-examining the Cold War: US-China Diplomacy, 1954–1973* (Cambridge, 2001).

[14] Robert Ross is a notable exception. He sees the common Soviet threat as the force that drove Washington and Beijing to cooperate, but directs his attention to the issue of how, through "continuous negotiations and mutual adjustments," the two sides were able to cooperate by managing their fundamental conflict of interest over the Taiwan issue. See Ross, *Negotiating Cooperation*, pp. 1–2.

U.S. Cold War strategy and policy was based on the identification of China as an implacable communist foe, worse even than the Soviet Union because more unpredictable and irrational. Wars had been, and were being, fought based upon this conviction. How was it possible that under Nixon, China shifted from being the United States' worst enemy to being its friend and even tacit ally? This suggests a serious alteration in perceptions and representations of China, a process with which available accounts do not engage in a sustained manner. These accounts are also silent on the issue of how and why Nixon and Kissinger managed to convince others of the rationality of their new policy. Policy changes do not occur automatically – the gap between the convictions of the policy elite, on the one hand, and policy output, on the other, is mediated by a political advocacy process that is often ignored by those who assume either universal rationality or an "imperial presidency." In Nixon's case, various bureaucratic, national, and international constituencies had to be convinced: among them, the China lobby and anticommunist conservative elements; the left wing, concerned with protecting détente with the Soviet Union; U.S. allies in Asia, worried about U.S. defense commitments; and even the Chinese leaders themselves.

This study aims to overcome the shortfalls of the available accounts of the Sino-American rapprochement using an approach that may be termed conceptual history. Rather than investigating the history of U.S. China policy or Sino-American diplomatic relations per se, it is primarily interested in identifying and tracing the changing perceptions of China and ideas about China policy associated with the rapprochement. The focus is on the themes and concepts within the debates about alternative policy positions in official American policy-making circles, and on the justification and implementation of the chosen policies from 1961 to 1974. The analysis of the official U.S. China policy discourse across the Kennedy, Johnson, and Nixon administrations is a significant departure from many available works on post-1949 U.S.–China relations, which tend to treat 1960s China policy thinking as an extension of that of the 1950s, and the Nixon administration as a watershed marking a new era in China policy.[15]

The alternative questions posed in this study may be recognized as the "how possible" queries emphasized by constructivists, in contrast

---

[15] See, for instance, Warren Cohen, *America's Response to China: A History of Sino-American Relations* (New York, 2000); Chang, *Friends and Enemies*; Harding, *A Fragile Relationship*; and James Mann, *About Face: A History of America's Curious Relationship with China, from Nixon to Clinton* (New York, 1998).

to the basic "why" questions that realists try to answer.[16] Constructivist approaches prioritize ideas and identity in the creation of state
interests because they work from the basis that all reality is socially
constructed.[17] The international system, for instance, does not exert an
automatic "objective" causal influence on states' actions. Rather, state
policy choices result from a process of perception and interpretation
by state actors, through which they come to understand the situation
that the state faces and to formulate their responses. Furthermore, actors may, by their actions, alter systemic structures and trends.[18] Even
beyond that, some constructivists argue that actors themselves change
as they evolve new ideas and conceptions about identity and political
communities. Thus, the constructivist understanding of "reality" cen-
ters upon the interaction of the material and the ideational.[19] The forging of this intersubjective context is a contentious process, but often
particular representations are so successful that they become a form of
"common sense," encompassing a system of understanding about a body
of subjects, objects, and issues with implicit policy consequences. This
structure of representation may be termed a discourse, and a radical
change in policy occurs when the prevailing discourse is challenged and
altered.

The key conceptual focus in this study is on discourses, rather than on
ideas, belief systems, or ideology, because the former conveys more effectively the multifaceted process by which meaning is constituted by policy
actors and by which policy choices are constructed, contested, and implemented. Discourses may be understood as linguistic representations and
rhetorical strategies by which a people create meaning about the world,
and they are critical to the process by which ideas are translated into

---

[16] On constructivist approaches in international relations, see Ted Hopf, "The Promise of
Constructivism in International Relations Theory," *International Security* 23(1) (1998),
pp. 171–200; Vendulka Kubálková, Nicholas Onuf, and Paul Kowert, eds., *International
Relations in a Constructed World* (London, 1998); and Alexander Wendt, *Social Theory of
International Politics* (Cambridge, 1999).

[17] On this theme, see especially Ralph Pettman, *Commonsense Constructivism, or the Making
of World Affairs* (New York, 2000).

[18] See Alexander Wendt, "Anarchy Is What States Make of It: The Social Construction
of Power Politics," *International Organization* 46(2) (Spring 1992), pp. 391–425; and
Katzenstein, ed., *Culture of National Security*.

[19] On this school of constructivism, see Nicholas Onuf, *World of Our Making: Rules and Rule
in Social Theory and International Relations* (Columbia, 1989); and Friedrich Kratochwil,
*Rules, Norms, and Decisions: On the Conditions of Practical and Legal Reasoning in Interna-
tional Relations and Domestic Affairs* (Cambridge, 1989).

policy in two ways.[20] First, they perform a constraining or enabling function with regard to state action, in the sense that policy options may be rendered more or less reasonable by particular understandings of, for instance, China, the United States, and the relations between them.[21] Second, discursive practice is an integral element of sociopolitical relations of power.[22] As a key means of producing the categories and boundaries of knowledge by which reality is understood and explained by society, discourses are often deliberate and instrumental. In representing subjects and their relationships in certain ways, political actors have particular objectives and specific audiences in mind.

Here, the focus on changing discursive representations of China and China policy in official American circles allows us to study in particular the policy advocacy process – within internal official circles, to the public, and to the other party in the bilateral relationship – in a significant policy reversal. Bringing to bear the understanding that the creation of meaning by discursive practice is an essential means of influencing political action, this book investigates the contested process by which the different actors and parties defined and redefined identities, generated new knowledge, and created new meanings in order to construct and maintain a new U.S.–China relationship.

In this study, each discourse about China may be understood to encompass the following elements: an image or representation of China; a related representation of U.S. identity; an interpretation of the nature of U.S.–China relations; and the "logical" policy options that flow from these representations. For ease of reference, each subdiscourse that is identified here is centered upon the core image of China upon which it is built. An image is simply the perception of a particular object or subject, the normative

---

[20] Karen Litfin, *Ozone Discourses: Science and Politics in Global Environmental Cooperation* (New York, 1994), p. 3. The concept of discursive formations and practices originates in Foucault's work on power/knowledge; see Michel Foucault, *The Archaeology of Knowledge* (London, 1972). See also Henrik Larsen, *Foreign Policy and Discourse Analysis: France, Britain and Europe* (London, 1997); and Gearoid Tuathail and John Agnew, "Geopolitics and Discourse: Practical Geopolitical Reasoning in American Foreign Policy," *Political Geography* 11(2) (1992), pp. 192–3.

[21] See Doty, "Foreign Policy as Social Construction"; and Jutta Weldes and Diana Saco, "Making State Action Possible: The US and the Discursive Construction of 'The Cuban Problem', 1960–1994," *Millennium* 25(2) (1996), pp. 361–96.

[22] Jim George, *Discourses of Global Politics: A Critical (Re)Introduction to International Relations* (Boulder, 1994), pp. 29–31; Jennifer Milliken, "The Study of Discourse in International Relations: A Critique of Research and Methods," *European Journal of International Relations* 5(2) (June 1999), pp. 225–54.

evaluation of it, and the identity and meaning ascribed to it.[23] The concept of images is employed here mainly as an analytical shorthand, as the image is but one of four subcomponents of each discourse.[24]

Discourses or images are not advanced as alternative explanatory variables for the U.S.–China rapprochement. Rather, this is an investigation of the existence and influence of groups of ideas of reconciliation with China, and of how these affected the ultimate policy outcome of rapprochement. In this sense, we are interested, above all, in the rapprochement as a process of change. The focus on discourse and process necessitates establishing a historical context and thus expands the temporal scope of this study to include the China policy debates in the 1960s and the implementation of rapprochement policy during the last two years of the Nixon administration. This book investigates official U.S. discourse on China during the period 1961–74 as a whole, focusing on alternative systems of representation, how one or more became dominant, and to what effect.[25] In contrast to the existing literature, this constructivist, discourse-based approach situates the prevailing *realpolitik* account of the rapprochement within the context of other ideas about reconciliation with China over a fifteen-year period. In the process, it offers new insights into critical issues of historical interest relating to the timing of, the motivations for, the bargains surrounding, and the evolving nature of the Sino-American rapprochement.

In 1969, there were, without doubt, significant material changes in relative international power that prompted strategic reassessments in Washington, Beijing, and Moscow. At the same time, however, these assessments were mediated by ideational factors. This constitutive relationship can be investigated if we first demonstrate that different groups of

[23] See Kenneth Boulding, *The Image* (Ann Arbor, 1956); Robert Jervis, *The Logic of Images in International Relations* (Princeton, 1970); and Ragnhild Fiebig-von Hase and Ursula Lehmkuhl, eds., *Enemy Images in American History* (Providence, 1997).

[24] This study may be distinguished from some notable historical-cultural works that emphasize the role of mutual images per se in Sino-American relations. See Tang Tsou, *America's Failure in China, 1941–50* (Chicago, 1963); Harold Isaacs, *Images of Asia: American Views on China and India* (New York, 1968); Akira Iriye, ed., *Mutual Images: Essays in American-Japanese Relations* (Cambridge, 1975); John Fairbank, *China Watch* (Cambridge, 1987); and Harry Harding, "From China, with Disdain: New Trends in the Study of China," *Asian Survey* 22(10) (October 1982), pp. 934–58.

[25] The analysis could have been extended further back to 1949, the year the PRC was formed, which has been the preferred starting point for most post–World War II works on U.S.–China relations. Time and space preclude such a broad time frame for this project.

officials read these same material changes in different ways and recommended different policy responses, depending upon their representations
of China, the Soviet Union, and the United States. Based on knowledge
about the wider context of U.S. China policy thinking across the Kennedy,
Johnson, and Nixon administrations, we begin by positing that in 1969,
Washington had at least four policy options in response to the changing
balance of power, all of which could have been justified on power political
grounds.

Option 1. Washington could have *done nothing*, allowed the intracommunist dispute to further weaken the opposing camp, and thus increased the relative strength of the U.S.-led Western camp. Indeed, this
was the policy effectively adopted by the Kennedy and Johnson administrations when they were faced with evidence of increased Sino-Soviet
tensions throughout the 1960s. It was a cautious policy of not wanting
to exploit uncertain divisions in the opposing camp in case these efforts
should backfire and cause the two communist powers to coalesce again
in common opposition to the United States.[26]

Option 2. The United States might have *supported the Soviet Union
against China.* Given that part of the Sino-Soviet feud centered on Beijing's
more militant and revolutionary views, this stance would have accorded
with the perception that China was the greater communist threat. Newly
available documentary evidence suggests that Kennedy and Johnson had
both considered the possibility of joint military action with the Soviet
Union against China's developing nuclear capabilities in 1963 and 1964.[27]
Furthermore, it has been suggested that in 1969, Nixon and Kissinger were
willing to condone a Soviet attack on China in return for Moscow's help
in ending the Vietnam War.[28]

Option 3. This is the option that Nixon and Kissinger claim to have
pursued, in which the United States would simultaneously improve relations with both the Soviet Union and China. By creating a *"triangular
relationship,"* they attempted to exploit the Sino-Soviet conflict. By maintaining better relations with Beijing and Moscow than they did with each
other, the United States would be able exert leverage both ways and to

---

[26] This was a public posture as well as an internal official policy stance; it was stated most
clearly at the end of the Kennedy administration and early in the Johnson years. The
documentary evidence and details are discussed in Chapter 2.

[27] William Burr and Jeffrey Richelson, "Whether to 'Strangle the Baby in the Cradle': The
United States and the Chinese Nuclear Program, 1960–64," *International Security* 25(3)
(Winter 2000/1), pp. 54–99. This is discussed in Chapter 2.

[28] Tyler, *A Great Wall*, pp. 62–3. This is discussed and evaluated in Chapter 6.

gain advantage on a wider range of issues.[29] In this classical realist concert model, the United States acts as a "balancer" in order to maintain equilibrium in the system through parallel détente with each of the two communist powers.[30] The aim would be to regain the pivotal hegemonic position that Washington had enjoyed in the international system after the Second World War, but which had been undermined by the Vietnam War.[31]

Option 4. Washington could have *supported China against the Soviet Union*. The latter was, after all, the United States' key superpower competitor, one with significant nuclear capabilities, while China was mainly a regional and subversive power. This would also have accorded with the realist stratagem of forming temporary alliances with weaker powers in order to balance the greater threat of a rising hegemon.[32] Of course, this strategy is closely related to, and might be a short-term element of, Option 3. However, as this study demonstrates, Kissinger and Nixon in fact moved significantly toward this model in practice, laying the foundations for a U.S.–China relationship that was substantively different from what would have ensued from pursuing Option 3.

In the sense that each of them was a viable option with a policy history and significant official proponents, the four options constitute the informal "dependent variable" in this study.[33] The relevant questions are then: why were Options 1 and 2 discarded; how did Options 3 and 4 become reasonable; which option was chosen, when, and for what reasons?

The analysis that follows is divided into three sections. Part I investigates whether significant rethinking of China policy was occurring within official circles during the 1960s, identifies these earlier discourses of

[29] Lowell Dittmer has characterized the resulting condition as a "romantic triangle," as distinct from the "stable marriage" situation that would result from the United States supporting either of the other two countries against the other. See Dittmer, "The Strategic Triangle: An Elementary Game-Theoretical Analysis," *World Politics* 33(4) (July 1981), pp. 485–515.

[30] Kissinger, *White House Years*, p. 1076; Kissinger, *Years of Upheaval* (London, 1982), p. 705; Nixon, quoted in *Time* 49 (3/1/72), p. 15. For good discussions on the classical realist concept of balance of power and equilibrium, see Peter Schoeder, "The Nineteenth Century System: Balance of Power or Political Equilibrium?," *Review of International Studies* 15(2) (1987), pp. 135–53; and Robert Jervis, "A Political Science Perspective on the Balance of Power and the Concert," *American Historical Review* 97(3) (1992), pp. 716–24.

[31] On how the Vietnam War "mortally threatened" this postwar hegemony, and how Nixon tried to recover a new global role of "centrality" for the United States, see Franz Schurmann's *The Logic of World Power* (New York, 1974); and Schurmann, *The Foreign Politics of Richard Nixon: The Grand Design* (Berkeley, 1987).

[32] Waltz, *Theory of International Politics*, Chapter 6.

[33] Note, however, that the constructivist approach here eschews the search for an independent causal variable.

reconciliation, and explores their substance and impact. It reveals that, in contrast to the hostile images of China as "Red Menace" and "Revolutionary Rival," there were also official proponents of two revisionist subdiscourses of China as "Troubled Modernizer" and "Resurgent Power," which entailed seeking better U.S.–PRC relations for reasons other than common opposition to the Soviet Union.[34] These revisionist discourses came to dominate in official circles from 1966 onward, before Nixon entered office, but bureaucratic politics and Chinese intransigence impeded a rapprochement during the 1960s.

While Part I explores the mostly midlevel official advocacy of revisionist approaches to China policy during the 1960s, Part II investigates the period of transition from 1969 to 1971, when the competing discourses "funneled" down to a more intense but contained interdepartmental policy debate about variations on the agreed theme of improving relations with Beijing in the face of a clear opportunity. How did the revisionist discursive context described earlier, representing China as a more "friendly" state, impinge on Nixon's and Kissinger's ideas and actions? As a background, the section first demonstrates that Nixon contributed to the discourse of China as a "Resurgent Power" during the late 1960s. Then it focuses on the transitional debate between the Nixon White House and the State Department over China policy, which resulted from differing interpretations of systemic changes. It shows how the White House captured the China policy apparatus and adapted the existing revisionist discourse in developing Nixon's and Kissinger's new conceptualization of triangular politics.

Part III, in turn, deals with how the Nixon administration's new China policy was advocated to the Chinese and justified to the various domestic constituencies as well as to international allies. From July 1971 onward, Kissinger and Nixon labored to "sell" the rapprochement to the Chinese leaders by means of cultivating an image of China as a noninimical partner, persuading them that areas of common interest existed, and negotiating new norms for the bilateral relationship consonant with their model of triangular relations. This discursive process also carried concrete policy consequences – notably in the Indo-Pakistan crisis of 1971 and in U.S. policy on Taiwan – for in order to convince the Chinese of their sincerity, Nixon and Kissinger had to demonstrate that Washington

---

[34] The terms "Red Menace" and "Troubled Modernizer" are borrowed from Richard Madsen, *China and the American Dream: A Moral Inquiry* (Stanford, 1995), pp. 28–52. However, the concepts are applied and developed here in different ways.

would act according to these new identities and norms. In a departure from existing works on the rapprochement, this section scrutinizes the implementation of the U.S. policy of rapprochement with China from 1971 to 1974.[35] It uses newly declassified documents to show the development of a later, neo-realist discourse of the U.S.–China rapprochement that consisted of an unspoken alliance intended to counter the worldwide influence of the Soviet Union, substantiated by American offers of closer intelligence and military relations. It elucidates the distinction between Options 3 (triangular relations) and 4 (support China against the Soviet Union) by demonstrating that Kissinger moved significantly toward Option 4 within a year of the "China opening," and by offering some explanation of why he did so. This distinction is not made within orthodox accounts of the rapprochement, which instead veer implicitly between these two variants of power balancing without engaging with the central paradox that Option 3 aims at the improvement of relations with Moscow, while Option 4 would result in the anti-Soviet alliance that Moscow had explicitly warned the Nixon administration against.[36]

Such analytical focus on the internal official China policy discourse in Washington has been made possible by the recent availability of a considerable amount of documentary material. The relevant volumes of the *Foreign Relations of the United States* series from the Kennedy and Johnson administrations, though not exhaustive, present a remarkably comprehensive record of the internal policy debates of the time. These sources are supplemented here by archival material from the presidential libraries and the National Archives, other State Department publications, oral histories, interviews, and memoirs. Nearly two-thirds of this book is based on newly declassified primary documents from the Nixon administration, most of which were not available to the authors of the existing key secondary accounts of the Sino-American rapprochement. On the other hand, this study is an analysis of what has been termed the *rapprochement* between the United States and the PRC. The term has been used to describe Nixon's "breakthrough" in effecting a reconciliation with mainland

---

[35] This is not an aspect usually dealt with in constructivist studies that are more interested in revealing "conditions of possibility," but it is a crucial one if we are interested in dynamic discursive contexts that are liable to reconstruction in practice. See Milliken, "The Study of Discourse in International Relations," pp. 234–6.

[36] For instance, Banning Garrett notes the difference between the two strategies, but in relation to Nixon's and Kissinger's initial rationale for rapprochement versus the more public calls for closer military relations with China beginning with the Ford administration. See Garrett, "Strategic Basis of Learning in US Policy Toward China," p. 229.

China in 1972, as opposed to the longer process of *normalization* leading
to the establishment of diplomatic relations, which eventually occurred
in 1979 under the Carter administration. In order better to understand
Nixon's and Kissinger's rapprochement with China in concept and in
practice, this analysis looks beyond the February 1972 summit to their
development of the new U.S.–China relationship by following events until
the end of 1974. It does not, however, venture beyond that, owing to the
constraints of space and time and because of the limited archival sources
from the Ford presidency.

PART ONE

COMPETING DISCOURSES, 1961–1968

2

"Red Menace" to "Revolutionary Rival"

Recasting the Chinese Communist Threat

...a great, powerful force in China, organized and directed by the government along Stalinist lines, surrounded by weaker countries...this we regard as a menacing situation.

President John F. Kennedy, 1 August 1963

We are facing the greatest menace to our freedom.

Indian Prime Minister Jawaharlal Nehru, November 1962

This Assembly would face the greatest menace to its future if it...admitted the...People's Republic [of China].

Adlai Stevenson, U.S. Representative to the United Nations, 22 October 1962

American attitudes toward China from the nineteenth century until the Second World War had been broadly paternalistic, assuming a "special friendship" with the Chinese people.[1] However, the situation altered dramatically in 1949 and 1950, when the communists won control of the mainland in the civil war and "Red" China subsequently allied itself with the Soviet Union. The communist victory seemed to signify Chinese rejection of American values and the American model of civil society, a rejection that gained enormous salience in the context of the rapidly developing Cold War. The Sino-Soviet alliance dramatically confirmed America's "loss" of China to its main enemy.[2] After the Second World War, the Soviet

---

[1] See Michael Hunt, *The Making of a Special Relationship: The United States and China to 1914* (New York, 1983); and James Thomson, Peter Stanley, and John Curtis Perry, *Sentimental Imperialists: The American Experience in East Asia* (New York, 1981).

[2] There was a short period from 1949 to 1950, prior to the Korean War, when some American officials, notably Secretary of State Dean Acheson, felt that the Chinese

Union was the only power capable of challenging American hegemony; and the communist leadership in Moscow coupled its rhetoric about a communist world revolution with action, expanding domination over its neighboring Eastern European states by setting up Soviet-backed communist regimes in them.[3] In view of this, American officials' initial response was to portray the Chinese Communist regime as a Soviet puppet. For instance, Dean Rusk, then assistant secretary of state for Far Eastern affairs, labeled the regime a "Slavic Manchukuo."[4]

China's entry into the Korean War, however, decisively cast it in the "communist aggressor" mould. Until then, China had been identified as "Red" but only an unwitting "Menace." But its unexpected dispatch of one million "volunteers" into North Korea convinced many Americans that China was a very real menace in and of itself. Beijing's intervention was a spectacular success, with Chinese forces fighting the U.S.-led United Nations troops to a standstill at the thirty-eighth parallel.[5] American officials now had little doubt that the Chinese Communists were full-fledged partners in Soviet aggression. There was widespread agreement in the Truman administration that the attack had stemmed "not so much from [Chinese] national interests as…from the Chinese Communist role as a member of the Moscow-directed International Communist front"; it therefore should be seen as part of a "global Communist program."[6]

Thus after the Korean attack, Communist China was identified by American officials in terms of the prevailing American representation of

communists were primarily nationalists and independent of the Soviets, and contemplated an accommodation with Beijing. On this "lost chance" debate, see Nancy Bernkopf Tucker, *Patterns in the Dust: Chinese-American Relations and the Recognition Controversy, 1949–1950* (New York, 1983); and the symposium in *Diplomatic History* 21(1) (Winter 1997).

[3] See Daniel Yergin, *Shattered Peace: The Origins of the Cold War and the National Security State* (London, 1978); and Thomas Paterson, *Meeting the Communist Threat* (Oxford, 1988).

[4] Dean Rusk, "American Friendship for the Peoples of China," speech at the China Institute, New York, 18 May 1951, *Documents in American Foreign Relations* [AFP] 1950–5, II, pp. 2473–4.

[5] There remains a debate about China's reasons for entering the Korean War. Authors working from American sources argue that it was defensive. See Allen Whiting, *China Crosses the Yalu: The Decision to Enter the Korean War* (Stanford, 1960); and Rosemary Foot, *The Wrong War: American Policy and the Dimensions of the Korean Conflict, 1950–1953* (Ithaca, 1985). But recent works based on Chinese and Soviet archives indicate a more coordinated and premeditated attack. See Chen Jian, *China's Road to the Korean War: The Making of the Sino-American Confrontation* (New York, 1994); *Cold War International History Project Bulletin* 6-7 (Winter 1995/6); and Sergei Goncharov, John Wilson Lewis, and Xue Litai, *Uncertain Partners: Stalin, Mao and the Korean War* (Stanford, 1993).

[6] DoS to Foreign Service Posts, 5 December 1950, quoted in Foot, *The Wrong War*, pp. 101–2.

Cold War international politics.[7] China's identity was now attached to that of the Soviet Union: it was an activist member of the Soviet bloc, propagating a renegade ideology, exercising domestic tyranny, and launching external military aggression – all of which threatened the established postwar international order. The "loss" of China and Beijing's entry into the Korean War heightened the fear with which Americans viewed the "communist threat." "Red China" became a powerful symbol during the McCarthy recriminations and witch hunts for communists in the State Department.

After Korea, the policy of containing communism was extended worldwide.[8] Other actions of the Chinese Communist regime at around the same time seemed to further prove its aggressive intentions: the invasion of Tibet in May 1950, the massing of Chinese troops opposite Taiwan and on the Indochinese border. Beijing's support for the communist war in Vietnam and its ties with Southeast Asian communist parties were construed as evidence of its aim to seize power across Asia. The United States responded by aiding the French in Indochina; constructing alliances with Japan, South Korea, the Philippines, Thailand, Australia, and New Zealand; and deploying forces to the region. It also recognized the Nationalist regime on Taiwan as the sole legitimate government of China and signed a mutual defense treaty with Taipei in 1954.[9] This was reinforced by a policy of nonrecognition and deliberate isolation of Communist China. With two claimants to sovereignty over "one China," labels were particularly significant, and "Red China" quickly came to denote the renegade mainland regime. This hard line was strengthened during the Eisenhower

[7] This portrayal is summed up by Jutta Weldes as the image of the United States as the "winner" of World War II, which bore the "burden of leadership" in "the free world," defending "democracy and freedom" against the "expansion and aggression" from the "totalitarian" Soviet Union and its international communist movement, which threatened America's very "way of life." See Weldes, "Constructing National Interests," *European Journal of International Relations* 2(3) (1996), p. 283.

[8] John Gaddis, *Strategies of Containment: A Critical Appraisal of Postwar American National Security Policy* (Oxford, 1982), pp. 109–26.

[9] On U.S. policy to contain China during the 1950s, see Yonosuke Nagai and Akira Iriye, eds., *The Origins of the Cold War in Asia* (New York, 1977); Marc Gallicchio, "The Best Defense Is Good Offense: The Evolution of American Strategy in East Asia, 1953–1960," in Warren Cohen and Akira Iriye, eds., *The Great Powers in East Asia, 1953–1960* (New York, 1990); and Robert Blum, *Drawing the Line: The Origin of the American Containment Policy in East Asia* (New York, 1982). On policy toward the Republic of China (ROC), see Robert Accinelli, *Crisis and Containment: United States Policy toward Taiwan, 1950–1955* (Chapel Hill, 1996); Nancy Tucker, *Taiwan, Hong Kong, and the United States, 1945–1992* (New York, 1994), Chapters 3, 4; and John Garver, *The Sino-American Alliance: Nationalist China and American Cold War Strategy in Asia* (London, 1997).

administration by Secretary of State John Foster Dulles, who consolidated the image of China as Red Menace over the two Taiwan Straits crises in 1954–5 and 1958.[10]

Accounts of Sino-American relations that portray the years between 1950 and 1970 as a period of continuing hostility and fear would assert that the predominant American representation of China revolved around Chinese aggression, expansionism, and extremism. Such hostile images clearly did exist among U.S. officials during the 1960s, but what were their origins, context, and parameters? The first section of this chapter shows how the stock hostile image of China as "Red Menace" was derived from the 1950s policy context, carried into the 1960s by particular key officials and reinforced by new events. American China policy thinking during the 1960s was not, however, a simple continuation of that of the 1950s; and as the limits of this particular image became apparent, the hostile discourse on China evolved into one more in keeping with Chinese actions during this period. As discussed in the second section, the new image of China as "Revolutionary Rival" reflected the preoccupation with the developing Sino-Soviet dispute but also offered a more moderated and ambiguous interpretation of the Chinese threat.

THE "RED MENACE": COMMUNIST CHINA AS EXPANSIONIST MILITARY AGGRESSOR

The "Red Menace" discourse of the 1950s and 1960s represented mainland China as both a domestic and an international threat. Internally, the communist regime was illegitimate and despotic; while externally, it was a proven expansionist aggressor developing ever more lethal offensive military capabilities.

Domestic Totalitarianism

American officials portrayed Red China as a menace to its own people. This representation derived from the characteristic totalitarianism implicit in the communist identity as posited by Americans, but it was also powerfully evinced by events in China. In the years immediately following the communist takeover, millions of landowners and other "bourgeoisie"

---

[10] See Chang, *Friends and Enemies*, pp. 116–42; Accinelli, *Crisis and Commitment*; and Zhang Shu Guang, *Deterrence and Strategic Culture: Chinese-American Confrontations, 1949–1958* (Ithaca, 1992), pp. 189–267.

were dispossessed, forced into labor, or killed in campaigns of "land reform" and "suppression of counterrevolutionaries." In 1957, after a brief experiment of "inviting criticisms," the regime again carried out brutal crackdowns. Dulles characterized the Chinese Communist Party (CCP) as a regime that "came to power by violence and . . . has lived by violence. . . . It retains power not by will of the Chinese people but by massive, forcible repression." It ruled through "Communist-type despotism" and suppressed differences under "international Communism's rule of strict conformity."[11] In response to those who pointed out that the CCP exerted effective control of the mainland, Dulles stated that the ability to govern did not in itself guarantee American approbation. He placed greater value on the test of whether, in Thomas Jefferson's words, the government reflected the "will of the nation, substantially declared."[12] The CCP, "which [held] mainland China in its grip, [was] a tiny minority comprising less than 2 per cent of the Chinese people," and its "regimentation [and] brutal repression . . . [had] resulted in extensive popular unrest."[13] Dulles's argument was based on the American ideal of liberal democracy, and its implication was that the Chinese Communist regime, because it was repressive and not built on popular consent, was illegitimate and unsustainable. Dulles argued publicly and privately that it was a "passing phase" whose passing the United States would assist by abstaining from any encouraging action.[14]

This argument continued to be used by the Democratic administrations of the early 1960s to justify extending the policy of isolation. A Senate debate in July 1961 set the tone for the new Kennedy administration when, one after another, conservative senators reiterated that the Chinese Communist regime was illegitimate: it did not "speak for its people"; it had "won power through brute force," "through usurpation"; it had

[11] John Foster Dulles, "Our Policies toward Communism in China," speech to the Lions International Club, San Francisco, 28 June 1957, *FRUS 1955–7*, III, pp. 558, 564.

[12] Ibid., p. 563.

[13] DoS, "Recognition of Communist China," 12 August 1958, *AFP 1958*, pp. 1141–2.

[14] Dulles, "Our Policies," pp. 566, 559; NSC meeting notes, 28 February 1957, *FRUS 1955–7*, III, pp. 491–2. Revisionist scholars have pointed out that Dulles and Eisenhower were more moderate and realistic in their China policy than this suggests. Nancy Tucker argues that Dulles, in particular, sought to restrain the Nationalists and worked toward a "two Chinas" solution. See Tucker, "John Foster Dulles and the Taiwan Roots of the 'Two Chinas' Policy," in Richard Immerman, ed., *John Foster Dulles and the Diplomacy of the Cold War* (Princeton, 1990). This thesis, however, does not detract from the crucial domestic political obstacles to a policy change and thus the rhetorical function, at least, of the "Red Menace" discourse that accompanied the policy of containment and isolation of Communist China.

committed "mass murder" and was "at war with its own people." Both
houses of Congress voted unanimously for a resolution against recognition.[15] This view was reinforced by the famines and other hardships that
accompanied the failure of China's "Great Leap Forward" at the end of
the 1950s. In 1962, this appalling situation, combined with the increasingly evident Sino-Soviet dispute, caused the key China-watching post in
Hong Kong to prophesy that the United States was entering the "har-
vest time" of the Dullesian policy of containing Chinese communism and
"forc[ing] them in on themselves." Hence, Washington ought to continue
this policy in order to reap its full benefits.[16]

Within the Kennedy administration, it was Secretary of State Dean
Rusk who most clearly articulated the image of the Red Chinese domestic
menace. He firmly upheld the conviction that a liberal democratic political system was most likely to meet human aspirations.[17] In one of his
definitive speeches as secretary of state, Rusk described the Cold War as
a clash of the "revolution of freedom" against the "counter-revolution of
coercion." The former he identified with Jeffersonian concepts of equality
and inalienable rights, of government "through the consent of the governed." The latter, of which China was a part, stood for the antithesis,
"the imposition of government based on will and force."[18] Rusk also
demonstrated his belief that the CCP regime was illegitimate by his persistent reference to "Peiping" rather than "Peking."[19] He alone among
Kennedy's advisers entertained Dulles's idea of the communist regime as
a "passing phase." In a key Policy Planning discussion about the likely
consequences of the Sino-Soviet split and Mao's death, Rusk suggested
studies into "the tradition of the turnover of governments in China" and
also "the possible recrudescence of Chinese warlordism and regionalism." Other officials did not agree about the possibility of such internal

[15] "Senate Concurrent Resolution 34," 28 July 1961, *Congressional Record* 107(10),
pp. 13950–62.
[16] ConGen/HK to DoS, "Implications for US Policy of Latest Developments in Communist
China," 18 July 1962, Box 15, Thomson Files, Kennedy Presidential Library (JFKL), p. 6;
ConGen/HK to DoS, "Trends and Prospects in Communist China: Implications for US
Policy," 1 February 1963, Box 3863, Central Foreign Policy Files (CFCP) (1963), Record
Group (RG) 59, National Archives (NA).
[17] Warren Cohen, *Dean Rusk* (New Jersey, 1980), p. 321.
[18] Dean Rusk, speech to symposium on Government and World Crisis, University of Ten-
nessee, 17 May 1962, *Department of State Bulletin* [*DSB*] 46, p. 896.
[19] "Peiping" [Beiping], the Nationalist name for the city, means "northern peace." The
communist regime reestablished this historic seat of power and its old name, "Peking"
[Beijing], meaning "Northern Capital."

challenges to the regime; Averell Harriman, assistant secretary for Far Eastern affairs, called it "overhopeful."[20]

External Aggression and Expansion

The strongest element of the Red Menace image envisaged the Chinese Communists routinely employing force to fulfil their expansionist ambitions. This belief was based primarily on Beijing's intervention in the Korean War, which greatly magnified the perception of China as a direct aggressor against the United States and against the UN, a symbol of the American-led world order.[21] An official justification for U.S. China policy was the argument that, far from ignoring Communist China, the United States had actually fought against its "huge invading army" in Korea. More importantly, China's attack epitomized the phenomenon of aggression that the world body had been set up to deal with. Indeed, the first collective UN action against aggression was in the Korean War. China had rejected the "code of civilized nations" and had been condemned as an aggressor by the General Assembly.[22]

American officials continued to emphasize such Chinese aggression during the 1960s. Rusk was committed to the world order as represented by the UN Charter, and he was particularly quick to highlight instances of Chinese transgression. He used the analogies of Korea and Munich and compared Beijing's involvement in the Vietnam War to that of the Japanese militarists in Manchuria and of Mussolini in Ethiopia.[23] This theme was echoed by U.S. representatives in the UN, where, until 1967, their speeches used some of the strongest invectives against China in order to muster increasingly uncertain international support for the U.S. policy of denying Communist China membership. Hence, Adlai Stevenson, who was personally in favor of a "two Chinas" policy, dutifully portrayed China as leading a "plague of warrior states," as "unregenerate," "the world's most warlike regime," intent on "shoot[ing] [its] way into our council halls."[24]

---

[20] Thomson to Harriman, memo of policy planning meeting, 12 January 1962, *FRUS 1961–3*, XXII, pp. 176, 179n.

[21] The Chinese attack caused 140,000 American casualties and the longest retreat in American military history.

[22] Dulles, "Our Policies," pp. 561–3.

[23] Cohen, *Dean Rusk*, p. 322; "United States Policy toward Communist China," statement by Secretary Rusk to the Subcommittee on Far East and the Pacific of the House Committee on Foreign Affairs, 16 March 1966, p. 5; *DSB* 57, p. 347.

[24] *DSB* 46, pp. 109–12; *DSB* 49, p. 755. On Stevenson's own views, see his article "Putting First Things First: A Democratic View," *Foreign Affairs* 38(2) (January 1960), pp. 191–208.

In the 1960s, the Korean War continued to provide the prime analogy for the type of Chinese Communist aggression that had to be contained. Yet none of Beijing's aggressive actions during the 1960s came close to the *"massive and direct use of Chinese Communist troops in overt aggression"* that was seen in Korea.[25] Apart from the feared invasion of Taiwan that never occurred, China launched a direct attack only once, but on a much smaller scale, during the Sino-Indian border war of October 1962. Kennedy immediately identified the Chinese attack as an "aggressive expansion of Communist power," signaling that "the subcontinent has become a new area of major confrontation between the Free World and the Communists."[26] India was of special significance because it was regarded as a political and socioeconomic counterweight to Chinese power in Asia.[27] Even before Nehru appealed for help, the Kennedy administration had decided to send arms and equipment to India. Yet the administration's response to the war was primarily the conscious exploitation of a "golden opportunity" to achieve two long-term American aims in South Asia: to woo nonaligned India into the American camp in the Cold War, and to foster an India-Pakistan rapprochement so that the subcontinent could be developed as an effective counterweight to Communist China.[28]

However, American aid to India was more limited than some pro-India officials would have liked. Rusk and Secretary of Defense Robert McNamara were unwilling to get directly involved, for fear of pushing Pakistan further toward a rapprochement with China or provoking a joint Moscow-Beijing reaction.[29] Moreover, there was general agreement that, rather than a full-scale invasion of India, Beijing's objective was limited to securing a disputed area in order to maintain control over Tibet.[30] Still, the Sino-Indian War was the main example of the Chinese Red Menace during the 1960s. To Rusk, it revealed "China's readiness to

[25] Stevenson to UNGA, *DSB* 49, p. 4 (emphasis mine).

[26] JFK to Ayub Khan, 28 October 1962; JFK to Harriman, 25 November 1962, *FRUS 1961–3*, XIX, pp. 359, 407.

[27] See John F. Kennedy, "If India Falls," *The Progressive* 22 (January 1958), pp. 8–11; Robert McMahon, *The Cold War on the Periphery: The United States, India, and Pakistan* (New York, 1994), p. 282.

[28] Rostow to Rusk, "Sino-Indian Confrontation," 2 November 1962; Komer to McGeorge Bundy, "Where Do We Go From Here," 7 December 1962, National Security Council Files [NSF] / Komer Files, Box 420, JFKL.

[29] Rusk to Galbraith, 20 November 1962, *FRUS 1961–3*, XIX, p. 401; Roger Hilsman, *To Move a Nation: The Politics of Foreign Policy in the Administration of John F. Kennedy* (New York, 1967), p. 337.

[30] Harriman mission memo, 3 December 1962, *FRUS 1961–3*, XIX, p. 418; Hilsman to Rusk, "The Five-Fold Dilemma: The Implications of the Sino-Indian Conflict,"

turn on even those who have tried to be a friend and to resort to overt aggression wherever its expansionist aims are thereby served."[31] A Policy Planning Staff paper written soon after the attack stated that pressure would be maintained on the "unregenerate regime" in view of its "active hostility . . . toward the non-Communist world." It argued that the offensive warranted continued trade sanctions and that a total Western embargo should be imposed if China resumed large-scale attacks.[32] India was a nation for which American liberals had great sympathy, and the Sino-Indian war hardened the attitudes of some officials, such as the ambassador to India, John Kenneth Galbraith, who had argued up until then that China was not expansionist.[33]

Offensive Capabilities

China's convincing defeat of the Indians demonstrated not only its aggressiveness but also its prowess. In launching an attack over what was some of the world's most difficult terrain, China had projected its power into the subcontinent for the first time, humiliating its key regional rival.[34] As William Bundy relates, in official circles the Sino-Indian war was viewed as evidence that China was "thrusting to become the dominant power in the area." It had demonstrated its considerable capacity for "sophisticated pressure-type action" and had acquired "much greater prestige and inspired much greater fear all around its borders."[35]

This display of strength exacerbated American officials' fears about the offensive capabilities underlying the Chinese Communist threat. China had traditionally been regarded as menacing primarily because of its "fantastically large" population.[36] In the 1960s, this concern was framed in

---

17 November 1962, Box 1, Hilsman Papers, JFKL; Komer to McGeorge Bundy, 24 November 1962, Box 420, Komer Files, JFKL.
[31] *DSB* 48, p. 642. See also Rusk to de Gaulle, 16 December 1963, *FRUS 1961–3*, XXII, p. 410.
[32] Policy Planning Council [S/P], "US Policy Toward Communist China," 30 November 1962, *FRUS 1961–3*, XXII, pp. 325–32.
[33] Chester Bowles, *Promises to Keep: My Years in Public Life, 1941–1969* (New York, 1971), pp. 475–7. At the height of the crisis, Galbraith (17 November 1962, *FRUS 1961–3*, XIX, p. 388) was moved to upbraid the State Department: "in light of our past lecturing on the aggressive designs of the ChiComs, we cannot now . . . confine our help in accordance with the assumption that the Chinese are lambs." These and other officials more sympathetic to China will be discussed in Chapter 3.
[34] Hilsman, *To Move a Nation*, p. 338.
[35] Bundy, draft manuscript, Chapter 7, Johnson Presidential Library [LBJL], p. 6.
[36] Isaacs, *Images of Asia*, p. 99.

two ways. First, American officials worried that the population pressure on resources would inevitably cause Beijing to look toward the Southeast Asian "rice bowl" to feed its population.[37] Bowles, especially, saw China as a "land-hungry, resource-hungry nation of exploding population with clearly expansionist aims."[38] Militarily, this huge population translated into one of the largest standing armies in the world, which American soldiers had encountered during the Korean War: they had been "swamped by a yellow tide," a "human sea" of Mao's volunteers.[39] Continuing wariness of this aspect of the Chinese military was evident in General Maxwell Taylor's 1963 statement that the United States should never again engage "the hordes of China" and that "any military contest with Communist China should be nuclear."[40]

The Kennedy administration was particularly concerned about China's developing nuclear capability. Rusk's controversial warning in 1967 about "a billion Chinese ... armed with nuclear weapons" is often cited,[41] but Kennedy had painted this scenario earlier, in 1963, when he had warned that China would soon be a power with "700 million people, a Stalinist internal regime, ... nuclear powers, and a government determined on war as a means of bringing about its ultimate success." Geography and ideology, backed by a new capability, would give rise to "a more dangerous situation than any we faced since the end of the Second World War."[42] In fact, it was generally acknowledged throughout the 1960s that the Chinese nuclear capability would remain very limited for some time and would not affect the overall strategic nuclear balance.[43] But Kennedy brooded about the imminent danger: he felt that even "relatively small [nuclear]

---

[37] S/P, "Review of US China Policy," 31 December 1957, *FRUS 1955–7*, III, p. 664; McNamara to Senate Armed Services Committee, 1964, quoted in Warren Cohen, *America's Response to China* (New York, 1990), p. 282.

[38] *DSB* 46, pp. 375–6. Bowles was convinced of a possible Chinese drive for *lebensraum* into Southeast Asia and tried to convince Kennedy to reduce this threat by selling food grains to China. See Chapter 3, this volume.

[39] S. L. A. Marshall, *The River and the Gauntlet* (New York, 1953), p. 210; Mark Clark, *From the Danube to the Yalu* (New York, 1954), pp. 87–101.

[40] Memo of NSC meeting, 11 May 1963, *FRUS 1961–3*, XXII, p. 367.

[41] *DSB* 57, p. 563.

[42] Press conference, 1/8/63, *Public Papers of the Presidents: John F. Kennedy [PPP:JFK]* (1963), p. 616. Kennedy expressed the same vivid worry to his advisers; see memo, 11 January 1963, *FRUS 1961–3*, XXII, p. 339.

[43] Johnson to Rostow, "The Implications of a Chinese Communist Nuclear Capability," 19 July 1963, Box 24, NSF, JFKL; Rostow to Johnson, "The Implications of a Chinese Communist Nuclear Capability," 17 April 1964, Box 237, NSF, LBJL.

forces in the hands of people like the ChiComs could be very dangerous to us all."[44]

Any nuclear capability would magnify the Red Menace because "people like the ChiComs" were implacably hostile, untrustworthy, and irrational. Working from the assumption of Chinese hostility, Rusk dismissed the defensive and symbolic reasons behind China's nuclear development. The Chinese nuclear capability, he told the Senate Foreign Relations Committee in 1966, would be used to intimidate "free" Asian countries or to create a regional nuclear "balance" in which China's "potentially almost unlimited" conventional forces could be used with increased effect. He warned that Chinese nuclear weapons would eventually be deployed against its neighbors and the United States.[45] McNamara expressed similar worries to the Joint Congressional Committee on Atomic Energy in the same year.[46]

Kennedy had hoped to prevent China from developing nuclear weapons by negotiating an international test ban treaty, but American officials generally saw Communist China as standing outside the reach of international norms, arguing that it had no intention of honoring international obligations, as shown by its abrogation of commitments in the Korean armistice, the Geneva accord on Vietnam and Laos, and the 1955 agreement to release American prisoners.[47] Hence there was a strong conviction that a nuclear China was dangerous because it would not adhere to arms limitation treaties even if it signed on to them.

Finally, American officials harbored a basic mistrust of Chinese Communists with nuclear weapons because of their perceived irrationality and inhumane attitude. For instance, Mao had said that in the event of a nuclear war, even if half the world's population were killed, "in a number of years there would be 2,700 million people again."[48] Kennedy told a French minister that a nuclear China would be "the great menace in the future to humanity, the free world, and freedom on earth" because the Chinese would not be restrained by nuclear deterrence – they "would be

---

[44] JFK to Harriman, 15 July 1963, *FRUS 1961–3*, XXII, p. 370.

[45] Rusk, "United States Policy," p. 4.

[46] McNamara to Joint Congressional Committee on Atomic Energy, 7 March 1966, in Congressional Quarterly, *China: US Policy Since 1945* (Washington, 1980), p. 160.

[47] Rusk to Gromyko, 21 September 1961, *FRUS 1961–3*, VII, pp. 184–5; JCSM-343–63, 29 April 1963, ibid., pp. 89–90. See Chapter 3.

[48] Tang, *America's Failure in China*, p. 576; John Lewis and Xue Litai, *China Builds the Bomb* (Stanford, 1988), p. 66.

perfectly prepared to sacrifice hundreds of millions of their own lives" to carry out their "aggressive and militant policies."[49]

Washington also worried about the psychological impact of Chinese nuclear capabilities in terms of Chinese prestige, security concerns on the part of its neighbors, and further nuclear proliferation.[50] These were considered serious enough for both the Kennedy and Johnson administrations to consider launching a preemptive strike at Chinese nuclear facilities with both conventional and nuclear weapons.[51] The idea of joint action with the Soviets to launch a preemptive strike against Chinese facilities was also broached.[52] McGeorge Bundy approached Dobrynin with the idea but received an unfavorable response.[53] A question remains as to whether the Kennedy administration was merely exploring various planning options or seriously contemplating such a strike, for aside from the nuclear issue, Kennedy was generally cautious and did not want war with China. Certainly, the interdepartmental planning group tasked with studying options for U.S. action argued that the political costs and military risks involved in a direct attack were not justified by the significance of the Chinese nuclear capability and would only delay, not destroy it.[54] Hence, the Johnson administration was more circumspect; when the Chinese exploded their first nuclear device in October 1964, Johnson confined himself to reassuring the American public that the administration had been expecting the event, that defense plans had taken it fully into account, and that U.S. defense commitments to its allies remained firm.[55]

---

[49] Quoted in Chang, *Friends and Enemies*, p. 236. The Defense Department, predictably, was inclined to take a similarly pessimistic stance. See DoD paper, "China as a Nuclear Power (Some Thoughts Prior to the Chinese Test)," 7 October 1964, National Security Archive China Fiche Document [NSA Doc.] 20.

[50] JFK to Macmillan, 29 March 1963, *FRUS 1961–3*, VII, p. 754; DoS draft position paper, 14 August 1964, *FRUS 1964–8*, XI, pp. 97–108; Hilsman to Rusk, "SE Asian Neutralist Reactions to a Chinese Communist Nuclear Detonation," 5 October 1962, Box 410, Komer Files, JFKL; NSC memo, "Effects of the Chinese Bomb on Nuclear Spread," 2 November 1964, Box 5, NSF, LBJL.

[51] JCSM-986-63, 31 July 1963, *FRUS 1961–3*, VII, p. 24*n*; NSC paper, "Destruction of Chinese Nuclear Weapons Capabilities," 14 December 1964, China Folder, Box 5, NSF, LBJL.

[52] Declassified documents from this period reveal oblique references to "radical steps" in a "joint program" – e.g., *FRUS 1961–3*, VII, pp. 22–3. For a more detailed discussion, see Chang, *Friends and Enemies*, pp. 242–5; and especially Burr and Richelson, "Whether to 'Strangle the Baby in the Cradle.'"

[53] Bundy memos, 15 and 25 September 1964, *FRUS 1964–8*, XXX, pp. 94, 104–5.

[54] S/P, "An Exploration of the Possible Bases for Action against the Chinese Communist Nuclear Facilities," 14 April 1964, ibid., pp. 39–40.

[55] *PPP:LBJ* (1963–4), II, pp. 1357–8.

Continuity and Limitations

The image of China as Red Menace was prominent among American policy makers in the 1960s. It was carried over from the definitive experience of the Korean War and the subsequent representation of a worldwide Cold War. In the 1960s, this discourse was fueled by further evidence of the totalitarian rule of the CCP, the Sino-Indian War, and growing Chinese offensive capabilities. The main reason for the continuity of this representation of China from the 1950s was that many key figures in office during the 1960s were Democrats whose perceptions of China had been formed during the traumatic Truman years. Bowles, Harriman, and Stevenson had all been there and, even if not personally convinced, were deeply aware of the Democrats' stigma associated with the "loss" of China and having been "soft" on communism, and were wary of hard-line public opinion regarding China. As a young congressman, Kennedy himself had attacked John Fairbank and Owen Lattimore for betraying China to the communists even before Joe McCarthy had leveled his accusations.[56] Rusk was assistant secretary for Far Eastern affairs at the time, and the experience of Korea especially hardened his attitude.[57]

Kennedy and Rusk were particularly assiduous in applying this inherited experience during their time in office. Rusk saw China as a renegade in relation to the international norms and the world order that he, with his "streak of messianic idealism" about the American place in the world, held in such high regard.[58] His resultant consistently hard line against China has earned him the dubious accolade of having been the persistent obstacle to changes in China policy during the 1960s.[59] But Kennedy adopted a harder stance toward China than is usually admitted – he specifically forbade Rusk from considering any change in China policy, and he acted to maintain the status quo by secretly promising Chiang Kai-shek to use America's Security Council veto to keep China out of the UN.[60] He also actively contemplated and ordered contingency plans for attacks on Chinese nuclear facilities. Clearly, Kennedy felt himself hamstrung during

---

[56] Cohen, *Dean Rusk*, p. 167.
[57] Ibid., pp. 59, 163; Rusk, *As I Saw It*, p. 250.
[58] Thomas Schoenbaum, *Waging Peace and War: Dean Rusk in the Truman, Kennedy and Johnson Years* (New York, 1988), p. 14.
[59] See, for instance, James Thomson, "On the Making of China Policy, 1961–9: A Study in Bureaucratic Politics," *China Quarterly* 50 (1972), p. 243; Bowles, *Promises to Keep*, pp. 307, 365–7, 403.
[60] JFK to Chiang, 16 October 1961, *FRUS 1961–3*, XXII, p. 160; Rusk, *As I Saw It*, pp. 282–4.

his first term by his marginal victory and by domestic political pressures.[61] That public opinion was indeed strongly against China during this period was demonstrated, for instance, in the dramatic poll result of March 1963 showing that a 47 percent to 34 percent plurality considered China to be a greater threat to world peace than the Soviet Union.[62] However, it would seem that he was also particularly suspicious of the Chinese Communists and, as Noam Kochavi suggests, had little understanding of Beijing's security fears of superpower encirclement and nuclear blackmail.[63]

Some limitations of the Red Menace discourse of the 1960s are clear from the foregoing analysis. First, it was an image of China confined to particular policy makers during the early 1960s, most obviously Kennedy and Rusk. Second, this image was articulated most loudly in the realm of public discourse; where it was presented in private exchanges, there was generally less invective. The image was conjured up in public rhetoric for the purpose of gaining and maintaining domestic and international support for the costly hard-line policies against China. Lastly, the aggression envisaged in the Red Menace image as derived from the Korean War example involved massive, direct Chinese military aggression. But instances of such action were almost nonexistent during the 1960s, apart from the Sino-Indian War, and even this was acknowledged to be a limited and restrained campaign. Instead, as the next section argues, the main form of Chinese hostility was indirect and often covert support for revolutionary movements. Thus, while there was a consensus that China was a threat to be contained and isolated within the prevailing Cold War structure, the analysis so far has shown that, in practice, the parameters of the "Red Menace" image of China as expansionist military aggressor were tightly drawn.

"REVOLUTIONARY RIVAL": COMMUNIST CHINA AS INDEPENDENT MILITANT CHALLENGER

The Chinese menace as identified by American policy makers in the 1960s was an evolving entity. Within the internal official discourse there

---

[61] Rusk, *As I Saw It*, p. 283. Kennedy was particularly constrained by Eisenhower's warning that the latter would reenter public life to oppose any attempt to recognize Communist China.

[62] Kusnitz, *Public Opinion and Foreign Policy*, p. 106. But Kusnitz also argues that this process was mutually reinforcing: "opinion had precluded any real changes in policy early in Kennedy's term and, having spurred on a tougher government stance, was now, in turn, being affected by it."

[63] Noam Kochavi, "Kennedy, China, and the Tragedy of No Chance," *Journal of American-East Asian Relations* 7(1–2) (Spring/Summer 1998), pp. 107–16.

developed a more well-defined hostile image of China, which differed in significant ways from the "Red Menace," even though it retained aggressive, renegade qualities and remained within the Cold War framework. This image of China as a "Revolutionary Rival" emphasized Beijing's goal of communist revolution rather than national expansion. Hence the means and focus of Chinese aggression were also reconceived. China was revolutionary because it posed a threat not so much in terms of direct military aggression against its immediate neighbors as through its provision of an alternative model of politico-economic development, and through its indirect support of "national liberation movements" in the Third World.[64] Moreover, Beijing's revolutionary fervor was increasingly stoked by the rivalry that attended the developing Sino-Soviet split. To Washington, China appeared to be the more radical and violent of the two leading communist states, and it was increasingly seen as an independent threat to, and the main enemy of, the United States.

"Aggression by seepage": Chinese Revolutionary Warfare

In its conduct of foreign policy after the Korean War, Beijing demonstrated considerable skill in manipulating the political and psychological elements of power. As seen in the Sino-Indian war, direct aggression by the Chinese tended to be opportunistic; it targeted weaker countries and employed Mao's "talk/fight, talk/fight" tactics, designed to achieve Chinese aims without massive military deployment. At the same time, Beijing was increasingly carrying the fight to the emerging smaller and weaker "in-between" states. Concentrating on the declared communist aim of "winning all the people of the world for socialism," China courted these new states diplomatically and with communist doctrine, and also appeared actively to be promoting and supporting so-called wars of national liberation within them.[65] Communist China thus embarked on "revolutionary warfare," which combined political subversion with guerrilla warfare.

That Beijing relied more on "revolutionary warfare" than outright military aggression was recognized by the Kennedy administration. A November 1961 special intelligence report stated that China was "almost certainly not going to attempt the open military conquest of any Far Eastern country" – its leaders believed that they could achieve their

---

[64] On Communist China's competing model of development, see Foot, *Practice of Power*, Chapter 8.
[65] Although – apart from Vietnam – Beijing apparently did not provide much concrete support for these movements. See Peter Van Ness, *Revolution and Chinese Foreign Policy: Peking's Support for Wars of National Liberation* (Berkeley, 1970).

objectives at far less cost and risk by using "Communist political warfare techniques" and, where appropriate, by supporting and guiding "guerrilla and terrorist action by indigenous forces."[66] This assessment appeared to be borne out in the Beijing-backed communist insurgency crises in Laos and Vietnam that faced Kennedy when he entered office. The tactic was the use of force in prolonged covert local action, involving the infiltration of forces trained outside the area to direct and accelerate the guerrilla war. In Vietnam, for instance, the United States charged that "terrorists" trained in the North were infiltrating and fighting in the South as the Vietcong.[67]

In this way, the Chinese were advocating a more subtle use of force, not across but within boundaries, in the form of "aggression by seepage."[68] The resulting threat was ambiguous: although it was often cited within the broad catalogue of Chinese misdemeanors by officials such as Rusk, the difficulty of lumping "revolutionary warfare" with overt military expansion was recognized. Hence, the administration felt the need to justify U.S. counteraction by making clear that revolutionary warfare was still "aggression." Deputy National Security Adviser Walt Rostow was at pains to emphasize that "[t]he sending of men and arms across international boundaries and the direction of guerrilla war from outside a sovereign nation is aggression"; it was especially important to clarify that "the operation run from Hanoi against [South] Vietnam is as clear a form of aggression as the violation of the 38th parallel by the North Korean armies."[69]

Kennedy himself, however, felt that communist revolutionary warfare constituted a new kind of threat because of the different means employed. In his May 1961 "Special Message to Congress on Urgent National Needs," he expressed his concern about the unorthodox threat of

---

[66] SNIE 13-3-61, "Chinese Communist Capabilities and Intentions in the Far East," 30 November 1961, *FRUS 1961–3*, XXII, pp. 172–3. The same assessment was made in 1962 and 1963 – see NIE 13-4-62, "Prospects for Communist China," 2 May 1962; NIE 13-63, "Problems and Prospects in Communist China," 1 May 1963, *FRUS 1961–3*, XXII, pp. 221–3, 365–6.

[67] Hilsman, "The Challenge to Freedom in Asia," speech on Cold War education, Florida, 14 June 1963, *DSB* 49, pp. 44–8.

[68] U. Alexis Johnson, "US Foreign Policy in the Far East," speech at a conference on foreign affairs, University of Nebraska, 20 June 1963, *DSB* 49, p. 79.

[69] Rostow, "Guerrilla Warfare in the Under-developed Areas," address at U.S. Army Special Warfare School, Fort Bragg, 28 June 1961, *DSB* 45, p. 236. Rostow was Kennedy's key adviser on counterinsurgency and himself favored a stronger military response to the communist insurgencies in Laos and Vietnam.

guerrilla warfare: "They have fired no missiles; and their troops are seldom seen. They send arms, agitators, aid, technicians and propaganda to every troubled area. But where fighting is required, it is usually done by others. . . . "[70]

Later, he told West Point graduates: "This is another type of war, new in intensity, ancient in its origins – war by guerrillas, subversives, insurgents, assassins, war by ambush instead of by combat; by infiltration, instead of aggression, seeking victory by eroding and exhausting the enemy instead of engaging him. . . . It requires a whole new kind of strategy, a wholly different kind of military training."[71]

The Joint Chiefs of Staff (JCS) and Vice President Johnson pushed for large-scale conventional military intervention to help the South Vietnamese, but Kennedy was convinced that communist revolutionary warfare was most effectively met by counterinsurgency techniques.[72] He personally promoted the use of Special Forces for counterguerrilla warfare, set up an interdepartmental "counter-insurgency" committee, and had the State Department establish a special "counter-insurgency" course for all officials posted to underdeveloped countries. In Vietnam, he adopted the strategy of isolating and securing "strategic hamlets" in order to cut off guerrilla supplies, a technique derived from the British counterinsurgency experience in Malaya.[73]

Kennedy's counterinsurgency program in Vietnam failed for reasons having to do with the porous and uncontrollable borders and infiltration routes in Laos and Cambodia and the unstable and unpopular South Vietnamese government.[74] However, the techniques that Kennedy chose reflected his representation of the Chinese Communist revolutionary threat in Southeast Asia. His analogies were the communist insurgencies in Greece, Malaya, and the Philippines rather than the Chinese attack in Korea.[75] While identifying the Chinese as the perpetrators, he dealt with the revolutionary war in Vietnam as a local affair; it was "their war," the United States could "help them . . . give them

[70] 25 May 1961, *PPP:JFK* (1961), p. 397.
[71] 6 June 1962, *PPP:JFK* (1962), p. 453.
[72] See Douglas Blaufarb, *The Counterinsurgency Era: US Doctrine and Performance* (New York, 1977), Chapters 1–4.
[73] Hilsman, leaving memo, 14 March 1964, *FRUS 1964–8*, I, pp. 179–82; Hilsman, *To Move a Nation*, pp. 438–9.
[74] See Lawrence Freedman, *Kennedy's Wars: Berlin, Cuba, Laos, and Vietnam* (Oxford, 2000), pp. 287–413; Yuen Foong Khong, *Analogies at War: Korea, Munich, Dien Bien Phu, and the Vietnam Decisions of 1965* (Princeton, 1992), pp. 91–5.
[75] Khong, *Analogies at War*, pp. 83–95.

equipment... send out... advisers," but the South Vietnamese would have to fight the communists themselves.[76] Kennedy was firmly against the "over-militarization" of U.S. involvement in Vietnam.[77] The image of China that emerges is one of an aggressor employing sinister means but ultimately posing an ambiguous threat in peripheral areas, one that did not justify conventional military resistance or a large-scale military commitment.

Sino-Soviet Split: China as "Revolutionary Rival"

While they recognized its unconventional "revolutionary warfare" tactics, American officials' perceptions of an aggressive China during the 1960s also evolved against the context of the Sino-Soviet dispute. Reports indicated that the rift centered upon Khrushchev's 1956 decision to seek "peaceful coexistence" with the West. Mao instead insisted on the inevitablility of war in the revolutionary struggle, condemned Soviet "revisionism," and challenged the Soviet position at the center of communist ideology. This ideological disagreement was central, because revolution, of either the class struggle or the anti-imperialism variety, lay at the heart of Maoism. Thus, "the negation of... violent revolution meant the negation of the universal applicability of the Chinese revolutionary model and the rejection of the 'unique contribution' [Mao] had made to Marxism-Leninism."[78]

Even though American officials could not decide at that time on the lasting significance of the Sino-Soviet dispute, the combination of Chinese polemics and evidence of China's growing support of communist insurgencies around the world was sufficient for them to identify China as the more militant communist threat. This in turn provided arguments against any relaxation of China policy. Rusk opposed the sale of food grains to

---

[76] CBS interview, 2 September 1963, *PPP:JFK* (1963), p. 652.

[77] This is not to say that the American commitment to South Vietnam under Kennedy was insubstantial: he increased the number of American military advisers, logistic units, and pilots from about 700 to 16,700. The radically expanded commitment in economic, military, and prestige terms formed a crucial basis for Johnson's decisions in 1965. See Lawrence Bassett and Stephen Pelz, "The Failed Search for Victory," in Thomas Paterson, ed., *Kennedy's Quest for Victory* (New York, 1989); Freedman, *Kennedy's Wars*, pp. 398–413.

[78] Yang Kuisong, "Changes in Mao Zedong's Attitude toward the Indochina War, 1949–1973," CWIHP Working Paper No. 34, p. 8. On the development of the Sino-Soviet dispute, see Dittmer, *Sino-Soviet Normalization*; Herbert Ellison, ed., *The Sino-Soviet Conflict: A Global Perspective* (Seattle, 1981); and Odd Arne Westad, ed., *Brothers in Arms: The Rise and Fall of the Sino-Soviet Alliance 1945–1963* (Stanford, 1998).

China in 1961, because Washington could not be seen to be softening its stance against China now that "Peiping seems to be splitting even from Moscow in pursuance of a more aggressive policy."[79] For the same reason, he refused to consider opening other lines of communication or to invite China to participate in disarmament negotiations the following year.[80]

By 1962, most American officials were convinced that the Soviets and Chinese were deeply divided.[81] The Cuban missile crisis and the Sino-Indian war at the end of 1962 presented important turning points. While the Chinese attack on India and its bellicose position during the Cuban missile crisis reinforced its more militant image, the Soviets markedly moderated their stance after the missile crisis. As the United States and the Soviet Union worked toward détente, Moscow seemed genuinely to want to avoid confrontation and seek "peaceful coexistence." The Partial Nuclear Test Ban Treaty was signed in August 1963, to vitriolic condemnation of superpower collusion by Beijing.[82] While intelligence sources were unanimous in assuring U.S. policy makers that the Chinese leaders were ultimately cautious and would not embark on irrational aggression, an NIE study warned that as a result of the coincidence of the deepening Sino-Soviet dispute and recent Soviet negotiations with the West, Beijing would become "more disagreeable" and could be expected to undertake "somewhat more assertive initiatives, in the hope of attaining limited but visible gains at minimum risk."[83] These actions would take place in Asia, where, even as Moscow's new moderation and the Cuban fiasco proved costly to Soviet prestige in Hanoi, Jakarta, and Pyongyang, Chinese influence was on the ascendance.

---

[79] DoS to Emb/Rangoon, 27 November 1961, FRUS 1961–3, XXII, p. 175n.

[80] NIE 11-5-62, "Political Developments in the USSR and the Communist World," 21 February 1962; Rusk to Rostow, 17 April 1962, FRUS 1961–3, XXII, pp. 207–8. Rusk's subordinate Walt Rostow had argued to the contrary that, given the apparent depth of the Sino-Soviet split, Washington ought to extend the carrot-and-stick approach in seeking dialogue and détente, while maintaining containment, to both Moscow and Beijing. See FRUS 1961–3, XXII, pp. 207–8. This is further discussed in Chapter 3, this volume.

[81] Foot, The Practice of Power, pp. 131–2; Hilsman, To Move a Nation, p. 344; Arthur M. Schlesinger, Jr., A Thousand Days: John F. Kennedy in the White House (London, 1965), p. 614; Thomson, "On the Making of China Policy," pp. 226–7.

[82] Summary of Zhou Enlai's conversation with representatives of the Kenyan African People's Congress, 5 September 1963, Zhou Enlai waijiao wenxuan (Beijing, 1989), pp. 335–9. On the Soviet-American détente, see Jennifer W. See, "An Uneasy Truce: John F. Kennedy and Soviet-American Détente, 1963," Cold War History 2(2) (January 2002), pp. 161–94.

[83] SNIE 13-4-63, "Possibility of Greater Militancy by the Chinese Communists," 31 July 1963, FRUS 1961–3, XXII, p. 371; INR, "Is Peiping Trying to Trigger World War III?," 22 July 1963, Box 24, NSF, JFKL.

Overall, therefore, the split from the Soviet Union promised increased Chinese activism and even ideological radicalism, an image that the Soviets helped to cultivate. Rusk could hardly ignore it when he was told by "a Foreign Minister beyond the Iron Curtain" that moving China toward "peaceful coexistence" was the biggest problem for peace in the world.[84] Soviet specialists within the administration – men like George Kennan, Charles Bohlen, and Llewellyn Thompson, all of them of higher stature than the generally middle-level China advocates – also argued that China was the more dangerous of the two communist powers and warned against any relaxation of China policy lest the developing Washington-Moscow détente be harmed.[85]

By 1964, nearly all official contact between the Chinese and the Soviets had been severed, their quarrel had degenerated into crude abuse, and it became clear that there was "virtually no chance of reconciliation" between the two.[86] American officials began to identify a separate "Asian Communism" arising from this dispersion of authority within the communist movement. A 1963 CIA report warned about the emergence of an "Asian Communist Bloc under the leadership of China." which, because of Beijing's "militant and intense anti-Western" line, would have "grave implications" for U.S. security interests in East Asia.[87] In order to deal with this separate branch of the communist movement, an Office of Asian Communist Affairs was formed within the Far East Bureau of the State Department in November 1963.[88]

A separate China-led militant wing of communism could be identified with clarity because of Chinese activism in the developing world during the first half of the 1960s. Beijing was trying to consolidate its bid for communist leadership by establishing itself as the champion and mentor of the underdeveloped nations.[89] It had its greatest impact in Southeast

[84] Testimony of Dean Rusk, *The Vietnam Hearings* (New York, 1966), p. 18.
[85] See e.g., Thompson to Rusk, "Policy re Treatment of Sino-Soviet Conflict," 26 February 1963, *FRUS 1961–3*, XXII, pp. 350–1; Thomson et al., *Sentimental Imperialists*, p. 283.
[86] NIE 10-2-64, "Prospects for the International Communist Movement," 10 June 1964, *FRUS 1964–8*, XXX, pp. 62–3.
[87] Ray Cline, "Sino-Soviet Relations," 14 January 1963, *FRUS 1961–3*, XXII, p. 340.
[88] Bureau of Far Eastern Affairs (EA) paper, n.d., ibid., pp. 397–8. But as Paul Kreisberg, who headed the ACA from 1965 to 1981, pointed out, this bureaucratic distinction also helped to foster an official "lobby" that was primarily interested in Communist China and "not just dealing with it as an enemy, but broadening and increasing the levels of contacts with it." Kreisberg oral history interview, 8 April 1989, Association for Diplomatic Studies and Training, Georgetown University Library, pp. 1–2.
[89] NIE 13-9-65, "Communist China's Foreign Policy," 5 May 1965, *FRUS 1964–8*, XXX, pp. 168–70.

Asia, with its activities in Indochina, but it also formed a close relationship with President Sukarno in Indonesia. Between 1960 and 1964, the Chinese leadership undertook an intense diplomatic offensive to promote ties with nonaligned and newly independent states, especially in Africa. To Rusk, Beijing's activities in Indonesia and Premier Zhou's presence in Africa were further evidence of Chinese "militancy."[90] Yet from Beijing's point of view, the diplomatic campaign was successful; by 1964, fourteen African states and, more significantly, France had recognized Communist China, dealing a severe blow to the American policy of nonrecognition.

China's activism in the developing world threatened America's position also because China appeared to be gathering a "Third World" coalition against the superpowers. Senator Walter Judd had expressed this worry back in 1949, when he imagined Communist China as a "dissident Bolshevism loose in Asia," trying to transform the world revolution into one of *"haves versus have-nots* on international lines."[91] In a key speech in 1965, Marshal Lin Biao seemed to affirm this view. Extrapolating from Mao's strategy of rural revolutionary war, he likened the developing countries of the world to the rural areas where proletarian revolutionary struggles had to be fought. The central developed imperialist world would be encircled, divided, and defeated by this developing periphery. Most menacing was Lin's emphasis on the "fundamental guiding principle" of "wars of annihilation."[92] In the context of the Chinese revolutionary activism of the time, Lin's speech appeared to be a blueprint for worldwide Chinese Communist aggression and reminded many American officials of Hitler's *Mein Kampf.*[93]

During the first half of the 1960s, therefore, a perception of Chinese communism as the more radical and aggressive revolutionary rival to Soviet communism was developing in parallel to Kennedy's perception of an unconventional and relatively limited form of Chinese "revolutionary warfare." By the period 1964–5, China had come to be seen by American policy makers as a separate, fiercer menace to the United States because

[90] Rusk to LBJ, memo of meeting with de Gaulle, 16 December 1963, *FRUS 1961–3*, XXII, p. 409.
[91] "Comments on China Policy, 1948/9," Judd Papers, Box 96, China, quoted in Chang, *Friends and Enemies*, p. 253.
[92] Lin Biao, "Long Live the Victory of People's War!," *Peking Review* 36 (3 September 1965), pp. 26–7, 18–9.
[93] Cohen, *Dean Rusk*, pp. 285–6. This analogy was used repeatedly during the Senate hearings on China in 1966, and even by Ambassador Cabot to his Chinese counterpart at the Warsaw talks. See Emb/Poland to DoS, "Cabot-Wang Talks," 15 September 1965, *FRUS 1964–8*, XXX, p. 204.

of its apparent achievement of broad influence across the Third World. Thus there was a tension in that what were perceived as relatively limited means were apparently being employed by the Chinese with greater efficacy, and toward more extreme ends. American policy makers generally overcame this cognitive dissonance by adopting the image of China as the most menacing of the new forces at work in the world, a separate radical communist power threatening American security interests. As William Bundy, then the assistant secretary of state for East Asia, put it, "while the American government was not alarmed about China to the extent of seeing grave possibilities of military attack, it did see in the total pattern of Chinese behaviour and expressed ideology a very great cause for concern, that had come to focus most specifically on Southeast Asia."[94]

Vietnam: Making Multiple Stances

American officials' perceptions of China as a militant Revolutionary Rival coalesced around the Johnson administration's Vietnam policies. American officials justified U.S. intervention in Vietnam in two ways. Within the broad Cold War framework, they were resisting international communist aggression and containing its expansion. More specifically, the United States wanted to disprove the efficacy of the militant Chinese brand of communist revolution. This entailed American policy makers in effect taking sides in the Sino-Soviet dispute, as they tried to boost Moscow's influence and its more moderate ideology. In its turn, this led to the precise outcome that Washington had tried to avoid in adopting the official stance of noninterference in the Sino-Soviet dispute. It was thought that it would be too risky to attempt to make hay out of the intracommunist split, as this might give cause for Sino-Soviet reconciliation.[95] Yet by escalating its intervention in Vietnam and trying to persuade Moscow to broker peace negotiations, the Johnson administration inadvertently brought about a situation of de facto cooperation between the two communist rivals as they competed to aid Hanoi against the common imperialist enemy.

Kennedy had seen the Vietnam conflict as a localized covert rebellion supported at a distance by the Chinese Communists. But Johnson

---

[94] Bundy, draft manuscript, Chapter 16, LBJL, p. 20.
[95] DoS and USIA to all U.S. diplomatic posts, "Info Policy Guidance on Sino-Soviet Relations," 24 July 1963, Box 3863, CFPF(1963); DoS to all U.S. diplomatic posts, "US Attitude Towards Sino-Soviet Relations," 7 May 1964, Box 2019, CFPF(1964–6); HK to DoS, "Communist China – US Policy Assessment," 17 February 1967, Box 1974, CFPF(1967–9), RG59, NA, p. 16.

inherited a failing counterinsurgency program, already-significant U.S. commitments to Vietnam, and general agreement that South Vietnam was falling into communist hands – all within the context of the heightened perception of China as an independent militant world revolutionary threat. Under Johnson, Vietnam came to be more firmly identified as China's war – Beijing's national interest was seen to be heavily imputed in the conflict because Vietnam was the crucial "test case for its vaunted doctrine of 'people's wars'... on which Mao's very claim to fame in the Marx-Lenin-Stalin lineage is based."[96]

The CIA warned in 1964 that communist victory in South Vietnam would support the Chinese Communists' aggressive tactical contentions against those of the more cautious Soviets and would thereby boost Chinese claims to world communist leadership. Beijing was already advertising South Vietnam as proof that the developing world was ripe for revolution, that the United States was a paper tiger, and that Maoist revolutionary warfare was a "cheap, safe, and disavowable technique for the future expansion of militant communism."[97] The prevailing view in the Johnson administration was that the United States must thwart Beijing's ambitions because even though the means were different, the ends were the same Cold War ones: Beijing and Hanoi were attacking South Vietnam in order to organize a communist coalition in Asia, which would pose a security threat to U.S. interests.[98] This "domino theory" was the basis of the Cold War strategy of containment. Vietnam was the first "war of national liberation," and the "hawks" argued that it had to be resisted as though it were conventional aggression, for "if we walk out of this one, we will just have to face others."[99]

In 1965, U.S. "resistance" was broadened to include systematic reprisal bombings in North Vietnam and a ground war in South Vietnam. When

---

[96] Draft memo, "The Chinese Equation," 27 April 1967, Box 1, NSF/Jenkins Files, LBJL. Although prevalent, this was not a conviction shared by all within the Johnson administration. The primary dissenter was Undersecretary of State George Ball, who argued against escalation in 1965 partly on the grounds that the rest of the world saw the Vietnam conflict as a civil war, and who was not convinced that the Vietcong were an instrument even of Hanoi, not to mention Beijing. Ball to Rusk, McNamara, and Bundy, "How Valid Are the Assumptions Underlying Our Vietnam Policies?," 5 October 1964, reprinted in *Atlantic Monthly* 320 (July 1972), pp. 35–49.

[97] CIA, 9 June 1964, *FRUS 1964–8*, I, pp. 485–7; Gen. Maxwell Taylor, "US Objectives in Vietnam," in *Highlights of the Hearings of the Senate Foreign Relations Committee* (Washington, 1966), p. 203.

[98] McNamara, draft memo to LBJ, "Courses of Action in Vietnam," 3 November 1965, *FRUS 1964–8*, III, pp. 514–15.

[99] General Earle Wheeler (Chairman, JCS), Vietnam meeting record, 21 July 1965, ibid., III, p. 204.

Hanoi and the Vietcong would not be dissuaded, American officials placed the blame squarely on Beijing. Intelligence reports in 1965 uniformly represented the Chinese Communists as "violent, unyielding, offering no avenue to settlement acceptable to the US," while Hanoi was "almost, but not quite as obdurate as the Chinese."[100] In the Senate hearings on Vietnam in 1966, Rusk elaborated on this subtle differentiation: although Hanoi was "the prime actor," the "instrument" of aggression, it was the "policy" of Beijing, its "doctrine," that was used to stimulate and support the aggression and to block negotiations.[101] Beijing was obstructing negotiations because it believed it could wear down the United States and eventually win the war, which would enormously enhance its position at both Soviet and American expense.[102]

By contrast, in the course of the Vietnam decisions of 1965 American policy makers acted according to the image of the Soviet Union as the more moderate arm of the communist movement. In their view, the Soviets actually wanted a peaceful settlement of the crisis but were being sucked into the conflict as a direct result of competition with their militant Chinese rivals. In early 1965, Moscow informed Western governments of its wish to settle the Vietnam conflict through negotiations, and the State Department took this as an indication of the Soviets' apparent commitment to better relations with the West. Rusk told the NSC in March that "[i]t is a pity that the US and the USSR are being dragged along by North Vietnam." He felt that there was "a difference between one country attacking another and the USSR supporting another socialist country."[103] In July, he was more candid: he saw "no real reason for a basic difference between the US and the USSR on Vietnam.... At the other end of the spectrum was Beijing, which was adamant against negotiations."[104] When they considered a pause in the bombing campaign in December, American officials hoped that the break might strengthen Moscow's hand in persuading Hanoi to negotiate.[105] Until the end of 1966, Johnson himself

---

[100] CIA briefing paper, 11 June 1965, *FRUS 1964–8*, II, p. 770.

[101] *Vietnam Hearings*, pp. 21, 269.

[102] NIE 11-12-66, "The Outlook for Sino-Soviet Relations," 1 December 1966, *FRUS 1964–8*, XXX, p. 484; Rostow, "A Strategy for Vietnam, 1967," 28 November 1966, *FRUS 1964–8*, IV, pp. 873–82.

[103] NSC meeting notes, 26 March 1965, *FRUS 1964–8*, II, p. 483.

[104] Bundy, "Meeting with Joint Congressional Leadership," 27 July 1965, *FRUS 1964–8*, III, p. 256.

[105] Bundy to Johnson, "Once More on the Pause," 27 November 1965; meeting on bombing pause, 18 December 1965, *FRUS 1964–8*, III, pp. 582–3, 658–69.

was still asking the Soviet Union to use its influence to end the war, to no avail.[106]

American officials explained that Moscow's apparent inability to persuade Hanoi to negotiate was a result of Chinese pressure. As Rostow told Johnson, Hanoi had to "live with China in the long run," which made it difficult for Hanoi to turn wholly to Moscow and its moderate advice.[107] These assessments were relatively accurate. When U.S. bombing appeared to cause Hanoi to consider Soviet proposals for peace talks in 1965, Mao strenuously opposed the idea, urging them to keep fighting. Mao Zedong redoubled his efforts to support violent revolution in Vietnam during this period – but this was also partly in response to the fact that, in a departure from Khrushchev's previous stance, Brezhnev had, in November 1964, declared that the Soviet Union would provide "all necessary support" to North Vietnam. Thus, Beijing was now forced to compete with Moscow not only ideologically, but also materially, in the DRV.[108] In 1965, the Soviet Union became the main source of military aid to Hanoi, providing some 70 percent to 95 percent of the equipment. Furthermore, the Soviets were supplying sophisticated equipment, such as surface-to-air missiles and antiaircraft guns, that the Chinese could not produce.[109] The State Department's Soviet specialists Kohler and Thompson argued that the Soviets had limited aims in spite of their support for Hanoi. They did not want to expand the war because they shared Washington's concerns about the risk of Chinese involvement, which would place before Moscow the "intolerable" dilemma of either becoming directly involved itself because of the 1950 treaty with China, or standing aside and dropping all pretense of communist solidarity.[110]

Because most American officials believed that Vietnam was China's war and that the Soviets wanted peace, the widespread explanation for Moscow's participation was that Washington itself had compelled the Soviet Union to aid Hanoi. Dobrynin claimed that continued

---

[106] LBJ to Gromyko, 10 October 1966; LBJ to Kosygin, 6 December 1966, *FRUS 1964–8*, IV, pp. 716–21, 906.

[107] Rostow to LBJ, 23 December 1965, *FRUS 1964–8*, III, p. 697. Hanoi's main concern beginning in 1964 was to juggle between Beijing and Moscow in order to get as much support in the war as it could; it did not seriously consider negotiations until late in 1968. See Ang Cheng Guan, *Ending the Vietnam War: The Vietnamese Communists' Perspective* (London, 2004).

[108] Yang, "Changes in Mao Zedong's Attitude toward Indochina," pp. 13–16.

[109] Intelligence report, "An Appraisal of the Effects of the First Year of Bombing in North Vietnam," 1 June 1966, *FRUS 1964–8*, IV, p. 432.

[110] Bundy, draft manuscript, Chapter 21, LBJL, p. 7.

American bombing of North Vietnam made any negotiation impossible.[111] American officials opposed to the escalation agreed, pointing out that the U.S. attacks furnished a "just cause" for communist aid to North Vietnam and that the Soviets could not now be seen to relinquish support of Hanoi.[112] Moscow was forced to compete with its Chinese rival in providing support for Hanoi in order to assert its leadership of the communist movement. According to this logic, escalation left the United States with the worst of both worlds, since the Soviets were forced to compete with the Chinese Communists on Beijing's terms and to act on parallel lines in order to support Vietnam.[113] This was an unresolved tension for many officials who, while believing that the more moderate Soviet Union was the best channel for negotiations, also maintained that firm resistance against Beijing and Hanoi was necessary.

China Policy Implications

The assumption that Vietnam was primarily Beijing's war reinforced the image of China as America's worst enemy. In this sense, the Vietnam War had stultifying implications for China policy. According to the Revolutionary Rival discourse, Washington was maintaining its policy of containing and isolating China by intervening in Vietnam. The United States had to adopt a tough stance in Vietnam to convince China that its "irrational militancy" could not succeed; any sign that the United States was softening its position toward China in other ways would imply that the United States was "rewarding" Chinese aggression. This was Rusk's consistent line against increasingly insistent pressure from allies and some officials in favor of UN membership for China.[114]

But as U.S. involvement in Vietnam deepened, one central ambiguity in American officials' image of China developed: an unexpected consensus on the perceived limits of Chinese aims. For our purposes, this forms an entry point into the other competing discourses about China during this

[111] Dobrynin to Thompson, 30 December 1966, *FRUS 1964–8*, IV, pp. 981–2.
[112] Ball and James Thomson, especially, had insisted that if it wanted peace through Moscow, Washington had to provide the Soviet Union with a political alternative, such as the submission of the whole problem to the UN Security Council for a great power–sponsored peace conference. Ball to LBJ, 13 February 1965, *FRUS 1964–8*, II, pp. 259–61.
[113] Vietnam Panel meeting notes, 8 July 1965, *FRUS 1964–8*, III, p. 140.
[114] Bundy, "Meeting with the President on United Nations Matters," 18 November 1964; Rusk to Canadian Secretary of State Paul Martin, 20 September 1966; Rusk to New Zealand Prime Minister Mike Pearson, 9 November 1966, *FRUS 1964–8*, XXX, pp. 126–7, 398–9, 421–2.

period. The internal policy debates about U.S. escalation forced a recognition that American attacks on North Vietnam would change the character of the war for China, as they would pose a direct threat to Chinese security on its southern border. The Vietnam policy makers were acutely aware – urged by Johnson's insistent probing – that U.S. escalation risked some form of direct Chinese reaction such as that in the Korean War, although they disagreed about the threshold at which this might happen.[115] George Ball persistently argued the worst case – that the Chinese would take fright at U.S. air attacks in the North and retaliate – but his was a lone voice within the inner circle of Vietnam policy makers.[116] Paradoxically, it was the "hawks," insisting on a strong stance against militant Chinese aggressors, who argued that Beijing would have a higher level of tolerance for U.S. attacks on North Vietnam because its ability to retaliate was constrained. The JCS and Rusk thought that because of its internal problems, and with no assured Soviet support, the Chinese would not risk a large-scale military adventure against the United States.[117] Intelligence officials concurred with the "hawks": intelligence estimates for 1965 assured Vietnam policy makers that China was unlikely to intervene with ground troops under conditions short of a U.S. ground attack on North Vietnam or U.S. air attacks on bases in southern China itself.[118] From Washington's key China listening post in Hong Kong, Consul General Edward Rice agreed that China would not intervene unless the "very existence" of the North Vietnamese regime was threatened. He agreed that China's ability to project power far beyond its borders was limited, and added that the North Vietnamese, who were traditionally wary of Beijing's control, did not want Chinese troops fighting in their country.[119]

---

[115] As Khong points out, the Korean War analogy eventually acted as a constraint by influencing Johnson's choice of graduated rather than heavy continuous air attacks – see *Analogies at War*, pp. 138 43.

[116] Apart from Ball, the only other high-level administration official who voiced misgivings about underestimating the likelihood of Chinese intervention was Vice President Hubert Humphrey. See Humphrey to LBJ, 17 February 1965, *FRUS 1964–8*, II, pp. 309–13.

[117] JCS to McNamara, "Vietnam and Southeast Asia," 22 January 1964, *Pentagon Papers*, pp. 283–5; Rusk memo, 19 April 1964, *FRUS 1964–8*, I, p. 252.

[118] CIA briefing paper, 11 June 1965, *FRUS 1964–8*, II, pp. 768–9.

[119] Rice to Bundy, 9 November 1965, *FRUS 1964–8*, III, pp. 556–9. Bundy agreed with this analysis – see Bundy to LBJ, 3 December 1965, ibid., p. 598. But the main thrust of Rice's argument, unlike that of the "hawks," was to assert that a U.S. escalation of the war would rather undermine these obstacles to overt Chinese intervention. See also Rice, "China's Major Problems Affecting US Policy," 7 January 1966; Rice to Bundy, telegram, "US Strategy in Vietnam and Possible Chinese Communist Intervention," 24 June 1966, Box 239, NSF, LBJL.

These arguments against the likelihood of Chinese military intervention
suggested that the Vietnam War was essentially a nationalistic war, with
Hanoi, and not Moscow or Beijing, at the center. More importantly, they
suggested limits to Chinese support for Hanoi, and hinted at a China that
was weak and essentially concerned about its national security. As some
scholars have pointed out, even though Beijing did deploy Chinese troops
in North Vietnam from 1964 onward, the Chinese presence was inten-
tionally communicated to U.S. intelligence. In this sense, the troops were
intended to act defensively, as a deterrent against an American invasion of
the North.[120] This sentiment was consistent with Chinese signals in 1965.
In a message sent via the British, Chinese Foreign Minister Chen Yi said
that China would not take the initiative to provoke a war with the United
States and would take part in the Vietnam conflict only if the war expanded directly into Chinese territory.[121] The Chinese also evinced their
worries at the regular Sino-American bilateral talks in Warsaw, where
the U.S. ambassador reported unusually "impassioned" ad-libbing by his
Chinese counterpart to the effect that the United States was "not only
committing aggression against Vietnam but...also posing [a] threat to
China every day," "jeopardis[ing] [the] security of...our...country."[122]

   Thus we find a significant ambiguity in American officials' image of
China as Revolutionary Rival. As the Sino-Soviet split deepened, and after
Kennedy's death and the failure of counterinsurgency, it appeared that
China posed an independent militant communist threat to both Soviet and
American positions. In the context of the Vietnam War, officials retained
a firm belief in the essential character of China as a threat – "in practice
the fear of China intervening in a defensive way tended to merge with the
fear of China pressuring and subverting in an offensive way."[123] Yet the
representations of China that prevailed among American policy makers

[120] Zhai Qiang, *China and the Vietnam Wars, 1950–1975* (Chapel Hill, 2000), pp. 137–
8; Allen Whiting, *The Chinese Calculus of Deterrence: India and Indochina* (Ann Arbor,
1975), p. 186.
[121] Chen Yi to British Chargé Hopson, 31 May 1965, *FRUS 1964–8*, II, p. 700.
[122] Emb/Poland to DoS, "Cabot-Wang Talks," 30 June 1965 and 15 September 1965, *FRUS
1964–8*, XXX, pp. 179, 204–5. The Johnson administration in turn reassured Beijing
about its limited intentions; this is discussed in the next chapter. On these ambassadorial
talks, which represented a continuous point of official Sino-American contact from 1955
to 1970, see Zhang Baijia and Jia Qingguo, "Steering Wheel, Shock Absorber, and
Diplomatic Probe in Confrontation: Sino American Ambassadorial Talks Seen from the
Chinese Perspective," and Steven Goldstein, "Dialogue of the Deaf? The Sino-American
Ambassadorial-Level Talks, 1955–1970," both in Ross and Jiang, eds., *Re-examining the
Cold War*.
[123] Bundy, draft manuscript, Chapter 32, LBJL, p. 38.

in 1965 suggested inherent limits to the capabilities of an independent but less secure Communist China. The next chapter discusses how some American officials' growing understanding of China's internal weakness and preoccupations led them to reconstruct China in less hostile ways, to attribute to Beijing possibly less menacing intentions in accordance with its diminished capabilities, and to argue for changes in China policy.

3

"Troubled Modernizer" to "Resurgent Power"

Revisionist Images of the PRC and Arguments
for a New China Policy

As the hostile policy discourse toward Communist China evolved and became more acute and yet also more ambiguous during the 1960s, a parallel revisionist discourse was developing both in reaction to events and as a result of personal convictions. Throughout the decade, a number of officials within the Kennedy and Johnson administrations worked to convince their colleagues of the need to alter the official U.S. position toward the PRC. This group combined liberal Democratic stalwarts such as Chester Bowles, Averell Harriman, and Adlai Stevenson; "old China hands" such as Edward Rice; and Asian and China specialists such as Roger Hilsman, Edwin Reischauer, James Thomson, and Robert Komer. They variously occupied the main China advisory positions in the State Department and the White House and headed key diplomatic posts.

These officials pushed for the relaxation of China policy and accumulated a "shopping list" of possible American initiatives that included lifting the travel ban on Americans wishing to visit China, removing trade restrictions on nonstrategic goods, inviting the Chinese to disarmament negotiations, and ending Beijing's exclusion from the UN on the basis of various "two Chinas" arrangements. They advanced arguments that were based on two central revised images of China, focusing in turn on its weakness and poverty, and on its pride and potential strength. Together, these two images identified China in ways that revealed potential common areas of understanding between the United States and China. Initially, the revisionist discourse was submerged within internal memoranda, waged as personal campaigns by midlevel officials. By the second half of the 1960s, however, it was boosted by China specialists outside of the government and was adopted to some extent within high-level official public discourse.

"TROUBLED MODERNIZER": CHINA AS AN UNDERDEVELOPED COUNTRY

The previous chapter showed that between 1961 and 1968, there was disagreement even at the highest levels in Washington about the nature and extent of the Chinese threat, and about the appropriate means with which to counter it. At the middle level of policy making, a number of key officials were also trying to convince their colleagues that the Chinese threat was heavily circumscribed by China's intractable internal problems. There were three distinct episodes during which Beijing appeared to be particularly weak, unstable, or domestically preoccupied: 1961–2, when the adverse consequences of the "Great Leap Forward" became apparent; 1965–6, when China suffered serious international diplomatic setbacks; and 1966–8, when Mao embarked on the Cultural Revolution. China was portrayed as a Troubled Modernizer by revisionist American officials and academics who argued that its problems stemmed from the failure of its political-economic system. They were convinced that China's economic dislocations would eventually force Beijing to concentrate on internal problems and bring to the fore moderate technocratic elements who would seek economic development within the world economy. The implication was that communism in China could be muted, not through rigid strategies of containment and isolation, but by advancing positive initiatives, which would strengthen such moderate leadership elements.

China in Trouble: Consequences of the "Great Leap Forward"

The "Great Leap Forward" (GLF) was a series of extreme agricultural and industrial development programs implemented by Mao in 1958 as an alternative to the Soviet (and Western) model of capital-intensive heavy industrial development. In an effort to mobilize China's vast population, the communist leadership implemented mass labor projects – first the large-scale establishment of agricultural communes, and then cottage industrial production, most infamously in the form of "backyard" steel furnaces. In 1961, Kennedy entered office just as the disastrous effects of the GLF program were becoming apparent.

U.S. intelligence reports of 1961 and 1962 vividly portrayed China's domestic crisis. Mao's ill-conceived development programs had failed dismally, causing not only massive structural dislocation in the economy, but also sociopolitical instability in the form of widespread food crises, public disaffection, and rising dissidence. Chinese industrial development, which had appeared promising in the first half of the 1950s, was now crippled by the backyard production policies and the withdrawal of Soviet technicians in July 1960. A special intelligence report in April 1961 estimated that the annual growth in industrial production had dived from 33 percent in 1959 to 12 percent and was unlikely to recover within the next few years. Another report estimated that industrial production had fallen by 41 percent in 1960–1 alone.[1] But the fundamental crisis was in agricultural production. The diversion of peasant labor away from farm production during the industrial GLF, combined with three successive years of bad crop weather, resulted in disastrous harvests in 1960 and 1961. Overall agricultural production fell by 30 percent between 1958 and 1960, and food output remained static while the population grew by 50 million during that time. One indication of the food shortage was that Beijing spent $200 million of its limited foreign currency reserves importing nearly three million tons of food grains during 1961.[2]

Although the scale of what we now know to have been a massive famine was not appreciated by American intelligence at the time, U.S. analysts were aware of the considerable social disruption engendered by the food shortages.[3] The CIA reported widespread hunger and exhaustion among the Chinese population and even within the army, which resulted in looting, arson, food riots, and the murder of communist cadres in certain areas.[4] The most obvious indication of popular disaffection and official demoralization was the sudden jump in the number of Chinese refugees entering Hong Kong, from the usual 100–200 per month to 1,500 in April 1962. In May, up to 5,000 refugees crossed the border each day.[5]

---

[1] SNIE 13–61, "The Economic Situation in Communist China," 4 April 1961, *FRUS 1961–3*, XXII, pp. 40–1; CIA, "The Situation in Mainland China," 27 July 1961, Box 22, NSF, JFKL.

[2] Ibid.

[3] The scale of the 1959–62 famine has only recently been established; estimates of the number of deaths range from 14 to 30 million. See Jasper Becker, *Hungry Ghosts: China's Secret Famine* (London, 1996). On the failure of U.S. intelligence to appreciate the scope of the disaster, see Noam Kochavi, "Mist across the Bamboo Curtain: China's Internal Crisis and the American Intelligence Process, 1961–1962," *Journal of American–East Asian Relations* 5(2) (Summer 1996), pp. 135–8.

[4] Lansdale to McNamara, 3 April 1961, *FRUS 1961–3*, XXII, p. 39; CIA, "Morale of Party Cadres and Armed Forces in Communist China," 18 May 1961, Box 22, NSF, JFKL.

[5] Hilsman, *To Move a Nation*, p. 315; ConGen/HK to DoS, 21 May 1962, *FRUS 1961–3*, XXII, p. 232*n*.

Although it was clear from intelligence information that China was undergoing a period of economic stagnation and even regression, American officials' perceptions of China's weakness were qualified in several ways. During 1961 and 1962, a number of officials within the Kennedy administration (most notably Bowles, Thomson, and Rice) proposed various food initiatives to China, such as allowing American companies to provide bunkering for foreign ships carrying food to China, offering gifts or emergency sales of food, and even lifting the embargo on food grains and medicines. Initially, it appeared that these would be humanitarian gestures that might help relieve bilateral tensions. The Chinese had supposedly expressed interest in food sales through American firms and through Burma, but these apparent openings failed to materialize.[6] Intelligence reports and even officials advocating a food initiative agreed that China was not likely to accept American food, even under famine conditions. It was felt that a domestically troubled Beijing needed to maintain the United States as its primary external enemy and was not about to temper its basic hostility toward Washington.[7] This view seemed to be vindicated when, in response to Kennedy's statement that he would consider food shipments to China if Beijing made a request, Chinese Foreign Minister Chen Yi retorted that China "need not be a beggar" for American aid.[8]

While the failure of the GLF severely weakened China's socioeconomic structure, it appeared to inflict less damage on the communist regime's power or on its ideological and strategic ambitions. Thus, in the aftermath of the GLF, Beijing maintained its enmity toward the United States, nurtured its dispute with the Soviet Union, launched a short military campaign against India, stepped up its support for revolutionary wars in Indochina and elsewhere, and pressed ahead with its nuclear weapons development program.

---

[6] In 1961, a Seattle firm claimed that China wanted to buy grain from it, but the government found no evidence for the claim. See Harriman to McGhee, 25 January 1962, *FRUS 1961–3*, XXII, p. 183n; and Department of Commerce, 26 March 1962, ibid., p. 209n. Bowles had also planned to travel to Rangoon to explore Chinese attitudes toward food sales with Burmese Prime Minister U Nu, but the latter was deposed in a coup before he arrived. Bowles to JFK, "US Initiative Regarding the China Mainland Food Crisis," 6 February 1962; Bowles to JFK, 27 June 1962, China Security 1962 Folder, Box 113A, President's Office Files (POF), JFKL; Bowles, *Promises to Keep*, pp. 470–1.

[7] SNIE 13–61, p. 41; U. Alexis Johnson to Rusk, "United States Policy on Shipments of Medicines and Food Grains to Communist China," 6 April 1962, *FRUS 1961–3*, XXII, pp. 213–4; Harriman to Rusk, 13 April 1962, ibid., pp. 216–7.

[8] Press Conference, 23 May 1962, *PPP:JFK 1962*, p. 431.

A Developmental Crisis

However, even as the Kennedy and Johnson administrations sought to deal with these hostile Chinese activities, its China watchers were gradually building up an image of China that emphasized its deep-seated economic crisis, which they predicted would eventually force Beijing to change its priorities radically. This image of China as "Troubled Modernizer" portrayed its internal problems as essentially a developmental crisis, a characterization drawn from assumptions of a universal path of development based on the Western model of industrialization and urbanization.[9]

The immediate sources of China's Troubled Modernizer image for American policy makers were the intelligence reports on China's economic situation from 1961 to 1966. These reports identified two key problems. First, China was an overpopulated country: its huge and rapidly growing population, combined with a low level of technology, rendered its arable land grossly inadequate. We have seen how China's enormous population was widely perceived to be the primary force contributing to Beijing's expansionist policies. By contrast, these intelligence reports portrayed China's population problem in developmental parlance, as "the race between food production and population growth." It was a problem that could be solved by inputs of modern technology and skills, accompanied by a birth control program.[10] In this sense, China's resource problem was similar to those faced by other "underdeveloped" countries.

However, China was in fact suffering a developmental crisis because of the misplaced priorities of, and the misallocation of scarce resources by, a communist leadership driven by ideological compulsions and extreme nationalism. Despite the lesson of the failed GLF, China's leaders quickly returned to their focus on military industrial development. From 1964 onward, American intelligence sources estimated that Beijing would revert prematurely to a policy favoring industrial development without committing enough resources to put agriculture on a sound footing, and would continue to sustain substantial military production even at the risk

---

[9] The classic work on this theory of development was in fact written by Walt Rostow: *The Stages of Economic Growth: A Non-Communist Manifesto* (Cambridge, 1960). On the impact of Rostow's theory during the 1950s and 1960s, see James Hagen and Vernon Ruttan, "Development Policy under Eisenhower and Kennedy," *Journal of Developing Areas* 23 (October 1988); and Kimber Charles Pearce, *Rostow, Kennedy, and the Rhetoric of Foreign Aid* (East Lansing, MI, 2001).

[10] SNIE 13-2-61, "Communist China in 1971," 28 September 1961; NIE 13-5-66, "Communist China's Economic Prospects," 13 January 1966, *FRUS 1961–3*, XXII, pp. 139, 241–2.

of serious economic difficulty. On this basis, they believed that "China [could] not become a modern industrial state for many years."[11] This was because, according to Western economic development models, industrial growth required large agricultural outputs such as industrial raw materials and food for urban workers. At the same time, in order to expand, agriculture needed basic inputs of chemical fertilizers and machinery – which Chinese industry could not provide either, because the distribution of skilled manpower and industrial production was skewed toward military production programs.[12]

American officials were concerned about the Chinese economic development process not because Mao was actively trying to subvert the "stages of economic growth" per se. They were mainly concerned with the implications of Mao's policies for social welfare and stability. Intelligence reports routinely predicted that the CCP would not commit sufficient resources to basic social needs. A 1961 SNIE anticipated that within the next ten years, China would rank among the world's top three producers of coal, steel, and electric power – but "its people [would] continue to subsist on a barely adequate diet in good [harvest] years, and suffer shortages in bad years."[13] A 1966 intelligence report juxtaposed this human deprivation with Beijing's determination to invest in costly weapons programs and concluded that "even in the face of a critical food emergency," the regime would probably make only "grudging and piecemeal cuts in its military programs."[14]

The key element of the discourse of China as a "Troubled Modernizer" is that those who held it believed in the universality of, and thus in the inevitable triumph of, Western socioeconomic liberalism.[15] These American officials saw Mao's economic policies, which systematically undermined basic social needs, as unsustainable. Hence intelligence reports warned

---

[11] NIE 13–64, "Economic Prospects for Communist China," 28 January 1964; NIE 13–3–65, "Communist China's Military Establishment," 10 March 1965, *FRUS 1964–8*, XXX, pp. 15–17, 152–4.

[12] This was discussed in detail by American officials – see Special State-Defense Study Group, "Communist China: Long Range Study," June 1966, ibid., pp. 332–43.

[13] SNIE 13–2–61, "Communist China in 1971," 28 September 1961, *FRUS 1961–3*, XXII, pp. 138–40.

[14] NIE 13–5–66, p. 241.

[15] On the endemic nature of the belief in the universal applicability of the American system and American values in guiding U.S. foreign policy, see Emily Rosenberg, *Spreading the American Dream: American Economic and Cultural Expansionism, 1890–1945* (New York, 1982); and Michael Mandelbaum, *The Ideas That Conquered the World: Peace, Democracy and Free Markets in the Twenty-first Century* (New York, 2002).

that "difficulties will accumulate in the economy, within the leadership, and between the regime and the people" and that "some future Chinese leadership will be forced to a fundamental concentration on China's economic problems."[16]

The time for such a domestic focus seemed to come in 1965, when the failure of the Chinese model of development was dramatized at the international level by a series of major diplomatic setbacks. China's standing within the developing world was dealt severe blows when it tried to block Soviet participation in a second Afro-Asian Conference modeled on Bandung. In Africa, a number of its diplomats were accused of subversive activities and expelled, while in Indonesia, Beijing's protégé Sukarno was overthrown and replaced by the fiercely anticommunist Suharto regime. Within the communist world, Chinese trade relations with Cuba broke down when Castro accused Beijing of "imperialist exploitation," and with even Albania drawing away, China found itself even more isolated. Soon after this external crisis, the Chinese Communist regime, as the United States had anticipated, turned its attention to domestic affairs – but not to economic reform. As the Cultural Revolution began in 1966, China retreated into isolation, convulsed by massive social upheaval and purges that further destabilized its socioeconomic structures.[17] Hence, if the "monumental miscalculations" of the GLF meant that Communist China "no longer interest[ed] developing countries as a model for rapid social and economic growth," the Cultural Revolution in turn "shattered the image of [the] collective leadership of the Chinese Communist regime [as] a homogeneous elite" and thus superior to the leadership of the Soviet and other movements.[18]

Dealing with the Troubled Modernizer

Throughout these three periods of crisis in China, revisionist American officials developed the Troubled Modernizer image. This represented China as a poor, underdeveloped, and overpopulated country, whose alternative "communization" model of development had ended in spectacular failure. Thus, these officials argued, China would inevitably have to carry out economic reform and enter the international economy. These officials

---

[16] NIE 13–64, p. 17; NIE 13–5–66, p. 242.
[17] See Roderick MacFarquhar, *The Origins of the Cultural Revolution*, vols. 1–3 (New York, 1974, 1983, 1997); and Andrew Wedeman, *The East Wind Subsides: Chinese Foreign Policy and the Origins of the Cultural Revolution* (Washington, DC, 1987).
[18] Barnett to Berger (EA), "China Strategy," 11 May 1967, Box 1, Jenkins Files, LBJL, p. 1.

also assumed that the domestic crisis would divide the Chinese leadership and encourage the emergence of more pragmatic elements, who would lead the impetus for reform. Therefore, the United States could help to edge China onto this inevitable path by relaxing its policy of isolation in order to encourage and strengthen those Chinese leaders eager to carry on with the business of modernization.

It began with the severe food shortages that Washington knew China to be suffering in the aftermath of the GLF. Although they agreed that any U.S. offer of food would be rebuffed, a number of officials urged that Washington take an interest in other Western food deals with the Chinese because these offered leverage over future Chinese behavior – the "food for peace" argument.[19] The State Department advised Western allies such as Australia, Canada, and France, which were already supplying China with wheat, that they might try to temper Chinese aggression by indicating "a relationship between the direction of any important change in its external behavior and continued availability to it of non-bloc foodgrains."[20] Even Walt Rostow, who was a hard-liner against the communists, argued in favor of opening up channels for possible food deals with China. He emphasized that China was generally being forced by the Sino-Soviet split to increase trade and other contacts with noncommunist countries. This increased dependence on the West showed that, despite its tough ideological rhetoric, China was becoming "just another nation in an increasingly diffused arena of world power," subject to the leverage and influence of other nations.[21]

Officials who adhered to the hostile images of China naturally opposed the idea of encouraging trade with Beijing. Rusk insisted that Washington should maintain the pressure to force Beijing to change its behavior instead of taking initiatives which would bail the Chinese Communists out of their failures.[22] However, revisionist officials countered that conciliatory

---

[19] See Bowles to JFK, 6 February 1962, *FRUS 1961–3*, XXII, p. 185.

[20] Rusk to JFK, "US Policy on Shipments of Medicines and Foodgrains to Communist China," 4 April 1962, ibid., pp. 208–11.

[21] S/P, "US Policy Re the Sino-Soviet Split," 2 April 1962, ibid., pp. 207–8; Rostow to Rusk, "State of the World," 17 September 1963, *FRUS 1961–3*, VIII, pp. 508–9. For food as quid pro quo for reducing tensions in Southeast Asia, see Rostow to JFK, 22 November 1961, Box 410, Komer Files, JFKL; and Noam Kochavi, *A Conflict Perpetuated: China Policy during the Kennedy Years* (Westport, 2002), Chapter 4. Kochavi dubs Rostow's approach "visionary revisionism" (p. 248) because of his messianic developmentalist attitude.

[22] Rusk to Macmillan, 24 June 1962, *FRUS 1961–3*, VIII, pp. 276–7; Kohler to Rostow, "Comments on the Possibility of Modifying US Economic Relations with Communist China," 8 March 1962, Box 15, Thomson Papers, JFKL; Komer to Kaysen, 24 January

initiatives were necessary in bringing about any positive change in Beijing's stance because these would appeal to the crucial section of the Chinese leadership that was predisposed to a moderation of hostilities. This point was first made in 1962 by Averell Harriman, then assistant secretary for Far Eastern affairs. He told Rusk that the difficulties following the GLF must have led to "inner battles" within the Chinese leadership, and "evidence that the US [was] willing to . . . [move] our relationship away from one of implacable mutual hostility might strengthen the hand of any element which might favor doing so."[23] Harriman's views were amplified in a State Department paper prepared for the president. While acknowledging that it was not possible to identify individual "dissident elements," the paper stated that "[t]here [were] bound to be among Chinese Communist leaders some who [were] basically more, and others . . . less, antagonistic towards the US, . . . who [might] see advantages . . . in a more conciliatory policy." The implication was that "[b]y inaction we would strengthen the hand of those advocating a line of maximum antagonism; by suitable action we might encourage those who are at the less hostile end of the spectrum – however narrow the spectrum."[24]

Food for China ceased to be an issue by the end of 1962, as the Chinese food crisis gradually diminished and, more importantly, the Sino-Indian War and China's international diplomatic activism seemed to dim the chances of any moderating change in Beijing.[25] A November 1962 S/P paper supported Rusk's stance that Washington should not end its trade embargo on China as this would only ease the pressure on the current regime. At the same time, however, it backed revisionist officials who pinned their hopes instead on the leadership changeover as the current aged leaders passed from the scene. The paper isolated the problem

1962, Box 410, Komer Files, JFKL. For a detailed analysis of the internal debates about the economic embargo on China within the Kennedy administration, which argues that the policy was effective in prising apart the Chinese and Soviets and in putting extreme pressure on Chinese leaders, see Zhang Shu Guang, *Economic Cold War: America's Embargo against China and the Sino-Soviet Alliance, 1949–1963* (Washington, DC, 2001).

[23] Harriman to Rusk, 13 April 1962, *FRUS 1961–3*, XXII, pp. 216–17.

[24] DoS draft paper, "Food Grains for Mainland China," 28 May 1962, ibid., pp. 231–3. There was apparently a group of Chinese foreign policy officials who advocated easing tensions with the Soviet Union, the United States, and India during the early 1960s, but this was rejected by the Party leadership. See Harding, *Fragile Relationship*, p. 33.

[25] For a useful detailed discussion of the Kennedy administration's deliberations and reactions to the Chinese famine, see Jean Kang, "Food for Communist China: A US Policy Dilemma, 1961–1963," *Journal of American–East Asian Relations* 7(1–2) (Spring/Summer 1998), pp. 39–72.

of leadership succession as the key "touchstone" for U.S. China policy changes. It made clear that the hard-line U.S. policy was specifically targeted only at the current "unregenerate regime" under Mao, and stated that if a new leadership were established via a coup, Washington should "assume optimum chances... [of] a basic reorientation and shape our policies accordingly."[26] This view was expressed publicly in a December 1963 speech by Roger Hilsman, then the assistant secretary for Far Eastern affairs. He identified tensions between the old "Long March" veterans and the upcoming "second echelon" of young Chinese leaders who were less doctrinaire. Referring to the Soviet leadership transition after Stalin's death, he said the United States hoped that a similar evolutionary process might bring to power the younger, more pragmatic leaders.[27]

It is useful to note, however, that these revisionist officials focused exclusively on the prospect of *peaceful* change on the mainland. Indeed, no U.S. official, not even those who held more hostile views of Beijing, seriously contemplated the possibility of more actively exploiting the political turmoil in China in order to force a regime changeover. This was made clear during the Taiwan Straits crisis of June–July 1962, when the PRC began a troop build-up opposite the offshore islands while Taipei agitated for an offensive against the mainland. In an attempt to manage the crisis, the Kennedy administration reined in the GRC and took the unprecedented step of trying to reassure Beijing via the British, the Soviets, and the Warsaw channel that it would not support any attack by Taipei.[28] This stemmed from an explicit recognition of Beijing's weak but proud position, and the assessment that the Chinese leaders were acting defensively to try to deter an attack in reaction to Nationalist provocation. Washington's priority was to prevent Beijing from "lash[ing] out in desperation."[29]

---

[26] S/P, "US Policy toward Communist China," 30 November 1962, pp. 325–6.

[27] Hilsman, speech to the Commonwealth Club of San Francisco, 13 December 1963, *DSB* (6 January 1964), pp. 11–17. The import of the message was not lost on the Chinese, who protested the American call to "overthrow" the regime – see ConGen/HK to DoS, telegram 1098, 16 December 1963, Box 3862, CFPF (1963), RG59, NA.

[28] DoS to Emb/UK, 22 June 1962; Emb/Poland to DoS, 23 June 1962, *FRUS 1961–3*, pp. 270, 273–5. The Chinese ambassador in Warsaw responded that if Taiwan attacked China, the United States and China might cooperate by continuing their talks "to restore the peace" – see Wang Bingnan, *Zhongmei huitan jiunian huigu* (Beijing, 1985), pp. 89–90.

[29] Hilsman to SoS, "Chinese Communist Military Positioning," ca. June 1962, Box 1, Hilsman Files, JFKL; ConGen/HK to SoS, 23 June 1962; Emb/Taipei to SoS, 26 June 1962, Box 25, NSF, JFKL; Ralph Clough oral history interview, 16 April 1990, ADST, GUL, p. 96.

It was not until 1965–6 that "revisionist" American officials could argue effectively for relaxing China policy based on Harriman's theme of exploiting divisions within the Chinese leadership to U.S. advantage. Indeed, the first half of 1966 presented a unique opportunity for improving Sino-American relations because of the coincidence of three factors. First, Beijing suffered a series of diplomatic setbacks. The State-Defense Study Group believed that China's failures at home and abroad had led to differences even within the old revolutionary leadership, and declared that "Peking is today in the twilight of the regime's revolutionary age."[30] From Hong Kong, Ed Rice reported in early 1966 that the way things had "gone badly wrong" externally was giving rise to a sense of isolation and paranoia within the Chinese leadership. Rice urged that Washington start relaxing its isolationist policies so as to influence the coming leadership succession in Beijing. This would strengthen the more pragmatic among the potential leaders, who wanted to "concentrate more on solving China's enormous internal problems and divert fewer resources to pushing world revolution."[31] James Thomson argued for "modified containment – plus subversion": "the careful use of free world goods, people, and ideas" to offer "doubting elements within the Chinese élite ... alternative patterns of relationships with the US" and to help induce more rational attitudes and behavior.[32]

These arguments for change were supported by a second factor: the escalation of U.S. involvement in the Vietnam War in 1965. Earlier, in 1962, officials in favor of a more aggressive U.S. military involvement in Vietnam had argued that China's economic crisis had inhibited Beijing's willingness to go to war on Hanoi's behalf and thus allowed Washington more leeway in Southeast Asia.[33] By 1965, Johnson's demonstrated toughness in Vietnam was perceived by even some officials who were not generally China policy revisionists as providing an opportunity to relax Chinese travel restrictions, because this would parry right-wing

---

[30] Special State-Defense Study Group, "Long-Range Study," pp. 333–4.
[31] Rice to DoS, 19 February 1966; Rice to Rostow, "US Policy Towards Communist China," 15 April 1966, *FRUS 1964–8*, XXX, pp. 256–9, 282.
[32] Thomson to McGeorge Bundy, "The US and Communist China in the Months Ahead," 28 October 1964; Thomson to Valenti, "Some Propositions on China Strategy," 1 March 1966; Thomson to Rostow, "Relaxation of US Embargo on Trade with Communist China," 4 August 1966, ibid., pp. 117–200, 262–4, 364–5.
[33] See, e.g., Rostow to Taylor, 31 July 1962, *FRUS 1961–3*, XXII, pp. 298–9. On the impact of perceptions of potential Chinese involvement and Kennedy's policies in Indochina, see Kochavi, *A Conflict Perpetuated*, Chapter 6.

criticism.[34] Johnson himself later made the same argument to the press, adding that the war in Vietnam had not prevented U.S. negotiations with the Soviet Union and need not be an obstacle to contacts with China either.[35]

The third factor was the evidence of public support for revisionist officials' arguments. This was provided especially by leading academic China specialists who testified at the highly publicized Senate Foreign Relations Committee hearings on China policy in the spring of 1966. With a remarkable degree of consensus, these China experts fleshed out the image of China as a "Troubled Modernizer." They confirmed that there was an ongoing struggle within the Chinese leadership, which, as Robert Scalapino suggested, pitted "the primitivism implicit in Maoist political-military doctrines" against "the professionalism ... implicit in the whole modernization program."[36] Doak Barnett identified the "primitives" within the Chinese leadership as the ideologues "preoccupied ... with political control ... keeping up political tension ... revolutionary momentum, and ... ideological fervor." The "professionals," on the other hand, were the "technical bureaucrats ... preoccupied with the practical problems of running the economy and other aspects of the country."[37] These academics also reiterated the idea that the move to a more pragmatic concentration on developmental issues was inevitable. As Donald Zagoria put it, "the kind of evolution that is already transforming Russia and the Eastern European Communist countries will have to come one day in China too."[38] The hearings produced a consensus that the United States should pursue a policy of "containment but not isolation" toward China, a recommendation that was echoed in other public discussions and publications by the Council on Foreign Relations, the National Committee on U.S.-China Relations, and the U.S. Chamber of Commerce.[39] In addition, most of the China experts who testified at the Senate hearings were subsequently drafted onto a new China Advisory

[34] William Bundy to Rusk, "Travel of Scholars and Representatives of Humanitarian Organizations," 16 June 1965; McGeorge Bundy to LBJ, "Paul Dudley White and Mainland China," 24 August 1965, *FRUS 1964–8*, XXX, pp. 172, 176, 196; Komer to LBJ, "Open Door for Red China?," 2 March 1966, China, Box 7, White House Confidential Files (WHCF), LBJL; Komer to LBJ, 16 August 1966; Box 239, NSF, LBJL.
[35] "Johnson Revives Bid for Contacts with Red Chinese," *New York Times*, 11 July 1967.
[36] Testimony of Robert Scalapino, 30 March 1966, in Iriye, ed., *US Policy toward China*, p. 61.
[37] Testimony of A. Doak Barnett, 8 March 1966, ibid., pp. 52, 130.
[38] Testimony of Donald S. Zagoria, 21 March 1966, ibid., p. 147.
[39] See Madsen, *China and the American Dream*, pp. 33–52.

Panel to serve as consultants to the State Department's East Asian Bureau.[40]

The expert views expressed at the Senate hearings reflected the changing social context within the United States and the reactions of the liberal elements of the establishment. As Richard Madsen has argued, these scholars objected to the means by which Chinese communism was being contained (but not to the ends) and sought ways that were more consonant with the values of liberal democracy. With the lingering specter of McCarthyism in the back of their minds, and at a time when "domestic controversy over Vietnam was starting to destroy the foundations of civil discourse, the opportunity for a new dialogue on China gave them a glimmer of hope that rational, factually based discussion about Asian affairs among responsible, self-disciplined people could still overcome the confusion created by bitter polarization."[41] Indeed, Madsen shows that something of an epistemic community had formed in 1964–5 around the National Committee on U.S.-China Relations, which consisted of elements of the church, academia, commerce, labor, and the media who sought to promote greater discussion and knowledge and to change public opinion about China. They were relatively successful, for during this period when the pro-Nationalist China lobby was in decline, the mass public began to evince greater interest in improved relations with Communist China.[42] Public opinion surveys did indicate that the American public remained anxious about the Chinese threat – a 1963 poll found a 47 percent to 34 percent plurality that considered China to be a greater threat to world peace than the Soviet Union, a plurality that grew to 71 percent to 20 percent in 1967.[43] But it was accompanied by a perception that negotiations could reduce this threat. In 1964, large (over 70 percent) pluralities were in favor of exchange visits and discussions with the Chinese about problems in Asia.[44] And in 1966, 56 percent favored UN membership for Communist China if this would help to reduce tensions in East Asia – an allusion to reducing U.S. involvement in the Vietnam War.[45]

[40] DoS to Emb/Taipei, State Department Press Release on China Advisory Panel, 7 December 1966, Box 2025, CFPF (1964–6), RG59, NA.
[41] Madsen, *China and the American Dream*, pp. 39–46.
[42] Thomson noted these trends in his memos to Bundy and Valenti.
[43] Leonard Kusnitz, *Public Opinion and Foreign Policy: America's China Policy, 1949–1979* (Westport, CT, 1984), pp. 106, 117.
[44] A. T. Steele, *The American People and China* (New York, 1966), p. 281.
[45] Kusnitz, *Public Opinion*, p. 115.

In 1965 and 1966, the Troubled Modernizer discourse filtered through to the highest levels of the Johnson administration. Although there were only very limited policy changes, there was a marked change in high-level rhetoric. Indeed, a new official language on Sino-American relations developed in 1966. Vice President Humphrey endorsed "containment without isolation," while McNamara talked about "the building of bridges" to China.[46] Johnson himself voiced the idea of inevitable Chinese moderation: "Sooner or later the pragmatic and compassionate spirit of the Chinese people will prevail over outmoded dogmatism."[47] And in a nationwide address in July, he echoed Thomson's line that "the greatest force for opening closed minds and closed societies is the free flow of ideas and people and goods."[48]

The window of opportunity during 1965–6 was a very small one, how-ever, as the Cultural Revolution that began in earnest in the second half of 1966 made any positive response from Beijing impossible. One of Mao's aims was to purge the leadership of his more moderate rivals. In trying to renew and radicalize revolutionary fervor, he was deliberately quashing the moderates' attempts to have China "settle down" as a developing na-tion seeking modernity.[49] But the proponents of the Troubled Modernizer discourse stressed instead that the awaited process of regime succession and evolution was finally beginning. A special CIA report in late 1966 highlighted the impact of the turmoil in exacerbating the fundamental economic crisis within the country and asserted that the long-term trend was moving inexorably against Maoist socialism. Only a pragmatic lead-ership could solve China's problems, while Mao's "desperate effort to reverse the tide may actually hurry his ultimate defeat."[50] Events over the next year seemed to bear out these estimates: the CIA reported on the "mess" and disorder that was affecting agricultural and industrial pro-duction and on the way in which central authority was being crippled by the continuing dissension within the leadership. It again predicted that Mao's extremism would not prevail.[51]

---

[46] Humphrey, speech to the National Press Club, Washington, D.C., 11 March 1966, *DSB* 54, pp. 523–8; McNamara, speech to the American Society of Newspaper Editors, 18 May 1966, Montreal, *AFP 1966*, pp. 14–21.

[47] Speech to the East-West Center, Honolulu, 18 October 1966, *PPP:LBJ 1966*, p. 1222.

[48] Speech to the American Alumni Council, 12 July 1966, ibid., pp. 721–2.

[49] Walt Rostow, *The Diffusion of Power: An Essay in Recent History* (New York, 1972), pp. 371–2.

[50] CIA, Special Memo 14–66, "The China Tangle," 23 September 1966, *FRUS 1964–8*, XXX, pp. 399–402.

[51] CIA, "Communist China's Troubles and Prospects," 22 February 1966, ibid., pp. 662–3.

Revisionist China watchers both inside and outside the administration seized the opportunity of the Cultural Revolution to lobby again for easing U.S. China policy in order to demonstrate the possibility of more peaceful relations with a more responsive successor regime.[52] In 1967, as the breakdown of order in China began to portend another food crisis, the China Advisory Panel and a meeting of the chiefs of mission in the Far East both recommended easing trade controls on shipment of food and medicine to China. In April, the ban on certain pharmaceuticals and some medical equipment was quietly lifted.[53] The China academics who had testified in the Senate in 1966 pressed their case with Johnson again in 1968, arguing that the continuing disorder in China provided an opportunity for the United States to lay the foundations for an eventual reconciliation with China.[54] In February 1968, even Rusk recommended the relaxation of trade controls on food, fertilizers, insecticides, and farm machinery.[55]

Yet there remained others who argued against such initiatives while the outcome of the Cultural Revolution was still uncertain. Al Jenkins, who took over from James Thomson in 1966 as the main China watcher on the White House staff, had initially been in favor of initiatives toward China.[56] But by 1967, he felt that Washington should stay its hand because of the "virtual certainty of non-reciprocation" from the Chinese; the "unpredictability" of the effects of U.S. actions; and the "unseemliness," even "unworthiness," of being more forthcoming with Communist China at a time when hard-liners were in fact on the ascendance in Beijing.[57] He

[52] ConGen/HK to DoS, "Communist China – US Policy Assessment," 17 February 1967; ConGen/HK to DoS, "Communist China – US Policy Assessment," 23 January 1968, Box 1974, CFPF (1967–9), NA.
[53] William Bundy to Rusk, "A New Approach to Our Trade and Transaction Controls against Communist China," 29 March 1967, *FRUS 1964–8*, XXX, pp. 541–3; Bundy to Katzenbach (undersecretary of state), "Licensing of Pharmaceuticals for Sale to Communist China," 18 September 1967, ibid., pp. 597–8.
[54] Jenkins, memo of China experts meeting with the president, 2 February 1968, ibid., p. 635.
[55] Rusk to LBJ, "Policy toward Communist China," 22 February 1968, ibid., p. 646. A good discussion of the Johnson administration's positive response to the Cultural Revolution as compared to the Kennedy administration's negative reaction to the GLF is provided in Victor Kaufman, "A Response to Chaos: The United States, the Great Leap Forward, and the Cultural Revolution, 1961–1968," *Journal of American–East Asian Relations* 7(1–2) (Spring/Summer 1998), pp. 73–92.
[56] Jenkins to Rostow, "Mainland Developments Demand a Clearer US Policy," 3 August 1966, Box 239, NSF, LBJL.
[57] Jenkins to Rostow, "Warsaw and US China Policy," 8 November 1967, Box 1, Jenkins Files, LBJL, pp. 2–3; Jenkins, "Thoughts on China," 22 February 1968, *FRUS 1964–8*, XXX, pp. 516, 656–9.

argued that in the Cultural Revolution climate of exceptional chauvinism and xenophobia, any American attempt to proffer relations with a successor government in Beijing would backfire.[58]

Essentially, Jenkins was cautioning against acting too hastily on the belief, implicit in the Troubled Modernizer discourse, in the eventual, even inevitable, triumph of the moderates seeking development and modernization in China. This assumption reflected American liberal ideals of "the good life," rooted in the belief in freedom of enterprise, conscience, and speech, obtained through individual success and personal self-expression within a competitive economy.[59] The perceived universality of these ideals was reflected in the expectation that the Western economic developmental experience would inevitably be repeated in other developing societies. Furthermore, the idea that there must exist contending individuals within the Chinese leadership accorded with the emphasis on individualism and diversity in American society.[60]

Fundamentally, the Troubled Modernizer image paved the way for a more constructive relationship with China because it emphasized not hostility and fear but the possibility of Sino-American mutual understanding. Rather than identifying China as an "Other" with antithetical characteristics, it represented China as moving – slowly but surely – toward America's own image. The failure of the GLF promoted the image of an underdeveloped country struggling with a backward economy and overpopulation. But as a "Troubled Modernizer," China was assumed to have ambitions and a developmental trajectory similar to those of the West, and to be ultimately understandable in the light of American liberal ideals. In this sense, even the terrible purges of the Cultural Revolution could be seen as a "curious, costly general election" that would bring about more moderate leadership.[61]

"RESURGENT POWER": CHINA AS FRUSTRATED REEMERGING MAJOR STATE

For American officials, the fundamental problem of Sino-American relations in the 1960s was how to get China to "behave" – to give up its menacing revolutionary aims and peacefully coexist with its neighbors and the noncommunist world. Those who saw China as a "Troubled Modernizer"

[58] Jenkins to Rostow, "Do as the Soviets Do?," 20 August 1967, Box 241, NSF, LBJL.
[59] William Sullivan, *Reconstructing Public Philosophy* (Berkeley, 1982), pp. 24–6.
[60] Madsen, *China and the American Dream*, p. 51.
[61] Quoted in Jenkins, "Thoughts on China," p. 658.

believed that the imperative of economic development would make this inevitable, and they thought that the United States could aid this process by encouraging progressive elements in China. During the second half of the decade, however, the revisionist discourse was boosted by a group of "old China hands" who posited an alternative image of China, accompanied by their own thesis on how to induce moderation in Beijing. They identified a central dilemma in China's current position. Because of its size and its ancient civilization, China was a natural and traditional major power in Asia. It had suffered a recent prolonged period of humiliating oppression by Western powers, but had begun to recover its major-power status again under communist rule. However, Beijing's resurgent ambitions contrasted sharply with its isolated, pariah status in international society – the result of what seemed like continuing Western suppression instigated by the United States.

This incongruity led to frustration on all sides. In Beijing, it reinforced extreme nationalism and heightened belligerent attitudes toward the United States and the "free world." Among America's Western allies, it drew increasingly insistent arguments that China, with its rising power and capabilities, could be "tamed" only by its inclusion in international society. In the face of these pressures, Washington's policy of containing and isolating Beijing in order to make it "behave" seemed increasingly futile. The Resurgent Power discourse thus suggested that by adopting attitudes and policies that accorded China some of the dignity due a regional great power, Washington would help to moderate Beijing's hostile stance and recover its own credibility. This was the most dynamic of the four main discourses on China policy of the 1960s, and the following analysis traces its development in three stages.

"China Is Here to Stay"

In 1961, the Kennedy administration faced a Communist China that had demonstrated its willingness and ability to use force against the "free world" in Korea, Indochina, and the Taiwan Straits. Moreover, it had obliged the world's major powers to deal with it on an equal basis at the 1954 Geneva peace conferences despite its pariah status. As a result, the international community was increasingly in favor of admitting China into the UN so that there could be greater international contact with, and a moderating influence on, a state that seemed bent on disrupting the world order. In the UN, the margin of states voting for a moratorium on the question of seating Communist China had steadily declined, and by 1961 three allies – Britain, Canada, and Brazil – had informed Washington that they would vote against the resolution.[62] Thus the United States risked a defeat in the 1961 vote that would damage its prestige if it did not agree to a debate on the issue.

This international pressure coincided with the first significant indications of China policy rethinking among U.S. public opinion leaders. In the aftermath of Dulles's brinkmanship during the second Taiwan Straits crisis of 1958, critics called for limiting U.S. commitments to Taiwan and allowing China to join the UN – moves toward a less potentially dangerous "two Chinas" policy. In 1959 and 1960, the Senate Foreign Relations Committee, academics, and noted Democrats such as Adlai Stevenson and Chester Bowles recommended such changes.[63] Kennedy himself said in a television debate with Richard Nixon that he favored persuading the Nationalists to give up the offshore islands.[64]

As a result of the impending crisis over the Chinese representation issue in the UN, China policy was subject to intense scrutiny and debate during the first months of the Kennedy administration. Midlevel revisionist officials quickly tapped into the international and domestic trends toward rethinking China policy. On the NSC, Robert Komer urged that Washington stop opposing UN membership for Communist China and deny support to the Nationalists on the indefensible offshore islands. It was "almost inevitable," he argued, that "some aspect" of China policy would have to be changed; and the administration ought to "disengage, as skillfully as we can, from unproductive aspects" of the policy. Komer stressed that these changes had to be made in order to "rationalize for the long pull," to

---

[62] The moratorium was a tactic devised by the Truman administration in 1950 to postpone discussion of Communist Chinese UN membership. In 1960, the vote was forty-two in favor of continuing the moratorium, thirty-four to discuss the issue, and twenty-two abstentions. It was felt that should the United States' main allies "defect" from its position, other, less important allies and neutrals would follow. See Foot, *Practice of Power*, pp. 32–8.

[63] Conlon Report, pp. 541–51; Alexander Eckstein, memo on China policy, November 1960, Box 14, Thomson Papers, JFKL; Stevenson, "Putting First Things First"; Chester Bowles, "The 'China Problem' Reconsidered," *Foreign Affairs* 38(3) (April 1960), pp. 476–86.

[64] "Transcript of the Third Kennedy-Nixon Television Debate," *NYT*, 14 October 1960. The islands of Jinmen (Quemoy) and Mazu (Matsu) lie off the Xiamen (Amoy) coast. The Nationalists maintained large garrisons on the islands, which the communists bombarded during the two Taiwan Straits crises of 1954 and 1958 and continued to shell periodically into the 1960s. The islands were strategically vulnerable but symbolically important: their contested status signified the continuity of the civil war and prevented a clear divide between the two Chinas being drawn down the Straits.

sustain the primary aim of containing Communist China.[65] This reflected
the basic understanding of the Resurgent Power image: Communist China
was now a significant world player, and American leverage and prestige
should not be wasted on trying to halt its inevitable international legiti-
mation. The administration should instead take a longer-term view and
concentrate on containing China's aggression in a defensible and sustain-
able way.

Edward Rice went further in a long S/P paper. He argued that in order to
"disengage skillfully" from its policy of strict isolation without the appearance of defeat, the United States had to show that it was not implacably
hostile to China. Washington should "hold ajar the door to a more satisfactory relationship" and take steps "to mute our shared hostility." Rice
suggested that the Kennedy administration remove unnecessary provocation to Beijing by denying support to covert mainland operations by
the GRC, refraining from infringements of Chinese territorial space, and
stationing U.S. nuclear weapons farther away from the mainland. China
should also be invited to participate in the disarmament negotiations and
test ban treaty.[66]

However, Kennedy quickly experienced the constraints of right-wing
opposition. The China lobby stepped up a campaign in public and
in Congress to deny recognition and UN membership to Communist
China.[67] Kennedy decided that the risk of setting off domestic "political
dynamite" over Chinese representation in the UN was too high.[68] At the
same time, there remained the more immediate need to protect American
prestige in the international arena. As Hilsman pointed out, giving in on

---

[65] Komer to McGeorge Bundy, 1 March 1961, *FRUS 1961–3*, XXII, pp. 19–20. Komer
to JFK, "Crossing Swords with Macmillan on Chirep Issue," 3 April 1961, Box 21A,
NSF, JFKL; Komer to Bundy/Rostow, "Operation Candor with the GRC," 2 May 1961,
Box 411, Komer Files, JFKL. Komer elaborated on his views in a forty-one-page paper,
"Strategic Framework for Rethinking China Policy," 7 April 1961, Box 22, NSF, JFKL.
A similar argument based on reduced U.S. leverage was later made in State Department
channels by Lindsay Grant, the head of the ACA. Grant to Green, "Proposed Restatement
of US Policy Concerning Communism," 22 October 1964, Box 16, Thomson papers,
JFKL.

[66] S/P draft paper, "US Policy towards China," 26 October 1961, *FRUS 1961–3*, XXII,
pp. 162–7.

[67] It also threatened to campaign for taking the United States out of the UN if Communist
China was given a seat. See Hilsman, *To Move a Nation*, pp. 306–10; and Stanley Bachrack,
The Committee of One Million: 'China Lobby' Politics 1953–1971 (New York, 1976).

[68] JFK to Australian PM Menzies, 24 February 1961; JFK to New Zealand PM Holyoake,
3 March 1961; JFK to Rusk, Stevenson, and Cleveland, 24 May 1961, *FRUS 1961–3*,
XXII, pp. 15, 21, 65.

the Chinese representation issue would represent the first time the United States had experienced a defeat in the UN on a matter that it felt to be "peculiarly of concern to its security." This would be politically undesirable for the new administration, and thus the issue had to be seen as a "power struggle requiring the commitment of everything we can put into it."[69] Thus, the administration eventually decided to manage the 1961 crisis in the UN by a change in tactics: the United States succeeded in having the China representation issue declared an "important question," one requiring a two-thirds rather than a simple majority vote.[70]

After the "important question" tactic proved effective in maintaining the status quo in the UN, the Kennedy administration's efforts at reconsidering its policy on Chinese representation flagged considerably. The administration also compromised on its general China policy stance. It adopted a "China must behave first" line, which remained predicated upon the image of China as a renegade menace that the United States had to "contain." As the S/P affirmed in 1962, there would be no relaxation of China policy "unless and until [Beijing gave] concrete evidence . . . of an intention . . . to alter its aggressive policy and actions and to modify its stance of active hostility towards the US and the non-Communist world."[71] This was echoed by Kennedy himself in his last press conference on 14 November 1963. As is often noted, he did say: "We are not wedded to a policy of hostility to Red China." But this was conditional: it was possible only "[w]hen the Red Chinese indicate a desire to live at peace with the United States, and with other countries surrounding it."[72]

It was not until December 1963 that Washington admitted publicly that the Chinese Communist regime was not a "passing phase." In a speech drafted by various revisionist officials, Hilsman told Americans

---

[69] Hilsman to Rusk, "The China Question," n.d., Box 411, Komer Files, JFKL, pp. 4, 6; JFK to Chiang Kai Shek, 15 August 1961, Box 113A, POF, JFKL, p. 3.

[70] The tactic worked – and continued to work for the next eight years. For details of the twists and turns of the Kennedy administration's deliberations surrounding the 1961 Chinese representation issue, see Foot, *The Practice of Power*, pp. 35–41; and Kochavi, *A Conflict Perpetuated*, pp. 61–9.

[71] S/P, "US Policy toward Communist China," 30 November 1962, *FRUS 1961–3*, XXII, pp. 325–32.

[72] *PPP:JFK 1963*, pp. 845–6. Beijing also set its own preconditions for improving relations with the United States, which Mao Zedong outlined to the Somalian Prime Minister on 9 August 1963: (1) the United States should "return" Taiwan to China; (2) the United States should recognize the PRC; (3) the U.S. trade embargo on the PRC should be lifted; and (4) the PRC should be allowed to enter the UN. Mao added that "we will not use force to liberate [Taiwan]" because that would entail a war with the United States. See *Mao Zedong waijiao wenxuan* (Beijing, 1994), p. 501.

that Washington could not ignore the reality of the communist regime in Beijing. He noted that although the mainland economy had collapsed after the failure of the GLF, the communist regime "retained firm command of the instruments of control" and had proved to be flexible and pragmatic "when their existence was threatened." Thus, "[w]e have no reason to believe that there is a present likelihood that the Communist regime will be overthrown."[73] Apart from tacitly acknowledging that Dulles's policy of isolation had failed, Hilsman's speech also indicated a more flexible stance – an "open door" – to the possibility of better relations with Communist China should it prove willing to modify its hostility.

The momentum of China's rising international status continued unabated into the Johnson administration, culminating in two major developments in 1964. In January, France recognized the PRC – the first major Western power to do so since the Korean War.[74] This caused great consternation in Washington, but not a public breach. Even Johnson reacted with a sense of inevitability, and conceded in private that "the time's going to come when we're going to have to recognize them."[75]

More significantly, China exploded its first nuclear device on 16 October. That even a very limited nuclear capability would greatly enhance China's international political leverage had been well understood from the time of the Kennedy administration. American officials anticipated that China would "strike a conciliatory stance from her new position of strength and wait for her neighbors to rush to the bargaining table." They even considered that "the colored peoples of the world might rally to a nuclear-armed China."[76]

The test itself brought to new heights international pressure for Beijing to be included in arms control negotiations and in the UN. The recognition of China's elevated position as a major world power was underlined by the UN Secretary General's call for five-power disarmament talks involving the United States, the Soviet Union, Britain, France, and China. Washington was forced to acknowledge that China would have

---

[73] Hilsman, San Francisco speech, pp. 12–13.

[74] De Gaulle made the decision in part to demonstrate independence from the United States. See François Fejtö, "France and China: The Intersection of Two Grand Designs," in Abraham Halpern, ed., *Policies toward China: Views From Six Continents* (New York, 1965).

[75] LBJ to Senator Richard Russell, telephone conversation, 15 January 1964, *FRUS 1964–8*, XXX, p. 3.

[76] Highlights of Policy Planning Meeting, "A Chinese Communist Nuclear Detonation and Nuclear Capability," 15 October 1963, *FRUS 1961–3*, XXII, pp. 399–402.

to participate in such talks "at some stage" if such agreements were to be effective.[77] Meanwhile, China capitalized on its new status by proposing alternative international nuclear control agreements.[78] Beijing sent a telegram to all heads of state suggesting a summit conference to negotiate nuclear disarmament.[79] It also presented the United States with a draft bilateral "no-first-use" agreement, stating that the Chinese were suggesting these alternatives because "the UN had proved incapable of handling [the] question of disarmament."[80]

Beijing's elevated international position further undermined U.S. China policy. As Komer pointed out, "Peiping's test . . . dramatically underlines [the fact] that *Red China is here to stay*," and the China watchers in Hong Kong were finally emboldened to state, in their annual review, that "we do not believe that Chinese Communism is a passing phenomenon."[81] It seemed that China would almost certainly be voted into the UN within the next year. Indeed, soon after the Chinese nuclear test, Canada, France, Britain, Italy, and Belgium indicated that they would not support the United States at the next UNGA. Combined with international opposition to American intervention in Vietnam, this left the United States in an increasingly isolated position. As the assistant secretary for international organizational affairs noted, "[V]irtually every government in the world now believes that we are gradually losing both the guerrilla war in South Vietnam and the parliamentary trench war in the UN."[82]

Shifting the Onus onto Beijing

Washington thus came under renewed pressure to relax China policy in order to protect the reputation of the United States and the legitimacy

---

[77] See, e.g., William Foster, Director, U.S. Arms Control and Disarmament Agency, speech to the Commonwealth Club, San Francisco, 4 June 1965; and US Representative Charles Yost to UNGA, 16 November 1965, *DSB* 53, pp. 81–2, 949.

[78] Emb/Poland to DoS, "Cabot-Wang talks," 7 August 1963, *FRUS 1961–3*, XXII, pp. 378–9.

[79] See *AFP 1964*, pp. 882–4, 1077.

[80] Emb/Poland to DoS, "Cabot-Wang talks," 25 November 1964, *FRUS 1964–8*, XXX, pp. 134–5.

[81] Komer to Bundy, 23 November 1964, ibid., p. 131; ConGen/HK to DoS, "Communist China and Recommendations for United States Policy," 6 November 1964, Box 16, Thomson Papers, JFKL, p. 1.

[82] Martin to Rusk, 30 November 1964, *FRUS 1964–8*, XXX, p. 139; Cleveland, "The Taming of the Shrew: Communist China and the United Nations," 31 October 1964, ibid., pp. 120–3.

of its position as a world leader.[83] "Revisionist" officials were quick
to invoke this image of the United States as an outflanked and potentially embarrassed world power in their quest for better relations with
China. Thomson wrote a long memorandum to McGeorge Bundy pep-
pered with references to improving "our look as a confident, realistic, responsible world power," projecting American "maturity and self-
confidence," establishing "greater rapport with our major allies," increasing "respect from the Third World," and lessening "the look of a defeated
obstructionist."[84]

However, as Komer had argued earlier in the context of Chinese representation, *"a shift in our policy will look like a defeat."*[85] It would appear that, after years of adhering to a righteous stance, Washington was
giving in to Chinese and international pressure. Yet, these revisionist officials pointed out, it was a necessary price to pay, and one that could
be minimized. Thomson and Komer argued that given the boost to its
status, Beijing had no intention of "behaving," and Washington could no
longer just "sit tight in increasingly lonely isolation" waiting for Beijing to
"change its spots." Instead, by taking unilateral steps such as acquiescing
to a "two Chinas" formula in the UN and relaxing restrictions on travel
and trade, the administration might actually begin to recoup its international standing. These steps would make Washington look less implacably
hostile to China and "shift the onus" for its own isolation onto Beijing
and its intransigence.[86]

Fundamental to this idea of "putting the monkey on the backs of
Chicom leaders"[87] was the conviction that China would not alter its attitudes sufficiently to allow any significant change to be effected. This was
particularly true of the Chinese representation issue: Beijing routinely insisted that it would enter the UN only if Taiwan were ejected, so a more

---

[83] This "soft" power aspect of U.S. relations with China has been analyzed by Foot, who
argues that Washington was not so much seeking a balance-of-power position as pivotal
world leader as fundamentally concerned about its ability to exercise power in its national
interest in the international arena. See Foot, *Practice of Power*, Chapters 1, 9. On "soft"
power, see Joseph Nye, *Bound to Lead: The Changing Nature of American Power* (New
York, 1991), pp. 70–1.

[84] Thomson to Bundy, "The US and Communist China in the Months Ahead," 28 October
1964, *FRUS 1964–8*, XXX, pp. 117–20.

[85] Komer to Bundy, 23 November 1964, p. 131.

[86] Ibid.; Thomson to Bundy, "The US and Communist China in the Months Ahead,"
28 October 1964, *FRUS 1964–8*, XXX, pp. 117–20. See also Rice to DoS, telegram 23,
7 July 1965, Box 238, NSF, LBJL.

[87] Rice to SoS, 7 July 1965, Box 238, NSF, LBJL.

reasonable "two Chinas" stance on the part of the United States would shift the blame for its exclusion entirely onto Communist Chinese intransigence. Both Thomson and Komer had argued this point back in 1961: U.S. support for "two Chinas" would maneuver Beijing into a position "where it is not us trying to keep them out of the UN, but they refusing to come in."[88] For this reason, the revisionist argument was tactically useful in overcoming the scepticism of "hostile" officials. For instance, after travel restrictions were relaxed slightly in early 1965, Rusk was able to use the argument that these "small steps...reflect our reasonableness and our desire to move towards some lessening of tensions," while Beijing's rejection of them "prove they are intransigent and their unreasonableness will cause them to become more and more isolated."[89] Thus, this tactic contributed to the aim of presenting the general U.S. stance as "that of a great nation which can afford to speak with moderation and dignity in response to the abuse and violence coming out of Peking."[90]

Still, for revisionists, shifting the blame for hostile U.S.–China relations onto Beijing was a short-term tactic. The longer-run aim, for Thomson and those of the "Troubled Modernizer" school, was to encourage a reconsideration of Chinese policies among moderates in Beijing.[91] At the same time, however, a parallel discourse on the need to bring the PRC into international society was developing, and from 1964 onward something of a consensus grew within the administration. This was because once China had become a nuclear-armed menace, the proponents of "hostile" images and "revisionist" images found common ground in agreeing that China could not be isolated and had to be treated as a legitimate state. This is best illustrated by the deliberations of the State Committee on Nuclear Proliferation in 1965. The committee was led by Soviet specialist Llewellyn Thompson and composed of the assistant secretaries and the S/P chairman – on the whole not a particularly "revisionist" group when it came to China policy. In its report to the president, it stated that China posed the biggest long-term problem to world peace because of its size, intransigence, and isolation – a standard "hostile image" representation.

---

[88] Komer to Bundy, 19 October 1961, p. 1; Thomson paper, "US Courses towards China," 30 March 1961, Box 14, Thomson Papers, JFKL, p. 3.

[89] Rusk to Gronouski, 5 February 1966, Box 2025, CFPF (1964–6), RG59, NA.

[90] DoS, "Public Statements on Communist China," 13 December 1966, Box 1, Jenkins Files, LBJL.

[91] Thomson to Rostow/Moyers/Valenti, "Peking's Response to Indications of US 'Flexibility' on China Policy," 2 April 1966, Box 17, Thomson Papers, JFKL.

But the report continued that in order for peace to be achieved, China had to be restrained from nuclear proliferation, and this was possible only if it joined the society of nations and participated in arms control regimes – a "join first" instead of "behave first" position.[92] The committee concluded that if the government was serious about nonproliferation, a "major high-level re-examination" of China policy was required.[93] Thus there was a gradual meeting of minds between officials working from the two initially opposite perspectives of improving Sino-American relations and containing Communist Chinese hostility.

The Chinese nuclear test also galvanized a change in American public opinion toward China. While polls still showed that Americans believed by three-to-one margins that China "would turn out to be a greater threat to the U.S." than the Soviet Union, they also revealed that the public was now more favorably disposed toward UN membership for the PRC than ever before. This led the State Department's opinion analyst to note a "growing feeling" that reality dictated greater Sino-American contacts.[94] In 1965 and 1966, both internal and external pressures for modifying U.S. policy toward the two Chinas came to a head. Voting did not take place in the 1964 UNGA because of a funding crisis, but in November 1965 a tied vote was cast for the first time on the question of seating Communist China and expelling the Nationalists. This did not carry the resolution, as the "important question" required a two-thirds majority, but the vote was sufficiently close to cause the Johnson administration to begin seriously to reexamine its China policy and to move toward "two Chinas."

Washington began to distance itself more strongly than before from the Nationalists' hope of returning to the mainland. In early 1966, Military Aid Program funding for the ROC was cut. The State and Defense Departments strongly reiterated that the U.S. obligation was purely defensive and that military assistance was not for mainland offensives. GRC forces were "too large in relation to the threat," and the United States was not

[92] The contention that institutional norms exert a conforming influence on members is, of course, the key claim of institutional and conventional constructivist approaches in international relations. See, for instance, Thomas Franck, *The Power of Legitimacy among Nations* (New York, 1990); Martha Finnemore, *National Interests in International Society* (Ithaca, 1996); and Amitav Acharya, *Constructing a Security Community in Southeast Asia: ASEAN and the Problem of Regional Order* (London, 2001).

[93] Committee discussion memo, 7–8 January 1965; committee report to the president, 21 November 1965, *FRUS 1964–8*, XI, pp. 166, 180.

[94] Kusnitz, *Public Opinion and Foreign Policy*, pp. 111–12.

prepared to continue underwriting their modernization.[95] In May 1966, Rusk himself recommended to Johnson that the United States move to adopt a "two Chinas" policy and concentrate on keeping the ROC in the UN rather than keeping the PRC out.[96]

Beginning in 1965, a second factor operating in favor of China policy changes was the escalation of American involvement in the Vietnam War. During the last quarter of 1965, concern about the possibility of Chinese intervention in Vietnam had grown in Washington, and this official worry was transferred to the public via the media and in televised hearings on Vietnam conducted by the Senate Foreign Relations Committee in March 1966. Polls at the time found that a 46 percent plurality of respondents expected that the United States would have to fight Chinese troops in Vietnam. This fear of war with China created in the public conciousness more interest in and receptivity to a China policy initiative that might help to stave off such a conflict.[97] Within the administration, too, there was a growing sense that a Vietnam policy increasingly unpopular both domestically and internationally could not be borne alongside an equally unpopular China policy. Thus William Bundy, the assistant secretary for Far Eastern affairs, successfully recommended that Washington accompany the intensification of the ground war in Vietnam with a lifting of the travel ban to China for doctors and scientists.[98] Also at Bundy's suggestion, the United States indicated that it was willing to admit Chinese journalists without reciprocity and suggested joint talks on alleged violations of Chinese territory by American ships and planes.[99] In mid-1966, Harriman urged that Johnson make a speech signaling "a spectacular change in attitude towards Red China," accepting "containment

---

[95] Thomson to McGeorge Bundy, "Moment of Truth with GRC Regarding Mainland Counter-attack," 3 February 1966; DoS to Emb/Taipei, "Joint State-Defense Message on Revised MAP Guidelines," 9 March 1966; Emb/Taipei to DoS, 11 May 1966, *FRUS 1964–8*, XXX, pp. 247–9, 266–9, 297–8.

[96] Rusk to LBJ, "Need for New Tactics on Chinese Representation," 14 May 1966, ibid., pp. 301–2. Johnson agreed, and Rusk was supposed to inform the GRC of this decision when he visited Taipei in July, but Chiang flatly refused to discuss it, and Rusk, for his own reasons, did not push the issue. See Emb/Taipei to DOS, "Chinese Representation," 1 July 1966; "Secretary's Discussion of ChiRep with GRC," 5 July 1966, ibid., pp. 344–50.

[97] See Kusnitz, *Public Opinion and Foreign Policy*, pp. 114–15.

[98] Bundy to Ball, "Proposed New Policy Initiatives for December 15 Warsaw Meeting," 4 December 1965, ibid., pp. 228–30; *DSB* 54, p. 90.

[99] DoS telegram, "Gronouski-Wang Talks," 16 December 1965, *FRUS 1964–8*, XXX, pp. 222–4. The two suggestions were rejected by the Chinese on the usual grounds that the Taiwan issue had to be settled first.

without isolation" and a "two Chinas" policy in order to establish greater credibility and so gain better public understanding of Vietnam policy.[100]

The Frustrated Resurgent Power

As discussed earlier, 1966 was the turning point for the revisionist discourse about China. Thomson has described 1966 as "the hopeful year, the central year of Johnsonian innovation" in China policy. A brief window of opportunity opened in the spring and summer of that year, when the Vietnam War and its critics seemed sufficiently stabilized to permit some high-level attention to be paid to China.[101] This coincided with the nation's exposure to the first extensive debate about China policy since the McCarthy era, sparked especially by extended hearings in both houses of Congress. Public opinion shifted perceptibly in favor of improving relations with China.[102] These circumstances produced two key changes in perceptions of China within the administration, changes that contributed vitally to the Resurgent Power discourse.

First, there was finally an explicit acknowledgment that China was a major power with considerable capacity for disruption, one that the international community excluded at its own peril. This was a point not made even by revisionist officials until 1966. In the expectation of high-level resistance, most of their recommendations had been carefully couched in terms of shifting the onus for its isolation onto China. On 1 March 1966, Thomson wrote a memorandum to Jack Valenti, Johnson's special assistant, which, for the first time, argued the importance of Chinese membership in international society on the basis of its power and destructiveness: "700 million people; the key to stability in Asia; the grandiose belligerent aims of Chinese Communist doctrine; Beijing's development of a nuclear capability."[103] Two weeks later, Rusk, in his testimony to the House Subcommittee on the Far East, acknowledged that "Communist China is a major Asian power today" and that "[w]e expect China to become some

---

[100] Harriman (ambassador-at-large) to Moyers (president's special assistant), 3 June 1966, ibid., pp. 318–19.

[101] Thomson, "On the Making of China Policy," p. 239.

[102] A Harris poll showed for the first time that a majority of those polled favored wide-ranging rapprochement with China, including diplomatic relations (57 percent in favor) and admission to the UN (55 percent in favor of membership for both Chinas). Harris Survey, 27 June 1966, Box 17, Thomson Papers, JFKL.

[103] *FRUS 1964–8*, XXX, p. 262.

day a great world power."[104] When Johnson made his landmark China speech in July, he emphasized China's crucial role in achieving peace in Asia and said that peace in Asia was possible only "through full participation by all nations in the international community under law" – implying that Beijing had to be included in the UN.[105]

The second, and key, change in perceptions of China that emerged in 1966 was the widely articulated image of China as a natural and historical great power, wronged in the past and frustrated in the present. A vista into pre-1949 China seemed suddenly to open at the Senate hearings in March 1966, where China specialists spoke at length on the histories of Chinese regional influence, the Chinese revolution, and Sino-American relations.[106] Officials began to use this historical angle in the internal China policy discourse. Some emphasized Chinese Communist attempts to resurrect the superior position that China had enjoyed in the past. For instance, the State-Defense Study Group portrayed Chinese history as engendering dangerous delusions of grandeur on the part of Beijing. It stated that the Chinese Communist leadership aspired to "regional hegemony and . . . acceptance as . . . the equal of the US and USSR." This desire had "psychological roots in China's long history during most of which China was the center and guiding light of its own world," and it posed a threat in that "by striving to achieve the unattainable," China might draw the United States into a war to protect its interests in Asia.[107]

Revisionists were more concerned with the interplay between this superiority complex and the "hundred years of ignominy" that China had suffered under unequal treaties imposed by Western powers after the Opium War of 1842. The China specialists at the Senate hearings presented an image of China derived from three main historical observations. First, it was historically "a very big, ancient, isolated, unified, and self-sufficient empire," and because of this, an intensely ethnocentric great power.[108] Second, because of its humiliation under the Western gunboat diplomacy of the nineteenth century, the Chinese were ultra-nationalistic and had a

---

[104] Rusk, "US Policy toward Communist China," p. 8.
[105] American Alumni Council speech, 12 July 1966, *PPP:LBJ 1966*, II, pp. 721–2.
[106] One legacy of the McCarthy years was the public silence on these subjects throughout the 1950s and official reticence that lasted well into the 1960s. Senators' questions about the historical aspects of Chinese power at the China hearings belied this general knowledge gap. See Iriye, *US Policy Toward China*, pp. 29–41.
[107] Special State-Defense Study Group, "Long-Range Study," p. 342.
[108] Testimony of John Fairbank, 10 March 1966, in Iriye, *US Policy Toward China*, p. 32.

fierce desire to prevent any recurrence of such humiliation.[109] Therefore, they were preoccupied with security and had "maximum conceptions" of their borders – hence the actions in Tibet, Korea, and on the Indian border. This was a concern that would have been shared by "any strong central government in Peking," communist or not.[110] Third, China was "a great power of a peculiar character": its traditional dominance of its neighbors was based not so much on military prowess as on the attraction of its great civilization, and relied less on military expansion than on tributary relationships.[111] In a similar way, the Chinese Communists were trying to find a new great-power position as head of the developing communist world by supplying ideological leadership rather than direct military involvement.[112]

Revisionist officials, on the other hand, were less interested in being apologists for Chinese aggression than in finding effective policy positions that could improve Sino-American relations by taking into account these historical factors. Edwin Reischauer and Edward Rice, from their posts in Japan and Hong Kong, respectively, mustered some of the most convincing arguments based on the image of China as a Resurgent Power. Reischauer pointed out that Beijing's dogmatism and ignorance were "fundamentally an expression of frustration on the part of the Chinese people, whose traditional pride and sense of superiority to all other nations have been gravely injured by a century of continuing humiliations" – a frustration exacerbated by China's present obvious weakness and backwardness.[113] Thus, he agreed with Fairbank's analysis that Beijing "shouts aggressively out of manifold frustrations," that behind its fierce and defiant rhetoric lay a craving for international prestige that would overcome past humiliations.[114]

As a result of this representation of China, the Resurgent Power discourse encompassed proposed policy changes based on assumptions very different from those of other revisionists. For instance, James Thomson also used the historical argument, but as a means to substantiate the Troubled Modernizer image. He urged that greater contact could help to combat the symptoms of China's humiliation – its "ignorance and

[109] Ibid., pp. 34–7.
[110] Testimonies of Benjamin Schwartz and Samuel Griffith, 16 March 1966, ibid., pp. 40, 91–3.
[111] Testimony of Hans Morgenthau, 30 March 1966, ibid., pp. 40–1.
[112] Testimonies of A. Doak Barnett, Fairbank, and Schwartz, ibid., pp. 82, 85, 89.
[113] Reischauer to DoS, 11 August 1966, *FRUS 1964–8*, XXX, p. 370.
[114] Fairbank testimony, p. 133.

fear" and the "acutely distorted view of the outside world that plots her encirclement and destruction."[115] However, Thomson essentially saw such initiatives toward Beijing as a form of benign internal "subversion" intended to encourage moderate elements that could then bring about a regime change in the long run.[116] Reischauer and Rice, on the other hand, saw their policy recommendations as ways to effect an overdue conciliation with the leaders of a major state. In so doing, they also rejected the earlier arguments that China was a renegade power and had to "behave first" before it became acceptable in international society, and those that saw limited unilateral U.S. initiatives as a way to "put the onus on Beijing" and defend America's international standing. Instead, they insisted that the onus was firmly shared by the United States.

This had been the basic thrust of Rice's 1961 S/P paper emphasizing the need to mute hostilities with China. In April 1966, as consul general in Hong Kong, Rice was able to develop this theme, taking advantage of the new awareness of China's historical pride and humiliation. He told Rostow that Beijing regarded the United States as its main enemy in part because of American attitudes and actions that had contributed to Chinese frustration. He gave three key examples. First, from Beijing's point of view, the U.S. alliance with a government on Taiwan whose main objective was to return to power on the mainland indicated that Washington was committed to the CCP's overthrow. Rice warned that Beijing would not accept the separation of Taiwan as final: "when China has been divided [in the past], nationalistic feelings have always created pressures for reunification." But the United States must dampen hostilities by clearly disassociating itself from the GRC aim of reconquest by covert as well as overt means. Second, Washington had undertaken actions that were not only hostile but insulting to Beijing, such as naval vessels that cruised up and down through China's claimed territorial waters. Rice argued that it served no purpose to cruise so near the Chinese coast: "If we and the Soviets do something similar with each other, neither of us feels humiliated, but the Chinese Communists remember all China's own

---

[115] Thomson to Valenti, *FRUS 1964–8*, XXX, pp. 262, 264.
[116] The Troubled Modernizer school, as well as Hilsman and those such as Komer and the Bundys who argued for shifting the onus onto Beijing, fall into what Kochavi calls "pedagogic" revisionists. Crucial to their views was the idea that China had first to fulfil certain standards of behavior, a starting point that precluded granting the PRC a more equitable status as suggested by the proponents of the Resurgent Power discourse. See Kochavi, *A Conflict Perpetuated*, p. 249.

past humiliations, know China cannot do to us what we do to them, and distrust us more than the Soviets do."

Finally, Rice turned to the hypocrisy of the U.S. policy on trade with China: "During the past century the West forced China to recognise that no country can refuse to trade with the rest of the world. We now enforce the opposite stand in our own embargo policy. With even the Chinese Government on Taiwan allowing at least some indirect trade with the mainland, we are being more Catholic than the Pope."

Rice's essential point was that the United States was in fact perpetuating China's ignominy by ignoring the fact that "Communist China . . . has national interests, both pretended and genuine." He advised that "we would do well to recognize by word and deed those of its interests which are legitimate."[117]

Reischauer pressed this point about U.S. arrogance, especially in its treatment of China as an illegitimate international pariah. He warned that the American pretense that "twelve million people on Taiwan and not the seven hundred million in continental China, represent the great historical entity known as China" severely undermined both American credibility and prospects for peace. He identified the greatest barrier to Beijing's readiness to seek rapprochement with the world as "the resentment of what they regard to be the callous pretense on the part of the world's greatest power that China does not really exist or that, if it does exist, it is so depraved or so unstable or so inconsequential that it should be barred from world society."[118]

Reischauer went further than Rice in suggesting that in order to assuage this Chinese bitterness, Washington had to adopt "a more realistic and more tolerant and appreciative attitude." It had to make clear that it regarded Communist China as a legitimate state with which it was prepared to have normal relations and whose sovereignty it would respect. Thus the United States should accept Communist China into the UN if it was willing to enter on the same basis as all other states; indicate that it was ready to live peacefully and to develop friendly cooperation with Beijing; and affirm its belief that the form of government on mainland China was for the people to decide, and that the United States had no intention of interfering in its domestic affairs. Moreover, Reischauer recommended a

---

[117] Rice to Rostow, "US Policy Towards Communist China," 15 April 1966, ibid., pp. 282–4. Similar observations, though not as strongly put, were made by Lindsey Grant a year earlier; see Grant to Green, "Communist China," 9 February 1965; and "Proposed Policy Initiatives," 18 March 1965, Box 16, Thomson Papers, JFKL.

[118] Reischauer to DoS, *FRUS 1964–8*, XXX, pp. 371–2.

little rhetorical "kowtowing": in his view, the United States had to "find ways to express our admiration for the great historic entity of China as not only the largest nation in the world today ... but as one of the truly great national units throughout human history."[119]

There were various other policy suggestions that reflected some of this Resurgent Power thinking, and that tried to demonstrate American regard for China's position. For instance, UN Ambassador Arthur Goldberg suggested that Johnson call for a foreign ministers' meeting between the United States and China. Johnson was apparently "fascinated" with the idea, and a proposal for such a meeting was drafted, but the plan was shelved because of an incident involving American and Chinese planes in North Vietnam.[120] Still, three months later Rostow reported that Rusk believed that "the proper way to proceed with respect to Communist China is to elevate the Warsaw talks to the Foreign Ministers level," but that he was waiting until the domestic situation in China had "settled down."[121] In 1967, Senate Majority Leader Mike Mansfield suggested to Johnson that the United States talk to China, rather than to the Soviet Union, regarding Vietnam. In a suggestion that clearly acknowledged China's important role in ensuring the region's stability, Mansfield offered to travel to Beijing to see Zhou Enlai in order to obtain "the Chinese view of what is needed for a settlement in Vietnam and for the restoration of more normal relations throughout the Western Pacific."[122]

However, it was the fear of Chinese intervention in the Vietnam War that forced the administration to take the steps that Reischauer had recommended to indicate America's peaceful intentions and respect for China's sovereignty. After the escalation of the U.S. war in Vietnam in 1965, and

[119] This point was apparently well accepted – it featured prominently in the 1966–7 edition of the State Department's annual "US Posture toward Communist China: Guidelines for Public Statements," Box 1, Jenkins Files, LBJL.

[120] Komer to LBJ, "Goldberg's Ideas on China," 19 April 1966; William Bundy to Rusk, "ChiCom-US Foreign Minister's Meeting," 13 May 1966; Bundy to Rusk, "Draft Warsaw Instructions," 20 May 1966, *FRUS 1964–8*, XXX, pp. 285–6, 299–300, 307. In January 1967, Rusk authorized Ambassador Gronouski to propose a foreign ministers' meeting if the Chinese reacted to U.S. bombing of Hanoi by trying to call off the Warsaw talks. But they did not, and the subject did not arise again. See Rusk to Gronouski, 11 January 1967, ibid., pp. 500–1.

[121] Rostow to LBJ, 30 April 1967, Box 6, NSF, LBJL.

[122] Mansfield to LBJ, 29 April 1967, *FRUS 1964–8*, XXX, p. 551. Rusk rejected the proposals, feeling that the internal turmoil in China made such a trip undesirable; and Rusk did not share Mansfield's conviction that Hanoi was under Beijing's control but felt instead that Hanoi was balancing its position between Moscow and Beijing. Rostow to LBJ, 30 April 1967.

after Chinese warnings that it would retaliate if American forces attacked Chinese territory, Washington used the Warsaw talks to reassure Beijing that "we intend no hostile actions against your country, have no intention of interfering in the internal affairs of the territory under your control, and...our actions in Vietnam are not directed in any way against your country."[123]

In June 1967, Johnson personally sent a message to Beijing via the Romanian prime minister that closely followed Reischauer's recommendations. Washington, he said, "did not want war with China, did not seek to change China's system of government, had no designs on Chinese territory, and wanted only to trade with China and get along to the extent that China would permit."[124]

These sentiments were repeated in major China policy speeches by William Bundy and Undersecretary Katzenbach in 1968.[125] The domestic turmoil of the Cultural Revolution, however, ensured that there was no positive Chinese response to these feelers.

China in a "Balance of Power"?

During the 1960s, Washington was forced to acknowledge to some extent China's status as a major world player, especially after it became a nuclear power in 1964. Beginning in 1966, China specialists sympathetic to Communist China introduced into the official discourse a recognition of China's historical status and experience and began to construct the Resurgent Power image, which stressed both the inevitability and peculiarity of Chinese power. China was a natural power that had traditionally exercised suzerainty over its neighbors. But its particular history of humiliation had engendered a fierce nationalism that found its expression in belligerent communism. Yet the historically benign form of Chinese influence could probably be resurrected if China were treated with sensitivity and respect. These "revisionists" argued, almost on moral grounds, that the United States had to alter its hostile stance against this returning power, and that the policy issues essentially revolved around a question of appropriate attitude, contact, and expectations. In other words, the

---

[123] FRUS 1964–8, II, pp. 700–1; Zhai, China and the Vietnam Wars, pp. 138–9; DoS to Emb/Poland, "Guidance for Gronouski-Wang Talks," 29 May 1967; 4 January 1968, FRUS 1964–8, XXX, pp. 577, 627.

[124] 26 June 1967, ibid., p. 583; XVII, pp. 430–5.

[125] Bundy to Emb/Taipei, 13 February 1968, FRUS 1964–8, XXX, pp. 638–41; Nicholas Katzenbach, speech to the National Press Club, Washington, D.C., 21 May 1968, DSB 58, pp. 737–40.

United States had to start relating to Communist China not as a "regime" but as a legitimate state and a major power. The United States had to recognize that in addition to sovereignty and security, China shared the very concerns about prestige, position, and influence with which the United States itself was so preoccupied.

However, insofar as any concrete steps were taken in this direction, they were taken with an eye on the Vietnam War and the growing uncertainty that accompanied the onset of the Cultural Revolution. The Resurgent Power discourse did not develop toward further consideration of how China was to be socialized into international society as a great power, or what its role in a peaceful East Asian region was likely to be. Although some, like Rusk, gave much thought to China's influence in the Asian region, they were loathe to concede that China would inevitably exercise some form of dominant influence over East Asia, because they saw Beijing's ideology and actions as aggressive and illegitimate.[126]

One person who did seriously consider this question was Alfred Jenkins, the China specialist on the White House staff beginning in late 1966. In one of his first reports to Rostow, Jenkins professed himself disappointed with the focus on issues of travel, trade, and Chinese representation in the UN. These struck him as "potentially useful but peripheral measures" in view of the uncertainties of the Cultural Revolution. He suggested that, for the moment, the administration should concentrate its planning resources on "issues ... to do with *China in the balance of power* in the Asia-Pacific" and proceeded to list a remarkably farsighted set of strategic issues that few other officials had emphasized in connection with China policy:

> ... *how China of whatever complexion relates* to the future role of Japan, the future status of Taiwan, the sort of Southeast Asia we want to see post-Vietnam and how much [commitment] it will require ... the possible future pull on China from successful Asian regional ventures, the desirability and degree of Soviet presence and investments in some of these ventures, the composition of probable future regional military coalescences ... the likelihood and desirability of Japanese participation and the need for US balancing of Japan ... the effects if Japan and/or India go nuclear ..."[127]

Jenkins explored the question of China and the Asian balance of power in a paper the following year. He bluntly acknowledged China's natural

---

[126] See, e.g. Rusk to Martin, 30 November 1964, *FRUS 1964–8*, XXX, p. 139.
[127] Jenkins to Rostow, "Highlights of China Panel Meetings," 3 February 1967, ibid., pp. 513–17.

role as a key power in East Asia: "China when strong has always had a sphere of influence on its periphery not unlike that which other strong nations throughout history have insisted upon." The main problem was the fact that China and Japan, the two indigenous powers of the region, were in "an unnatural state of affairs" – China "contained" because of its aggressive ideology and actions, and Japan an economic power but not a military one. The heavy American presence in the region, Jenkins argued, could not be sustained in the long run because it would become an "affront to Asian sensibilities of perhaps irreparable severity." Thus, "we must contrive a rebalance, with China principally in mind." There was a need to "strengthen non-Communist Asia, with a view to ultimate reduction of the US component in the balance of power in the region." This was an important precursor to Richard Nixon's 1969 Guam Doctrine, and it tapped into the public discourse increasingly recognizing China's role as a major power.[128] However, regarding the specifics of China's role in the Asian balance of power, Jenkins concluded that Beijing would begin to help maintain a peaceful balance of power in Asia only when it had given up "pretensions of leading global revolution" and could accept a world of "cooperative diversity." In other words, a constructive role for China still awaited its moving out of the "Maoist-Stalinist" phase.[129]

The foregoing analysis of American officials' image of China as Resurgent Power shows that it was the most dynamic of the four competing images of China in the 1960s. It had progressed logically in response to the pressure of events in 1961, 1964, and 1966, and had only really come to light in 1966 before it was forced to come to a halt. More than any of the others, the Resurgent Power subdiscourse reflected the strong sense during the second half of the 1960s that things awaited a redefining change, a breakthrough.

While there was some degree of overlap in the two revisionist discourses, they were distinct in their underlying image of China, their expectations of how and how much the United States could hope to change Chinese behavior, and the particular aims of the suggested policy changes. The Troubled Modernizer discourse was essentially a "visionary" one, envisaging the eventual and inevitable transition of the currently weak and backward PRC to American-style capitalism and democracy, which would bring with it domestic and foreign policy moderation. This process

---

[128] See Chapter 5.
[129] Jenkins, "Further Thoughts on China," 9 October 1968, FRUS 1964–8, XXX, pp. 709–18.

would be aided by American "subversion" of the communist dictatorship using goods and ideas, which would strengthen the moderates within the Chinese leadership and encourage them to bring about regime change. However, these alterations on the part of the Chinese could come only with time, and in the interim, Troubled Modernizer proponents were happy to shift the onus for apparent U.S. intransigence onto China.

The Resurgent Power proponents, on the other hand, aimed for more immediately obtainable changes in U.S. attitudes and policies. They accepted the fact that the communist regime was permanent and that it harbored essentially Chinese nationalist interests and sentiments. Given the legitimacy of some of Beijing's key complaints about U.S. actions, and the increasing international recognition of the importance of the PRC, they emphasized that Washington ought to look first to moderating its own position in the hope of developing a more constructive engagement with China, without setting preconditions about how Beijing ought to "behave" first.[130] The intersections between the two subdiscourses – James Thomson, for instance, borrowed arguments of historical ignominy to support his arguments for travel and trade links, and Edward Rice pushed for revisions in the trade and travel restrictions – were inevitable given the small circle of revisionist officials and the need for discursive consolidation for the purposes of bureaucratic persuasion. However, as discussed in this chapter, the underlying thrust of the two sets of subdiscourses remained distinct.

[130] For a somewhat similar distinction drawn for the revisionist discourse during the Kennedy administration, see Kochavi, *A Conflict Perpetuated*. Kochavi's categories of "visionary" versus "temperate" revisionism reflect the distinction drawn here between Troubled Modernizer and Resurgent Power, but we place different officials within our categories, mainly because Kochavi's concern was more with the policy stances of individuals, while mine is with the internal logic of different discourses to which different individuals may have contributed in different ways.

4

The Revisionist Legacy

The Discourse of Reconciliation with China by 1968

The two preceding chapters analyzed the China policy debate within the Kennedy and Johnson administrations and traced American officials' arguments for and against relaxing China policy in the 1960s. They demonstrated that four distinct subdiscourses about China existed within the internal official discourse, each a representation of the perceived identity and characteristics of China, of the Sino-American relationship, and of resulting U.S. interests and policy stances. These are summarized in Table 4.1.

Table 4.1 highlights how each discourse focused on particular aspects of China's identity, used separate frames of reference, and made distinct policy recommendations. The Red Menace image emphasized China's aggressive hostility toward the noncommunist world, working from the 1950s international framework of two opposing rigid blocs in a Cold War. The second hostile discourse based on the image of China as Revolutionary Rival used the less rigid international framework resulting from the Sino-Soviet split to suggest selective opposition to the more militant Chinese brand of communism. The two revisionist subdiscourses of China, on the other hand, stressed indigenous aspects of Chinese identity. The Troubled Modernizer image was concerned with China's poverty and "basic needs" crises, viewed through the lens of Western models of socio-economic development. The policy recommendation was that Washington should try to encourage the ascendance of the moderate elements of the Chinese leadership that wanted to concentrate on these internal problems, thereby muting China's external hostility. The Resurgent Power discourse, in turn, centered upon China's frustrated reemergence as a major international player, asserting that U.S. policies had served to exacerbate

TABLE 4.1. *Summary of the four subdiscourses of China in U.S. official discourse, 1961–8*

Images	Chinese Identity and Characteristics	U.S. Identity and Characteristics	Policies (Proposed and Actual)	Aims
Red Menace	Soviet ally, totalitarian, aggressive, expansionist; growing offensive capability	Democratic, peace-loving, leader of "free world"	Containment and isolation: support for noncommunist Asian states; defense and recognition of Taiwan; nonrecognition	Limit Chinese expansion and ability to threaten "free world"; undermine communist regime
Revolutionary Rival	Proponent of militant ideology and revolutionary warfare; rival to Soviet influence and leadership in developing and communist worlds	As above, but with willingness to deal with communist power that would lower hostilities	Counterrevolutionary warfare; conventional warfare	Contain international communist expansion; demonstrate failure of Chinese model of militant communism as opposed to Soviet détente model
Troubled Modernizer	Weak developing country; division in leadership between ideologues and modernizers	Universal model of socioeconomic development	Selective humanitarian aid, free flows of people and nonstrategic goods	Encourage moderate elements in Chinese leadership eager to focus on socioeconomic development
Resurgent Power	Rising international player and traditional great power frustrated by historical humiliation and current weakness	Dogmatic, unrealistic world leader, insensitive to Chinese wounded pride	"Two Chinas," reduce hostile/provocative actions, show appreciation of Chinese historical status	Shift onus onto China; recoup international credibility; placate and reduce Chinese hostility

historical Chinese grievances and resentment. Notably, one of the key concerns within this discourse was with the declining credibility of the United States as a world leader, and hence with policies that would help to salvage the American position.

These four subdiscourses coexisted and interrelated with each other throughout the 1960s, constituting a "salad" of ideas about China within the policy realm. Far from a simple extension of 1950s policy thinking about China, the prevailing discourse about China as a Red Menace to be contained and isolated was modified and challenged. The proponents of these distinct subdiscourses usually harbored the primary aim of justifying existing policies, or of advocating new policies on what was becoming an increasingly controversial issue. This gave rise to a dynamic context characterized by competing discourses and various groups jostling for policy influence. An analysis of this process allows us to assess the extent of internal U.S. China policy rethinking by 1968, and to contribute to answering the question of how this related to the rapprochement in 1972.

COMPETING DISCOURSES

The four subdiscourses of China found within American official discourse from 1961 to 1968 were akin to the four stages in the evolution of China policy thinking during the 1960s. However, the transition from one discourse to another was not clear-cut; they overlapped in time, with one or two subdiscourses prevalent during each phase. This competitive process is discussed here with the aid of Table 4.2, which illustrates the prominence of each image over this period in relation to major events and actual U.S. policy changes. All four images of China were held by various key officials throughout the period. However, the advocates of each associated policy discourse were more vocal at certain times than at others, as events at the domestic and international levels lent credence to the characteristics that they propounded. The high-level, mostly public articulations of the Red Menace image peaked in connection with the 1962 Sino-Indian War and the first Chinese nuclear test in 1964. The Revolutionary Rival image rose rapidly between 1963 and 1965, as the Sino-Soviet split widened and China stepped up its support for revolutionary warfare, particularly in Vietnam. The Troubled Modernizer refrain was probably the most consistently articulated across this period, clustering around the effects of the GLF failure of 1961–2, China's diplomatic setbacks of 1965–6, and the internal turmoil of the Cultural Revolution of 1966–8. The articulation of the Resurgent Power image peaked after China's acquisition of nuclear weapons capability in 1964, the 1965 tied vote in the UN, and especially after the Senate hearings of 1966.

The discourses were competitive in the sense that they experienced ascendance and decline relative to each other within each phase, and because they overlapped and provided contesting interpretations of key events. As Table 4.2 shows, the Troubled Modernizer and Red Menace discourses predominated during the Kennedy administration. The year 1961 opened with an immediate contest of alternative representations of China in the wake of the failure of the GLF. Proponents of the Red Menace image, including Rusk and members of the China lobby in Congress, saw the GLF as an instance of the domestic tyranny of the Chinese Communists and anticipated that its failure might undermine the regime. Liberal Democratic stalwarts Bowles and Harriman, by contrast, articulated the Troubled Modernizer thesis as a way to explain the failure and to justify relaxing China policy in response. The course of events over the first two years favored the Red Menace proponents. The GLF failure did not significantly weaken Beijing, which instead attacked India, providing a great boost to its image as an expansionist communist aggressor. Although the Chinese campaign was evidently limited, available revisionist images of China could not sufficiently challenge the Red Menace account of the war.[1]

The Red Menace image was very influential during the Kennedy administration, partly as a result of policy inertia from the 1950s but also because it was boosted by tenacious advocates such as Rusk and Kennedy himself. Kennedy's lukewarm responses to the "food-for-peace" pressures from the Troubled Modernizer camp, and to early Resurgent Power arguments for moving toward a "two Chinas" policy, reflected at least his insecurity in the face of domestic opposition, if not a personal animosity toward Communist China. The Cuban missile crisis was a turning point in the Cold War, resulting in the search for a Cold War détente that included a slight softening toward China in 1963. However, the Sino-Soviet split worked to strengthen the trend toward hostile images of China, which gradually evolved into the Revolutionary Rival discourse beginning in 1963.

There was more marked competition among the four discourses during the Johnson administration – Table 4.2 illustrates the intense contestation,

---

[1] Later, the China specialists who articulated the "Resurgent Power" image of China portrayed the attack as arising from historical, nationalistic Chinese territorial claims, rather than from communist expansionism. See Iriye, ed., *US Policy toward China*, pp. 91–3, 112.

TABLE 4.2. *The relative ascendance of the four discourses in relation to significant events for China and the United States and U.S. China policy initiatives, 1961–8*

Year	Significant Events (China)[a]	Peak Articulation of Images[b]				Significant Events (United States)	U.S. China Policy Landmarks
		RM	RR	TM	RP		
1961	GLF failure effects			▓			Reciprocal journalist exchange proposed; "important question" tactic in UN China representation
1962	GLF effects; Taiwan Straits crisis; Sino-Indian war	▓				Cuban missile crisis	Possibility of grain sales
1963			▓			Search for détente with Soviet Union; JFK assassinated	Permanence of CCP regime recognized; better relations if it "behaved first"
1964	French recognition; first nuclear test	▓	▓	▓	▓	Elections – LBJ elected	
1965	Diplomatic setbacks					Vietnam escalation	Travel ban lifted for medical and scientific personnel; proposed admission of Chinese journalists, meeting on disarmament; joint exploration of U.S. infringement of Chinese air and sea territory

					Senate hearings	Travel ban lifted on scholars; "containment without isolation" accepted by LBJ
1966	Cultural Revolution					
1967						Trade embargo lifted on some pharmaceuticals and medical equipment
1968					Vietnam peace talks	

a Domestic or international events that had significant effects on Sino-American relations.

b This section indicates the key years n in which each image was most prominently articulated by its proponents in the internal discourse. Unshaded boxes do not signify that the particular image was not being articulated, only that it was not a "peak" year. No attempt has been made to quantify these trends. The relative rise or decline is plotted for each image, but not across images, i.e., the table brings out the main contending images for any given year, but does not indicate which particular image was most powerful in that year. RM = Red Menace; RR = Revolutionary Rival; TM = Troubled Modernizer; RP = Resurgent Power.

especially in the years 1964 and 1965. China's first nuclear test in October 1964 was a key event that featured in three out of the four competing discourses. It stimulated the Red Menace discourse by providing its proponents with evidence that Beijing would soon have maximum offensive capabilities to support its aggressive ideology. According to the subtler Revolutionary Rival discourse, however, the test was above all an important symbol in China's bid to lead a Third World coalition or a rival group within the communist movement. The test provided the first big boost to the Resurgent Power image among revisionist American officials: it was irrevocable evidence of Beijing's international significance, especially when accompanied by increasing international pressure for China's inclusion in the UN and arms control regimes. Proponents of the Troubled Modernizer image, for whom the nuclear test was not a definitive event, nevertheless interpreted it as further evidence of the gross misallocation of resources that would inevitably force Beijing to focus on basic social needs. In the short run, the Revolutionary Rival representation "won" in terms of policy outcome – the Johnson administration publicly discounted the strategic significance of China's new nuclear capability and reinforced its commitment to resisting Chinese aggression in Vietnam.

The Vietnam War was the definitive event in the Johnson administration's Asia policy, and it viewed China very much through the lens of the campaign. The war was decisive in the redefinition of the dominant hostile image of China from Red Menace to Revolutionary Rival because it allowed Washington to demonstrate its discrimination between coexistence with peaceful communist powers (the Soviet Union) and firm resistance to militant ones (China). And yet Vietnam also proved to be an important factor facilitating arguments for relaxing China policy. First, there was a fundamental ambiguity within the Revolutionary Rival image of China: Washington wanted to oppose firmly Chinese support for revolutionary warfare in Vietnam, but it did not want to fight China itself. Hence, even nonrevisionist American officials advocated initiatives intended to reassure China that the United States did not want to extend the war. At the same time, Washington's increasing understanding of Beijing's defensive security concerns in the war added to its appreciation for the fact that China would not fight the United States except in the extreme circumstances of a threat to its territory or the destruction of the DVN.[2] Beijing's subsequent internal preoccupation during the Cultural

---

[2] Indeed, some authors have argued that Washington and Beijing reached a modus vivendi of sorts in the conduct of the Vietnam War in order to manage the mutual threat during the

Revolution also helped to dampen the hostile images of China in official American minds. Second, revisionist officials argued that given its demonstrated containment of communism in Vietnam, the administration could afford, in domestic political terms, some relaxation of China policy.

These effects coincided with the strengthening of the two revisionist discourses: the Troubled Modernizer image was reinforced by Beijing's diplomatic setbacks of 1965–6, while proponents of the Resurgent Power image were spurred on by the tied vote in the UNGA on Chinese representation in 1965 that followed the Chinese nuclear test. Thus, 1965 was a turning point in the internal American official debate over China policy: after that, all three of the main competing discourses of China pulled in the same direction. The Revolutionary Rival discourse did continue to constrain improvements in Sino-American relations, but it also contained an inherent element of ambivalence, and its positive impact on the American side is evident from the number of U.S. initiatives to relax China policy in 1965 and 1966. The trend toward relaxing U.S. China policy was greatly enhanced in 1966, when the revisionist discourse was reinforced by China specialists at the Senate hearings. Although their arguments were based on contrasting characteristics – China's poverty and weakness, and its pride and potential strength – both subdiscourses advocated reducing China's isolation.

This revisionist trend also permeated the Johnson administration's public discourse on China, which increasingly emphasized China's weakening position and thus coalesced around the theme of Troubled Modernizer. In a late 1967 interview, Johnson expressed the hope that the Chinese leaders would learn from their failures in Africa, Latin America, and Asia and move toward "a better understanding and a more moderate approach to their neighbors."[3] Chinese militancy was really a source of weakness; Rusk often reminded the public that China's militant stance had isolated it even within the international communist community, and that it now appeared to be a major issue of contention within China itself, in its "great agony over the directions of policy and the identity of leadership."[4] At

later part of the 1960s. See Chen Jian and James Hershberg, "Informing the Enemy: Sino-American 'Signalling' and the Vietnam War, 1965," paper presented at CWIHP workshop on New Evidence on China, Southeast Asia, and the Vietnam War, January 2000, Hong Kong University; and Robert Schulzinger, "The Johnson Administration, China, and the Vietnam War," in Ross and Jiang, eds., *Re-examining the Cold War.*
[3] LBJ, interview with joint television networks, 19 December 1967, *PPP:LBJ 1967*, p. 1172.
[4] Rusk, "American Purposes and the Pursuit of Human Destiny," address to the American Legion National Convention, Boston, 29 August 1967, *DSB* 57, pp. 34–7.

the same time, the administration also acknowledged publicly the reduced Chinese threat. By 1967, even Rusk had admitted on television that the Chinese were not "actively involved" in the Vietnam War, while Rostow pointed out that the Chinese were militarily cautious and averse to the risk of a major confrontation with the United States, and that Hanoi's nationalist impulses were essentially separate from the Chinese Communist aims.[5] The latter also asserted that militancy and overreach had exacerbated China's developmental problems: "some time during the coming generation, mainland China will have to acknowledge more fully and act on the proposition that agricultural and population control is its fundamental problem; and it may need the help of the world community to avoid mass starvation." Rostow hoped that when it emerged from the Cultural Revolution, Beijing would concentrate on this primary task of the "modernization of the life of the nation."[6] The fact that "China is no longer the wave of the future"[7] thus opened up possibilities for change and peaceful coexistence.

However, the stronger element of the revisionist discourse at this time was that of the Resurgent Power, primarily because this image stood up better in the face of the Cultural Revolution. By promoting hard-liners, Mao's purges during the Cultural Revolution appeared to dash – for the time being, at least – Troubled Modernizer hopes of the rise of more moderate elements within the Chinese leadership. Although its proponents were convinced of the inevitability of Chinese moderation, initiatives to increase contact with China failed to strike a chord with any element of the internally preoccupied Chinese leadership, and the outside world was left guessing as to how long the chaos in China would last or what the complexion of the new leadership would be. Proponents of the Resurgent Power image, on the other hand, saw the Cultural Revolution as the latest evidence of China's frustrations and proposed unilateral steps more appropriate to the circumstances, steps that would reduce American hostility and thus temper the rising Chinese paranoia that accompanied the internal turmoil. They did not make regime change in Beijing a condition for improving U.S.–China relations. This posture of "quiet reasonableness" and the fact that Washington did not try to take sides against Mao

---

[5] Rusk, interview with British Independent Television network, 1 February 1967; Rostow, "The Great Transition: Tasks of the First and Second Postwar Generations," Sir Montague Burton Lecture, University of Leeds, 23 February 1967, *DSB* 56, pp. 195, 493–4.

[6] Ibid., pp. 497, 501–2.

[7] Rusk, "American Purposes and the Pursuit of Human Destiny," p. 34.

during this period of internal upheaval helped to keep the door open to improving bilateral relations later on.[8]

More importantly, the Resurgent Power discourse most clearly identified the need to change China policy with immediate American interests. It was articulated in relation to the declining U.S. credibility as a world power, and it proposed changes explicitly aimed at improving America's leadership image among its allies and the international community. Also, these policy changes might help to salvage the domestic standing of the Johnson administration: the moralistic historical reasons for which Resurgent Power arguments claimed the need for altering American attitudes toward China were important at a time of widespread domestic disillusionment with Vietnam. By focusing on these American self-interests, the Resurgent Power discourse helped to bring official China policy thinking to the doorstep of rapprochement in 1968.

The foregoing is a narrative of the process of China policy rethinking among American officials from 1961 to 1968, based on the four competing strands this study has identified within the discourse. The relative ascendance and decline of each image has been explicitly related to particular international and domestic events, and in this sense "discourse" and "image" are not used here as explanatory variables. They are rather instruments that facilitate a multilevel understanding of the process of change. These discourses were derived from central representations of China by specific individuals, and they related to particular understandings of different aspects of American self-identity. Furthermore, contending interpretations of the same key events provided by proponents of each competing discourse do indicate that the particular outlook and understandings associated with a specific image affected the context within which officials understood external events and subsequently formulated policy positions.[9]

Thus there was an active process of debate and rethinking about China policy among American officials from 1961 to 1968. This process was

---

[8] On the possibility that the Johnson administration might have misplayed its hand during the Cultural Revolution, see Victor S. Kaufman, *Confronting Communism: US and British Policies toward China* (Columbia, 2001), Chapter 8.

[9] This two-way effect is labeled "mutually constitutive" by constructivists. See Emmanuel Adler, "Seizing the Middle Ground: Constructivism in World Politics," *European Journal of International Relations* 3(3) (1997), pp. 319–63. However, I would not go so far here as some constructivists who argue that domestic ideology or self-identity drive changing perceptions of national interest. See the articles in Katzenstein, ed., *Culture of National Security*.

encapsulated within the competition among four distinct subdiscourses, which evinced the following characteristics. First, it was a constructive process: each subdiscourse tended to build upon, rather than simply to displace, another. Revolutionary Rival was an updated version of Red Menace, while its ambiguities about Chinese strengths in turn made room for Troubled Modernizer, which emphasized Chinese weakness. Resurgent Power in turn incorporated the knowledge of current Chinese weakness in its understanding of Chinese frustrations in light of its historical status. Second, these images produced a cumulative trend toward a deeper and more complex American official understanding of China. This understanding placed greater emphasis on factors endogenous to China – Maoist ideology, China's internal weakness, divisions within the regime, China's historical experience – rather than those derived from its association with the Soviet Union. It also encompassed Chinese strengths and weaknesses in the past, present, and future. Third, the revisionist trend viewed China less as an "Other" and more in terms of common identity characteristics, such as universal goals of socioeconomic development, and especially the attributes of major powers. Fourth, accompanying the eventual predominance of the Resurgent Power image was the primary framework of viewing China in relation to preserving American self-identity and self-interest.

THE DISCOURSE OF RECONCILIATION WITH CHINA, 1968

There was an active process of reassessment of China policy under Kennedy and especially during the Johnson administrations. From 1966 onward, revisionist representations of China gradually came to dominate internal and public official discourse. By 1968, therefore, the official status quo thinking about China policy leaned toward reconciliation based on two nonstrategic discourses that may be loosely termed "liberal" as opposed to "realist." They stemmed from four main concerns. The first was a moralistic or humanitarian concern for the Chinese people on the part of "China hands," China friendship groups, missionary groups, and other sympathetic elements. Second, officials needed to rationalize China policy in the face of declining international and domestic support for its harsher elements. In the short run, therefore, the urge was to shift the onus for hostile U.S.–China relations onto Beijing and its intransigence. In the longer run, revisionist officials ultimately aspired to end China's isolation and to socialize it into international society as a responsible major power.

These ideas of reconciliation with China and the attending policy recommendations predated the significant systemic changes of 1968–9 that
apparently motivated Nixon and Kissinger's search for rapprochement.
However, the underlying Sino-Soviet dispute was evident, and it deepened in the course of the 1960s. Yet the theme of exploiting Sino-Soviet
differences to U.S. advantage did not feature prominently in the 1960s
discourse of reconciliation with China. This was due in part to the same
general caution that had led to Washington's official "neutral" stance regarding the dispute – officials were by and large uncertain about how
best to exploit it. Some, like William Bundy, did contemplate the matter
in relation to worsening Sino-Soviet polemics and the search for peace in
Vietnam beginning in late 1965. Bundy suggested that raising the profile
of the U.S.–PRC ambassadorial talks might "stimulate the Soviets to increase their efforts to ensure a role for themselves in bringing the Vietnam
war to a peaceful conclusion," and might bring the broader advantage of
"increase[ing] the elements of uncertainty" for Soviet policy makers. The
problem, though, was that Beijing would most probably not want to play
the game. Bundy judged that the Chinese would have more to lose if they
were perceived to be collaborating with the United States.[10]

In the following year, there was a series of suggestions from out-
siders (such as Zbigniew Brzezinski, then a professor of international
relations at Columbia) and NSC staff members that Washington should
"flirt with" the PRC as part of a "series of calculated moves to stimulate
anxiety among the Soviets." The Johnson administration's China hands
joined with Soviet specialists to object to this. Al Jenkins argued that the
arms control negotiations with Moscow were at stake, and that the plan
could backfire and engender greater Soviet hostility and withdrawal from
détente. In terms of China policy itself, he felt that it would jeopardize
"our genuine efforts to maintain an openness of attitude toward China
and [to] take steps ... toward a better relationship."[11]

Together, the nature of the 1960s discourse of reconciliation with China
and the official reservations of the Johnson administration regarding the
Sino-Soviet split suggest that, had it been faced with the dramatic deterioration of Sino-Soviet relations that occurred in the spring of 1969, the
Johnson administration would most likely have chosen to continue with

[10] Bundy to SoS, "US Position on Possible Change of Location of US-Chicom Ambassadorial Talks," 21 December 1965, "Jenkins memos" folder, Box 5, NSF, LBJL, pp. 5–6.
[11] Jenkins to Rostow, "Cater Memo Suggesting We Pretend We Are Flirting With Red
China," 19 January 1967, Box 1, Jenkins Files, LBJL.

the policy of neutrality (Option 1). Certainly, in light of the developing consensus on the representation of China as a weak but influential power with which the United States had to engage as soon as possible, collaborating with Moscow against Beijing (Option 2) would not have been a likely choice. In the event, however, the choice did not fall to a Johnson (or Humphrey) administration.

Even so, does the foregoing analysis suggest that there was a chance for a different type of "liberal" rapprochement with China in the latter part of the 1960s?

Apart from the ideational developments, in actual policy terms the 1960s were in fact not as barren as they are often portrayed. Contrary to the impression that there was no mutual contact, there was sustained bilateral communication between the two countries in the form of the ambassadorial talks at Warsaw, which had begun in the late 1950s and continued regularly until 1967, after which they became more sporadic. Although the concrete effectiveness of these talks is often dismissed, they may have represented the most comprehensive bilateral contact of any state with the PRC over this period, and they proved to be a valuable channel of communication in times of crisis. From 1965 onward, American officials at the highest levels toned down their rhetoric against China and offered the possibility of better relations. At the same time, the Johnson administration took the first steps in relaxing the travel ban and trade embargo, so that by 1968 doctors, scientists, and academics could apply to travel to China, and U.S. firms were allowed to export pharmaceuticals to China.

Yet these policy changes represented very limited progress in comparison to changes in public opinion and new policy proposals within the administration.[12] The reasons are to be found in constraining factors within the domestic political context on both sides. On the U.S. side, high-level resistance to alterations in China policy played a significant role for much of the 1960s. In particular, there is no doubt that Rusk's stubborn opposition presented a significant bureaucratic "stone wall" to the revisionist discourse generated from middle levels. From a policy point of view, Kennedy shared Rusk's reservations for both personal and domestic political reasons; in particular, he had a large civil rights domestic agenda and did not wish to alienate the conservatives in Congress.[13] Johnson, on the

---

[12] Foot, *Practice of Power*, pp. 84–5, 93–103; Foot, "Redefinitions," pp. 14–18.
[13] For an alternative study of the efforts of revisionist officials to change China policy from 1961 to 1963 and the limitations posed by Kennedy's bureaucratic apparatus, personal

other hand, was preoccupied with the Vietnam War and its domestic repercussions.[14] It is possible that as a mutual understanding of sorts developed
between Washington and Beijing regarding the limits of the U.S. intervention in Vietnam after 1966, the impetus for changing China policy was
diminished. It is more likely that, because of the need to marshal domestic
support, Johnson did not feel able to undertake major initiatives toward
China that would fundamentally call into question the raison d'être of
the Vietnam War.[15] Johnson was not particularly confident in the field
of foreign policy, and often deferred to his senior advisers.[16] This lack of
bureaucratic consensus prevented significant policy response to the revisionist discourse on China policy.[17] And yet the foregoing analysis has
demonstrated that, from 1966 onward, there was a notable move toward
something of a consensus on the need to soften Washington's stance on
China, if only to improve America's international image and to assuage
Beijing's security concerns with regard to the war in Vietnam. By 1967,
even Rusk had acknowledged the inevitability of UN representation for
the PRC, recommended a relaxation of the trade embargo, and approved
suggestions for a bilateral foreign ministers' meeting.

The key impediment to the process of rapprochement after the turning
point in internal American official thinking in 1965 was the lack of response from Beijing. There were several important attempts by Washington
to substantiate the high-level American desire for better relations –
for instance, proposals for journalistic exchange visits, a disarmament
meeting, and a meeting about U.S. incursion into Chinese territory during

---

suasion, and lack of policy leadership, see Kochavi, *A Conflict Perpetuated*, esp. Chapter 3.
Kochavi also offers a more moderate interpretation of Rusk's attitude toward China,
documenting his willingness to take small steps toward Beijing as early as 1961.

[14] The latter point is made strongly in Nancy Tucker, "Threats, Opportunities and Frustrations in East Asia," in Warren Cohen and Nancy Tucker, eds., *Lyndon Johnson Confronts
the World* (Cambridge, 1994).

[15] Kusnitz, *Public Opinion and Foreign Policy*, pp. 116–17.

[16] David Kaiser, "Men and Policies: 1961–69," in Diane Kunz, ed., *The Diplomacy of the
Crucial Decade: American Foreign Relations during the 1960s* (New York, 1994), pp. 31, 25.
However, Johnson's key policy staff members are unanimous in pointing out his personal
flexibility and practicality toward relaxing China policy – he was primarily concerned
with eradicating "ignorance, poverty, disease" and reconciliation with "all these hungry
people who have no long-term reason to hate us." William Bundy, draft manuscript,
Chapter 16, LBJL, p. 15; James Thomson Oral History interview, LBJL, p. I–47; Walt
Rostow Oral History interview, LBJL, p. I–95.

[17] For the parallel bureaucratic consensus explanation of the Chinese decision for rapprochement, see Rosemary Foot, "The Study of China's International Behaviour: International Relations Approaches," in Ngaire Woods, ed., *Explaining International Relations
since 1945* (Oxford, 1996), pp. 270–2.

the Vietnam War – but the Chinese rejected these out of hand. In a sense, this was the cycle of "bad timing" in U.S.–PRC relations reasserting itself, as Mao's Cultural Revolution plunged China into isolation and internal chaos just as the most positive signals were being sent from the United States. The Chinese foreign policy apparatus broke down during the Cultural Revolution; Mao and other top leaders were preoccupied with internal affairs, and between 1966 and 1969 all but one ambassador were recalled from their posts, while the foreign ministry was incapacitated by attacks from a rebel ultra-leftist faction.[18]

However, we should underestimate neither the degree of Chinese antagonism nor the deep ideological and political roots of the Chinese Communist leadership's portrayal of the United States as its enemy, *throughout* the 1960s. China scholars emphasize the revolutionary character of the Maoist regime on the mainland, and assert that its two key goals were domestic political mobilization for regime security and international competition with the Soviet Union for influence in the communist and Third World liberation movements.[19] These two elements were intrinsically linked. As the Sino-Soviet dispute worsened from 1958 onward, Mao adopted an ultra-leftist "dual adversary" posture, which pitted China against both the Soviet Union and the United States. In 1962, he dismissed suggestions that China might improve its security situation by reducing its antagonism with the United States as evidence of Soviet "revisionist thinking" that had infiltrated the CCP.[20] Mao's fundamental ideological opposition to Soviet "revisionism" made impossible any contemplation that Beijing might follow Moscow down the path of seeking détente with the West. Moreover, the PRC had two key national security reasons for antipathy toward Washington: the Taiwan issue and, more importantly during this period, the Vietnam War. Beijing's support for Hanoi had

---

[18] Li Jie, "Changes in China's Domestic Situation in the 1960s and Sino-US Relations," pp. 307–9; and Gong Li, "Chinese Decision Making and the Thawing of Sino-US Relations," pp. 321–7, both in Ross and Jiang, eds., *Re-examining the Cold War*.

[19] See, for instance, Zhai Qiang, "China and America: A Troubled Relationship"; and John Garver, "Food for Thought: Reflections on Food Aid and the Idea of Another Lost Chance in Sino-American Relations," in *Journal of American–East Asian Relations* 7(1–2) (Spring/Summer 1998), pp. 93–106. On the theme of domestic mobilization in Chinese foreign policy, see Thomas Christensen, *Useful Adversaries: Grand Strategy, Domestic Mobilization, and Sino-American Conflict, 1947–1958* (Princeton, 1996), Chapters 5 and 6.

[20] Li, "Changes in China's Domestic Situation," pp. 301–6; Zhang Baijia, "The Changing International Scene and Chinese Policy towards the United States, 1965–1970," in Ross and Jiang, eds., *Re-examining the Cold War*, pp. 56–66.

stemmed from the belief that Vietnam was an ideal test case for Mao's revolutionary ideology. But Chinese sources suggest that from 1964 to 1965, increased U.S. intervention in Vietnam also seriously heightened the Chinese leadership's paranoia because it proved that Mao's previous belief that the United States was a vacillating power was wrong. This in turn had domestic implications, because the sense of external threat led Mao to his attempt to secure the Chinese revolution sufficiently that China could better counter a large-scale U.S. campaign in Southeast Asia.[21]

The limits of the official discourse of reconciliation with China during this period reflected these two constraining factors in a striking manner. The proponents of the Troubled Modernizer discourse were essentially playing a waiting game, while the imperative of "shifting the onus onto Beijing" as well as the Resurgent Power idea of unilaterally redressing injustice may be argued to have hampered the deeper development of thinking regarding a "real" opening to China. Revisionist officials argued for the relaxation of China policy using rationales and actions that did not require a response from the Chinese; indeed, they assumed that the Chinese would not respond. Such assumptions, while they did overcome the most immediate perceptual stumbling blocks on the U.S. side, presented inherent limits to the development of the 1960s revisionist discourse. For instance, by accepting the fact that the Chinese would remain adamantly intransigent, they precluded (or at least did not encourage) detailed studies of options for resolving or overcoming the basic and complex bilateral dispute about Taiwan. All revisionist officials consistently advocated a move to an eventual "two Chinas" stance. Yet these same officials recognized that both the PRC and the ROC would not accept the idea. Indeed, one might argue that the concept was bandied about with ease precisely because of the low political cost of articulating "two Chinas" during the 1960s. No one had a plan for how it was going to happen in practice, but the ideal had the advantage of making the speaker appear reasonable and just, while shifting the onus for Sino-American hostility onto Beijing. This tactic had served Kennedy well in the 1960 election debates, and was readily acknowledged by Komer, Thomson, Rice, and other revisionist officials in their internal memoranda.

Indeed, some PRC reaction to U.S. gestures during the 1960s might have prompted or forced U.S. officials into more serious consideration of how a two-sided rapprochement might be developed. Given the inherent limits to 1960s revisionist thinking about reconciliation with the

---

[21] Odd Arne Westad et al., eds., "77 Conversations," pp. 2–3.

Chinese and, importantly, the fact that a "two Chinas" policy was consistently advocated by revisionists as the solution to the Taiwan problem, a case cannot convincingly be made that a rapprochement was possible on the U.S. side during the 1960s. There was a real opportunity, in terms of official American attitudes, for the unilateral relaxation of China policy, but this is qualitatively different from a bilateral rapprochement or reconciliation.

By 1967, therefore, it seemed that the Johnson administration had moved as far as it could in terms of both official attitudes and policy initiatives toward China. A large number of policy proposals intended to further increase contact, mute hostilities, and show appreciation for China awaited better possibilities of Chinese reciprocation for their implementation. In 1968–9, the time appeared to be at hand, as the Vietnam peace talks began and the Cultural Revolution seemed to be winding down. In some of the last memoranda of the Johnson administration, Jenkins, Rusk, and Rostow urged that the time was right to continue the process of relaxing China policy.[22]

---

[22] Jenkins to Rostow, 5 December 1968; Rusk to LBJ, 4 January 1969; Rostow to LBJ, 6 January 1969, *FRUS 1964–8*, XXX, pp. 725–6, 729–30.

PART TWO

DISCURSIVE TRANSITIONS, 1969–1971

5

Nixon's China Policy Discourse in Context

> Great ideas can change history, but only if great leadership comes along
> that can give those ideas force. . . . What lifts great leaders above the second-
> raters is that they are more forceful, more resourceful, and have a shrewd-
> ness of judgment that . . . enables them to identify the fleeting opportunity.
>
> Richard Nixon[1]

Richard Nixon's opening to China in 1972 has been indelibly associated
with balance-of-power politics and its attendant assumption of a sudden, almost automatic realist reaction to structural changes from 1969
onward. Yet Nixon had been a prominent figure in the U.S. government
since the 1950s and had maintained a high-profile involvement with communist and Asian affairs during the 1960s, when he was out of office.[2]
This chapter traces Nixon's thinking about China policy prior to, and
during the first two years of, his presidency and investigates its relationship to the developing discourse of reconciliation in official and informed
public circles during the 1960s.[3] Did Nixon, in keeping with his front-line

---

[1] Richard Nixon, *Leaders* (New York, 1982), p. 330.
[2] This chapter does not discuss Kissinger's thinking about China prior to 1968 because
Nixon was the key driver behind the idea of reconciliation with China in the early days
of his administration. By his own admission, Kissinger had paid relatively little attention
to Asia per se before he served under Nixon – he was a specialist in European and nuclear
politics – and did not seriously consider bringing about a China opening until the Sino-
Soviet border war in March 1969 offered a geostrategic opportunity. See *White House
Years*, pp. 165, 172, 177.
[3] A combination of primary and secondary sources are used here to analyze Nixon's private
and public discourse on China from 1952 to 1971. Note, however, that documentary
sources for the period when he was out of office, from 1961 to 1968, were remarkably

Republican conservative position, perceive China as a "Red Menace" to be ruthlessly contained and isolated? How then did he turn to the discourse of reconciliation with China that accompanied his moves toward rapprochement when he took office?

"TOUGH COEXISTENCE": NIXON'S CHINA POLICY THINKING AS VICE PRESIDENT, 1952–1960

Nixon's early political career was built significantly upon anticommunist foundations. Shortly after being elected a congressman from California in 1947, he was appointed to the Herter Committee, which undertook a study tour of Europe in preparation for the Marshall Plan. This first-hand experience of the threat of communism to democracy in postwar Europe engendered a lasting engagement with the complex issue of the "international communist threat." During his subsequent time in Congress, Nixon earned a reputation for being a staunch anticommunist through his prominent involvement in the Alger Hiss case, and he emerged as a leading critic of the Truman administration's Asia policy after the outbreak of the Korean War. This high profile was instrumental in Nixon's selection as Eisenhower's running mate in the 1952 presidential election.[4]

In spite of his reputation as one of the ultimate "Red baiters" of the time, there are indications that Nixon's thinking about U.S. China policy during his eight years as vice president was more nuanced than some of his public rhetoric indicated. Publicly, Nixon sometimes came across as an extreme hard liner – for instance, during the offshore islands crisis in 1954–5, when he openly considered the use of nuclear weapons.[5] In private, though, he sought more practical means to put pressure on the Sino-Soviet relationship and indirectly to influence the Chinese toward moderation, while emphasizing the need to be vigilant and to support the GRC.

Nixon's efforts on this front were strongest in 1953 and 1954, during the period following his extensive tour of Asia and before the onset of the first offshore islands crisis. During his 1953 trip, Nixon made many public statements of U.S. support for the GRC, which "truly represents the

---

thin at the time of this writing because of the paucity of declassified private material from the Nixon Library in Yorba Linda.

[4] On this early period, see Stephen Ambrose, *Nixon: The Education of a Politician, 1913–1962* (London, 1987), pp. 141–270; and Irwin Gellman, *The Contender, Richard Nixon: The Congress Years, 1946–1952* (New York, 1999).

[5] *NYT*, 18 March 1955, p. 16.

Chinese nation and the Chinese people," and promised to "oppose vigorously" the admission of Red China into the UN.[6] In his national report, he declared that "China is the basic cause of all our problems in Asia."[7] In his internal report to the NSC,[8] though, Nixon qualified his stance on how to deal with Communist China. While strongly recommending the continuation of the policy of containment and diplomatic isolation, he argued against the strict economic blockade of China. The administration was conducting a review of China policy, and there was a growing internal debate about whether the trade embargo on China ought to be lowered to conform with the trade restrictions against the Soviet bloc.[9] Nixon argued that "in practical terms," "trade is inevitable" – the outside world, not least U.S. allies and American businesses, would want to conduct business with China. And since the United States could "trade with China without recognizing her," this was an issue that Washington could concede.[10]

Moreover, Nixon identified an important role for trade as part of the "wedge strategy" to divide the Soviets and the Chinese. Against the notion that restricting Western aid to China would force it to rely more and more on Soviet aid and thereby generate friction in the unequal relationship between the two communist powers,[11] Nixon argued that spreading American economic influence on the mainland would help to strain the Sino-Soviet alliance even faster, as it would soon become apparent that the Soviets could not compete with the West in providing for China's needs. Eisenhower liked the idea that the best way to influence the Chinese people against the communist government might be to allow Chinese junks

[6] *NYT*, 9 November 1953; Nixon's radio statement, Taipei, 8 November 1953, Box 1, Series 370, Nixon Pre-Presidential Papers (NPPP), National Archives–Pacific Rim (NA-PR).
[7] Nixon, nationwide radio and television address reporting on vice presidential trip to Asia, 23 December 1953, Box 1, Series 369, NPPP, NA-PR, p. 4.
[8] The National Security Council apparatus was set up in 1947 under Truman. Eisenhower created the position of special assistant to the president for national security affairs and revamped the NSC to act as a center of policy making that would allow the heads of various agencies to debate and advise the president on key policy issues, and through which presidential decisions and policy guidelines would be disseminated. See Robert Bowie and Richard Immerman, *Waging Peace: How Eisenhower Shaped an Enduring Cold War Strategy* (Oxford, 1998), Chapter 5; and John Prados, *Keeper of the Keys: A History of the National Security Council from Truman to Bush* (New York, 1991), pp. 57–96.
[9] NSC 166/1, "US Policy towards Communist China," 6 November 1953; NSC Planning Board to NSC, "US and Free World Controls over Transactions with Communist China," 3 March 1954, *FRUS 1952–4*, XIV, pp. 278–302, 371–6.
[10] Memo, 177th meeting of the NSC, 23 November 1953, ibid., pp. 348–9.
[11] NSC 166/1, pp. 280–2.

to sail to Japan "to fill up with everything they could buy," and he tried
to persuade the Defense Department that the trade "weapon" should be
explored.[12]

In the run-up to the Geneva Conference held in May and June 1954,
Nixon reiterated that an offer of trade could be used as a "negotiating
point" in the talks, which offered a slim opening for direct contact with the
Chinese. He argued that the United States had very few bargaining chips,
and, in spite of ideological differences, it was necessary to be "calculating
and hard-boiled" – the time had come "to determine under what conditions, what level of trade, would best serve the interests of the US vis-à-vis
Communist China." After all, the United States had traded with the Soviet
Union in the 1930s before recognition.[13] Nixon's argument here was situated more broadly within the idea that China was "too important" to
the United States to be ignored or isolated. It was "the key to Asia," the
"great dynamic force in Asia," and Washington simply had to engage
with the issue of China in its Asian strategy. In his view, the United States
had to be strong and not concede to China a "sphere of influence"; but
on the other hand, it could not try to eliminate the Chinese threat by war,
as this would be unacceptable to domestic opinion and to allies. Therefore, Nixon asserted that Washington must seek a middle path of "tough
coexistence," a "third option...in between war and appeasement,"
based on the aim of "driving a wedge" between China and the Soviet
Union.[14]

Nixon's internal official policy views during this period clearly indicated his sharp interest in the centrality of the Sino-Soviet relationship
and his pragmatism regarding unofficial trade and contact with China.
But domestic politics in the 1950s did not allow the public articulation

---

[12] "Minutes of 192nd NSC Meeting," 6 April 1954, Box 6, NSF, Whitman Files, Eisenhower
Library (DDEL); Memo, 193rd NSC meeting, 13 April 1954, *FRUS 1952–4*, XIV, pp. 409–
11. Defense, however, was not convinced that the United States could fight and trade
with the Chinese Communists at the same time. This logic was not unique – it had been
contemplated since 1948 and was a lasting point of contention between Washington and
its British ally. See John Gaddis, "The American 'Wedge Strategy', 1949–1958," in Harry
Harding and Yuan Ming, eds., *Sino-American Relations 1945–1955: A Joint Assessment of
a Critical Decade* (Wilmington, 1989); and Kaufman, *Confronting Communism*.

[13] 193rd NSC meeting, pp. 409–11.

[14] Memo, 211th NSC Meeting, 18 August 1954, *FRUS 1952–4*, XIV, p. 536; Philip Pope,
"Foundations of Nixonian Foreign Policy: The Pre-Presidential Years of Richard M.
Nixon, 1946–1968," unpublished Ph.D. dissertation, University of Southern California,
August 1988, pp. 233–4, 518.

of this view. Congressional sentiment was such that it opposed even the idea that the U.S. delegation should meet separately with the Communist Chinese delegation at Geneva; and when there was serious flooding in China in late 1954, even though Dulles and Nixon discussed the possibility of offering disaster relief, nothing was done, in part because of the expected opposition from the China lobby.[15] Subsequently, the September 1954 offshore islands crisis certainly forced a toughening of the administration's line against Communist Chinese aggression and reinforced its support for the GRC.[16] Yet Nixon retained his ideas about the best approach to the China problem. During the presidential election of 1960, he told an audience of newspaper editors that he approved of China being brought into disarmament negotiations, even though he would not recognize Beijing. This accorded with his idea that China was an important power that had to be engaged separately by the United States. Notably, Nixon also indicated that his opposition to recognition of the PRC need not be permanent; the United States would change this policy once China "qualifie[d] for recognition and admission to the UN as a peace loving nation in its international policies." And this was a change that he expected to happen: "Looking to the future, I would say that there will be certain facts and circumstances which will be motivating them toward a change in direction of their policies."[17]

In this sense, Nixon echoed what revisionist historians have shown to be Eisenhower's and Dulles's own inclinations toward a more realistic policy vis-à-vis Communist China.[18] Moreover, Nixon went a little further in trying to articulate such a policy within official circles, and his arguments during this period foreshadowed some of the key elements of his later China policy.

---

[15] Dulles, telephone conversation with Nixon, 9 July 1954, Box 2, Dulles Files, DDEL.

[16] See Accinelli, *Crisis and Containment*, pp. 157–252; and J. H. Kalicki, *The Pattern of Sino-American Crises: Political-Military Interactions in the 1950s* (Cambridge, 1975).

[17] Nixon address and question-and-answer session before the Convention of the American Society of Newspaper Editors, Washington, D.C., 23 April 1960, Folder 9, Box 132, Series 207, NPPP, NA-PR.

[18] Eisenhower thought that the United States ought to trade with the PRC and allow it into the UN, while Dulles tried to pursue a "two Chinas" policy. See David Mayers, "Eisenhower and Communism: Later Findings," in Richard Melanson and David Mayers, eds., *Reevaluating Eisenhower: American Foreign Policy in the 1950s* (Urbana, 1987); Qing Simei, "The Eisenhower Administration and Changes in Western Embargo Policy against China, 1954–1958," in Cohen and Iriye, eds., *Great Powers in East Asia*; and Tucker, "John Foster Dulles."

CHINA AS "KEY PLAYER": THE DEVELOPMENT OF
NIXON'S CHINA STRATEGY, 1960–1968

During Nixon's "wilderness years,"[19] the period during which he was out
of office in the 1960s, his idea of China as the "key player" in Asia developed even more strongly toward the conviction that a rising China had to
be reckoned with sooner rather than later using a mixture of "soft" and
"hard" policies. While this paralleled the rise of the "Resurgent Power"
discourse in Washington during the latter half of the 1960s, Nixon's China
strategy was also an outgrowth of his own pragmatic predilections dating
back to the 1950s. In addition, the way in which his ideas developed during the late 1960s also reflected a wider discursive trend among a group
of international leaders as well as within the domestic political context.

Nixon traveled widely during the 1960s and was well received by leaders in Europe and Asia whom he had met previously when he was vice
president. Through his trips to Asia in 1964, 1965, and 1967, Nixon
built up something of an expertise on the Vietnam War, which helped
to propel him back into the public eye and into politics. On this issue,
he developed the "tough containment" arm of his China strategy. In articles and speeches in 1964 and 1965, he asserted that the risks of war
with China would in fact be slimmer if the United States stuck to a determined course than if it were to negotiate with the communists. He argued
that the Vietnam War was a "showdown" with Communist China that
Washington had to face now, rather than having to face "a bigger war
later, when the Communists would be stronger" as a result of having been
allowed to overrun Indochina. Also, Washington had to check communist expansion now while Beijing was weakened by the Sino-Soviet split,
rather than in ten to twenty-five years when it had become one of the great
powers.[20]

At the same time, however, the "coexistence" arm of his China strategy was being exercised during his encounters with European leaders,
especially with French President Charles de Gaulle and ex–West German
Chancellor Konrad Adenauer in 1963 and 1967. Both men argued that
Washington should improve relations with, and eventually recognize,

---

[19] The term is Jonathan Aitken's, in *Nixon: A Life* (London, 1993).

[20] Nixon, speech delivered to San Francisco Commonwealth Club, 2 April 1965, Box 3,
Series 207, NPPP, NA-PR, pp. 1–11; "Nixon Urges Quarantine in Vietnam," *Boston
Herald*, 16 April 1964, p. 2; Nixon, "Needed in Vietnam: The Will to Win," *Reader's
Digest*, August 1964, p. 43; Nixon, *Memoirs*, pp. 270–1; Stephen Ambrose, *Nixon: The
Triumph of a Politician, 1962–1972* (London, 1989), pp. 68–79.

Communist China on the basis of two essentially realist power considerations. First, they counseled that the United States should tilt its policy
toward Communist China in order to counterbalance the growing Soviet
threat – an argument that was emphasized in 1967 as Western European
fears that the United States was losing its focus on NATO grew with
Washington's increasing involvement in the Vietnam War.[21] De Gaulle
also preached the value of conciliation from a position of strength. It was
crucial, he told Nixon, that the United States negotiate with China now,
while the latter needed American friendship (against the Soviets), instead
of waiting until Washington was compelled to talk to Beijing because of
the latter's strength.[22]

This idea of temporary weakness and eventual resurgence was the over-
lapping point between the two arms of Nixon's China strategy. In March
1966, he saw Johnson and urged an unspecified "diplomatic communication" with China as soon as possible, advising that "time is on their side.
Now is the time to confront them on the diplomatic front."[23] Of course,
there was an element of cognitive dissonance in this twin formulation of
the need to contain China while it was weak but also to negotiate with it
before it became too strong. By 1967, however, Nixon had found a way to
overcome this: he began to shift the preconditions for better relations with
China away from Chinese behavior in general and toward the ending of
the Vietnam War in particular. In March 1967, he told Romanian Communist Party Secretary General Nicolae Ceauşescu that once the war was
over, Washington could establish "effective communications" and "take
steps to normalize relations" with Beijing.[24] By placing less emphasis on
the need for Beijing to change its spots in general, Nixon was, like the revisionist China officials, implicitly acknowledging that U.S. China policy
was increasingly untenable in the face of demonstrable Chinese influence
on international affairs vital to U.S. interests.

In addition to power balancing motivations, de Gaulle also introduced
to Nixon a version of the "Resurgent Power" image closer to that held

---

[21] Nixon, *Memoirs*, pp. 280–1; "Notes on Germany," Box 1, Series 17, NPPP, NA-PR, p. 1.
[22] Aitken, *Nixon*, pp. 318–19; Nixon, "Notes on France," Box 1, Series 17, NPPP, NA-PR,
pp. 1, 4. By the time they met again in early 1969, Nixon told de Gaulle that he would
want to talk to China even as he negotiated with the Soviets; it was essential to have
more communication with China before it got too strong. Nixon–de Gaulle memcon,
1 March 1969, Box 1023, NSF, Nixon Presidential Materials (NPM), pp. 8–9.
[23] Nixon, *Memoirs*, pp. 272–3.
[24] Emb/Bucharest to DoS, "Visit to Romania by Former Vice President Richard M. Nixon,"
29 March 1967, Box 2633, CFPF(1967–9), RG59, NA, p. 10.

by revisionist U.S. officials and academics at the 1966 Senate hearings. In 1965, he told Nixon that France had recognized China because "it is so big, so old and very much abused . . . by Western colonial power."[25] In 1967, he advised Nixon that China should not be "isolated in rage."[26] Thus, the longer-term threat of China lay also in the likelihood that its attitude would be further colored by its continued perceived ill-treatment at the hands of the international community. The corollary of this was the Western world's capacity to influence Chinese attitudes by changing some of its policies – precisely what Nixon had been advocating in private, though in a more limited way, since the 1950s.

The clearest enunciation of Nixon's resulting China strategy took the form of an article in *Foreign Affairs*, which he wrote with the help of his campaign aide Leonard Garment, published in October 1967.[27] In it, Nixon portrayed China as still a danger and a threat in Asia. He wrote that Asia's future hinged on "four giants": China, "the world's most populous nation and Asia's most immediate threat"; the United State, "the greatest Pacific power"; India, "the world's most populous non-communist nation"; and Japan, "Asia's principal industrial and economic power."[28] He argued that the "clear, present and repeatedly and insistently expressed" threat of China would be augmented by a "significant deliverable nuclear capability" within the next three to five years. If that capability was developed outside of any nonproliferation agreement, there was a distinct possibility that Beijing would "scatter its weapons among 'liberation' forces anywhere in the world."[29]

Thus, working on his theme of China as a "key player," Nixon now stated: "Any American policy toward Asia must come urgently to grips with the reality of China."[30] He went on to present his old "tough co-existence" strategy in detail, separating its two arms into "short-range" and "long-range" policies. The long-range aim, he asserted, borrowing de Gaulle's words in the much-quoted paragraph, was to pull China back into international society: " . . . we simply cannot afford to leave China

---

[25] Quoted in Speer, "Nixon's Position on Communist China," p. 343; Herbert Parmet, *Richard Nixon and His America* (Boston, 1990), p. 622.
[26] "Notes on France," p. 2.
[27] Nixon, "Asia after Vietnam," *Foreign Affairs* 46(1) (1967), pp. 111–25.
[28] He deliberately excluded the Soviet Union as a Pacific power, writing that despite its spatial dominance of the Asian continent, it was essentially a European power. Nixon, "Asia after Vietnam," p. 119.
[29] Ibid., pp. 113, 122.
[30] Ibid., p. 119.

forever outside the family of nations, there to nurture its fantasies, cherish its hates and threaten its neighbors. There is no place in this small planet for a billion of its potentially most able people to live in angry isolation."

Nixon often repeated this key passage during his presidential election campaign in 1968, sending the message to audiences beyond the academic and policy elite.[31] He also stated that in the long run, the United States would have to resume contact and develop détente with China, as it was trying to do with the Soviet Union. It would be in the interest of world peace to persuade them to give up the idea of nuclear confrontation.[32]

However, this long-term goal could be achieved only through *short-range* policies that clearly recognized the danger posed by Communist China and the fact that "the world cannot be safe until China changes." Thus, the short-term aim would be to "persuade China that it *must* change...that its own national interest requires a turning away from foreign adventuring and a turning inwards toward the solution of its own domestic problems." Rushing to grant Beijing recognition or UN membership, or even to "ply it with offers of trade," would not work. Such tactics would only serve to strengthen the Chinese leaders in their present course.[33] In publicly stating his China strategy, Nixon was careful to adopt a harder stance than he had articulated in private. He changed his earlier position on trade, for instance; and he was even more forthright in speaking to campaign audiences, calling China "an outlaw nation" that "we should not now under any circumstances" recognize, trade with, or admit to the UN.[34]

Instead, Nixon argued that the United States had to create conditions that would force Beijing to see the wisdom of reaching some form of limited accommodation with the West. As in the postwar European economic recovery program and the Atlantic Alliance, the United States had to strengthen noncommunist Asia and build it up as a buffer to Communist China. Thus, Nixon defined the criteria for better relations: "Only as the nations of non-Communist Asia become so strong – economically, politically and militarily – that they no longer furnish tempting targets

---

[31] See, for instance, "Answers by Richard Nixon to Detroit Free Press," 29 September 1968, and p. 14; "To Keep the Peace," CBS nationwide radio broadcast, 19 October 1968, Speech File, Richard Nixon Library (RNL), p. 9.

[32] "Transcript of Oregon Telethon – Tape Two," 26 May 1968, Speech File, RNL, p. 6.

[33] Nixon, "Asia after Vietnam," p. 121.

[34] "Oregon Telethon," p. 6; "Transcript of Interview with Phil Clark," 12 July 1968, Speech File, RNL, p. 16.

for Chinese aggression, will the leaders in Beijing be persuaded to turn
their energies inward rather than outward. And that will be the time when
dialogue with mainland China can begin." In short, while holding out the
prospect of conciliation in the long run, Nixon advocated a short-term
policy of "firm restraint . . . [and] . . . creative counter-pressure designed to
persuade Beijing that its interests can be served only by accepting the basic
rules of international civility."[35]

At this juncture, therefore, Nixon's argument differed substantively
from that of the revisionist academics and Johnson administration officials. In his view, the "containment without isolation" line introduced by
the Johnson administration "cover[ed] only half the problem." It did not
employ sufficient pressure to persuade; and Nixon asserted that, along
with the longer-term prospect of conciliation, there was a need for "a
marshalling of Asian forces both to keep the peace and to help draw off
the poison from the Thoughts of Mao."[36] "Resurgent Power" proponents
recommended that the United States extend to Beijing understanding, respect, and inclusion – all of which Nixon would term "appeasement."
Instead, he would first apply firm pressure on Beijing to change its spots.
Also, while the "Troubled Modernizer" revisionists would try indirectly
to back more moderate elements of the Chinese leadership in the hope
of bringing about a leadership change, Nixon wanted to force *any* realistic Chinese leader to recognize China's external limits and to focus on
its more urgent internal development. Overall, then, Nixon managed to
breach the policy gap between the orthodox and revisionist arguments
about China policy by presenting a harder-line stance tailored to conservative audiences.

Still, Nixon's two-pronged 1967 China strategy was not completely
novel. The Johnson administration was grappling with the dilemma of
trying to reduce bilateral tensions with Beijing while fighting a war in
Vietnam that was ostensibly an exercise in containing militant Chinese
Communist–sponsored aggression. In order to overcome this dilemma, it
was also forced at times to adopt a similar line of immediate resistance
to aggression along with the hope of eventual conciliation with China.
This was evident in Rusk's controversial comments at a news conference
in October 1967, when he made an argument very similar to Nixon's.[37]

---

[35] Nixon, "Asia after Vietnam," pp. 122–3; Theodore White, *The Making of the President 1968* (London, 1969), p. 414.

[36] Nixon, "Asia after Vietnam," p. 123.

[37] This is perhaps not surprising, since Rusk was the most consistently hard-line of high-level officials in terms of China policy.

In explaining why U.S. national security was at stake in Vietnam, he played up the Chinese menace, warning that "within the next decade or two, there will be a billion Chinese on the mainland, armed with nuclear weapons, with no certainty about what their attitude toward the rest of Asia will be." At the same time, Rusk also explained that Washington's aim in Vietnam was not to contain communism per se but to help "free Asia" to live in peace, and to influence Chinese attitudes by "turn[ing] the interests of people in mainland China to the pragmatic requirements of their own people and away from... ideological adventurism abroad."[38] Thus, operating from the Johnson administration's perceived need to assure China that U.S. operations in Vietnam were not directed against it, Rusk had arrived at the same justification that Nixon had put forward for continued U.S. involvement in Asia.

However, there remained significant differences between Nixon's China discourse and that of the Johnson administration. Overall, the rhetorical thrust of the latter's reconciliation discourse was "peaceful coexistence." There was some genuine hope – in the "Troubled Modernizer" mold – that the chaos of the Cultural Revolution might indeed prove to be the straw that would break the back of Chinese revolutionary fervor, that the "original violence" of the Chinese Communists would "spend itself," bringing forth moderate leaders with "an attitude of peaceful coexistence."[39] The Johnson administration also hoped to obtain Beijing's support to end the Vietnam War. Various officials hinted broadly that Sino-American relations could be improved by "a desire on the part of Beijing to cooperate peacefully with others," which could be demonstrated by Beijing's ceasing to support Hanoi and throwing its influence on the side of unconditional negotiations for a peaceful settlement of the Vietnam conflict.[40] These strands stood in significant contrast to Nixon's assumption of a still-aggressive China, the lessons he drew from the U.S. experience of containing the Soviet Union in Europe after the Second World War, and his representation of the Vietnam War as a "showdown" with China – all of which led to his "tough coexistence" strategy.

---

[38] Rusk news conference, 12 October 1967, *DSB* 57, pp. 563–4.
[39] Rusk, interview on the "Today" program, NBC, 12 January 1967; interview with National Educational Television network, 5 May 1967, *DSB* 56, pp. 169, 788.
[40] Rusk, interview with British Independent Television network, 1 February 1967, *DSB* 56, p. 195; David Popper (deputy assistant secretary of state for international organizations), "China, the United Nations, and the United States," address to the Public Affairs Fellows of the Brookings Institution, Washington, D.C., 28 March 1967, *DSB* 56, p. 695.

PRESIDENT NIXON'S CHINA POLICY DISCOURSE, 1969–1971

The "Peacemaker" and the "Next Superpower"

During the 1968 presidential election campaign, however, Nixon began to move from his "tough coexistence" position on China toward the Democrats' emphasis on reconciliation and peace. To an electorate suffering from Vietnam fatigue, and in the context of the Johnson administration's efforts at peace talks, all the key candidates argued for better East-West contacts and relations. From April onward, Vice President Hubert Humphrey advocated a shift from containment and confrontation to "reconciliation and peaceful engagement," "building bridges" through trade and communications with both the Soviet bloc and mainland China.[41] Nelson Rockefeller confirmed his bid for the Republican nomination on 1 May, calling for more "contact and communication" with China.[42] Two months later, the nuclear nonproliferation treaty was signed by sixty-two countries, including the United States and the Soviet Union, and by August Nixon had followed with the promise to move from an "era of confrontation" to an "era of negotiation" and "peaceful competition," in which the United States would extend the "hand of friendship" to both the Soviet and the Chinese people. He agreed with Humphrey that the next president had to be prepared to negotiate with the Soviet leaders and, eventually, with the leaders of "the next superpower, Communist China."[43] This was not a radical change in Nixon's personal position – he had told Ceausescu privately in 1967 that he thought it would be possible to open communications and seek normalization with China after the Vietnam War. Neither was it unconditional – both parties reaffirmed that China had first to cease to "endanger other states by force or threat" and be ready to be a "responsible member of the international community."[44] But it was Nixon's first public articulation of a positive "reconciliation" discourse, centered on the need to reduce Cold

---

[41] Humphrey, speech to the Overseas Press Club, New York, NYT, 23 March 1968, pp. 1, 29; speech to the Commonwealth Club, San Francisco, NYT, 13 July 1968, p. 1.
[42] NYT, 1 May 1968, pp. 1, 30.
[43] Nixon interview, NYT, 7 August 1968, p. 28; speech accepting Republican Party nomination, NYT, 9 August 1968, p. 20.
[44] Republican campaign platform, NYT, 5 August 1968; Democratic campaign platform, NYT, 27 August 1968, p. 26. The former sounded a stronger note, specifically stating that the United States would not "condone aggression, or so-called 'wars of national liberation,'" or "naively discount the continuing threats of Moscow and Beijing," and pledging to continue opposition to Communist China's admission to the UN.

War conflict and to negotiate peaceful coexistence.[45] While not abandoning his conservative image and audiences, he muted his more belligerent rhetoric to take into account the public desire for peace.

Shortly after his election, Nixon was able make this conciliatory public discourse a more permanent change in policy because of supporting events. On 21 August 1968, the Soviet Union invaded Czechoslovakia, and the enunciation of the Brezhnev Doctrine heightened Chinese nervousness about the possibility of more belligerent Soviet action stemming from their border dispute.[46] On 26 November, Beijing indicated that it would resume the Warsaw talks with the new administration, causing speculation that Communist China was finally prepared for greater communication and contact with the United States.[47] In his inaugural address, therefore, Nixon strongly signaled both to his domestic audience and to Beijing that he would pursue reconciliation. He deliberately situated this policy stance within a new image of the United States and a revised conception of its role in the world. He told the war-weary nation that America under Nixon would be a "peacemaker." This, he claimed with characteristic flamboyance, was "our summons to greatness," the chance to lead the world onto "that high ground of peace that man has dreamed of since the dawn of civilization." As a great and responsible power carrying out its mission to "make the world safe for mankind," "all our lines of communication will be open." Combining elements of Johnson's 1966 speech with his own catch phrases, Nixon stated that his administration sought "an open world – open to ideas . . . exchange of goods and people – a world in which no people great or small, will live in angry isolation."[48] Washington would "try to make no one our enemy." Nixon invited adversary nations

---

[45] Apparently, Beijing had listened with interest to Nixon's new public line. When Premier Zhou Enlai met Nixon in February 1972, he remarked that "in your campaign speech . . . you also recognized the realities of China, the success of the Chinese people. It [is] also because of that [that] we are meeting today." Memcon, 22 February 1972, Box 87, President's Office Files (POF), NPM, p. 17.

[46] Robert Sutter, *China Watch: Toward Sino-American Reconciliation* (Baltimore, 1978), pp. 67–75; He Di, "The Most Respected Enemy: Mao Zedong's Perception of the United States," *China Quarterly* 137 (March 1994), pp. 145–58.

[47] *NYT*, 27 November 1968, p. 1. This is discussed at greater length in the next chapter, in relation to triangular politics.

[48] This section of Nixon's speech was in contrast to what Kissinger had in mind when he helped draft it, which was a more limited message to the *Soviets* – "some statement to the effect that we believe in open lines of communication to Moscow." The references to exchanges and angry isolation meant for the Chinese were Nixon's own. Kissinger to RN, 8 January 1968; Kissinger, "Proposed Foreign Policy Section of Your Inaugural Address," 14 January 1968, Inaugural Folder, Box 1, NSF/HAK, NPM.

to "peaceful competition" and promised to achieve this through "patient and prolonged diplomacy." However, he retained the idea of negotiating from strength and warned that the United States would remain "as strong as we need be for as long as we need be."[49]

Reconfiguring the Chinese Threat

In the 1960s, Nixon had played up the Chinese threat in the context of his arguments for a more robust U.S. involvement in the Vietnam War, in line with his right-wing, anticommunist reputation, and mostly to conservative audiences. But his entry into office was accompanied by the convergence of two political trends that allowed him to pursue the more realistic policy toward China that he had been advocating since the 1950s: the domestic desire for reduced American military involvement overseas and a generally lower risk of future conflict; and the opportunity to reduce tension and increase contact with a China that was now apparently ready to resume talks. In making the transition from his "tough coexistence" line to his new reconciliation discourse, Nixon drew a clearer distinction between the immediate Chinese threat – which he now argued had diminished significantly – and China's potential as a major power in the longer term.

Once in office, however, Nixon emphasized China's current weakness and difficulties, which rendered it a reduced threat. In part, this reflected Nixon's wider conciliatory foreign policy stance that stemmed from the need to address public wariness of U.S. overseas military commitments that might necessitate "another Vietnam." Hence, like Johnson, he had argued the need for noncommunist Asian states to develop their own regional collective defense arrangements in 1967.[50] As president, in July 1969, Nixon elaborated on this Asian strategy in some remarks to journalists during a Pacific tour, enunciating a policy that came to be called the Guam, or Nixon, Doctrine.[51] It pledged that while the United States

---

[49] Inaugural Address, 20 January 1969, *PPP:RN 1969*, p. 3. Mao Zedong read Nixon's speech with interest and marked it for distribution to Party cadres; a commentary on it was also published in the *People's Daily*, thus reaching a wider Chinese audience – Gong Li, *Mao Zedong yu Meiguo* (Beijing, 1998), pp. 195–6.

[50] Nixon, "Asia after Vietnam," pp. 111–23. On Johnson's encouragement of Asian regionalism, see Rostow, *Diffusion of Power*, pp. 426–9.

[51] The remarks were made before the policy had been thoroughly discussed in Washington and caused widespread alarm among many Asian governments. See Robert Litwak, *Détente and the Nixon Doctrine* (Cambridge, 1984).

would keep all its treaty commitments and maintain a nuclear shield for allies and vital states, Washington would expect those states to assume the primary responsibility for providing the manpower for their defense.[52] During this same session at which he anticipated the scaling down of the U.S. presence in the region, Nixon pointed out that Chinese Communist influence in Asia was on the wane. This was evident in the "minimal role" that it was playing in Vietnam as compared to the Soviet Union. China's capacity to inspire wars of national liberation had been significantly reduced because of its internal problems as well as the economic and political development of noncommunist Asia.[53] Taken together, his remarks implied that the United States could afford less direct involvement in the region because of the reduced Chinese threat.

In other speeches, Secretary of State William Rogers backed up Nixon's thesis with a "Troubled Modernizer" portrayal of China, asserting that the Chinese feared not so much encirclement by the military strength of the United States as "the real threat [that] comes from the superior performance of open societies" in the form of the economic development of neighboring noncommunist Asian states.[54]

This reconfiguration of the Chinese threat occurred in the context of less cautious reassessments of the Chinese menace presented by liberals of both parties in Congress and in academic circles, who had resumed their drive for a change in China policy. Senator Edward Kennedy, a prominent proponent of this cause, told the first conference of the National Committee on U.S.–China Relations that the old image of China as "an illegitimate Soviet puppet, expansionist, and evil" was no longer accurate. The Sino-Soviet clashes had showed conclusively that China was independent of the Soviets, and Beijing's other clashes with its neighbors had been "relatively limited," unlike the Soviet takeover of Czechoslovakia. Republican Senator Jacob Javits urged "new and unorthodox thoughts about China," and Doak Barnett, that long-time proponent of policy change, called for a new Sino-American relationship as "limited adversaries."[55] In October, a *New York Times* editorial saw the meeting between Kosygin and Zhou Enlai in Beijing to defuse the border tension as evidence that the Chinese leaders were "rational men able to weigh the costs and advantages of

---

[52] Informal remarks in Guam with newsmen, 25 July 1969, *PPP:RN 1969*, pp. 546–8.
[53] Ibid., pp. 554–5.
[54] Rogers, "Vietnam in the Perspective of East Asia," address to Associated Press luncheon, New York, 21 April 1969, *DSB* 60, pp. 398–9; address to the National Press Club, Canberra, Australia, 8 August 1969, *DSB* 61, pp. 179–80.
[55] *Washington Post* [WP], 21 March 1969, p. A8; *NYT*, 23 March 1969, p. 10.

alternative policies." Beijing's willingness to discuss differences with Moscow suggested a similar opportunity for U.S.–China relations, and the *Times* recommended that Nixon offer to visit Beijing.[56] In the Senate, the chairman of the Foreign Relations Committee, William Fulbright, asked for ministerial-level talks with the Chinese. Edward Kennedy went further, suggesting that consular missions be set up on the mainland as a prelude to diplomatic recognition.[57] And Senator Mike Mansfield again offered to travel to Beijing to meet Zhou Enlai in order to "improve the climate" between the two countries and to help resolve the Vietnam conflict.[58]

The effect on the Nixon administration of this continuing liberal discourse on reconciliation with China was twofold. On the positive side, it helped to facilitate the move toward a greater public consensus on the need for more peaceful relations with China. However, it also exerted indirect pressure on the administration, especially with respect to the 1972 elections, adding to Nixon's worry that the Democrats might get to Beijing before he did. Still, in 1969 Nixon could not take the more extreme unilateral steps suggested, although in that year the administration did take three key public steps toward reducing tensions with China. First, it agreed to resume the Warsaw talks in February. Second, on 21 July the trade and travel ban was eased slightly to allow U.S. citizens abroad to buy up to $100 worth of Chinese communist goods and to allow some categories of citizens to visit China. This was accompanied by private feelers through de Gaulle and Pakistani President Yahya Khan seeking expanded talks with Beijing. In public, Rogers explained that the administration sought peaceful contacts with China in order to "remove irritants in our relationship and . . . help remind people on mainland China of our historic friendship for them."[59]

In the event, however, the Chinese canceled the planned Warsaw talks and did not respond to any of the other gestures.[60] This left Washington open to conservative charges of "turning soft" on the communists, and Rogers and Nixon were obliged to display caution in public and to try to

---

[56] *NYT*, 9 October 1969, p. 46.

[57] *NYT*, 25 January 1969, p. 6; *WP*, 21 March 1969, p. A8.

[58] Mansfield letters to Sihanouk and Zhou, 17 June 1969, attachments; Bryce Harlow to RN, 23 June 1969, CO 34-2 (1969–70) Folder, Box 6, White House Confidential Files (WHCF), NPM.

[59] National Press Club address, 8 August 1969, p. 180.

[60] Washington's China watchers gauged that this was the result of disagreements among the leadership in Beijing about U.S. policy. See the detailed discussion in the next chapter.

shift the onus for the stalemate onto Beijing, much as the Johnson administration had done. When pressed in a news conference in Taipei, Rogers said the aim of relaxing trade and travel restrictions was "to make it clear that the reason Communist China is not a member of the international community is because of its own attitude ... the US ... is willing to try to have more friendly relations ... [but] they refuse to."[61] He told Congress that "our ability to influence the rate of improvement [on the mainland] is very limited," and he did not lift the ban on travel to China early in 1969, as was widely expected, for fear of conservative criticism.[62]

Thus, in 1969, official public policy still emphasized waiting for Beijing to demonstrate a change in its attitude before substantial improvements in relations could occur. But the sense that this would happen sooner rather than later was reinforced by the Chinese initiative suggesting a resumption of the Warsaw talks in the first place, and by the escalation of the Sino-Soviet dispute into a border war in March. Indeed, Beijing was beginning to shed its isolation, and reappointed many of its ambassadors overseas from May onward. In response, the Nixon administration lowered its conditions for better relations with China: Nixon and Rogers both stated publicly that the signal they now sought was merely Beijing's agreement to resume talks with the United States, in Warsaw or any other mutually acceptable site.[63]

Realism and Reconciliation, 1970–1

Beijing agreed to resume the Warsaw talks in January 1970. For its part, Washington removed all restrictions on nonstrategic U.S.–China trade, third-country trade in Chinese goods, and the $100 limit on tourist purchases of Chinese-made goods in December 1969. During this period, Nixon and Kissinger began to construct a more coherent public account of China policy that would justify the new moves to a variety of audiences. The two key tenets of this discourse were found in Nixon's annual foreign policy reports to Congress, which were written by Kissinger and his NSC staff.[64] First, it was a policy of strength: while it was motivated

---

[61] News conference in Taipei, 3 August 1969, *DSB* 61, pp. 180, 183.
[62] Rogers testimony to Senate Foreign Relations Committee, 27 March 1969, *DSB* 60, p. 312; *NYT*, 30 March 1969, p. E4.
[63] Nixon, address before the twenty-fourth session of the UN General Assembly, 18 September 1969, *PPP:RN 1969*, p. 728; Rogers, National Press Club address, p. 180.
[64] There was a dispute between the State Department and the NSC over this responsibility. State was cut out of the process despite having been the first to produce a large report in

by the lofty aim of ensuring international peace through negotiation, the Nixon administration would not make concessions to communists. Second, it was not based on the hope of exploiting the Sino-Soviet split, but rather on the constructive engagement of China as a vital and major power.

In his first report in February 1970, Nixon formally presented his foreign policy strategy: the pursuit of a realistic foreign policy from a position of strength, which would also allow negotiation with adversaries in order to achieve international peace. But now, in anticipation of the administration's first talks with the Chinese at Warsaw, there was a need to assure conservative audiences that Nixon was not abandoning his principles in order to consort with communists. Hence, he explained that "the 'isms' have lost their vitality" – ideology had become less of a rallying point with the Sino-Soviet split and Soviet-American arms reduction negotiations, and new great-power relations had to be based on hard-headed "national interest." American interests dictated that Washington make "patient and precise efforts to reconcile conflicting interests on concrete issues" in order to reduce tensions with its communist adversaries and the chances of nuclear miscalculation.

On the other hand, in the face of rumors about Moscow's seeking Washington's support for joint action against Chinese nuclear facilities and media speculation about a new Sino-American relationship that would exploit the dispute between the two communist powers, Nixon had to try to mute Moscow's, and primarily Beijing's, concerns about U.S. intentions. Thus, he pointed out that the Guam Doctrine symbolized U.S. determination "not to seek hegemony" in the Asia-Pacific region. In its desire for better relations with China, the United States was not trying to forge "any condominium or hostile coalition of great powers." He asserted that Washington stood above the intracommunist dispute and had no interest in exacerbating Sino-Soviet hostilities, which would only endanger wider international peace.

Instead, his administration's openness to China was based on the recognition of China's significance and the talents and potential contributions of the Chinese people. Nixon repeated his 1967 argument that China's massive population should not be isolated from the international community; putting "Resurgent Power" imagery to good use, he argued that a stable

1969. See Seymour Hersh, *The Price of Power: Kissinger in the Nixon White House* (New York, 1983), p. 114.

international order required the contributions of this "great and vital," "gifted and cultured" people. Moreover, Washington recognized that the Chinese tradition of self-imposed isolation had been terminated when "an internally weak China fell prey to exploitation by technologically superior foreign powers," and it would keep in mind this "unique past" of "isolation and incursion . . . pride and humiliation" when it attempted to redefine its relationship with China. Specifically, it would not try to exploit the Sino-Soviet rift to China's disadvantage.[65]

From the second half of 1970 onward, prospects for new Sino-American contacts gained rapid momentum through a series of public and back-channel signals and messages. By the time Nixon delivered his second foreign policy report to Congress in February 1971, the White House had received a secret invitation from Zhou Enlai for an American emissary to visit Beijing.[66] With these plans for Kissinger's secret trip to Beijing in hand, Nixon's report tried to prepare the public for dramatic events ahead. It presented the most coherent account so far of the new China discourse within the context of his foreign policy strategy, and one can clearly detect elements of Kissinger's *realpolitik* approach.

First, Nixon reiterated the theme of how the international system had moved beyond the rigid bipolar structure of the Cold War, and how the United States had to adapt its foreign policy to these changes. The "fluidity of [this] new era of multilateral diplomacy" offered opportunities for "*creative diplomacy.*"[67] Second, Nixon tried to situate the coming breakthrough within the development of the U.S. role as world peacemaker: the purpose was to "work with other nations to build *an enduring structure of peace.*" In pursuing this task, Nixon's new approach encompassed not only "coexistence" but also "accommodation" and "partnership," which, at its fullest extent, "encompasses adversaries as well as friends."[68]

In the case of China, "partnership" would entail imparting a new sense of equality and respect – essential if the national security advisor and the president would be holding direct talks with the Chinese leaders. Thus, Nixon referred to China by its official title, the People's Republic of

---

[65] RN, "First Annual Report to Congress on US Foreign Policy for the 1970s," 18 February 1970, *PPP:RN 1970*, pp. 116–22, 144, 178–82.

[66] This sequence of back-channel communications is discussed in greater detail in the next chapter.

[67] RN, "Second Annual Report to Congress on US Foreign Policy," 25 February 1971, *PPP:RN 1971*, pp. 219–20. Emphasis mine.

[68] Ibid., pp. 221–2.

China, and did not once refer to the Chinese "threat."[69] He wrote that the
international order would remain insecure as long as China, as a major
power, stood outside of it; and the administration's new policy toward
China embodied his goal of creating a "balanced international structure
in which all nations will have a stake." At the same time, the report tacitly
recognized China's desire for international influence commensurate with
its size and history. The new international structure, Nixon promised,
would provide full scope for "the influence to which China's achievements entitle it."

Nixon went on to outline the terms for improving relations with China,
in part to assure conservatives that he was not "going soft" on the Chinese
Communists. First, in establishing a dialogue with Beijing, the administration would not accept Chinese "ideological precepts" or "the notion
that Communist China must exercise hegemony over Asia." Second, the
Taiwan issue had to be resolved "by peaceful means." Third, the PRC
could not dictate as a condition of its entry into the UN the expulsion of
the ROC. Yet, in the midst of this, Nixon added enigmatically, "neither
do we wish to impose on China an international position that denies
its legitimate national interests."[70] Furthermore, in a nationwide radio
address, he declared that "[w]hen the government of the People's Republic of China is ready to engage in talks, it will find us receptive to
agreements that further the legitimate national interests of China and its
neighbors."[71]

A few months later, in the wake of Ping-Pong diplomacy and in the run-
up to Kissinger's secret trip to Beijing, Nixon again imparted the message
that China was a major power with which the United States had to deal
on an equal basis. In extempore remarks at a number of domestic policy
briefings, he told business groups that China would become one of the
five "economic superpowers" of the world in five to fifteen years' time.
China's very real economic potential derived from its people, who were
"creative . . . productive . . . one of the most capable . . . in the world"; and
"800 million Chinese are going to be, inevitably, an enormous economic
power, with all that means in terms of what they could be in other areas
[meaning military, and especially nuclear, power]." Thus, in order to avoid
the attendant dangers of an isolated, angry, and economically powerful

[69] Nixon's first use of Communist China's official name was in a toast to Ceauşescu three
    months before – 26 October 1970, *PPP:RN 1970*, p. 947.
[70] Report to Congress, pp. 276–8.
[71] RN, radio address about the "Second Annual Foreign Policy Report," 25 February 1971,
    PPP:RN 1971, p. 216.

China, Nixon told his audiences that he intended, in the long term, to normalize relations with China.[72]

It might seem that Nixon had come full circle, back to his stance in the 1967 article. Yet the difference here was that by July 1971, the time was ripe to begin the process of achieving the "long-range" aim of reconciliation with China.

NIXON'S DISCOURSE OF RECONCILIATION IN CONTEXT

When Kissinger's secret trip to Beijing and the subsequent invitation for Nixon to visit China were announced on 15 July 1971, administration spokesmen were ready to provide an explanation of the radical change in China policy, made more coherent by their ability to refer to a bank of Nixon's writings and statements from 1967 onward, all of which apparently pointed to this consistent and logical development. The main elements of the public rationale for the Nixon "breakthrough" were that it did not represent a radical change in policy, that it was conducted in the pursuit of peace, and that the unexpected development of a summit meeting resulted from a Chinese initiative and invitation.[73]

The foregoing discussion has shown that Nixon's stance on reconciliation with China did not develop out of a radical change in his worldview in the late 1960s.[74] Rather, Nixon's China policy grew out of the discursive culmination of a position that he had begun to formulate more than a decade before. He had actively considered more pragmatic policies toward China during the 1950s, and in the 1960s he had utilized and built upon the twin elements of the revisionist discourse – its image of China as a "Troubled Modernizer" but also a "Resurgent Power" – in arguing for bringing China back into the international community. From 1967 onward, domestic and international political conditions allowed Nixon to consolidate and publicly articulate this policy stance to a wider audience. Thus, while Nixon's ideas were developed in a personal, unofficial,

---

[72] RN, remarks to Eastern media executives, Rochester, New York, 18 June 1971; remarks to Midwestern news media executives, Kansas City, Missouri, 6 July 1971, *PPP:RN 1971*, pp. 758, 806.
[73] This reasoning was usefully summarized in Holdridge to Kissinger, "Your Briefing on China for Billy Graham and Influential Conservatives," 9 August 1971, HAK Folder, Box 15, WHCF, NPM.
[74] Authors who suggest this include Earl Mazo and Stephen Hess, *Nixon: A Political Portrait* (New York, 1968), pp. 306, 312–13; Michael Handel, *The Diplomacy of Surprise: Hitler, Nixon and Sadat* (Cambridge, MA, 1981), Chapter 4.

and international context, he did engage with, contribute to, and develop, the official discourse of reconciliation. By the time he was elected, therefore, Nixon had shaped his own semiconciliatory "tough coexistence" discourse. During the first two years of his presidency, Nixon advanced particularly the image of China as a major power that it was in the American interest to negotiate with, accommodate, and even make a partner of, as the United States was doing with its superpower rival.

However, Nixon's discourse of reconciliation with China differed from that of the Johnson administration in two key respects. First, Nixon was able to combine the two ideas of current Chinese weakness and backwardness and potential Chinese strength by distinguishing between short-range and long-range images and policies. Second, by emphasizing the need to continue in the strong but modified containment of China through building up noncommunist Asian states following the Marshall Plan model, Nixon was able to recast "containment without isolation" in a mold more acceptable to conservatives.

The successful "selling" of Nixon's new China policy stemmed from two factors. First, it was carefully situated within an overall foreign policy strategy, as set out in the _Foreign Affairs_ article, elaborated in the Guam Doctrine, and updated in the annual foreign policy reports. In contrast to the China policy discourse of the 1960s, which tended to address China as a bilateral issue without an overarching strategy, Nixon's China policy appeared to be deliberate, orchestrated, and even statesmanlike, and thus better avoided the impression of having been adopted out of duress or fear of the communists. Second and most crucially, however, were the particular political circumstances at the time, which prompted the Chinese to respond to Nixon's overtures. Johnson's overriding problem had been China's persistent disregard for his initiatives; by contrast, Nixon not only received a response from Beijing but was able to negotiate exchanges at the highest official level, without having to make public concessions.

The issue of exactly what the "bargain" was would crop up prominently in the wake of Nixon's visit. Certainly, at the time of Kissinger's trip, many of the preconditions for better relations that had been set out at various times by the Americans had not been met. Beijing had not renounced force in the Taiwan Straits, altered its conditions for entry into the UN, or ceased support for revolutionary warfare in Southeast Asia. The clearest set of "goal posts" through which Beijing had kicked its diplomatic ball, though, was precisely the minimum conditions that Nixon and Rogers had stated at the end of 1969 – that China had to abandon its isolation and show that it was ready for peaceful contact with the outside world, and particularly with the United States. For the moment, this alone was sufficient to justify Nixon's China opening in terms of avoiding the dangerous "angry isolation" of a major power. In order for the new relationship to be defined and developed, however, it would be necessary to explore the key reason for China's readiness for new relations with the United States. Although conscientiously played down in public by the Nixon administration, it was geopolitical considerations that made it possible for China and the United States to become "former enemies." This rationale played an important part in the internal official discourse of reconciliation with China, and will be discussed in the next chapter.

6

Debating the Rapprochement

"Resurgent Revolutionary Power" versus "Threatened Major Power"

For the Nixon administration, the period from 1969 into the first half of July 1971 constituted the initial phase of transition toward a new conception of China and China policy. It was a contested process, with a number of different strands moving ahead at varying speeds within the bureaucracy, in the public discourse, and through secret channels. In contrast to the previous chapter on Nixon's China discourse and broad foreign policy strategy before and shortly after taking office, this chapter focuses on the official China policy discourse in the State Department, the intelligence agencies, and the Defense Department, as well as in the National Security Council and the White House, at a time when the new administration was debating, deliberating, and defining the shape of its China policy.

This analysis sheds particular light on the much-vaunted difference between the State Department's approach to China and the White House's strategy and preferred paths. The received notion – from the accounts of Kissinger and other NSC staff members – is that State Department officials were obsessed with issues of secondary importance, such as trade and Taiwan, and missed the larger geopolitical picture, while Kissinger and Nixon were very much alive to the opportunity offered by China's strategic need for better relations with the United States, given the threat of a Soviet attack. Contemporary documents reveal, however, that most officials did recognize the potential advantages of triangular politics after the outbreak of Sino-Soviet hostilities in March 1969. The key area of contention lay instead in the assessment of the implications of the Sino-Soviet conflict in general, and of China's intentions in particular, for U.S. policy.

NEW OPPORTUNITIES AND OLD DOUBTS AT THE BEGINNING OF THE NIXON ADMINISTRATION

Nixon took office at a time when two events dominated the scene for all China watchers: the chaos of the Cultural Revolution within China and the increasingly severe nature of the Sino-Soviet conflict, now evinced by rising border tensions. While its domestic preoccupation had foreclosed any possibility of response to earlier U.S. overtures, China's confrontation with the Soviet Union was becoming Beijing's top concern, particularly after the Soviet invasion of Prague in August 1968. Three months later, Beijing responded positively to a State Department proposal to resume the ambassadorial talks at Warsaw, announcing that Chinese policy had always been "to maintain friendly relations with all states, regardless of social system, on the basis of the Five Principles of Peaceful Coexistence."[1] This excited speculation that Beijing was at last adopting a more forth-coming policy toward the United States, since the "five principles of coex-istence" was a product of the milder Chinese foreign policy of the 1950s. Certainly, it seemed that the drastic deterioration in Sino-Soviet relations that followed the border clashes beginning in December 1968 would cause Mao to turn his attention away from ideological revolution and toward national security.[2] Thus, at the beginning of 1969 there seemed to be an early opportunity for the new administration to explore the possibility of improved relations with China.

However, this opportunity occurred in the face of considerable reserve among the intelligence communities and the State and Defense Depart-ments about the reasons for, and implications of, this apparent soften-ing of the Chinese stance. While there was clear recognition of the new strategic triangle, there was also disagreement and skepticism about how Washington might best turn the Sino-Soviet conflict to its advantage.

Because of the general recognition that China was motivated by Soviet pressures, early analyses suggested that Beijing was not interested in im-proving U.S.–PRC relations for their own sake. In one of the earliest studies of the developing U.S.–USSR–PRC relationship, the director of the

---

[1] John Holdridge, *Crossing the Divide: An Insider's Account of Normalization of US-China Relations* (Lanham, 1997), pp. 25–6; INR, "Peking's Foreign Policy in Flux," 23 December 1968, Box 1963, SNF(1967–9), RG59, NA, p. 1.

[2] Chinese sources bear out this expectation. See especially Yang Kuisong, "The Sino-Soviet Border Clash of 1969: From Zhenbao Island to Sino-American Rapprochement," *Cold War History* 1(1) (2000), pp. 21–52. Gong Li argues that Mao in fact overperceived the Soviet threat after the invasion of Czechoslovakia and thus overreacted to Soviet provo-cations – see "Chinese Decision Making and the Thawing of US-China Relations," p. 331.

State Department's Bureau of Intelligence and Research (INR) pointed out that the way in which Beijing publicized the resumption of the talks and deliberately fed press speculation about a possible rapprochement suggested that, rather than a "fundamental shift" in Sino-American relations, China was seeking to play on long-standing Soviet fears about the possibility of a U.S.–China reconciliation.[3] The Defense Department also acknowledged that, while the Soviets and Chinese now appeared to "regard one another with more active hostility than they regard the US," and while each was likely to use its own relations with the United States as a means of "checkmating the other's policies," the Chinese would not go so far as to make a "deal" with the United States. Ultimately such a reversal would only serve Soviet propaganda purposes about Chinese "revisionism."[4]

The various agencies were not optimistic about the prospects for better U.S.–China relations because they continued to see the relationship as an adversarial one in terms of basic conflicts of interest and ideology. INR assessed that beyond the central dispute about Taiwan, current Chinese Communist foreign policy objectives – the promotion of communism abroad and Chinese influence in Southeast Asia, the neutralization of Japan, and membership in international organizations – "would necessarily be achieved against the US rather than through collaboration with it."[5] Defense also perceived that Beijing still adhered to "hard line militancy" and the aim of undermining America's position in East Asia by political means and by means of insurgency.[6] This view of an "unremittingly hostile" China was boosted by a CIA warning that ideology would soon be supplemented by new capabilities – a China "that was beginning to realize some of its potential in the economic and advanced weapons fields could become a far more formidable force in Asia than is Maoist China."[7] These assessments reflected Nixon's thinking about China in the early days of the administration. In his 1967 *Foreign Affairs* article, he had argued for a collective Asian security system to guard against growing

[3] INR to SoS, "Sino-Soviet Relations: Schism, to Triangle – to Quadrilateral?," 11 February 1969, Box 1974, CFPF(1967–9), RG59, NA, pp. 1, 7–8.
[4] DoD, "Response to NSSM 9," 20 January 1969, NSA Doc. 40. NSSM 9 was one of Kissinger's first directives as national security adviser and addressed the specific question of whether the PRC would "try to make a deal with the United States at the expense of the Soviet Union" and if Beijing was "really interested in peaceful coexistence with the US." NSSM 9, "Review of the International Situation," 23 January 1969, NSA Doc. 38.
[5] INR, "Sino-Soviet Relations," pp. 8–9.
[6] DoD, "Response to NSSM 9."
[7] NSC study, "Communist China," ca. February 1969, NSA Doc. 42; CIA, SNIE 13–69, "Communist China and Asia," 6 March 1969, NSA Doc. 67.

Chinese capabilities.[8] After he took office, Nixon reiterated his distrust of the "less rational" Chinese Communist leaders, presenting his decision to press forward with developing Johnson's initiative of a limited antiballistic missile system as primarily a safeguard against a possible Chinese nuclear attack.[9]

Furthermore, the new administration retained a primary interest in developing relations with the Soviet Union, and it was not clear that a rapprochement with China would play to the American strategic advantage. The Nixon administration's priorities lay in ending the Vietnam War with Soviet cooperation and developing a superpower détente through arms control agreements and a summit.[10] It would seem that, in the first months of 1969, the White House remained undecided in its assessment of Chinese intentions and China policy, in part because it was more focused on the U.S.–USSR relationship. This preoccupation was evident in early February, when, in response to a probe by a Polish diplomat about the new administration's attitude toward China, Nixon told Kissinger to "give every encouragement to the attitude that this Administration is 'exploring possibilities of rapprochement with the Chinese'" among the Eastern Europeans.[11] Planting this idea was obviously an early playing of the "China card," aimed at exploiting Soviet worries about a possible improvement in U.S.–PRC relations in order to exert pressure on Moscow to be more forthcoming toward Washington.[12] This strategy was conducted with the understanding that the United States would not go so far as to seek a "deal" with China. The Soviet Union was capable of inflicting direct, unacceptable damage on the United States and was in active competition for power and influence with Washington "almost everywhere in the world." By contrast, the Chinese danger was more long-term, localized, and indirect. Therefore, chances of a serious U.S. rapprochement with China were "remote," since it did not need China as a military counterweight to the Soviet Union, and the costs of alienating Moscow would be too high.[13]

---

[8] Nixon, "Asia after Vietnam," pp. 112–17.
[9] RN to French Ambassador Charles Lucet, memcon, Part IV, "Communist China," 21 February 1969, Box 2635, SNF(1967–9), RG59, NA; "President Nixon Discusses the Vietnam Peace Talks and the ABM Safeguard System," 25 March 1969, DSB 60, p. 316; Nixon news conference, 14 March 1969, *PPP:RN 1969*, p. 208.
[10] See, for instance, Hersh, *Price of Power*; Bundy, *Tangled Web*.
[11] RN to Kissinger, 1 February 1969, Box 341, NSF, NPM.
[12] Kissinger, *White House Years*, p. 169.
[13] INR, "Sino-Soviet Relations," pp. 8–9.

"REVOLUTIONARY RESURGENT POWER": THE STATE
DEPARTMENT RETHINKS CHINA POLICY

In spite of the general climate of skepticism in the various agencies and in
the White House regarding China's intentions during the first two months
of 1969, the State Department's East Asia Bureau was engaged in an
active reformulation of China policy. This represented a consolidation into
official policy of the revisionist "containment without isolation" approach
to China articulated by the Johnson administration in 1966 and 1967.
It was a process that was developed in parallel with the deliberations
about U.S. policy toward the Sino-Soviet split. It followed the established
trend of emphasizing bilateral issues, and it developed from the previous
consensus on the need to improve Sino-American relations for reasons
lying outside triangular politics, as discussed in Part 1. As a result, at this
early stage State was in fact ahead of the White House in proposing new
policy probes toward China.

Two key State papers prepared in 1969 provide a good account of its
representation and assessment of China during this period. The first was
a discussion paper on the proposed February Warsaw talks prepared by
the Asian Communist Affairs desk (ACA) for Nixon; the second was a
China policy study undertaken between February and August in response
to NSSM 14, which was to be the first detailed statement of the Nixon
administration's China policy.[14]

Both studies acknowledged that the national aims and interests of
China and the United States remained in conflict, and that Beijing was
looking to be treated as a "major world power" and "the primary source
of revolutionary ideological leadership"[15] – that is, as both the "Revolutionary Rival" to the Soviet Union and the "Resurgent Power" that it
was presumed to be. However, State was prepared to recognize the basis for China's drive for major-power status. The ACA paper stated that
Washington had to "achieve some *modus vivendi* with the Government
which now speaks for a quarter of the world's population and is one of
the dominant power factors in East Asia."[16] Essentially, though, this determination was underlain by the conviction that, although conflicts of
interest persisted, there was a distinct possibility of change in Beijing's

[14] Kissinger to SoD, SoS, Director of CIA, "NSSM 14," 5 February 1969, NSA Doc. 43.
[15] "NSSM 14," pp. 7–8, 2–3.
[16] Paul Kreisberg, DoS discussion paper on Warsaw talks, 4 February 1969, Box 1973,
CFPF(1967–9), RG59, NA, p. 3. Kreisberg was a China specialist who had been involved
in the Warsaw talks since 1965.

attitude. The NSSM 14 study stated that in the short term, China was neither a major economic power nor a military power on a par with the United States or the USSR, and that it faced serious internal economic and political problems that hampered its ability to attain its foreign policy objectives.[17] However, this relative weakness was combined with an intransigent leadership, which meant that any U.S. efforts to reduce Chinese hostility would achieve "extremely limited" results.[18] In the longer term, China would strengthen militarily and would pose a bigger threat to the region and to the United States. On the other hand, it was "more likely that China's policy ultimately will moderate, given an international climate conducive to moderation [because of] domestic economic pressures and the emergence of a more pragmatic leadership."[19] U.S. China policy, then, was in some sense a patient and calculated waiting and probing game.[20]

In considering its approach to the proposed first Warsaw meeting of the new administration, the ACA paper reflected the above assessment. Beyond the chance provided by the Sino-Soviet dispute, it was an "opportunity presented by the advent of [a new] Administration, the subsidence of the Cultural Revolution . . . and the prospect of a negotiated settlement in Vietnam."[21] The resumption of the Warsaw talks would allow Washington "to determine how far Peking may be prepared to move from its current positions . . . to negotiate with us on some specific issue rather than polemicizing."[22] Reiterating the Troubled Modernizer argument, ACA was confident that "there may . . . be Chinese leaders who . . . in the not-too-distant future may be able to re-evaluate Sino-US relations in a different context and for whom . . . a reformulation of our policies *now* may be critical considerations in a . . . policy debate in Peking."[23]

Proceeding from this familiar revisionist discourse, however, State developed policy probes that signified notable departures from those of the 1960s. ACA recommended that at the renewed Warsaw talks, the United

---

[17] "NSSM 14," pp. 1–3.
[18] Ibid., p. 9.
[19] Ibid., p. 3.
[20] This take on China policy reflects Nixon's approach in his 1967 *Foreign Affairs* article, discussed in the previous chapter. However, while Nixon emphasized the need for continued containment of China in the short run, State was more focused on constantly probing for evidence of changes in Beijing's attitude that would allow reconciliation.
[21] Kreisberg, discussion paper on Warsaw talks, p. 12.
[22] In his first presidential news conference on 27 January, Nixon expressed a similar view that the talks would be an opportunity to see "whether any changes of attitude on their part on major substantive issues may have occurred." *PPP:RN 1969*, p. 16.
[23] Kreisberg, discussion paper on Warsaw talks, pp. 1–2.

States should now move away from proposals about "people-to-people" exchanges, in which the Chinese had been manifestly uninterested, to dialogue about more general "political" issues. Given the unique opportunity at the beginning of 1969, ACA wanted to address directly Beijing's key concern about Taiwan and the central question of how the United States could move toward normal relations with the PRC without abandoning the GRC. Washington needed to find a way forward that would avoid the quagmire of a "two Chinas" or "one China, one Taiwan" stance that neither Beijing nor Taipei would accept. Here, Kreisberg made the crucial specific suggestion that Washington should indicate its willingness to review its military presence in the Taiwan area if the PRC agreed to renounce the use of force in the Taiwan Straits.[24] This was the origin of an approach that would provide a vital compromise and facilitate rapprochement later on. It would help to reduce the military aspect of this key bilateral disagreement between the United States and the PRC and provide an "obfuscating and face-saving" means of dealing with the U.S. defense commitment to Taiwan. The two parties could emphasize the "small, unimportant but visible aspect of a *physical* US military presence on Taiwan and ... downplay or even ignore the important but invisible aspect of the actual US commitment to defend Taiwan."[25]

The assistant secretary for East Asia and the secretary of state, however, felt that the ACA proposal went "one notch too far at the present moment," and it was watered down to a suggestion that the U.S. side should "vaguely hint at a connection" between the U.S. military presence and Beijing's refusal to renounce force in the Taiwan Straits area.[26] Kissinger was even more cautious on this point. In transmitting the draft proposal to the president, he eliminated any implication that the United States might be prepared to remove its presence from Taiwan, in order to reduce the risk of "misinterpretation" that there was a fundamental change in U.S. policy.[27] Kissinger's reserve stemmed from his agreement with the view that Beijing was not serious about improving relations with the United States and wanted to open talks with Washington mainly as

[24] Ibid., pp. 6–7.
[25] Ibid., p. 9.
[26] Bundy to U. Alexis Johnson, "Warsaw Draft Instructions," 28 January 1969; Rogers to RN, "US Policy toward Peking and Instructions for the February 20 Warsaw Meeting," n.d., POL CHICOM-US 1 January 1969 folder, Box 1973, CFPF (1967–9), RG59, NA.
[27] Kissinger to RN, "US Policy towards Peking and Instructions for the February 20 Warsaw Meeting," 12 February 1969, Box 700, NSF, NPM.

leverage against Moscow. He also thought that the Chinese wanted to probe for "softness" in the new administration's thinking on Taiwan.[28] Kissinger's caution might be attributed to his lack of experience with China policy, but it was also consistent with his admission that he did not perceive the potential of triangular politics until the Sino-Soviet border war erupted later in the year.[29]

In the event, Beijing called off the February 1969 talks two days beforehand, citing the defection of a Chinese diplomat to the United States, but State's intelligence sources concluded that the postponement was more the result of leadership disagreements and indecision at the highest levels in China.[30] Thus, events seemed to bear out the revisionists' conviction that divisions over Sino-American relations were developing within the Chinese leadership. Accordingly, State indicated to the Chinese that it remained "ready at an early date" to resume the Warsaw talks.[31]

At this point, events overtook expectations: the Sino-Soviet conflict developed into direct military clashes at the border from March onward, causing alarm in international circles about the possibility of an all-out war.[32] In Washington, these developments forced the administration to seriously reconsider its attitudes toward China and the Soviet Union and provided impetus for policy decision and action.

For the State Department, the outbreak of hostilities served to emphasize China's current weakness and vulnerability. In considering which party was the "aggressor," the State Department's East Asian Bureau (EA), INR, and the Hong Kong consulate judged that Beijing, concerned about

[28] Kissinger to RN, "Warsaw Talks," 11 February 1969, Box 700, NSF, NPM.
[29] Kissinger, *White House Years*, pp. 172, 177; Raymond Garthoff, *Détente and Confrontation: American-Soviet Relations from Nixon to Reagan* (Washington, DC, 1994), p. 243.
[30] INR, "Communist China/US: Peking Calls Off February 20 Warsaw Meeting," 18 February 1969, Box 1973, CFPF(1967–9), RG59, NA. It was likely that this period in the run up to the Ninth Party Congress in April 1969 saw an intensification of the factional infighting around Mao, but Mao was also preoccupied with other matters, such as reacting to Sino-Soviet clashes at the border.
[31] DoS to Emb/Warsaw, "Letter to ChiComs on Continuation of Talks," 12 March 1969, Box 1973, CFPF(1967–9), RG59, NA.
[32] On the history of the border conflict, see Thomas Robinson, "The Sino-Soviet Border Conflict," in Stephen Kaplan et al., *Diplomacy of Power: Soviet Armed Forces as a Political Instrument* (Washington, DC, 1981); Yang, "The Sino-Soviet Border Clash of 1969," pp. 22–5; Viktor Gobarev, "Soviet Policy toward China: Developing Nuclear Weapons 1949–1969," *The Journal of Slavic Military Studies* 12(4) (1999), pp. 37–47; and Christian Osterman, ed., "East German Documents on the Border Conflict," *CWIHP Bulletin* 6–7 (1995/96), pp. 186–93.

the "overwhelmingly superior" Soviet border deployments, had opened limited hostilities as a means of deterring a Soviet attack and forestalling "another Czechoslovakia."[33] In the event of a large-scale Sino-Soviet war, State's China watchers predicted that "Soviet military might well outgun China in the initial stage" and that there was "no Chinese capability to prevent the conflict from being waged inside China." In this context, they recommended that, while the United States had to remain officially neutral, Washington would have to convey a "pointed" statement to Moscow deploring the use of force, while reassuring China that it would not get involved in the conflict. As the Hong Kong China desk pointed out, this stance, while "objectively neutral," was "actually beneficial" to the Chinese.[34] Still, if forced to choose between the two sides, State would in effect have opted for what I have previously labeled Option 1 – "do nothing."

Ultimately, though, there were clear limits to State's perception of Chinese weakness relative to the Soviet Union. Even at the height of the war scare, State took a more sanguine and aloof stance toward the possibility of a large-scale Sino-Soviet war than did the White House. In August, a spate of intelligence information about Soviet military activities suggested that "Moscow may be preparing to take action against China in the near future," including the option of a non-nuclear strike against Chinese nuclear facilities.[35] At the same time, members of the Soviet embassy staff probed State officials about potential U.S. responses to a Soviet attack on China. Yet Secretary of State William Rogers advised Nixon that the chances of a Soviet attack on Chinese nuclear installations were "substantially less than fifty-fifty." Echoing the findings of Kennedy and Johnson era studies, State analysts argued that such a "surgical strike" was unlikely because it would not permanently remove the Chinese nuclear threat, and that a Soviet attack would more likely take the form of

[33] INR, "Peking's Tactics and Intentions along the Sino-Soviet Border," 13 June 1969; "Implications of Sino-Soviet Developments: Meeting of June 21," 23 June 1969, Box 1975; Nethercut to Thayer, 7 July 1969, Box 1974, CFPF(1967–9), RG59, NA. Chinese sources confirm that Mao had initiated the Zhenbao Island confrontation in March 1969 as a defensive counterattack in response to perceived Soviet provocations in 1968 – see Yang, "The Sino-Soviet Border Clash of 1969," pp. 27–31.
[34] Comments by ConGen/HK on contingency study on Sino-Soviet conflict, enclosed with Nethercut to Thayer, 7 July 1969, Box 1974, CFPF(1967–9), RG59, NA.
[35] INR, "Communist China/USSR: Peking Accentuates the Positive," 11 August 1969, Box 1975, CFPF(1967–9), RG59, NA; William Burr, "Sino-American Relations, 1969: The Sino-Soviet Border War and Steps towards Rapprochement," *Cold War History* 1(3) (April 2001), pp. 86–90.

a controlled "punitive attack" along the border. They did not believe that Moscow wanted to escalate the conflict.[36]

Short of the extreme war scenario, however, State officials appreciated the strategic opportunities offered to Washington by the escalated Sino-Soviet conflict. In a conversation with Nixon on 10 June, Assistant Secretary of State for East Asian Affairs Marshall Green observed that moves toward China would help to increase Soviet worries, making it "less prone to take us for granted and [persuading it to] do things to improve relations with the US if only to prevent a US-Peking drift."[37] EA, INR, and Europe desk staffers agreed that the situation opened up significant opportunities for both "attracting and needling the Soviets to greater cooperation," especially in Indochina, through "direct US initiatives toward the Chinese."[38] The secretary of state himself developed a *realpolitik* tone in a December memorandum to Nixon recommending that the administration modify trade controls against China. Rogers argued that this would "introduce an additional complicating factor into the Soviet leadership's assessment of our intentions towards China – and towards the USSR." This would "serve our long-term interest of forestalling an eventual, more fundamental rapprochement between the USSR and China."[39] The secretary of state had come to the same strategic conclusion as Kissinger – that the United States would derive greatest benefit from developing better relations with the Soviet Union and China than they had with each other and from acting to maintain the Sino-Soviet gulf short of war.[40] This was a radical departure for State, which had consistently maintained throughout the 1960s that the United States should not try to exploit the Sino-Soviet dispute as it might provide cause for reconciliation between the communist adversaries.

Ultimately however, the State Department – or more accurately, the East Asian bureau – retained as its main focus the improvement of relations with the PRC. The altered strategic context provided an impor tant boost to the endeavor, but other potential geopolitical gains vis-à-vis the Soviet Union were really incidental. While State officials clearly

---

[36] Rogers to RN, "The Possibility of a Soviet Strike against Chinese Nuclear Facilities," 10 September 1969, DEF 12 CHICOM folder, Box 1529, CFPF(1967–9), RG59, NA; INR, "Implications of Sino-Soviet Developments."

[37] Bundy, *Tangled Web*, p. 104.

[38] INR, "Implications of Sino-Soviet Developments."

[39] Rogers to RN, "Next Moves in China Policy," 2 December 1969, Box 1973, CFPF(1967–9), RG59, NA. Nixon agreed to implement the moves to relax trade policy.

[40] See Kissinger, *Diplomacy*, p. 729.

appreciated Washington's strategic opportunity in the Sino-Soviet split, EA was primarily concerned with seeking signs that the Chinese were contemplating a less adversarial relationship with the United States.

Soon after the March border clashes, Hong Kong reported that the Soviet Union had "replaced the US in Peking's eyes as the primary threat to the nation's security." Now, "[l]ogic would appear to encourage efforts by Peking to improve relations with the US . . . as a means of dealing more effectively with the Soviet threat."[41] Thereafter, EA redoubled its efforts to probe for Chinese readiness using the tools of key bilateral issues. When INR detected a more receptive mood in Beijing as Sino-Soviet tensions escalated from September onward, Green quickly returned to the table ACA's previous suggestion that Vietnam-related U.S. troops in Taiwan be withdrawn gradually. Furthermore, he asked that the Chinese be informed privately about the cessation of the Taiwan Straits patrol, which the U.S. government had decided to eliminate for budgetary reasons.[42] The latter was put into practice sooner than Green had anticipated: in mid-October, Kissinger asked the Pakistanis to inform the Chinese that the United States was removing its two destroyers from the Taiwan Straits, in "an effort to remove [a bilateral] irritant." Nixon added to Kissinger's report of the meeting, "also open trade possibilities."[43]

Yet given their focus on bilateral relations, when Beijing did begin to respond positively to such moves, State's China hands returned to their doubts about Beijing's intentions regarding genuine reconciliation with Washington. In December, the breakdown of the Sino-Soviet border talks appeared to generate new momentum in both Soviet-American and Sino-American relations. First, the Soviets agreed to resume the SALT talks with the United States. Kissinger read this as a Soviet attempt to impress Beijing with the possibilities of a Soviet-American rapprochement at

[41] ConGen/HK to DoS, "Communist China's Foreign Policy," 15 April 1969, Box 1962, CFPF(1967–9), RG59, NA. At the start of 1969, Mao and Zhou had requested four marshals to undertake a review of China's relations with the Soviet Union and the United States. They produced a first report for the Politburo in July 1969, which stated that "the Soviet revisionists have made China their main enemy, imposing a more serious threat to our security than the US imperialists" and noted that "both China and the United States take the Soviet Union as their enemy thus the Soviet revisionists do not dare to fight a two-front war." – "A Preliminary Evaluation of the War Situation," 11 July 1969, CWIHP 11, pp. 166–7.
[42] INR, "Communist China: Increased Curiosity about US Asian Policy," 8 September 1969, Box 710, NSF, NPM; Green to undersecretary of state, "Next Steps in China Policy," 6 October 1969, Box 1973, CFPF(1967–9), RG59, NA.
[43] Kissinger to RN, "President Yahya and Communist China," 16 October 1969, Box 623, NSF, NPM.

China's expense.[44] In the same month, the Chinese leadership appeared to come to a resolution of the internal debate about policy toward the United States.[45] Beijing released two detained American yachtsmen with much publicity, and in early December it agreed to resume the Warsaw talks. INR, in turn, interpreted this as a symbolic reminder to the Soviets that the Chinese also had the option of dealing with the United States.[46] The White House, on the other hand, had more definite confirmation of Chinese motives. On 19 December, Kissinger and Nixon received a note from Beijing through the Pakistani channel informing them that the yatchsmen had been released in response to the earlier message received from the United States and the news of the withdrawal of the destroyers.[47]

State was not informed of this. At the same time, it also had to contend with other signs of intransigence from the Chinese on the key bilateral issue of Taiwan. Even as Beijing began to send out relatively moderate signals toward Washington in September, it continued to demand American concessions over Taiwan. For instance, a senior Chinese official was reported to have asserted that relaxations in trade and travel restrictions were "chickenfeed." Before talks could begin, the United States would have to withdraw the Seventh Fleet from the Taiwan Straits, and eventually remove all troops from Taiwan. He also insisted that Beijing would not renounce the use of force in settling the Taiwan question. Thus, it seemed that even at the height of the Sino-Soviet crisis, Chinese officials did not see the strategic impetus as sufficient to change their policy toward the United States.

[44] Kissinger to RN, "Recent Soviet Policy Developments: SALT, China and Germany," 23 December 1969, Box 711, NSF, NPM.

[45] INR, "Communist China: The Sino-Soviet Dispute and Domestic Politics," 17 December 1969, Box 1962, CFPF(1967–9), RG59, NA. This was an accurate reading. The Four Marshals had submitted a second report to the Politburo in September, which asserted that "the Soviet revisionists indeed intend to wage a war of aggression against China" and that "we must wage a tit-for-tat struggle against both the United States and the Soviet Union, including using negotiation as a means of fighting against them." Marshal Chen Yi went further to push for a "breakthrough" in Sino-American relations, suggesting ministerial level meetings and talks on strategic issues "without preconditions." Together, these reports stimulated Mao's change in policy toward the United States. See "Our Views about the Current Situation," 17 September 1969; and "Further Thoughts by Marshal Chen Yi on Sino-American Relations," *CWIHP Bulletin* 11 (Winter 1998), pp. 170–1.

[46] INR, "Peking 'Responds' to the December 3 US Initiative," 9 December 1969, Box 2188, SNF(1970–3), RG59, NA.

[47] Memcons, 19 and 23 December 1969, Box 1031; Kissinger to RN, "Word from China through Pakistan," 23 December 1969, Box 624, NSF, NPM.

Combined with State's assessment that the Soviet threat to the PRC was not a particularly serious one, the China specialists' emphasis on signals within bilateral issues exacerbated State observers' suspicions that other signs of relative moderation probably did not represent basic changes in Beijing's stance toward the United States, but rather "tactical adjustments" in the context of the Sino-Soviet conflict.[48] In other words, Beijing was still mainly concerned with the competition with its rival for communist ideological leadership, and China remained a "revolutionary" power whose basic interests conflicted with those of the United States. This wariness would be exacerbated by a gradual process of bureaucratic isolation that allowed the White House's China discourse to hold sway during this period of transition.

"THREATENED MAJOR POWER": THE WHITE HOUSE RECONCEPTUALIZES CHINA

The Nixon White House did not pay particular attention to China in its initial months, and a discernable White House discourse about China really developed only in response to the militarization of the Sino-Soviet dispute from March 1969 onward. In contrast to State's China policy discourse, the White House focused heavily on the potential scenario of a Sino-Soviet war. As Kissinger and Nixon have recounted in their memoirs, this rethinking process did indeed contain a strong *realpolitik* flavor and centered on the issue of how to play the "China card" to American advantage vis-à-vis the Soviet Union. In the process, the White House discourse on China itself was reoriented to emphasize both Chinese weakness and the importance of China's security to international peace and stability.

With the outbreak of hostilities at the Sino-Soviet border, the difference between State and White House reactions lay in their assessment of how and to what extent the United States should respond, and the type and means of action that ought to be taken to turn the situation to U.S. advantage. The White House explored more ways of making advances toward the Chinese and advocated stronger action to deter the Soviets from attacking China.

Initially, the White House was not overly alarmed about the escalation of the Sino-Soviet conflict, but rather gave its attention to the potential strategic opportunity that the border war provided for Washington.

---

[48] INR, "Increased Curiosity about US Asian Policy," pp. 2–3. See also Burr, "Sino-American Relations, 1969," pp. 95–6.

Indeed, the Soviets themselves helped to draw attention to this opportunity through "heavy-handed diplomacy." Soon after the border clashes, Soviet Ambassador Anatoly Dobrynin insisted to Kissinger that the Chinese were "everybody's problem."[49] A month later, in the midst of other Soviet probes about the state of U.S.–China relations, Dobrynin obliquely suggested to Kissinger that "there was still time for the two superpowers to order events."[50]

In response to Moscow's obvious preoccupation with its Chinese adversary and worry about a possible U.S.–PRC rapprochement, Nixon and Kissinger began to play the "China card." Nixon sent a message to Premier Kosygin, assuring him that the United States had "no interest in seeing [the Soviet Union and China] in conflict and...[had] no intention to exploit their present difficulties." As Kissinger pointed out, the implication was that Washington had the capacity to do so if it chose.[51] By June, Kissinger reported his conviction to Nixon that the "growing obsession of the Soviet leaders with their China problem...suggests that [they] may become more flexible in dealing with East-West issues...if they are in fact attempting to ensure our neutrality in their Chinese containment policy, if not our active cooperation." Nixon suggested that they "subtly encourage" Eastern bloc countries to establish diplomatic relations with Beijing and that they find ways to increase Soviet "anxiety" about a possible Sino-American "anti-Soviet coalition."[52]

Accordingly, Nixon made some moves toward China. In June, he approved the relaxation of restrictions on academic, scientific, and journalistic travel to China and agreed to ease some trade controls.[53] Furthermore,

[49] *White House Years*, p. 172. For an official internal Soviet account of the clash, see "Soviet Report to GDR Leadership on 2 March 1969 Sino-Soviet Border Clashes," 8 March 1969, in Ostermann, ed., "East German Documents," pp. 189–90.

[50] DoS memcon, "US-Communist China Warsaw Talks," 14 January 1969, NSA Doc. 37; Buchanan to Kissinger, "Meeting," 20 May 1969, Box 1, Top Secret Files (TSF) (1969–74), RG59, NA; DoS memcon, "Soviet Attitude Toward US-Chicom Relations," 9 October 1969, NSA Doc. 80; Kissinger, *White House Years*, p. 173. In his memoir, Dobrynin comments that "we were making a mistake from the start of displaying our anxiety over China to the new administration." Anatoly Dobrynin, *In Confidence: Moscow's Ambassador to America's Six Cold War Presidents* (New York, 1995), p. 202.

[51] Emb/Moscow to DoS, "Oral Statement by Ambassador Jacob D. Beam to Soviet Premier Alexei Kosygin," 23 April 1969; Kissinger, *White House Years*, p. 173.

[52] *White House Years*, pp. 178–9; Nixon, handwritten comments on letter from Knorr to Kissinger, 10 June 1969, Box 822, NSF, NPM.

[53] "Restrictions Eased on US Travel to Communist China," 21 July 1969, *DSB* 61, p. 126; Kissinger to secretaries of state, treasury, and commerce, "National Security Decision Memorandum 17," 26 June 1969, NSA Doc. 71. Nixon directed that at the earliest

the following month, during his "Guam Doctrine" press briefing, he portrayed China as a troubled adversary and a reduced threat.[54] Such public indications of a less hostile approach to China were accompanied by secret attempts to communicate to the Chinese leaders the administration's interest in a new relationship. At the beginning of August, Nixon asked both Romanian President Ceauşescu and Pakistani President Yahya Khan to convey to Chinese Premier Zhou Enlai his interest in accommodation with China. During a trip to Asia, he informed regional leaders that the United States opposed the Soviet idea of a "cabal" against China and believed that "no real peace is possible [in Asia] without China's playing a role."[55]

During the second half of 1969, however, intelligence reports raised concerns in Washington that Moscow was seriously contemplating a major attack on China. In early July, Kissinger commissioned an interagency study on the alternative U.S. policy options for various scenarios of "military clashes" between the Soviet Union and China.[56] The study has not yet been declassified, but John Holdridge, the NSC representative on the study group, reports that the main outcome consisted of contingency plans for the United States to "direct a strong political campaign against the Soviets in the United Nations and in other public forums" in the event of a war.[57] Thus, the emphasis was now on restraining the Soviet Union from attacking China: both White House and State Department officials appeared to have converged on a consensus that China was clearly the weaker of the two communist powers, and that Washington might not want to see it seriously attacked by the Soviet Union.

On this point, Patrick Tyler has suggested, on the contrary, that Nixon considered a "deal" with Moscow by which the United States would have acquiesced to a Soviet attack on Chinese nuclear facilities in return

---

opportunity, restrictions should be modified to allow foreign subsidiaries of U.S. firms to carry out nonstrategic transactions with China; to allow U.S. citizens traveling abroad to buy Chinese goods; to permit exports of food, agricultural equipment, fertilizers, and pharmaceuticals to China; and to modify import and export controls to allow trade in nonstrategic goods.

[54] Informal remarks in Guam with newsmen, 25 July 1969, *PPP:RN 1969*, pp. 546–8. See Chapter 5, this volume.

[55] Memcon, "Private Meeting between President Nixon and Ceausescu," 2 August 1969, Box 1023, NSF, NPM; Bundy, *Tangled Web*, p. 105; Kissinger, *White House Years*, pp. 180–1; Holdridge, *Crossing the Divide*, pp. 31–2.

[56] NSSM 63, "US Policy on Current Sino-Soviet Differences," 3 July 1969, Box 7, RG273, NA.

[57] Holdridge, *Crossing the Divide*, p. 35.

for Soviet cooperation to end the war in Vietnam.[58] As Burr observed, this choice of what I have labeled Option 2 – support the Soviet Union against China – would have been "wholly out of synch with the idea of [U.S.–PRC] rapprochement, but would have reflected the higher priority of the Vietnam problem."[59] Tyler's account is based on interviews, and there is no archival evidence so far to support his hypothesis.[60] However, some Soviet specialists did see the potential advantage to the United States of a Sino-Soviet war. Kissinger's own NSC adviser William Hyland – acknowledging that it was a "highly personal and apparently minority" view – noted that allowing the Soviet Union to attack China in a limited war might pave the way for an early Vietnam settlement and solve the Chinese nuclear problem.[61]

It is clear, however, that as the evidence mounted for Soviet militancy and a possible strike against China from August 1969 onward, Nixon decided to take more obvious cautionary steps to warn Moscow to show restraint, and conciliatory steps to reassure China that the United States would not cooperate with the Soviet Union against it. In the months that followed, the White House worked with State to send the public messages to Moscow and Beijing that the United States would not exploit the Sino-Soviet conflict, wanted to improve relations with both sides, and would be markedly concerned by a Soviet attack on China.

This stance toward the Sino-Soviet conflict stemmed from two key representations of China. First, it was a relatively weak and threatened state. In the White House, the border war, more than the Cultural Revolution, dramatically demonstrated Chinese vulnerability. According to Kissinger, when the border clashes first began, the White House assumed that the Chinese were the provocateurs, based on the perception that they were irrational and more aggressive than the Soviets.[62] However, after the new border clashes in the Xinjiang region in May, and with the Soviet probes in August, Nixon and Kissinger appear to have changed their minds. The White House's reconceptualization of China was encapsulated at a meeting on 14 August, when Nixon told the Cabinet that the Soviet Union was the more aggressive party in the conflict and that it was not in America's

[58] Tyler, *A Great Wall*, pp. 62–3.
[59] Burr, "Sino-American Relations, 1969," p. 84.
[60] Tyler's principal source is then Secretary of Defense Melvin Laird, but all of the ex-officials interviewed by this author in 2001 denied that such a deal was under consideration.
[61] Hyland to Kissinger, "Sino-Soviet Contingencies," 28 August 1969, Box 700, NSF, NPM.
[62] Kissinger, *White House Years*, p. 172.

interest for China to be "smashed" in a Sino-Soviet war.[63] In late August, Kissinger had what he later claimed to be a definitive discussion with Allen Whiting, a RAND China expert who had previously served in INR, in which he was in turn convinced that "the Russians were much more likely to attack China than the other way round." He was apparently impressed by Whiting's warning that the Soviet border buildup was in preparation for a strike against Chinese nuclear facilities.[64]

Second, the White House–inspired discourse identified China as a major state whose security was vital to international stability. In the existing revisionist discourse, China was a "Resurgent Power" whose constructive participation in international society was vital to ensuring international peace. Now Kissinger argued that China's very national security vis-à-vis the Soviet Union was vital to the maintenance of international order. As Rogers stated in a public address, the administration did not regard it as "a good thing" to let the Soviet Union and China engage in a "sizable war," because this would be "injurious to all."[65] It might involve nuclear weapons, and it would seriously disrupt the balance of power in Asia.

Essentially, therefore, Nixon and Kissinger's policy contained two elements along a sliding scale. The first, overt element was triangular politics – Option 3, as set out in Chapter 1 – playing the "China card" with the aim of attaining an equilibrium, with the United States as the pivot. The longer-term objective was to improve substantially Washington's international power position and to recover a new centrality for the United States in world affairs. With the Vietnam fiasco and the Sino-Soviet split, America's identity as the leader of a worldwide anticommunist crusade had been called into question both domestically and abroad. Nixon and Kissinger now attempted to reconstruct the United States as the force that would prevent war between the communists. At the same time, by keeping the focus on the central superpower contest, they tried to recoup

[63] Memcon, "Conversation with the President Concerning China and US-Chinese Contacts," 9 September 1969, Box 1973, SNF(1967–9), RG59, NA; Kissinger, *White House Years*, p. 182. Nixon said the same thing to a smaller group of advisers at a meeting in San Clemente on 18 August – see William Safire, *Before the Fall: An Inside View of the Pre-Watergate White House* (New York, 1975), p. 370.

[64] Kalb and Kalb, *Kissinger*, pp. 226–7; Allen Whiting, "Sino-American Détente," *China Quarterly* 82 (1980), p. 336; Holdridge, *Crossing the Divide*, p. 34; Whiting to Kissinger, "Sino-Soviet Hostilities and Implications for US Policy," 16 August 1969, Box 839, NSF, NPM.

[65] *NYT*, 29 August 1969.

and reiterate America's identity as the undisputed leader and center of the Western alliance.[66] In the context of triangular politics in 1969, the "ostentatious renunciation of collusion" with either Moscow or Beijing served as an "invitation to each to improve relations with Washington" and thereby boost America's relative strategic position.[67] However, this would work only short of the limiting situation of a war between the two communist powers. As long as both the PRC and Soviet Union regarded the other as a greater threat than the United States, Washington could pursue even-handed "parallel détente," but in the extreme event of an outright Soviet attack on the PRC, the United States would have to side with China, in deference to the greater goal of maintaining international equilibrium and peace.[68] At the time, the Nixon administration hinted – leaving the means unspecified – that if it should come to a larger war, Washington would move toward Option 4, which was to support China against a Soviet attack.

Nixon's primary intention was to restrain the Soviets, and in a public warning gesture he asked the CIA director to brief the media about Moscow's overtures concerning action against China and to convey Washington's concern about the rising possibility of a Sino-Soviet war.[69] On 5 September, Undersecretary of State Elliot Richardson, in a speech to the American Political Science Association, asserted that "in our own national interest," Washington wanted good relations with both sides and would neither let Chinese "invective" dampen its efforts to cooperate with Moscow, nor let "Soviet apprehensions prevent us from attempting to bring Communist China out of its angry, alienated shell." However, Richardson declared that while intracommunist ideological differences were "not our affair," a Sino-Soviet war was a different matter: Washington "could not fail to be concerned" if the quarrel escalated into a "massive breach of international peace and security."[70]

At the same time, Kissinger and Nixon also worked toward a more positive approach to the Chinese. In spite of the diffusion of Sino-Soviet

---

[66] This is Schurmann's argument in *The Foreign Politics of Richard Nixon*, in which he asserts that Nixon's grand design was aimed at regaining a new, central global role for the United States and at preventing a slide into isolationist sentiment after Vietnam.

[67] Henry Kissinger, *Diplomacy* (New York, 1994), p. 725.

[68] Ibid.; *White House Years*, p. 836; *Years of Upheaval*, p. 54.

[69] "Russia Reported Eyeing Strike at China A-Site," 28 August 1969, "Western Envoys Differ on Soviet Threat to China," 29 August 1969, *WP*.

[70] Richardson, "The Foreign Policy of the Nixon Administration: Its Aims and Strategy," 5 September 1969, *DSB* 61, p. 260.

tensions after the Zhou–Kosygin meeting at Beijing airport on 11 September, Kissinger continued to urge Nixon to make it even plainer that the United States was not "siding with the Soviets," in order to encourage those in China who wanted a "more rational" relationship with the United States. He recommended that the State Department instruct its foreign embassies to deplore the Soviet idea of a preemptive strike against China.[71] Making advances to China was now not just a tactic to persuade the Soviets to be more forthcoming in cooperating with Washington; it was a serious attempt to develop closer relations with China in accordance with Kissinger's balance-of-power belief that "it was more advantageous to align oneself with the weaker of two antagonistic partners, because this acted as a restraint on the stronger."[72] In this sense, the theme of encouraging restraint on Moscow's part provided a meeting point at which Options 3 and 4 merged in the White House's China policy discourse in 1969.

DEBATES AND DEPARTURES: THE RENEWED WARSAW TALKS, 1970

The Nixon administration held two sessions of ambassadorial talks with the Chinese at Warsaw in January and February 1970. The preparations for these talks provided a focal point for the competing China discourses of the State Department and White House and perpetrated the eventual bureaucratic rupture between them over China policy.

Initially, the resumption of the talks generated much optimism in Washington, and the guidelines for the January talks submitted to Nixon by the secretary of state bore some significant departures in policy. The American ambassador's introductory statement reflected a point of agreement between State and the White House:

The US intends to honor its commitments but...has no intention of attempting...to exclude the PRC from developing normal, friendly relations with its Asian neighbors and pursuing its own legitimate national interests in this area.... Whatever constructive contribution your Government can make toward reaching a just and equitable peace in the area and in easing the legitimate concerns of other Asian governments would contribute toward more rapid achievement of the goal of a reduction of military tension in the area and a reduced American

---

[71] Kissinger to undersecretary of state, "Response to Soviet Probe of Our Position on China," 24 September 1969, Box 710, NSF; Kissinger to RN, "The US Role in Soviet Maneuvering against China," 29 September 1969, Box 337, NSF, NPM.

[72] Kissinger, *White House Years*, p. 178.

military presence in Southeast Asia, which we recognize is near the southern border of China.[73]

This was designed as a deliberate re-representation of China away from
the image of an aggressive, hostile adversary and toward that of a major
regional power and potential partner in peace. Rogers explained to Nixon
that in order to signal "a new beginning" in Sino-American relations, it
was important to "dispel earlier characterizations of China as a potential aggressor and threat to its Asian neighbors" and to express the new
"assumption that the PRC does not intend to undertake overt aggression
against other Asian states." Additionally, by offering to carry out bilateral disarmament negotiations, Washington would signal its recognition
of China as a "major power and an essential element in the disarmament
picture."[74]

At the same time, State continued in its efforts to test the waters by
addressing the vital bilateral issue of Taiwan. The U.S. ambassador was
instructed to reiterate the American commitment to the U.S.–ROC defense
treaty, but to insist that this was "without prejudice to any future peaceful
settlement" between the PRC and the GRC. Washington also offered the
strong reassurance that "we will also not support and in fact will oppose"
any Nationalist offensive against the mainland. On this point, State was
willing to go further than the White House to reassure the Chinese. First, it
did not ask the Chinese for a commitment to peaceful reunification. Rather
than making it conditional upon a renunciation of force by the Chinese, as
the Defense Department and the intelligence community preferred, State
linked the withdrawal of U.S. troops from Taiwan to the more general
prospect for the growth of "peace and stability in Asia." In this respect,
State made important headway in setting out the basic U.S. position in
negotiating on the Taiwan issue. The idea that the United States was
not committed to a permanent military presence on Taiwan but would
unilaterally reduce its forces as tensions in the area diminished was subsequently inscribed as an official position by State in a 1971 NSSM study.[75]

---

[73] DoS to Emb/Warsaw, "Draft Instructions for 135th Sino-US Ambassadorial Meeting,"
17 January 1970, Box 2187, SNF(1970–3), RG59, NA.

[74] Rogers to RN, "Guidance for Sino-US Ambassadorial Meeting, January 20, 1970,"
14 January 1970, Box 2187, SNF(1970–3), RG59, NA.

[75] DoS, "NSSM 106 Issues Paper – What Price Improved US-PRC Relations and a More
Constructive International Role for Peking?," 6 March 1971, Box 3, LOT 72D504,
RG59, NA. This position led to running battles with the Defense Department, which
wanted to extract from Beijing an agreement to renounce the use of force in the Taiwan
Straits before undertaking any force reduction. See "DoD Position Paper on option A-5

Second, State's original instructions for the January 1970 Warsaw talks contained the phrase, "we do not intend to interfere in whatever [peaceful] settlement may be reached." As the ROC desk later protested to Green, this position would have precluded Washington from exercising any influence with the GRC on issues such as political reform on the island.[76] Taken further, it might limit Washington's ability to help to protect Taipei's right to choose independence for Taiwan. In the event, the sentence was deleted after Kissinger advised Nixon that it suggested that Washington was encouraging the Chinese Communists and the GRC to "make a deal."[77] However, in introducing the new principle that the United States would not interfere in the settlement of the Taiwan issue as long as it was peaceful, State moved Washington toward the explicit recognition that Taiwan was an internal affair of the Chinese, with the caveat that the United States retained its right to defend its ROC ally if the PRC used force. This set the direction for the "one China" policy that Kissinger and Nixon would eventually adopt.[78]

The most important result of the January 1970 talks was the parallel proposals for higher-level meetings by both sides. The United States offered to send a special representative to Beijing or to receive a Chinese representative in Washington, while the Chinese proposed talks at a "higher level" or through "other channels acceptable to both sides."[79] Somewhat paradoxically, this development caused the State Department to withdraw into caution about Chinese intentions. This would appear to support Kissinger's complaints about State's unimaginative conservatism. Yet Kissinger's own NSC staff credited State with the high-level emissary initiative in the first place.[80] Certainly, the notion of higher-level talks was not a new one on the seventh floor – it had been brought up during the early 1950s, and Rusk had considered it in 1967. On the other

of the NSSM 106 Study," ca. March 1971, Green to Rogers, "Senior Review Group Meeting on NSSM 106 – China Policy – Briefing Memorandum," 22 February 1971, ibid.

[76] Shoesmith to Green, "Warsaw Talks: Preserving US Options in Possible Future GRC-PRC Negotiation on Status of Taiwan," 20 January 1969, Box 2187, SNF(1970–3), RG59, NA.

[77] Kissinger to RN, "Guidance for Warsaw Talks," n.d., Box 700, NSF, NPM. Yet Kissinger and Nixon would have to make this very commitment to Beijing in 1971, when they began serious discussions on the terms of rapprochement with the Chinese.

[78] See Chapter 8, this volume.

[79] Emb/Warsaw to DoS, "Stoessel-Lei Talks: Report of 135th Meeting, January 20, 1970," 24 January 1970, Box 2187, SNF(1970–3), RG59, NA.

[80] Holdridge, *Crossing the Divide*, pp. 35–6.

hand, Rogers had presented the suggestion of higher-level talks to Nixon as a test of Chinese intentions, pointing out that "[s]hould the Chinese wish to signal their willingness to improve relations, they could accept this offer without compromising any of their principles." But he had not really expected China to respond positively: "[a]cceptance of such an offer at present is unlikely, but they will find it interesting as evidence of US interest in further development of relations."[81] Such thinking adhered to the lines of the 1960s revisionist discourse, which would test Chinese intentions and shift the onus for its isolation onto Beijing but without really expecting a Chinese response, or any further U.S. action, in the short term.

Thus, State tried to deflect the issue of a higher-level meeting, holding out instead for Chinese willingness to move on other bilateral issues such as prisoners and exchanges.[82] Rogers suspected that Beijing wanted "purely optical evidence" of agreement with the United States in order to achieve its main aim of demonstrating to Moscow that it could negotiate an easing of tensions with the United States.[83] A discussion paper stated that "we cannot yet assume that Peking... is motivated by any desire for a genuine long-term improvement in Sino-US relations or that it will alter... its broad revolutionary goals."[84]

When, at the February talks, the Chinese responded that they would be prepared to receive "a representative of ministerial rank" or a "special presidential envoy" in Beijing, Rogers again counseled caution.[85] He reiterated to Nixon that Washington should ascertain whether a higher-level meeting would be productive by first developing at the Warsaw ambassadorial level some basic areas of mutual understanding. Specifically, State suggested six principles that could provide a basis for discussion:

(1) Disputes relating to Taiwan should be resolved peacefully between those parties on the mainland and on Taiwan which are directly concerned;
(2) The US will not interfere in such a settlement;
(3) As tensions relating to the area diminish, the US military presence in the Taiwan area will be gradually reduced;

---

[81] Rogers to RN, "Guidance for Sino-US Ambassadorial Meeting, January 20, 1970."
[82] Green to Rogers, "Sino-US Ambassadorial Talks on January [*sic*] 20, 1970 – Action Memorandum," 4 February 1970, Box 2187, SNF(1970–3), RG59, NA.
[83] Rogers to RN, "Sino-US Negotiations in Warsaw," 7 February 1970, Box 2188, SNF(1970–3), RG59, NA.
[84] DoS memo, "US Strategy in Current Sino-US Talks," ca. February 1970, POL CHICOM-US (2 May 1970) folder, Box 2188, SNF(1970–3), RG59, NA.
[85] Stoessel to Rogers, "Sino-US Talks: February 20 Meeting," 20 February 1970, Box 2188, SNF(1970–3), RG59, NA.

(4)   The US and the PRC will resolve disputes which arise between them through peaceful negotiations;
(5)   It is desirable from the standpoint of both sides to expand mutual contacts and trade;
(6)   The principles of peaceful coexistence are consistent with the foregoing.[86]

There was no disagreement between State and the White House on these basic principles. These were precisely the issues that Kissinger negotiated at length with the Chinese leaders when he went to Beijing in July and October 1971, and at the February 1972 summit.

At this point, the disagreement lay in the *means* of communicating and negotiating with the Chinese leaders once it became clear that they were ready to do so. The White House was determined to take it up to higher levels, while Rogers wanted first to hammer out the basis for any agreement at Warsaw, with lower stakes involved. As secretary of state, Rogers was influenced by the consideration that a higher-level meeting would be "a major international event, receiving the widest public attention and with widespread and substantial international and domestic political consequences."[87]

In the White House, Kissinger in particular was convinced that the direct Soviet threat to its national security was a sufficient motivation for Beijing to hold serious talks and to make substantial improvements in relations with the United States. As he explained to Nixon, while the "immediate" Chinese purpose was indeed "to show the *appearance* of the ability to deal with us ... primarily for Soviet consumption" rather than to "talk much substance," Washington could take the opportunity to work at convincing them of "the desirability of appearing to be able to make deals with us." This would then make it easier for the Chinese leaders to "justify seeking the *substance* of understandings."[88] In other words, with sustained high-level contacts and the correct strategic persuasion, Washington could exploit the China opening and deepen it into some form of modus vivendi. Kissinger also argued that playing for higher stakes would benefit Washington because Beijing had more to lose if these overtures failed, since China was in need of strategic help from the United States. A higher-level meeting would unnerve Moscow, Taipei, and other U.S. allies and friends. On the other hand, the Chinese would

---

[86] Rogers to RN, "Higher-Level Meeting with the Chinese," 10 March 1970; DoS to Kissinger, "Revised Warsaw Instructions," 31 March 1970, Box 2188, SNF(1970-3), RG59, NA; Green oral history interview, in Tucker, *China Confidential*, pp. 238–9.
[87] Rogers, "Higher-Level Meeting with the Chinese."
[88] Kissinger to RN, "The Warsaw Talks," 12 January 1970, Box 700, NSF, NPM.

face the same problems in receiving a U.S. "imperialist" in Beijing. More-over, they would have significant incentive to consider making conces-sions to the United States regarding Taiwan, because the collapse of such a high-level contact would "encourage the Soviets to believe that Chinese [explorations] of the US option had failed and that the Chinese now had to face the Soviets on their own."[89]

Most important for Nixon and Kissinger, however, was the consider-ation that contacts through a presidential emissary would be controlled directly from the White House. Indeed, they were busy trying to offer the Chinese, through the Pakistani back channel, an alternative "direct White House channel to Peking ... on which we could guarantee total se-crecy."[90] In the event, the Warsaw talks did not continue after February 1970, as the U.S. incursion into Cambodia caused the next meeting to be cancelled.[91] As the Warsaw channel dried up, State's role in the conduct of China policy also declined, and the China discourse was eventually captured by the White House through a process of bureaucratic isolation. Nixon and Kissinger stepped up their search for an alternative secret chan-nel of communication with Beijing during the second half of 1970. After trying channels via Paris, Romania, and Pakistan, the big breakthrough came in the form of a reply from Zhou via the Pakistanis on 9 December 1970, inviting a presidential envoy to Beijing to discuss "the vacation of Chinese territories called Taiwan."[92] After delays over the next few months on the Chinese side, they eventually reiterated the invitation in April 1971, and by June had agreed to receive Kissinger secretly in Beijing in July to discuss Taiwan and other issues of common concern.[93]

CONCLUSION

During the period of transition from 1969 to early 1970, different inter-pretations of the significance of changes in the strategic context led to

---

[89] Kissinger to RN, "Chinese at Warsaw Talks Suggest US Send High-Level Representative to Peking," n.d., Box 700, NSF, NPM.

[90] Kissinger to RN, "Message from President Yahya on China," 23 February 1970, Box 1032, NSF, NPM.

[91] DoS to Kissinger, "May 20 Sino-US Talk in Warsaw," 28 April 1970, NSA Doc. 171; Rogers to RN, "Chinese Cancellation of May 20 Warsaw Meeting," 19 May 1970, Box 2188, SNF(1970–3), RG59, NA.

[92] Note from Zhou Enlai, dictated by Hilaly in Kissinger's office, 9 December 1970, Box 1031, NSF, NPM.

[93] See "Exchanges Leading Up to HAK Trip to China, December 1969–July 1971" folder, Box 1031, NSF, NPM.

debates within the Nixon administration regarding preferred policy positions. In spite of their contempt for the bureaucracy, Nixon and Kissinger relied upon the State Department's China expertise, and there was an active exchange between State and the White House during this initial process of hammering out the ideational foundations for a China policy.

During this time, State managed to combine the previous revisionist rationale for a new China policy with the opportunities offered by the new geopolitical circumstances, and it formulated vital details of the steps that it thought the United States could take regarding the central Taiwan issue in order to work toward better relations with China. However, the foregoing analysis shows that during the China policy debates from 1969 to 1970, State differed from the White House on two main issues: how blatantly to play the "China card" with the Soviets, and at what level to carry out negotiations with the Chinese.

On both counts, State's more reserved position stemmed from the perception that China was a resurgent but still revolutionary power, and a conviction that the Chinese had yet to demonstrate that they were serious about pursuing better bilateral relations. Fundamentally, precisely because of its recognition of the importance of triangular politics, State firmly identified Beijing's anti-Soviet motivation, imputing to the Chinese short-term opportunistic aims rather than a genuine change in attitude toward the United States. State's China hands disagreed with Kissinger and Nixon that the strategic imperative alone would be sufficient to persuade Beijing to moderate its revolutionary aims and to effect a concrete improvement of relations with the United States. This caution reflected many China hands' experience of the long wait over the 1960s for the Chinese to come around to the idea of reconciliation, and their knowledge of the intractability of the basic problems that divided the two sides.

Throughout the period between 1969 and 1971, State sought further indications from the Chinese that they were serious about negotiating a basic understanding for better relations. It would seem, therefore, that State might have been swayed from its ambivalence had it been made aware of the secret back channel communications from December 1970 onward.[94] State might have concluded that Beijing's release of prisoners and detainees, the beginning of U.S.–PRC exchanges in the form of

---

[94] Rogers missed an important opportunity to discover the Pakistani channel in December 1970. The U.S. ambassador in Islamabad reported remarks by Yahya Khan about having conveyed a message from Nixon to Zhou, but the cable was intercepted by Kissinger's office. See Haig to Kissinger, enclosing Emb/Islamabad to Rogers/Kissinger, "President Yahya on US-China Relations," 14 December 1970, Box 1031, NSF, NPM.

"Ping-Pong diplomacy" and associated journalistic travel, and the invitation to a high-level emissary and the president went beyond unilateral symbolic gestures aimed at unsettling the Soviets. While the anti-Soviet motivation remained, these were signals and initiatives taken in response to Washington's own actions. They were designed to bring about a significant public resumption of official Sino-American talks at which the Chinese agreed to discuss a range of issues of interest to both sides – concrete evidence of the high stakes Beijing placed on the opening.

In the White House, meanwhile, the focus in China policy thinking shifted firmly away from Nixon's public discourse about peace and the need to end China's isolation in order to help fulfill its potential as a major power. Under Kissinger's guidance, it was steered toward the appreciation that this was China's moment of vulnerability and need, during which there was a unique Chinese readiness to approach the United States. Thus, the White House discourse now represented China as a "Threatened Major Power" and focused policy on "interests" rather than ideology – it was assumed that in order to achieve its most immediate national security needs, Beijing would change its attitude toward Washington sufficiently to develop a new relationship. A key difference between the State and White House positions was that Kissinger was convinced that by taking some bold steps, Washington could persuade Beijing to move from an opportunistic opening toward rapprochement and eventual normalization.

At this point, a vague distinction was already being drawn between the two variants of the "balance of power" strategy. On the one hand, Nixon and Kissinger wanted, above all, to play the "China card" for its effects on Moscow, Hanoi, and domestic politics. In this regard, they were most concerned about personalizing and dominating the means of communication with Beijing, and – something the State Department did not appreciate – with seeking a dramatic opening to China as soon as possible. On the other hand, during the second half of 1969, when the White House was especially concerned about the possibility of a large-scale Sino-Soviet war, it hinted that in such an eventuality, the United States would side with China in order to maintain international stability. In doing so, Nixon signaled publicly that his administration regarded China as a vital major power under threat, in whose security Washington perceived itself to have a significant interest. The potential ramifications of this representation of China were considerable, and the way in which Kissinger and Nixon deliberately developed these ideas during the rapprochement will be analyzed in Part III.

PART THREE

DISCOURSES OF RAPPROCHEMENT IN PRACTICE, 1971–1974

7

"Principled" Realist Power

Laying the Discursive Foundations of a New Relationship, July 1971 to February 1972

> Kissinger: "Many visitors have come to this beautiful, and to us, mysterious land.... All have departed with new perspectives...."
> Zhou: "You will find it not mysterious. When you have become familiar with it, it will not be as mysterious as before."[1]

As the president's personal envoy, Henry Kissinger flew secretly to Beijing from Pakistan on 9 July 1971 and stayed for two days of talks with Zhou Enlai. Upon his return, Kissinger characterized those discussions as "the most searching, sweeping and significant...I have ever had in government." These meetings, he reported to Nixon, marked a "major new departure in international relations," and the Nixon administration now had the opportunity to "transform the very framework of global relationships."[2]

In spite of the prior back channel messages, Kissinger's first trip was in some ways a step into the unknown, and his fundamental task was to establish whether the Chinese leaders were indeed ready to relate to the United States in a nonhostile and nonmilitant fashion. Kissinger found that the small coterie of Chinese leaders he met were people whom he could deal with. More than that, he was clearly in awe of Zhou, and drawn to admiration and respect for the man whom he felt "ranks with Charles De Gaulle as the most impressive foreign statesman I have met."[3] By

---

[1] Zhou-Kissinger memcon, 9 November 1971, Box 851, NSF, NPM, p. 6.
[2] Kissinger to RN, "My Talks with Chou En-lai," 17 July 1971, Box 851, NSF, NPM.
[3] Ibid., p. 7. Nixon held Zhou in similarly high regard; in his book on great leaders who "changed the world," he chose – alongside de Gaulle, Churchill, and Adenauer – not Mao Zedong but Zhou Enlai. See Nixon, *Leaders*, Chapter 7.

virtue of his mission and position, Kissinger was uniquely responsible for articulating the image of the new China that the United States could begin to deal with in noninimical terms. The China that Kissinger described was a "principled" realist power, with leaders who were at once foreign and familiar. While they stuck firmly to Maoist ideology and retained revolutionary fervor, they also shared Nixon's and Kissinger's pragmatic strategic vision and would privilege the current common strategic interests of the United States and PRC over the outstanding bilateral issues of contention.

Kissinger made two preparatory trips to Beijing in 1971 – the secret one in July, and a publicized visit in October. This was followed by an advance trip by Alexander Haig, his deputy, in January 1972, ahead of Nixon's summit the following month. These trips covered much more than logistical preparations; the dialogues were occasions for the crucial mutual construction of the shared interests that motivated the opening, and for articulation of the principles and norms that would guide action in the new relationship. Most secondary accounts of the rapprochement tend to portray both sides as having sought the new relationship with their realist rationale and needs clearly defined and calculated in advance, and with a clear conviction that the other side was similarly convinced. However, the available documentary accounts of the Sino-American talks of this period clearly indicate a process of mutual investigation and negotiation. In their direct contacts with the Chinese leaders and their representatives, Kissinger and Nixon very consciously tried to articulate common interests, delimit areas of difference, and probe for Chinese aims and potential compromises. The Chinese did the same, in a process that revealed that they did not always have the same interpretation of all the key aspects of the strategic situation – the most notable examples being the U.S.–Japan relationship and its effects on Chinese security, and Soviet aims in Europe and Asia.

Thus, this chapter (and the rest of Part III) deals with the dynamics of the implementation of the policy of rapprochement – a set of processes quite distinct from the internal policy debates and advocacy discussed in the previous sections. The direct interaction and negotiation between the Americans and the Chinese involved the mutual construction of identities and interests. In what was a relatively "closed" process, the importance of discursive constructions in the evolution of policy stances may be more clearly discerned.

Kissinger and his NSC staff devoted the seven months between his secret trip and the summit to nurturing the basis for the new relationship, employing a multilevel process of identifying and developing areas of strategic agreement and cooperation with the Chinese along realist balance-of-power lines. This may be regarded as a two-tier process of advocacy. First, Kissinger brought back from his encounter with the Chinese leaders the first high-level official first-hand experience and representations of China in more than twenty years. He needed to convince Nixon that the administration could now deal with the China and Chinese that he had found. This was not a difficult task, as it was mainly a confirmation of the new identity of the Chinese consonant with the new relationship they had in mind. Second, the White House had to act upon and develop its initial image of China as a Threatened Major Power and former enemy in the course of preparing for subsequent dialogues. Kissinger and Nixon had to persuade the Chinese leaders of the new American image of China, the commonalities between the United States and China, and the shared realist logic of the rapprochement.

KISSINGER'S NEW REPRESENTATION OF THE CHINESE

The process of the presidential envoy's getting to know China and the Chinese leaders after more than twenty years of estrangement was to be a crucial one: Kissinger's new representation of the Chinese and Sino-American interests would provide the vital ideational bridge to allow the smooth transition from the old policy of containment and isolation to a new one of rapprochement.[4] Kissinger's impressions would be important because there still existed significant doubts about Chinese motivations for inviting high-level U.S. officials to Beijing.

In the background papers for the trip, Kissinger's staff seriously considered aspects of the discourse perpetuated by the State Department and others suspicious of Beijing, which portrayed the PRC as a "Resurgent Revolutionary Power" acting opportunistically to reap symbolic political gains at the expense of the United States. They conceded that among the major political gains that the Chinese could anticipate from the mere fact of Kissinger's trip and a summit were: an increase in the PRC's prestige, the erosion of the ROC's international position, the possible replacement of the ROC by the PRC in the UN, leverage over Moscow in the Sino-Soviet conflict, and disarray among America's Asian allies and friends. The NSC staff also considered the possibility that Beijing might be hoping for

---

[4] Akin to a modern-day Marco Polo – indeed, Kissinger's secret mission was code-named "Polo."

an "even more sensational" gain by demanding at the meeting that the United States withdraw completely from Asia as a precondition for the further development of Sino-American relations. This would humiliate the United States and strengthen China's ideological standing among its domestic and allied constituencies.[5]

However, Kissinger firmly advised Nixon that such tactics would not square with the circumstances under which the Chinese had agreed to his visit.[6] Instead, in the course of the two trips he made to Beijing in 1971, Kissinger developed his previous representation of China as a Threatened Major Power. He presented the new image of China as a "Principled" Realist Power, which was motivated by national security concerns to conduct a serious bilateral dialogue with Washington, and which could be expected to negotiate reasonably in the search for "normalized" relations.

The Realist Power

Kissinger reiterated that China was a realist, rather than revolutionary, power. In the background paper for the July trip, he surmised that Beijing was "now governed more by practical considerations than by militant ideology"; it had taken initiatives toward Washington "in response to the Soviet military threat along their borders" and hoped to use the United States as a "counterweight" to the Soviets. In view of this key motivation, in geopolitical terms it would be counterproductive for Beijing to offend Washington, which might then decide to "stand aside" if the Soviets chose to attack China. In the same vein, Kissinger pointed out that the Chinese probably recognized that a U.S. withdrawal from Asia would not necessarily suit Chinese purposes, since it would leave "areas of vacuum into which the Soviets could move quickly" and would remove a restraint upon Japan, which was increasingly viewed by Beijing as a "rival and potential threat."

Furthermore, Kissinger observed that, apart from the symbolic political gains associated with the visit, Beijing sought concrete objectives through a bilateral dialogue. These included the reduction of U.S. forces on Taiwan, a formal U.S. acknowledgement of the importance of China

---

[5] This was a possibility that worried some officials most closely involved in the secret opening to China. For instance, Vernon Walters, the military attaché who handled logistical communications in the Paris channel, felt obliged, even after Kissinger's successful July trip, to express these same doubts regarding the upcoming summit meeting. Walters to Kissinger, 24 December 1971, Box 849, NSF, NPM.

[6] NSC, "POLO – Scope Paper," n.d., Box 850, NSF, NPM, pp. 1–2.

in world affairs, and some form of bilateral nonaggression agreement.[7] Thus, Kissinger saw a basis for doing business with the Chinese, and he identified as one of his main tasks working out the "parameters for the *quid pro quo*" Washington sought. The latter included Chinese help with moving Hanoi toward a peaceful settlement, a modus vivendi on the Taiwan issue, channels for future bilateral communication, and an understanding of the Chinese view of "the Soviet role in world affairs and how this relates to Soviet military capabilities."[8]

During his secret trip to Beijing, Kissinger found further evidence of Chinese realism and sincerity in the opening to the United States. In a detailed report of this first encounter written for Nixon, Kissinger described the Chinese leaders as "tough, idealistic, fanatical, single-minded and remarkable"; he was impressed by their "inward philosophical tension" but also by their "inward strength." Kissinger took pains to emphasize the difficulty and momentousness of the occasion for Beijing. While this was a relatively unemotional, tactical "major new turn in international relations" for Nixon and Kissinger, it was "no less than a personal, intellectual, and emotional drama . . . of philosophical contradictions" involving "profound moral adjustment" for the Chinese.[9] These Chinese veteran leaders of the Long March, the Great Leap Forward, and the Cultural Revolution were now talking to the "arch-capitalists" even as a "war of liberation" was being fought at their southern borders. They were in "anguish." To Kissinger, the fact that the Chinese leaders were willing to contemplate the prospect of "friendship and cooperation" with the United States in spite of this "wide chasm of ideology and isolation" indicated their seriousness and sincerity.[10]

Kissinger was fundamentally convinced that hardened ideologues like Mao and Zhou could execute a *volte face* of this magnitude because of

---

[7] In fact, in May 1971 the Chinese Politburo established eight principles to guide dealings with the United States, which included requirements that a deadline be set for the withdrawal of U.S. troops from Taiwan; U.S. recognition of the PRC as the sole legitimate government of China; and the Chinese position that U.S. armed forces should be removed from Indochina, Korea, Japan, and Southeast Asia in order to ensure peace in the region. A bilateral nonaggression agreement was not contemplated, and the Politburo seemed prepared to view normalization of relations as a longer-term possibility, if and when Washington agreed to meet its conditions on Taiwan. See Zhang, "The Changing International Scene," p. 74. The Taiwan issue is discussed in detail in Chapter 8.

[8] NSC, "POLO – Scope Paper," pp. 2–6.

[9] "My Talks with Chou En-lai," pp. 6; also Kissinger to RN, "My October China Visit: The Atmospherics," 29 October 1971, Box 851, NSF, NPM, pp. 7–8.

[10] "My Talks with Chou En-lai," p. 6.

his belief that the Chinese leaders' pragmatic, realist character had been brought to the fore by the direct Soviet threat at their northern border. In his report to Nixon, Kissinger affirmed this "realist" identity of the Chinese leaders he had met. They were not seeking a rapprochement with the United States because they had suddenly changed their ideology or attitudes.[11] These remained dangerous men: "they do not wish us well"; they are "fanatically tough" propagators of a "distasteful" ideology. In dealing with them, the "risks will be great." On the other hand, these negative aspects proved the hardheaded, interest-driven motivation for the rapprochement. For, as Kissinger pointed out, the present generation of Chinese leaders understood "big conceptions"; they were "deeply worried about the Soviet threat to their national integrity . . . and see in us a balancing force against the USSR." Also, "they actually do appreciate the balancing role we play in Asia."[12]

A "Principled" Leadership

Apart from the strategic vision that allowed them to move beyond ideology to reach out to the United States, the Chinese leaders' grasp of the "big" issues was also reflected in their qualities as dialogue partners. Kissinger was most impressed with their negotiating style; they displayed a "largeness of spirit," were "matter-of-fact," "concentrated on essentials," and eschewed the "ploymanship, rigidity and bullying" associated with the Soviets.[13] During the July trip, he did not take to heart various disconcerting performances, such as when Zhou appeared to draw back from a presidential visit by suggesting that they should first establish diplomatic relations, or when the Chinese disagreed on who had initially suggested the summit.[14] He was also ready to overlook the "fits and starts" in the process of negotiating a joint announcement at the end of the visit, during

---

[11] However, for a discussion of the ways in which Beijing's ideological boundaries were shifting in accompaniment to the opening to the United States, see Chen, *Mao's China and the Cold War*, pp. 238–44. Chen argues that although geopolitics and security concerns were vital to Beijing's decision, the rapprochement was pursued at a time when the status of Mao's revolution was in decline in the wake of the Cultural Revolution. This facilitated certain "subtle structural changes" in ideology that accompanied the rapprochement, such as the radical redefinition of the concept of "imperialism" that represented Moscow as having replaced Washington as the "bastion of reactionary forces in the world."

[12] "My Talks with Chou En-lai," pp. 7, 10.

[13] Ibid., pp. 2, 5.

[14] Memcon, 10 July 1971, 12.10–6pm, Box 851, NSF, NPM, pp. 5, 13–19, 33–5; Kissinger to RN, "My Talks with Chou Enlai," p. 8. In both cases, Kissinger had been obliged to play a cool hand and suggest the postponement of the summit if the Chinese were not ready.

which the Chinese drafters did not turn up for hours, obliging him to carry out negotiations in the early hours of the morning. Instead of seeing these as calculated pressure tactics, Kissinger attributed the problems to the fact that "it is hard for life-long revolutionaries to act against their own principles, and we must be exceptionally careful not to drive them away." Kissinger also observed to Nixon that once they had reached basic agreement, most of the negotiation about the announcement was "free of the pettiness and elbowing we have experienced with the Russians."[15]

The Chinese style came across more strongly during Kissinger's second trip to Beijing in October 1971, a key purpose of which was to negotiate the details of the joint communiqué that would be issued at the end of the upcoming summit. In his report of the painful process – they exchanged seven drafts during eleven hours of negotiations over two and a half days, during which the American party was obliged to postpone its departure twice – Kissinger made clear how "tough and skillful but also reasonable and broad in outlook" Zhou was. Apart from the tricky issue of Taiwan, Kissinger informed Nixon that Zhou was able to "empathize" with Washington's difficulties and was "restrained" in presenting Chinese requirements. As a result, the Chinese draft read "very mild[ly] in comparison to standard Maoist expressions."[16]

This "principled" style was reflected most clearly in the structure of the Shanghai Communiqué itself. During the October 1971 trip, Kissinger initially proposed what he admitted was a "conventional" draft, designed to "glide over" differences while stressing "fuzzy areas of agreement." Zhou had rejected the American approach as one that submerged differences in "banality," a document of the type that the Soviets would "sign but neither mean nor observe." He insisted that the Chinese, who kept their promises, were not afraid to state disagreements. Otherwise, given the well-known differences between the two sides, the communiqué would have a blatantly "untruthful appearance."[17] The Chinese side introduced an alternative model by which each party would state separately its stances on various international issues, highlighting areas of agreement where they existed.[18]

---

[15] Ibid., pp. 8–10. On the use of deadlines as a calculated pressure tactic in Chinese negotiating behavior, see Richard Solomon, *Chinese Negotiating Behavior: Pursuing Interests through 'Old Friends'* (Washington, DC, 1999), pp. 143–7.

[16] Kissinger to RN, "My October China Visit: Drafting the Communiqué," n.d., Box 846, NSF, NPM, pp. 7–8.

[17] Ibid., p. 1–2.

[18] Marshall Green had made a similar suggestion a month before that the United States and China issue "separate, simultaneous public statements" of their respective minimum

In his post-trip report, Kissinger enthused that this was an ideal solution; it would be an "honorable" document in which the two sides "vigorously and inoffensively" set forth their differing views. It reflected the "basic reality" that there were fundamental differences between Beijing and Washington, but also that they did share certain common interests. This would indicate "both realism and forward movement" and would serve to reassure each party's friends and allies.[19] Kissinger observed to Nixon that such a communiqué would portray the Chinese and American leaders as statesmen who "stuck by their principles but had the largeness of perspective to move relations forward despite profound disagreements."[20]

Indeed, Kissinger and Nixon emphasized throughout this opening period the importance of sticking to principles in dealing with the Chinese. Even as he stressed the ideological dilemma that the Chinese leaders faced in opening up to the Americans, Kissinger was acutely aware of similar difficulties that the Nixon administration would have in justifying the China opening to conservative domestic constituencies and allies. Hence he had told Zhou in his opening statement that "as we move to formalize these contacts... we must both be true to our principles, because neither of us can play a responsible world role or build a lasting peace if we abandon our principles."[21] For the United States, this pertained particularly to the central issue of Taiwan. In the background paper prepared prior to the July trip, Kissinger's staff had characterized their recommended approach to the issue as a "principled" one – Kissinger would have to tell the Chinese that U.S. ties with the ROC could not lightly be set aside; while the Nixon administration understood that to Beijing, Taiwan was a part of China, "the US as a great nation simply will not sell out its friends."[22] The principle in question was a great power's credibility, which Kissinger found that the Chinese leaders shared. For instance, in spite of Kissinger's gentle entreaties, Zhou repeatedly insisted that Beijing could not negotiate on behalf of, or seek to influence, Hanoi regarding a settlement of the Vietnam War. Beijing would not "trade in principles" when it came to its support for allies such as North Vietnam and North

positions on the Taiwan question. See Green to Rogers, "President's Visit to China – Scope Paper," "Suggested Negotiating Position on Taiwan," 25 September 1971, Box 2696, SNF(1970–3), RG59, NA. This was the second time that State had made this suggestion; it was first put forward for a Warsaw meeting in 1961. See Emb/Warsaw to DoS, "The 104th Warsaw Talks," 18 April 1961, *FRUS 1961–3*, XXII, p. 52n.

[19] Kissinger, "My October China Visit: Drafting the Communiqué," pp. 6–7.
[20] Ibid., p. 1.
[21] Memcon, 9 July 1971, p. 6.
[22] NSC, "POLO – Taiwan," 3 July 1971, Box 850, NSF, NPM, p. 1.

Korea.[23] As Kissinger noted, this line was consistent with Beijing's "virtuous stance of championing the cause of smaller nations and re-fusing to be a superpower with its characteristics of bullying and over-involvement."[24]

On the issue of Taiwan, though, Beijing's emphasis on basic princi-ples helped to pave the way for the modus vivendi sought by Nixon and Kissinger. In his first conversation with Zhou in July, Kissinger set out the Nixon administration's "principles" on Taiwan, which the Chinese could "count on": the United States would remove the two-thirds of its forces on Taiwan related to the Vietnam War within a specified time af-ter the war ended; it would reduce the other forces on Taiwan "as our relations improve"; it would not advocate a "two Chinas" solution or a "one China, one Taiwan" solution to the political future of Taiwan; and it would not support the Taiwan Independence Movement. However, he drew a distinction between these fundamental principles and the issue of the "timing of political steps."[25] He had told Zhou frankly that there was "no possibility" of Washington extending formal recognition to the PRC as the sole legitimate government of China during Nixon's first term in office, although this could probably be accomplished fairly early in his second term. Zhou proved amenable, stating that the exact timing for recognition could be discussed later. He only insisted that the "general di-rection," the fact that the United States was "willing to move towards the establishment of normal relations," should be established.[26] By October, Kissinger reported to Nixon that the Chinese approach distinguished be-tween "principle" and "policy execution" – they "had to have" principles such as troop withdrawals and sovereignty over Taiwan, but they did not insist on deadlines.[27]

Finally, Kissinger judged that the Chinese leaders' "principled" con-duct would extend to trustworthiness and reliability in developing the new relationship. He assured Nixon that the Chinese could be expected to be "meticulous" in their diplomacy and in keeping agreements.[28] These

[23] Memcon, 9 July 1971, pp. 34–8; 10 July 1971, 12.10–6pm, p. 27; 21 October 1971, 4.42–7.17pm, pp. 10, 18; 22 October 1971, 4.15–8.28pm, pp. 7, 16, Box 851, NSF, NPM.
[24] Kissinger to RN, "My October China Visit: Discussions of the Issues," Box 851, NSF, NPM, p. 3.
[25] Memcon, 9 July 1971, pp. 12–15.
[26] Memcon, 9 July 1971, pp. 14–16; 10 July 1971, 12.10–6pm, p. 16.
[27] Kissinger, "My October China Visit: Drafting the Communiqué," p. 5.
[28] Ibid., pp. 5–6; Memcon, 11 July 1971, 10.35–11.55am, pp. 7–8. As Kissinger told Zhou, in the course of the SALT negotiations the Soviets had tried to use a different English announcement from the Americans, saying that it was their translation from the Russian text.

were "men of honor" with whom one could make a "gentlemen's agreement."[29] Part of this confident assessment might have arisen from the
fact that Kissinger and Nixon needed the Chinese leaders to trust them
in turn – as they told Zhou, because of domestic politics the American
side could "do more privately than we can say publicly."[30] For instance,
the commitment not to support the independence movement on Taiwan,
the agreement to withdraw troops related to the defense of the ROC as
U.S.–China relations improved, and the promise to normalize relations
in the first half of Nixon's second term were made in secret. Thus, while
Kissinger was assuring Zhou that "any agreement that he makes with us
will be kept in the letter and in the spirit," he could hardly have wanted
anything but reciprocity from the Chinese.[31] So it was that in his first private meeting with Zhou,[32] Nixon rather sycophantically told Zhou that
"[i]n the eight years in which I was Vice President, in the three years I
have been President, and in the six years I was member of Congress, I
have never seen a government more meticulous in keeping confidences
and more meticulous in keeping agreements than your government."[33]
This was regardless of the fact that the two sides had at that point not
come to any concrete agreement on which the Chinese could keep or not
keep their word. It also ignored the consideration that such remarkable
confidentiality was bought at the price of the iron control wielded by an
authoritarian communist state.

Chinese Statesmanship

Kissinger's contemporaneous report of his secret meetings in Beijing in
July 1971 is a more telling account of his awe at the event and his early admiration for the Chinese leaders he encountered than his memoir written
eight years later. It is clear that a large element of his positive assessment of
the Chinese was derived from the deep impression left by Zhou Enlai. The
nature of the secret high-level meeting determined from the outset that the
new relationship would depend in large measure upon the personalities

---

[29] Memcon, 11 July 1971, 10.35–11.55am, p. 8.
[30] Memcon, 10 July 1971, 12.10–6pm, p. 2.
[31] Memcon, 9 July 1971, p. 22.
[32] Memcon, 22 February 1972, Box 87, POF, NPM, p. 4. Transcripts of the 1972
Nixon–Zhou talks can also be accessed on the National Security Archive website:
<http://www.gwu.edu/~nsarchiv/nsa/publications/DOC_readers/kissinger/nixzhou/>.
[33] He repeated it in the penultimate meeting – memcon, 26 February 1972, Box 87, POF,
NPM, p. 8.

involved. Moreover, Kissinger found Zhou particularly impressive because he thought him a statesman and a realist of deep convictions and firm principles.[34] Zhou was the most cosmopolitan of the Chinese leaders of the time, and he remains one of the most highly respected modern Chinese leaders today. It is not surprising that Kissinger was impressed by his urbanity and eloquence; his command of philosophy, history, and current events in the United States; and by his remarkable personal modesty, hospitality, consideration, and "easy egalitarianism."[35]

At the same time, the China opening was significantly personality-driven as a result of the distinctive Chinese negotiating style. Richard Solomon, who began his involvement with China as a member of Kissinger's staff in 1973, has pointed out that the "cardinal principle" for Chinese leaders in dealing with foreigners was to establish deep personal bonds or *guanxi* with their counterparts, admitting the outsider to "guest membership" in Chinese society and entertaining him "with informality and frankness." This represented a conscious cultivation of personal and political stakes, which could then be used as a "halter" in pressing for the development of the relationship.[36] Of course, this process works both ways. For instance, by October 1971 Kissinger was able confidently to observe that the personal political stakes Mao and Zhou had invested in the opening to the United States made it vitally important for them, too, that Nixon's summit be seen to succeed.[37]

In summing up his impressions of the Chinese in July, Kissinger was careful to acknowledge that the leaders he met were probably unique – they were "the cream of their current elite," and it was "inconceivable that the next generation . . . will produce leaders tempered by such experiences." On the other hand, Kissinger claimed that almost all the positive qualities he observed were "Chinese, not communist, and can be found in Taiwan or Singapore or San Francisco." Kissinger's key point was that Zhou and the other leaders in Beijing were more Chinese than they were

---

[34] Nixon called Zhou China's "Metternich, Molotov, and Dulles" – see *Leaders*, p. 231. UN Secretary General Dag Hammarskjold remarked that when he first met Zhou during the Korean War peace talks, he had felt "uncivilized in the presence of a civilized man." Related by Charles Freeman, oral history interview, in Tucker, *China Confidential*, p. 252.

[35] See Dick Wilson, *Chou: The Story of Zhou Enlai* (London, 1984); Ronald Keith, *The Diplomacy of Zhou Enlai* (London, 1989); and Wang Junyan, *Da Waijiaojia Zhou Enlai* [Zhou Enlai: The Great Diplomat] (Beijing, 1998).

[36] NSC background paper, "Chinese Principles and Assumptions," ca. February 1972, Box 847, NSF, NPM; Solomon, *Chinese Negotiating Behavior*, pp. 20–2, 100–4.

[37] Kissinger, "My October China Visit: The Atmospherics," 29 October 1971, p. 8.

communist. In spite of the ideological antipathy between Washington and Beijing, the current Chinese leadership was realist, primarily motivated by national security concerns, and possessed an array of good qualities that would allow the two sides to work together. Taken together with his calculatedly unfavorable comparison between the Soviets and the Chinese, Kissinger was also articulating, in his by now authoritative voice and actions, the idea that the Chinese and Soviet communists could be dealt with not as a united bloc but as separate and even antithetical states. This coincided with what he told Zhou was Nixon's own policy of dealing not with communism "as an abstract crusade" but rather with "specific communist states on the basis of their specific actions toward us."[38]

In summary, the image of the Chinese as presented by Kissinger was that they were serious and sincere in seeking rapprochement; that they were motivated by national security concerns and were pragmatic realists who shared Nixon's strategic vision; that they were "principled" and reliable; and that their leaders were worthy of respect and admiration. These qualities marked China out as a potentially friendly nation and significantly reinforced the geopolitical opportunity for a concrete change in U.S.–China relations moving toward friendship and cooperation. Having ascertained that the Chinese, like the Americans, desired a more constructive and stable relationship, Kissinger and Nixon now had to formulate the details of this new relationship.

NEW IDENTITY, NEW INTERESTS: ARTICULATING THE COMMON GROUND FOR A NEW RELATIONSHIP

The process of making a friend out of an implacable enemy involves more than simply re-representing the other. Analyses of the "images" held of one party by another suggest personal, subjective perceptions of others, which may be altered as a result of interaction, changing behavior, or external circumstances. This study of the U.S.–China rapprochement in *practice* examines the intersubjective process by which the U.S. side not only reconstructed images of the Chinese, but also actively tried to bring the two sides' perceptions of each other's characteristics and key interests into line with the desired new relationship. In this vein, Kissinger's and Nixon's dialogues with the Chinese leaders contained two key elements: clarification and persuasion.

---

[38] Memcon, 9 July 1971, p. 22.

First, direct talks crucially allowed the two sides to articulate and ascertain certain mutual contextual beliefs. For instance, it was vital that they should confirm that among the various "realist" power political options available given the strategic situation, they had both chosen the same one. For the United States, this meant that it would not side with Moscow against Beijing but rather would be even-handed and, in the limiting case, prevent a Soviet attack on China. Beijing, on the other hand, had to demonstrate to Kissinger and Nixon that it had decided to improve relations with the United States rather than make concessions to, or conciliate with, Moscow. This amounted to a mutual assurance that they interpreted the material context in similar ways in order to derive common interests, which in turn would allow mutual understanding, reduction of bilateral tension, and provide the focus for coordination needed to develop a new relationship. Second, the dialogues consisted of a significant degree of advocacy in the areas of outstanding disagreement, such as Vietnam, Japan, and Taiwan. The Americans had to convince the Chinese that they shared some common interests even on these issues, in the process of defining the common ground and the norms on which to base the new relationship and by which to conduct bilateral affairs. Together, these elements constituted the process of constructing a structure of knowledge that set out shared interests and motivations and the "principles" that would govern action in the relationship.[39]

China: A Great Power

Kissinger recognized, as did the State Department, that one of China's key political aims in the rapprochement was to be accepted as a legitimate great power. Beijing anticipated that the presidential visit would constitute "spectacular proof" that China had "arrived at great power status" and was "unequivocally one of the 'big five' [nations]."[40] As part of his effort to establish the "right," "positive" climate at their first meeting, therefore, Kissinger hastened to assure Zhou that Washington certainly viewed China as a major power with which the United States would deal on a basis of "equality and mutual respect." On account of its "achievements, tradition, ideology, and strength," it was time for China to "participate

---

[39] For a constructivist account of how, through their speech acts, actors create the foundations upon which they erect new political structures and institutional arrangements, see Nicholas Onuf, "Constructivism: A User's Manual," in Kubálková et al., eds., *International Relations in a Constructed World.*

[40] NSC, "Polo – Summit," n.d., pp. 1, 4.

on the basis of equality in all matters affecting the peace of Asia and . . . the world."[41]

At the same time, Nixon was conveying this message in the public realm, first in his second foreign policy report issued in February 1971, and then in a speech in Kansas City during Kissinger's trip, when he referred to China as potentially one of the five major world economic powers.[42] Later, in person, Nixon pointed out that China, like the United States, was "by destiny . . . a world power."[43] The Chinese leaders appreciated Nixon's and Kissinger's deliberate emphasis on the two sides' treating each other as equals; Zhou affirmed that "equality" and "the principle of reciprocity" were of first importance in their dealings.[44] However, he added that Beijing sought equality not in the sense of great power status – China was "comparatively not developed" and even with economic development was determined "absolutely not [to] become a superpower" and not to "spread our hands all over the world." On the contrary, Beijing sought a greater international justice whereby "all countries, big or small, [would] be equal" – that is, without the hegemony of big powers. As Kissinger noted, this was in line with Beijing's self-identification as the champion of small and underdeveloped nations.[45]

There was one obvious danger in playing up the image of China as a great power in Beijing. As Kissinger's staff pointed out, his trip and a presidential visit were bound to "gratify the 'Middle Kingdom' instincts which the Chinese leaders of today unquestionably share with their predecessors." However, the image of these modern-day "imperialist barbarian[s]" bringing tribute to Beijing was a political and symbolic price that Washington would have to pay. As a superpower, the United States could afford some magnanimity.[46] It would seem that Nixon agreed, for in his personal preparatory notes in advance of the February 1972 summit, in a culmination of what the "Resurgent Power" proponents had advocated in the late 1960s, he wrote that he would treat Mao "as Emperor."[47] In any case, those who brought tribute were historically rewarded with

[41] Ibid., p. 8; Memcon, 9 July 1971, p. 4.
[42] RN, "Second Annual Report to Congress on US Foreign Policy," 25 February 1971; "Remarks to Midwestern News Media Executives," Kansas City, Missouri, 6 July 1971, *PPP:RN 1971*, pp. 219–20, 806. Zhou made a point of noting the latter, mentioning it to Kissinger in the course of their talks – memcon, 9 November 1971, p. 36.
[43] RN–Zhou memcon, 21 February 1972, pp. 6, 9.
[44] Memcon, 9 July 1971, p. 7.
[45] Ibid., p. 37; 10 July 1971, 12.10–6pm, p. 3; 11 July 1971, 10.35–11.55am, pp. 16–17.
[46] NSC, "Polo – Scope Paper," pp. 1–2.
[47] RN, handwritten notes, 18 February 1972, Box 7, President's Personal Files (PPF), NPM.

even more valuable gifts, and Washington expected Beijing to be willing to pay a price for this symbolic gain. Kissinger was also convinced that its prestige value made the summit more important to the Chinese than to the United States – the Chinese wanted it more, and this could be used to U.S. advantage in pressing for a meeting that would serve its objectives.[48]

China: The Former Enemy

In itself, the recognition of China as a great power to be related to on "equal" terms did not suggest that U.S.–China relations would necessarily be friendly. In addition to giving the Chinese leaders "face" by demonstrating appreciation of their nation's international status and influence, therefore, Kissinger had to convey to Zhou the Nixon administration's view that the PRC was no longer an enemy. Specifically, because Washington was not opposed to Beijing and did not regard it as an aggressive, implacable foe with necessarily conflicting interests, the United States would not cooperate with China's other enemies to attack it and indeed would undertake not to work against Beijing's interests.

Addressing himself to what Washington perceived as Beijing's key concern about encirclement and collusion, Kissinger stated as his first substantial point in the opening meeting with Zhou: "we will never collude with other countries against the [PRC], either with our allies or . . . opponents."[49] When Zhou later spoke about Chinese war preparations and the worst-case scenario that China "would be carved up once again" by the united forces of the United States, the USSR, and Japan, Kissinger assured him that there was "no possibility" of any such action. Indeed, in a remarkable statement, Kissinger told Zhou that it would be inconceivable for the United States to encourage or cooperate with another power to destroy China, since – apart from the Taiwan issue, which he fully expected to be resolved in the "relatively near future" – the United States and China had "*no conflicting interests at all.*"[50] Indeed, "a strong and developing [PRC] poses no threat to any essential US interest."[51]

The reasoning was fleshed out by Nixon when he met Zhou and Mao the following February. Fundamentally, Nixon pointed out, the United States and China posed no threat to each other or to each other's key interests: they did not "threaten each other's territories," and neither

---

[48] NSC, "Polo – Summit," p. 5.
[49] Memcon, 9 July 1971, p. 6.
[50] Memcon, 10 July 1971, 12.10–6pm, pp. 7, 28. Emphasis mine.
[51] Memcon, 9 July 1971, p. 6.

wanted to "dominate the world." Therefore, they could find "common ground, despite our differences, to build a world structure in which both can be safe to develop in our own ways."[52] More basically, Kissinger also earnestly tried to reconstruct the expansionist, aggressive image that Washington had previously held of Beijing. He recounted to Zhou how he had changed his mind about the Chinese being the aggressors in the Sino-Soviet border clashes in the summer of 1969 when he noticed that the incidents took place near a Soviet supply point, not a Chinese one.[53] He even ventured the questionable statement that "we believe a strong China is not expansionist because this is your tradition" – presumably referring to Beijing's historical practice of tributary relations with smaller neighbors rather than direct military conquest – but was immediately corrected by Zhou, who pointed out that China did have an "expansionist tradition" and had "committed aggression" against Vietnam, Burma, and Korea in the past.[54]

Nevertheless, Kissinger asserted that now, in "relations among large countries," the United States will be "your *supporter* and not your opponent." As evidence of this, he was authorized to extend the president's assurance that Washington would not take any "major steps affecting your interests without discussing them with you and taking your views into account." Specifically, he was prepared to provide any information Beijing might wish to have regarding "any bilateral negotiations we are having with the Soviet Union on such issues as SALT, so as to alleviate any concerns you might have." Washington would also try to conduct these talks "in a way that ... do[es] not increase the opportunity for military pressures against you."[55] Furthermore, the Nixon administration was prepared to make with Beijing as well any arms control agreement that it concluded with Moscow, particularly the agreements on accidental war and a hotline. The Chinese politely declined these offers.[56]

At the same time, however, Kissinger and Nixon made clear to the Chinese leaders at the opening stages of the rapprochement that treating China "equally" also meant that Washington would be even-handed in

---

[52] Memcon, 21 February 1972, in Burr, *Kissinger Transcripts* (New York, 1999), pp. 63–4.

[53] Memcon, 10 July 1971, 11.20–11.50pm, p. 4.

[54] Memcon, 9 July 1971, p. 42. Ironically, given Kissinger's original attempt to shift the focus away from the United States' more contentious recent relations with the communist regime by alluding to China's ancient history, Zhou pointedly attributed China's current nonaggressive philosophy to the Maoist system and ideals.

[55] Memcon, 10 July 1971, 12.10–6pm, pp. 28–9; 9 July 1971, p. 6. Emphasis mine.

[56] Memcon, 11 July 1971, 10.35–11.55am, p. 8; 22 October 1971, pp. 32–3.

developing both U.S.–PRC and U.S.–USSR relations. As Kissinger's staff expressed it in a briefing paper for the October trip, Washington needed to make clear that it had too much "big concrete business" to do with the Soviets, which would affect stability in many parts of the world, to move to an "overt pro-PRC policy."[57] As Kissinger told Zhou, in contrast to concrete superpower negotiations, Washington and Beijing still had broad "political issues" to settle.[58]

During his October trip, Kissinger delivered a stronger message to the Chinese that the United States would continue to negotiate with the Soviets even though there might be unintended negative side effects for Beijing. This was probably because Washington found, in the wake of the announcement of Kissinger's secret July trip to Beijing and the coming summit, that the Soviets were responding to the Sino-American rapprochement by being more forthcoming about the U.S.–USSR summit and other negotiations, such as those over Berlin. Kissinger informed Zhou that "we recognize that when we make a settlement with the Soviet Union . . . this can have the objective consequence of increasing your problems" – that is, of freeing Soviet hands to concentrate on the East. However, the Nixon administration did not negotiate with the Soviets for this purpose; Washington fully intended to "pursue our interest with Moscow while we try to improve our dialogue with Peking," but "we cannot be held accountable when the objective consequences of such dealings" complicated China's problems.[59] The subtext, as Kissinger's aide Winston Lord later explained, was: "We are making some progress with the Soviets, and you Chinese should be sure that you keep up with us and improve relations with us, so that we don't get ahead of you in relations with the Russians."[60] This was, of course, the exercise of triangular politics – my Option 3 – derived from the interest-based realist rationale of Nixonian foreign policy.

China and the United States: Common Interests, Potential Partners

As presented to the Chinese leaders, the Nixon administration's foreign policy strategy consisted of three key elements: it was consciously realist and therefore based on the assessment of national interest; it was

---

[57] NSC briefing paper, "Polo II – Soviet Union," 7 October 1971, p. 14.
[58] Memcon, 10 July 1971, 12.10–6pm, p. 36.
[59] Memcon, 22 October 1971, p. 30; "My October China Visit: Discussions of the Issues," p. 29. Zhou's phlegmatic response was that "it does not matter."
[60] Oral history interview, in Tucker, *China Confidential*, p. 278.

not aimed at fostering conflict among the major powers and would thus be even-handed; but it also was anti-hegemonic and so would prefer a strong PRC, which could help to act as a counterweight against the Soviet Union. Within this framework, Nixon and Kissinger sought to persuade the Chinese that Washington and Beijing did have significant common ground on a host of major international issues on which a strategic basis for their new relationship could be built.

To begin with, it was crucial for Beijing to know that the American leaders shared its pragmatism and realism. At the February summit, Nixon discussed with Zhou the factors that had brought the two sides together. While the public line emphasized the "basic friendship between our peoples," they both knew that "the basis on which an established relationship must rest" could not be "friendship alone." In Nixon's legalistic parlance, "a contract was only as good as the will of the parties concerned to keep it"; "as friends, we could agree to some fine language, but unless our national interests would be served by carrying out agreements set forward in that language, it would mean very little."[61]

In the course of the dialogues in 1971 and 1972, Kissinger and Nixon presented to the Chinese two key areas in which their national interests coincided: the need to restrain Soviet and Japanese militarism and expansionism, and the need to contain creeping Soviet influence in Asia. As Nixon put it, China and the United States shared these congruent interests in terms of "national security," not in terms of "philosophy" or "friendship."[62] He added that "[w]e are not... being philanthropic.... it is in the interest of the US that China be a strong independent country and that China's neighbors not engage in carving it up."[63] Thus, "as we look at the... balance of power of the world, there is no reason for the PRC and the US to be enemies, and there are many reasons why [we] should work together for a... peaceful world."[64]

On the other hand, Nixon's China policy was "not an attempt to create a power combination."[65] Working for peace using triangular politics meant that even as the United States was absolutely not looking to collude with the USSR against China, neither was it seeking a Sino-American condominium against the Soviets. The United States was not looking for Sino-Soviet conflict, because upsetting the balance of power would cause

[61] Memcon, 22 February 1972, Box 87, POF, NPM, pp. 8–9.
[62] Ibid., pp. 9–11.
[63] Memcon, 23 February 1972, p. 20.
[64] Memcon, 21 February 1972, Box 87, POF, NPM, p. 5.
[65] Kissinger to Zhou, 20 October 1971, p. 3.

the resulting conflict to spread.[66] Thus, "w[e] want good relations with
the PRC and we want good relations with the Soviet Union. And we
would welcome better relations between the Soviet Union and the PRC."
Nixon's principle was that "any nation can be a friend of the US without being someone else's enemy."[67] This was rhetoric that the Chinese
shared: Zhou responded that "we don't have the least opposition to the
improvement of relations between the US and Soviet Union" either.[68]

The Soviet Union: Common Adversary. While it was certainly true that
Washington sought good relations with both Moscow and Beijing,
Nixon's statement that he wanted better Sino-Soviet relations was not entirely accurate. According to the model of triangular politics as set forth
in Kissinger's memoirs, while the United States did not seek a Sino-Soviet
war, it needed at least some frigidity in Sino-Soviet relations in order for
the strategy of parallel détente to work. The aim of the policy was to create
a power equilibrium within the triumvirate, managed essentially by the
United States' "maintaining closer relations with each side than they did
with each other."[69] This would work only so long as the Chinese regarded
the Soviets as a greater threat than the Americans, and vice versa.

In his memoirs, Kissinger states that he did not have to wield any
"card" to try to influence Chinese foreign policy decisions; the PRC simply cooperated with the United States out of the obvious coincidence of
interests.[70] The following discussion shows, by contrast, that Kissinger
and Nixon felt it necessary to devote considerable effort and time in their
talks with the Chinese leaders to building up the image of the Soviet Union
as a shared adversary – but, crucially, as a greater threat to the Chinese.
This was done in three ways: by emphasizing Soviet aggressiveness in general and the Soviet threat to the PRC in particular; by explaining that the
United States perceived Soviet militarism as a menace to international stability and U.S. security; and by offering Beijing various means of support
in preparing for a Soviet attack.

---

[66] Memcon, 23 February 1972, p. 20.
[67] Memcon, 25 February 1972, Box 87, POF, NPM, p. 6. This was also Nixon's public
line when he announced Kissinger's secret trip in July 1971 – see RN, television address,
15 July 1971, *PPP:RN 1971*, p. 819.
[68] Memcon, 22 February 1972, p. 18; also Zhou to Kissinger, memcon, 20 October 1971,
p. 21.
[69] Kissinger, *White House Years*, p. 1076; Henry Kissinger, *Years of Upheaval* (London, 1982),
p. 705.
[70] From Kissinger's realist systemic interest-driven account, the card, if it existed, was automatic – it "played itself" – *Diplomacy*, p. 729.

In his preparatory notes for the February 1972 summit, Nixon wrote, as the first item under the heading "How can we work together?," "Your opponents are ours." This was an obvious reference to the Soviets, against whom Washington and Beijing had to "maintain [the] balance of power" and "restrain their expansion."[71] In the earlier dialogues, Kissinger was probably inclined to emphasize the Soviet menace because the Chinese were relatively taciturn on the subject. In the July talks, Zhou referred obliquely to "our northern neighbor" and "the other superpower" but did not initiate any discussion on the issue, except to say that Beijing would prefer it if Nixon went to Moscow before coming to China, as it did not want to "deliberately create tensions."[72] This was the only sign of Chinese disquiet over their confrontation with the Soviets.[73]

However, Kissinger put Zhou's reticence down to a sense of "face." After the October trip, he informed Nixon that "a deep and abiding Chinese hatred of the Russians" came through repeatedly in his conversations with Zhou, even though Zhou had placed the Soviet Union last on a list of six key issues on the substantive agenda for the talks and had declared that Beijing was not opposed to U.S.–USSR relations. Kissinger noted that these remarks were "for the record" and that the Chinese were displaying bravado in the face of the Soviet threat.[74] He made it a point to highlight to the Chinese the Soviet menace, which was directed mainly at them. As a member of the U.S. party noted, even at the public banquet Kissinger used "anti-Soviet play" and deliberately "always [used] Soviet examples as bad guys."[75] In private, he spelled out to Zhou that in the wake of the Sino-American rapprochement, the fact that Moscow had reached agreement with Washington on Berlin and SALT, and was pushing for a European Security Community, indicated its "great desire to free itself in Europe so it can concentrate on other areas" – specifically, in the eastern direction, toward China.[76] Kissinger supplemented this message via the Paris channel in August, when he informed Ambassador Huang Zhen that, in bilateral negotiations about an agreement to prevent accidental nuclear war, the Soviets had tried unsuccessfully to get the United States to agree to make the provisions of the agreement applicable to other countries, which

[71] RN, handwritten China notes, 21 February 1972, Box 7, PPF, NPM.
[72] Memcon, 10 July 1971, 12.10–6pm, p. 35.
[73] Kissinger, "My Talks with Chou En-Lai," 17 July 1971, p. 8.
[74] Kissinger, "My October China Visit: Discussions of the Issues," pp. 5, 7, 29.
[75] Dwight Chapin, "Zhou – dinner 10/24," 25 October 1971, Box 27, Chapin Files, NPM.
[76] Memcon, 22 October 1971, pp. 29–30.

would oblige the United States to report on nuclear events in China and France.[77]

In January 1972, Kissinger's deputy Alexander Haig headed an advance team to China for a "rehearsal" of the president's visit, and the White House tried to use Haig's brusque military style to convey more forcefully this message about the Soviet threat. For instance, Haig told Zhou that in the wake of the South Asian crisis, Washington assessed that Soviet policy on the subcontinent had undergone a "precipitous" shift, from one content with keeping India and Pakistan divided to one of greater involvement in order to "encircle the PRC with unfriendly states." Evidence that Moscow was stepping up its attempt to encircle China included its recent announcement of support for Bangladesh, its offer of assistance to Pakistan, its increased material support for Hanoi, and Gromyko's planned visit to Japan. Haig explained that the United States objected to these Soviet moves because "we felt that the future viability of the PRC was of the greatest interest to us and a matter of our own national interest." Bluntly, Washington was convinced that the Soviet strategy was first to "neutralize the [PRC] and then turn on us."[78]

To underline the pragmatic interest-driven nature of U.S. policy, Haig employed an appropriate, but perhaps unflattering, analogy: just as Churchill was willing to cooperate with Stalin against the greater danger of Hitler's Germany, Washington felt that the United States and the PRC "must concert at this critical juncture." It was also General Haig's task to make Washington's first substantial offer of cooperation with the PRC against the greater threat of the Soviet Union. He told Zhou that the United States would use its "resources," as it had done during the crisis between India and Pakistan, to attempt to "neutralize" Soviet threats on the PRC's periphery and to "deter threats against the [PRC]."[79] Specifically, the White House would – "unilaterally and without any reciprocity" – provide Beijing with available U.S. strategic and tactical intelligence pertaining to the Soviet threat to China.[80]

---

[77] Memcon, 16 August 1971, Box 330, Lord Files, LOT 77D112, RG59, NA, pp. 4–5. But Garthoff argues that Kissinger misread the Soviet position, which was not intended to be anti-Chinese – see *Détente and Confrontation*, pp. 202, 272.

[78] Zhou–Haig memcon, 3 January 1972, Box 1037, NSF, NPM, pp. 2–4.

[79] U.S. actions during the South Asian crisis are discussed in Chapter 8.

[80] Zhou–Haig memcon, 3 January 1972, p. 6; NSC, talking points for Haig trip, n.d., Box 1037, NSF, NPM, pp. 6–7. Haig's presentation did not go down well. Mao reportedly commented, "To worry about us, [the Americans] are the cat who is crying over the death of a mouse! When [the Soviets] are in Vietnam, they want to surround China from Indochina, and again, when they are in the subcontinent, the Russians want to

Nixon repeated this offer during the February 1972 summit, assuring Zhou that the United States would "oppose" any attempt by the Soviets to engage in "aggressive action" against China.[81] While Nixon did not elaborate on how he intended to oppose potential Soviet aggression, there is documentary evidence for at least one meeting, on 23 February 1972, during which Kissinger – along with his aides Winston Lord, Jonathan Howe, and John Holdridge – briefed Marshal Ye Jianying, the vice chairman of the Military Commission, and Qiao Guanhua, the vice minister of foreign affairs, about the deployment of Soviet forces along the Sino-Soviet border. The briefing included details about ground forces, tactical aircraft and missiles, strategic air defense systems, and strategic attack forces, especially nuclear forces.[82] Kissinger's assistant Robert MacFarlane has revealed that he and other aides provided intelligence briefings to the Chinese on each of Kissinger's subsequent trips to Beijing.[83] Lord confirms that these briefings occurred, but he adds that they were "more a gesture to back up the verbal exchanges than of significant substance"; the main purpose was "to build trust, confidence, a sense of shared danger." There was also a degree of "political symbolism": according to Lord, the White House assumed that the Soviets might well "get to hear of it" and thus, by implication, had regarded this action as a means to further load the "China card."[84] The significance of the intelligence information

encircle China from the subcontinent.... What about Taiwan, the Philippines, and South Korea? Do all these countries need [U.S.] protection? Isn't it dangerous that China's independence and living should be protected by you?" Accordingly, Zhou took umbrage at Haig's remarks, stating that he was "surprised" that the United States seemed to be "all of a sudden express[ing] doubts over China's viability, asserting that it wants to maintain China's independence and viability." Zhou retorted that China would never rely on "external forces" to maintain its independence and viability, since this would make it "a protectorate or a colony." Gong Li, "Chinese Decision Making," pp. 352–3; Hong Zhaohui, "The Role of Individuals in US-China Relations, 1949–1972," in Li Hongshan and Hong Zhaohui, eds., *Image, Perception, and the Making of US-China Relations* (Lanham, 1998), p. 358; Memcon, 7 January 1971, Box 1037, NSF, NPM, pp. 4, 2.
[81] Nixon–Zhou memcon, 23 February 1972, Box 87, POF, NPM, p. 21.
[82] See Nixon–Zhou memcon, 22 February 1972, Box 87, POF, NPM, p. 10; Kissinger–Ye memcon, 23 February 1972, Box 92, NSF, NPM. These documents are also available at <http://www.nsarchive.org/NSAEBB/NSAEBB106/index.htm>.
[83] See Robert MacFarlane, *Special Trust* (New York, 1994), pp. 149–69. MacFarlane writes that apart from detailed briefings about Soviet military dispositions and readiness at the Chinese border, they also provided information on Soviet military aid to North Vietnam and other Third World countries and guerrilla movements.
[84] Author interview with Winston Lord, 7 March 2001, New York. Moscow apparently did learn about the provision of intelligence information: Anatoly Dobrynin, the Soviet ambassador in Washington, told Kissinger in March that Moscow had it from

provided over this period is debatable, as there is little documentary evidence available as yet. However, the fact that in 1972 the White House secretly provided Beijing with regular intelligence information regarding Soviet disposition of forces at the Sino-Soviet border indicates that in spite of their rhetoric about even-handedness, Nixon and Kissinger were prepared covertly to lean toward Beijing in order to strengthen the image of the Soviet Union as a shared adversary. In this sense, they practiced Option 4 – support Beijing against Moscow – to some extent, even short of the exigency of a large-scale Sino-Soviet war, although both Chinese and American rhetoric during the talks subscribed to even-handed dealings within the strategic triangle.

The Chinese were more cautious. Marshal Yeh responded positively to the intelligence briefing, but his remark that the information was "an indication of your wish to improve our relationship" appeared to suggest that the Chinese appreciated it mainly as a demonstration of mutual trust and confidence.[85] Zhou himself was circumspect in response to Nixon's somewhat obvious but indirect references to the Soviet threat,[86] agreeing that the Soviets pursued a "policy of expansion" but insisting that China was willing to solve the boundary dispute and to improve relations with Moscow.[87] He observed that the Soviets were "really very frightened that the US and China are coming closer" and were "a little bit hysterical" regarding the Beijing summit.[88] Zhou's presentation appears to accord with official Chinese accounts, which report that Mao's understanding of the "basic issue" in the Sino-American rapprochement was that "[n]o matter whether it is the United States or China, neither of us could fight simultaneously on two fronts." That is, the Chinese leaders were primarily seeking détente, but not a de facto

Chinese sources that Kissinger had given the Chinese "a complete rundown of the 'dislocation' of Soviet forces on the Chinese border, as well as of the location of Soviet missile installations." Kissinger denied it. See Memcon, 9 March 1972, Box 493, NSF, NPM, p. 3.

[85] Kissinger–Yeh memcon, p. 20.

[86] For instance, Nixon told Mao that the United States and the PRC did not want to dominate each other or to "reach out and control the world," but "this cannot be said of some other nations"; and he observed to Zhou that China was "so significant a power that the Soviet Union has more units on its border with China than it does on the border with Western Europe." RN–Mao memcon, 21 February 1972, in Burr, *Kissinger Transcripts*, p. 64; RN–Zhou memcon, 21 February 1972, p. 10.

[87] Memcon, 23 February 1972, pp. 22–36; Memcon, 25 February 1972, pp. 4–5.

[88] Memcon, 23 February 1972, pp. 30, 36–7. Nixon promised that "we will ... make every effort to see that no pretext will be created by this meeting to indicate we are setting up a condominium against them."

alliance, with the United States in order to concentrate on their main Soviet adversary.[89]

Be that as it may, the Shanghai Communiqué signed at the end of the summit carried clear anti-Soviet overtones. The short list of five issues on which the two sides agreed included the following: "neither should seek hegemony in the Asia-Pacific region, and each is opposed to efforts by any other country or group of countries to establish such hegemony; and neither is prepared to negotiate on behalf of any third party or to enter into agreements or understandings with the other directed at other states."

As Kissinger pointed out in his memoir, this boiled down to an agreement not to cooperate with the Soviet bloc, and to oppose any attempt by any country to dominate Asia. Since the Soviet Union was the only other country capable of such domination, the text suggested that "a tacit alliance to block Soviet expansionism in Asia was coming into being."[90] This reflected the centrality of the Soviet threat to the developing U.S.–PRC relationship, and foreshadowed the way in which Kissinger's progressive construction of this threat would bring the Nixon administration closer to a U.S.–China coalition against the Soviet Union.[91]

Japan: Restraining a Potential Regional Hegemon. In the eyes of the Chinese leaders, however, there was a second potential hegemon in Asia: Japan. At his first meeting with Kissinger, Zhou expressed more concern about the Japanese menace than the Soviet threat. He charged the United States with "rearming the Japanese militarists," asserting that Japan's economic expansion, facilitated by the U.S. defense umbrella, would now "of necessity lead to military expansion." Not only had Japan's defense spending increased dramatically, Tokyo had – in the 1969 Sato communiqué – "openly decreed that Korea, Taiwan and Vietnam are linked to [Japan's] security."[92] Pursuing the encirclement theme, Zhou suggested that the Nixon administration was willing to consider withdrawing troops from

[89] Gong Li, "Chinese Decision Making," p. 353.
[90] Kissinger, *Diplomacy*, p. 728.
[91] The way in which this was subsequently developed is discussed in Chapter 10.
[92] "Joint Communiqué between President Richard Nixon and His Excellency Prime Minister of Japan," 21 November 1969, Box 924, NSF, NPM. The sections to which Zhou referred read: "[Sato] stated that the security of the Republic of Korea was essential to Japan's own security.... [T]he maintenance of peace and security in the Taiwan area was also a most important factor for the security of Japan.... Japan was exploring what role she could play in bringing about stability in the Indochina area."

the region precisely because Japan was strong enough to serve as its "vanguard... in controlling Asian countries."[93]

Thus, Japan appeared to be the most difficult issue of contention. Because the nature of this disagreement extended to the heart of U.S. security policy in Asia as a whole, Kissinger was obliged to work hard during this opening phase to convince Beijing that the U.S.–Japan defense relationship was in the Chinese interest. First, he agreed with Zhou that Japan had militaristic and expansionist tendencies because of its history and economic drive. However, he sought to placate the Chinese leader's concern about collusion using an argument similar to the one employed for the Soviet Union. Drawing on the logic of power balancing, he acknowledged that according to one variant of "the sort of theory which I used to teach," the United States could withdraw from Japan and allow it to rearm, thus leaving Japan and China to "balance each other off," to their mutual disadvantage vis-à-vis the United States. But Kissinger insisted that Washington would not do this, because Japan could repeat its expansionist policies of the 1930s, which would eventually draw the United States and others into a wider war; thus "using Japan against you... would be much too dangerous for both of us."[94]

Instead, Kissinger and Nixon argued that the U.S. defense relationship acted as a restraint on potential Japanese rearmament, military expansion, and nuclear weapons development. Because it provided a defensive shield for Japan, Washington could use its influence to discourage potentially aggressive policies that might be "detrimental to China." On the other hand, if Tokyo should feel "forsaken" by its American ally, it would build up its own military capability. American and Chinese interests were thus "very similar" – neither wanted to see Japan "heavily rearmed."[95] This was particularly true in the case of nuclear weapons, about which Zhou expressed great concern.[96] Accordingly, Kissinger pointed out that "if we were to withdraw, their peaceful nuclear energy program gives them enough plutonium so they could easily build nuclear weapons.... the alternative is really a Japanese nuclear program which would be very much less desirable."[97] Working on this Chinese concern, Nixon reminded himself in preparation for the summit: "Don't say

---

[93] Memcon, 9 July 1971, pp. 29, 37; 10 July 1971, 12.10–6pm, pp. 10–11.

[94] Memcon, 9 July 1971, p. 42.

[95] Ibid.; RN–Zhou memcon, 22 February 1972, p. 12; 23 February 1972, p. 19.

[96] This portion appears to have been sanitized in the transcripts but is reported in Kissinger to RN, "My Talks with Chou En-Lai," p. 15; NSC briefing paper, "Polo II – Japan," p. 2.

[97] Memcon, 21 October 1971, 4.42–7.17pm, p. 24.

'We oppose rearmament of Japan' ... [say instead] 'We oppose [a] nuclear Japan.'"[98]

In the course of the 1971 meetings, Kissinger offered Zhou three U.S. "principles" regarding Japan. First, Washington favored the conventional rearmament of Japan to limits adequate for the defense of the four Japanese islands and "nothing else." Second, it opposed the nuclear armament of Japan. Third, it firmly opposed any military expansion by the Japanese, particularly into Taiwan or Korea.[99] The last point was of special concern to Zhou, who expressed apprehension over potential Japanese intervention in Taiwan during the transition process between U.S. withdrawal and reunification. Zhou saw a "great possibility" that Chiang Kai-shek would approach Japan as an alternative guarantor if he felt the United States to be "unreliable," and cautioned that Washington was responsible for preventing Japan from "meddling" in Taiwan's affairs.[100]

Finally, Kissinger and Nixon argued that the U.S. defense relationship with Japan was to China's advantage because it served to prevent Soviet influence on Tokyo. This reasoning gained credence when, following the announcement of Kissinger's July 1971 trip to Beijing, there was evidence that both Moscow and Beijing were exploiting the uncertainty over U.S.–Japan ties and competing to improve relations with Tokyo. The Soviets invited Japanese cooperation in jointly exploiting Siberian resources, and opened talks with Tokyo on the subject of the disputed Kurile Islands. Beijing, meanwhile, attempted to influence the struggle for a successor to Prime Minister Sato by openly supporting potential candidates who were in favor of establishing diplomatic relations with the PRC on the

[98] RN, handwritten China notes, 18 February 1972. Seymour Hersh has suggested that Nixon went so far as to subtly threaten Beijing that if it did not accede to the continued U.S.–Japan defense relationship, Washington would allow Japan to develop nuclear weapons. See Hersh, *Price of Power*, pp. 380–1. There is as yet no documentary evidence for this, although the declassified transcripts of the dialogues between Kissinger and Nixon and Zhou do contain several sanitized sections within suggestive contexts relating to the reversion of Okinawa and U.S.–Japan defense policy. Michael Schaller also documents some indications that Nixon and Secretary of Defense Melvin Laird had hinted to the Japanese that the United States would favor a nuclear-armed Japan – see "Détente and the Strategic Triangle," in Ross and Jiang, eds., *Re-examining the Cold War*, pp. 365, 377–8.

[99] Memcon, 10 July 1971, 12.10–6pm, p. 27; 22 October 1971, pp. 9, 24. During his visit to China, Nixon took pains to emphasize to Zhou the connection between maintaining the U.S. alliance with and troop presence in Japan, and preventing Japan from interfering in Taiwan or Korea. See RN–Zhou memcon, 23 February 1972, pp. 18–19; and RN–Zhou memcon, 24 February 1972, Box 87, POF, NPM, pp. 12–13.

[100] Memcon, 10 July 1971, 12.10–6pm, pp. 7, 9, 19.

latter's terms.[101] In October, Kissinger was obliged to warn Zhou that Beijing should not attempt to undermine U.S.–Japan relations, not least because of their concerns about Soviet attempts to improve relations with Tokyo.[102] As Nixon put it, "the US can get out of Japanese waters, but others will fish there."[103] Indeed, by February 1972, Chinese attitudes toward Japan appeared to have changed somewhat: Sino-Japanese talks were in the pipeline; the United States had removed nuclear installations from Okinawa; and Zhou admitted that Japanese attention was now not so much on Taiwan or South Korea as on the Kuriles.[104] He told Nixon that Beijing would improve relations with Tokyo; they were pinning their hopes on "the next Japanese government" to establish diplomatic relations and conclude a peace treaty.[105]

Although Zhou did not appear to come around to Kissinger's point of view regarding Japan until later, it was evident even at this opening stage that Chinese concerns about a threatening Soviet Union and a resurgent Japan converged on the conclusion that only the United States was in a position to deter both. This was a point that Kissinger and Nixon made assiduously, against Zhou's accusation that the United States was over-extended and should withdraw its troops from Asia. Nixon told Zhou, "I believe the interests of China as well as the interests of the US urgently require that the US maintains its military establishment at approximately its present levels and that the US...should maintain a military presence in Europe, in Japan, and...our naval forces in the Pacific." The world was in fact "much safer...[with]...two superpowers, rather than just one," since the United States could balance the Soviet Union and deter it from aggression.[106] And in Asia, the end of U.S. involvement would open a power vacuum that would be filled either by the Soviets or the Japanese. For instance, "would he [Zhou] prefer to have Japan or [the] US as [the] ROK's friend?"[107] Thus, continued strong U.S. involvement and commitments in Asia were in fact in the Chinese interest.

Vietnam: An Honorable Settlement. Ending the Vietnam War and "extricating" American troops from Indochina in an honorable manner

[101] NSC, "Polo II – Japan," pp. 5–8.
[102] Memcon, 22 October 1971, p. 19.
[103] Memcon, 22 February 1972, p. 12.
[104] Memcon, 23 February 1972, p. 18.
[105] Memcon, 24 February 1972, Box 87, POF, NPM, pp. 25–6.
[106] Memcon, 22 February 1972, pp. 9, 13.
[107] RN, handwritten China notes, 21 February 1972.

was the key preoccupation of the Nixon administration. It featured most prominently in Nixon's and Kissinger's triangular diplomacy, in which they calculated that they could isolate Hanoi by means of parallel superpower détente with both its Soviet and Chinese allies, accompanied by "madman bombing."[108] Privately, Nixon initially placed great emphasis on Vietnam in the opening to China, instructing Kissinger to build on Chinese fears of what he might do in the event of a stalemate in the war, and listing "some progress" on the issue as a prerequisite for a summit.[109] Kissinger tried to secure Beijing's help in reaching a settlement by arguing that this would be to China's advantage in terms of undermining Soviet influence in Indochina, quickening U.S. military withdrawal from Indochina and Taiwan, and removing a key bilateral conflict. On the surface, this gambit was a failure. No "deal" was ever done, and in the course of their dialogues the Chinese flatly refused to help and went out of their way to establish for the record their support for Hanoi.

In July 1971, the first concrete suggestion of cooperation that Kissinger made to Zhou pertained to the Vietnam War. He suggested that Beijing and Washington might, "in a gesture of goodwill," guarantee a settlement in Vietnam. This would be more successful than the 1954 attempt, Kissinger assured Zhou, because the two sides would be treating each other "not from the point of view of hostility but of cooperation."[110] But the Chinese would not be drawn in: Zhou stuck to his "principled" position that Beijing would support its North Vietnamese ally and could not negotiate on its behalf. The basic Chinese position was that all foreign troops should be withdrawn from Indochina and that its peoples should be left to decide upon their own respective governments.[111]

At the same time, Zhou indicated Chinese interest in an "honorable" exit for the United States and wished Kissinger well in his negotiations in Paris. He also did not object to the way in which the U.S. side had, since the Warsaw talks in early 1970, linked the issues of troop withdrawals from Taiwan and the winding down of the Vietnam War.[112] Furthermore, the two sides did agree that a continuation of the war would only benefit

---

[108] See Jeffrey Kimball, *Nixon's Vietnam War* (Lawrence, 1998). Kimball argues that Vietnam formed the main "link" in the "Nixinger" policy of linkage.

[109] WH Memo, "Meeting between President, Dr. Kissinger and General Haig," 1 July 1971, Box 1036, NSF, NPM, p. 2. Indeed, as Kissinger told Dobrynin, China's role in the Vietnam War "introduced distortions" to China's relative power. Memcon, 18 November 1971, Box 492, NSF, NPM, p. 7.

[110] Memcon, 9 July 1971, p. 28.

[111] Ibid., p. 24; Memcon, 10 July 1971, 12.10–6pm, pp. 23–6.

[112] Memcon, 11 July 1971, pp. 12–13; Kissinger, "My Talks with Chou En-Lai," p. 14.

the Soviets. As Kissinger pointed out, Moscow hoped to "embarrass" Beijing by competing for influence with Hanoi and eventually to "create a bloc against you." Zhou responded in turn that Moscow hoped that the United States could be tied down in Indochina.[113]

Still, the Chinese refused to try to persuade Hanoi to agree to a settlement on American terms and scrupulously stated that the resolution of the Vietnam conflict should take precedence over the Taiwan issue. They also rejected, because of his close involvement in the Paris talks,[114] the suggestion of Ambassador David Bruce as an alternative presidential emissary for the October trip. In the run-up to the summit, Beijing turned down American requests to help moderate Hanoi's negotiating position in Paris and to arrange meetings between the Americans and Le Duc Tho in Beijing.[115] According to his notes, Nixon had hoped up until the summit that he could persuade the Chinese that "Taiwan-Vietnam = trade-off" and that "it *is* in your interest for US to get out (2/3 of Taiwan forces)."[116] In the event, Zhou reiterated that "[o]nly the Indochinese themselves have the right to . . . negotiate with you," and said that it was up to the United States to take "more bold action" if it genuinely wanted to withdraw. Nixon had asked for "any moves, any influence to get negotiations," but he was forced to add that "[w]e don't expect anything, however, and if we cannot get any assistance we understand." By the end of the summit, he had to accept that "[o]f course . . . the Prime Minister is telling us . . . he cannot help us in Vietnam."[117]

There would seem to be very little reason to believe that the Chinese could or would help the United States in Vietnam, given the extent to which they had already compromised their communist and revolutionary credentials through the rapprochement with the United States. Indeed, they not only made vociferous statements of support for Hanoi but also stepped up their military assistance for North Vietnam after 1971.[118] On

[113] Memcon, 21 October 1971, 4.42–7.17pm, pp. 11, 19–20; see also Haig–Zhou memcon, 3 January 1972, p. 3.
[114] Huang Zhen–Kissinger memcon, 26 July 1971, Box 330, Lord Files, RG59, NA.
[115] Walters, *Silent Missions*, pp. 454–6; Ross, *Negotiating Cooperation*, p. 49.
[116] RN, handwritten China notes, 15 February 1972, 6am; 23 February 1972.
[117] Memcon, 22 February 1972, pp. 20–7; 24 February 1972, pp. 15–17.
[118] Chinese aid to Hanoi peaked in 1972 and 1973 – see Zhai, *China and the Vietnam Wars*, pp. 136, 196. Indeed, in this sense Kissinger's linkage strategy failed in the short run, as détente with Moscow and Beijing instead exacerbated to some extent Sino-Soviet rivalry in supporting Hanoi to demonstrate that they had not betrayed the communist cause. This increased moral and material support stymied the peace talks and allowed the war to be extended.

the other hand, as was the case within the key triangular U.S.–USSR–PRC relationship, the mere fact of the reversal of Chinese policy toward the United States conveyed a sufficient message regarding Beijing's reassessed priorities and interests. The decision for rapprochement had nullified Washington's rationale for the Vietnam War, which had been to contain the revolutionary expansion of Communist China. And the fact that Zhou and Mao were meeting with Kissinger and Nixon against the backdrop of a stepped-up U.S. military campaign in Cambodia and Laos justified Kissinger's observation that the war did not pose a real obstacle – "we indeed understood each other; the war in Vietnam would not affect the improvement of our relations."[119] There is some evidence that Beijing did try to influence Hanoi toward an early settlement, which suggests that, despite its rhetoric, Beijing recognized that it was in the Chinese interest for the war to be settled on American terms so that Sino-American relations could proceed.[120] Indeed, the rapprochement played a key role in the breakdown of Sino-Vietnamese relations over the 1970s, culminating in the war of 1979.[121]

CONCLUSION: DISCURSIVE FOUNDATIONS

The foregoing analysis has shown how, in the course of four sets of high-level meetings in 1971 and 1972, Kissinger and Nixon established the understanding that the Chinese were ready, willing, and could be relied upon to develop new, less hostile relations. This was achieved by means of the representation of China advocated by Kissinger, and also by the mere fact of the meetings. The discursive foundations of this new relationship consisted of three elements. First, the articulation of new identities: China was represented as an unquestioned great power, to be dealt with on an equal basis by the United States, and the United States was reconstructed as the PRC's supporter rather than opponent in international affairs. Second, the identification of common interests: the two sides agreed in private and in public that they were united in opposing "hegemony" and attempts at hegemony in Asia. In private, the Americans particularly emphasized their shared interest in containing the Soviet Union in Asia, offering Beijing intelligence assistance against the Soviet threat. Third, the management,

---

[119] Kissinger, *White House Years*, p. 1087.
[120] See Westad et al., eds., "77 Conversations," pp. 138–40, 176; Zhai, *China and the Vietnam Wars*, Chapter 9.
[121] See Stephen Hood, *Dragons Entangled: Indochina and the China-Vietnam War* (New York, 1992); and William Duiker, *China and Vietnam: The Roots of Conflict* (Berkeley, 1986).

muting, and even overcoming of strategic disagreements: this pertained especially to the rise of Japan and the Vietnam War. The two sides also went some way toward codifying these elements in a formal agreement in the form of the Shanghai Communiqué.

These discursive foundations were crucial, but they were fundamentally conceptual, and there remained the question of whether the two sides would *act* in accordance with their declared interests when put to the test. Thus, the establishment of an understanding that both sides desired new relations was accompanied by a keen awareness of the need to convince each other that they had the capacity and willingness to bring about this new relationship. The next chapter focuses on Kissinger's and Nixon's efforts to convince the Chinese by their policy actions that the developing norms of their new relationship applied not only in principle, but also in practice.

8

Principles in Practice

*Policy Implications of the U.S. Decision
for Rapprochement*

> Kissinger to Nixon: "The crucial factor... will be the Chinese judgment of
> our seriousness and reliability: this litmus test will determine their future
> policy.... Our essential requirement is to demonstrate that we are serious
> enough to understand the basic forces at work in the world and reliable
> enough to deliver on the commitments we make."[1]
>
> Zhou to Nixon: "... in view of the current interests of our two countries...
> we may find common ground. But this common ground must be truly re-
> liable. It should not be a structure built upon sand, because that structure
> will not be able to stand."[2]

In the process of constructing a new relationship with Beijing, Washington
had not only to cultivate a convergence in worldviews and in the appreciation of certain common national interests, but also to demonstrate its
willingness to act in accordance with the basic principles governing the
relationship. The latter included the agreement to counter hegemony in
Asia and the aim of working toward normalization of relations. Between
1971 and 1972, the two sides established regular high-level channels of
contact that would allow bilateral communication and policy coordination. This took two forms: Kissinger's occasional trips to Beijing and, in
between, his secret meetings, first with the Chinese Ambassador Huang
Zhen in Paris and then with the Chinese UN Representative Ambassador
Huang Hua in a CIA "safe house" in New York after the PRC gained UN
representation in October 1971. The purpose of these meetings was to

---

[1] Kissinger to RN, "Mao, Chou and the Chinese Litmus Test," 19 February 1972, Box 13,
NSF/HAK, NPM, pp. 1, 6.
[2] Zhou-Kissinger memcon, 22 February 1972, Box 87, POF, NPM, p. 14.

allow Kissinger and Nixon to carry out their promise to keep the Chinese "meticulously" informed about issues that affected them. Also, Kissinger began to build up a record of coordinating policy positions with Beijing on major issues such as the Korean situation.

However, the key tests of the solidity of the "common ground" during this period lay in two outstanding U.S. policy issues, South Asia and Taiwan. In these two areas, the Nixon administration established new policies as part of the effort to convince Beijing of its seriousness and reliability regarding the new relationship. The South Asian crisis was an early opportunity in the rapprochement, one that allowed the White House to demonstrate dramatically its readiness to act in accordance with two key principles: Washington's recognition and support of legitimate Chinese interests in the region, and the shared strategic antipathy toward attempts at "hegemony." The Taiwan issue, on the other hand, was a key bilateral obstacle, but one that posed a constructive challenge to the two sides to put their ingenuity and determination to normalize relations to the test. The new norms negotiated were aimed at allowing the two sides to set aside this conflict of interest for the time being, but they nevertheless significantly changed the character of U.S. policy toward Taiwan.

TEST OF FRIENDSHIP: THE 1971 SOUTH ASIAN CRISIS

The Indo-Pakistani crisis of 1971, which eventually led to war in December, provided the first opportunity for the White House to demonstrate to Beijing that the United States and China did have compatible interests in Asia; that Washington would act upon this coincidence of interests through concrete policy formulation, coordination, and cooperation; and that Washington recognized and supported legitimate Chinese interests in Asia. The Nixon administration's handling of the 1971 South Asian crisis has been characterized as a "fiasco" by some, and there is general agreement that Kissinger and Nixon miscalculated and exaggerated the intent and involvement of the Soviet Union and China in the conflict.[3] Insofar as much documentary evidence remains unavailable, it would be premature to conduct an analysis of Kissinger's and Nixon's "misperception" of "reality" at this juncture.[4] However, on the basis of available accounts, it is possible to show that Kissinger, in particular, was predisposed to

---

[3] Bundy, *Tangled Web*, p. 269; Christopher Van Hollen, "The Tilt Policy Revisited: Nixon-Kissinger Geopolitics and South Asia," *Asian Survey* 20 (April 1980), pp. 339–61.

[4] Robert Jervis, *Perception and Misperception in International Politics* (Princeton, 1976).

construct the crisis as a Sino-Soviet contest in which the United States had to demonstrate its support for China and its Pakistani ally against the Soviet Union and its Indian ally. Moreover, new evidence from the transcripts of Kissinger's talks with the Chinese ambassadors in Paris and New York during the latter part of 1971 makes clear the pro-China motivations behind such thinking, and the extent to which the White House was prepared to act upon such beliefs.

The 1971 Indo-Pakistan crisis was the culmination of a series of conflicts resulting from the partition of the subcontinent after World War II, which left India flanked to its east and west by two parts of Pakistan. The internal tension between Bengali East Pakistan and the West, which contained the seat of government, erupted with a Bengali rebellion against the Islamabad regime at the end of 1970. Yahya Khan's brutal repression of the Bengali revolt triggered a crisis as millions of refugees fled into India, threatening to destabilize an already disaffected region. While U.S. aid agencies quickly provided relief supplies and funds, Nixon and Kissinger resisted domestic and bureaucratic pressures to cut military aid to Pakistan and to censure Islamabad. This was probably due in large part to the "special relationship" with Yahya, who was acting as a secret intermediary between Washington and Beijing during this period.[5]

By contrast, the White House viewed the Indians and Soviets with distrust. The superpower dimension to the conflict was brought to the fore when the Indo-Soviet Friendship Treaty was signed in August 1971. While this was clearly a reaction to rising Indo-Pakistani tensions, Zhou also believed that the timing of the treaty was related to Kissinger's July trip to Beijing.[6] Kissinger's own reading of the treaty was that "for all practical purposes [it] gave India a Soviet guarantee against Chinese intervention if India went to war with Pakistan. By this action the Soviet Union deliberately opened the door to war on the subcontinent." The Soviet specialists on the NSC staff agreed that the Indo-Pakistani conflict had become "a sort of Sino-Soviet clash by proxy."[7] However, the treaty itself fell some distance short of an alliance: it provided only for Indo-Soviet consultations in a crisis, and pledged each country against cooperation with a third country against the other.[8] Still, more active Soviet

[5] Kissinger, *White House Years*, pp. 851–2, 863.
[6] See Zhou-Haig memcon, 3 January 1972, Box 1037, NSF, NPM, p. 12.
[7] Sonnenfeldt and Hyland, quoted in Kissinger, *White House Years*, p. 767.
[8] See Dennis Kux, *Estranged Democracies: India and the United States, 1941–1991* (London, 1994), pp. 286, 292–5.

involvement turned the South Asian crisis into an issue of superpower concern, and when India and Pakistan moved their troops close to their shared borders in October, Washington exerted pressure on New Delhi, via Moscow, to accept a mutual troop withdrawal proposal.

At the same time, Kissinger and Nixon also threatened to withdraw U.S. economic assistance to India. Kissinger warned the Indian Ambassador on 8 October, "If you start a war we will cut off all economic aid and you must include that in your cost calculation."[9] A month later, Nixon more indirectly cautioned Prime Minister Indira Gandhi that "the American people would not understand if India were to initiate military action against Pakistan." He observed that the Indo-Soviet treaty was "not popular" with the United States, and expressed doubt that an Indo-Pakistani war could be limited, since it would have "implications and possibly great dangers for the whole framework of world peace."[10] However, Nixon did not like the new Indian leader and was left with the impression that she was ready to go to war with Pakistan.[11]

The South Asian crisis clearly had repercussions for China, and the need to protect the developing U.S.–China rapprochement and Nixon's summit was foremost in the minds of many in Washington. The State Department and the White House agreed that there was a need to explain U.S. policy to Beijing, but they differed in their perceptions of what the Chinese should be encouraged to do. The interagency Special Action Group (WSAG) for the crisis thought it desirable to communicate with the Chinese about the issue, principally to "stress the parallel interests we have in discouraging war in the area." In this context, it was important to ensure that China "not miscalculate its involvement with the Pakistanis, in ways which might lead to Pakistani overconfidence" and thus to war.[12] On 16 August, Kissinger brought up the subject with Huang Zhen. He explained that the pro-Indian sentiment in the United States made it difficult for the administration to continue providing military supplies to Pakistan, but assured Huang that Nixon would not take India's side. He informed Huang about Washington's threats to cut off economic aid if India started military action, adding, "it is important that Pakistan not

[9] NSC background paper, "Action to Reduce Tensions in South Asia," 23 November 1971, Box 571; memcon, 8 October 1971, Box 570, NSF, NPM, p. 1.
[10] Memcon, 4 November 1971, Box 919, NSF, NPM, p. 4.
[11] Nixon, *Memoirs*, p. 132; Kissinger, *White House Years*, pp. 878–81. Kissinger called these "the two most unfortunate meetings Nixon had with any foreign leader."
[12] DoS to Kissinger, "Contact with the Chinese on the South Asian Crisis," 27 August 1971, Box 2189, SNF(1970–3), RG59, NA.

start a war." Nevertheless, he also made it clear that the United States would "understand" if Pakistan's other friends, such as the PRC, provided it with military equipment.[13]

In late November, Indian forces supported Bengali insurgents in incursions into East Pakistan, creating a tense situation just short of outright war. The Chinese responded by informing Washington that "should Pakistan be subjected to aggression by India, China will support the Pakistan Government and people," adding that it had agreed to "continue to provide military assistance" to Pakistan, but Beijing urged the United States to "exert its influence to prevent the further deterioration of the situation through persuasion."[14] Kissinger and Nixon reacted by giving Islamabad similar assurances. They privately assured the Pakistanis that they regarded the United States as having a commitment to come to Pakistan's aid against India as a result of the 1959 executive agreement concluded under Eisenhower – even though this agreement was envisaged to guard against Soviet, not Indian, aggression, and even though State challenged its validity.[15]

At the same time, Kissinger made an even greater effort to convince Pakistan's Chinese ally about the U.S. "tilt" toward Pakistan. On 26 November, at a meeting with Huang Hua, Kissinger took it upon himself to provide the Chinese with detailed intelligence information about Indian deployments, noting that "this violates every security rule." He also informed Huang about unconfirmed reports that the Indians were moving their divisions away from the Chinese border toward East Pakistan.[16]

On 3 December, war broke out between India and Pakistan when Yahya Khan launched an attack in western India. Indian forces were engaged in Kashmir and the Punjab, but nevertheless continued to advance steadily in the East, and it became apparent that they would soon control East Bengal. The State Department reacted by suspending all arms shipments, economic aid, and development assistance to India. At the same time, the UN General Assembly passed a resolution calling for a ceasefire and the withdrawal of Indian forces from East Bengal. However, Kissinger clearly felt that more had to be done. He was convinced, based on an intelligence

---

[13] Memcon, 16 August 1971, NSA Doc. 216, pp. 6–8.
[14] Chinese note attached to memo, Kissinger to SoS, 22 November 1971, Box 330, Lord Files.
[15] Bundy, *Tangled Web*, pp. 276–7; Kissinger, *White House Years*, pp. 894–5. This was contentious because executive agreements, by definition, do not have to be submitted to Congress for approval.
[16] Memcon, 23 November 1971, Box 330, Lord Files, pp. 12–13.

report, that Gandhi was bent on extending the Indian campaign in order to liberate Kashmir and to decimate the Pakistani army and air force. Thus, the "survival of [West] Pakistan itself" was at stake.[17] In the "geopolitical perspective" of the White House, therefore, the conflict was a "ruthless power play by which India, encouraged by the Soviets," was exploiting the weakness of Islamabad in order to gain new dominance on the subcontinent. For Kissinger, this Soviet-Indian "collusion" represented an "assault on international order," and strong action was needed on the part of the United States to counter the growing Soviet influence on the subcontinent.[18] This was an extension of the superpower contest, and American credibility was at stake: "if we collapse now the Soviets won't respect us...[and] the Chinese will despise us." And it was particularly crucial because for the first time Washington and Beijing found themselves on the same side. Thus, as Kissinger told Nixon, "We really don't have any choice. We can't allow a friend of ours and China's to get screwed in a conflict with a friend of Russia's."[19]

The White House proceeded to exert pressure on the Soviets to restrain India, to encourage Pakistan to resist Indian aggression by diplomatic means and by a show of U.S. support, and to urge China to complicate the situation for India and the Soviet Union. Nixon sent a note to Brezhnev threatening to cancel the Soviet-American summit if Moscow did not help to end the war. Subsequently, he also warned that the United States would provide military assistance to Pakistan in accordance with their "treaty."[20] On 10 December, circumventing the secretary of defense and the Joint Chiefs of Staff, Kissinger directly ordered the preparation for a naval task force to sail to the Indian Ocean.

Against this backdrop, Kissinger asked for another meeting with the Chinese UN Ambassador in order to "inform Peking fully about our various moves concerning South Asia and *to indicate our approval of Chinese support for Pakistan, including diversionary troop movements.*"[21] In

[17] See Kissinger, *White House Years*, pp. 896, 901; Bundy, *Tangled Web*, p. 278.

[18] Kissinger, *White House Years*, p. 897; interview with Helmut Sonnenfeldt, 26 February 2001.

[19] Kissinger, *White House Years*, pp. 897–8; Nixon, *Memoirs*, p. 527. The State Department, JCS, and CIA disagreed with the White House, and there was "open rebellion" by the WSAG – see *Haldeman Diaries*, p. 381.

[20] Kissinger, *White House Years*, pp. 900–1; Bundy, *Tangled Web*, pp. 278–9. On the way in which Nixon and Kissinger persisted in attributing "maximum offensive aims" to both Moscow and India, see Garthoff, *Détente and Confrontation*, pp. 296–314.

[21] Kissinger to RN, "My December 10 Meeting with the Chinese in New York," NSA Doc. 233, p. 1. Emphasis mine.

his attempt to demonstrate U.S. support for China and its ally, Kissinger made his first offer to Beijing of U.S. satellite intelligence information about Soviet troop movements: "we would be prepared at your request, and through whatever sources you wish, to give you whatever information we have about the disposition of Soviet forces."[22] He followed up the offer with the statement that "the President wants you to know that... if the PRC were to consider the situation on the Indian subcontinent a threat to its security, and if it took measures to protect its security, the US would oppose any effort of others to interfere with the PRC." The intention clearly was to encourage the PRC to move its troops to the Indian border as a way to divert Indian military attention away from Pakistan, by helping to ensure that Beijing was able to monitor its northern flank at the same time. According to Kissinger, "an active if tacit collaboration" developed.[23]

Huang Hua responded that Beijing supported both the UN principles – that India should call a ceasefire and that it should withdraw from East Bengal. However, he added that the Soviet-backed Indian action on the subcontinent was "a step to encircle China" and that "we are prepared to meet attacks coming from the east, west, north, and south." Kissinger's rejoinder reemphasized U.S. support for China and the fact that they were on the same side in this crisis, since "Pakistan is being punished because it is a friend of China and because it is a friend of the US."[24] Kissinger has claimed that Huang's presentation persuaded him that the Chinese were ready to intervene militarily if the situation worsened.[25] However, the transcripts show that he made what amounted to an offer of a strategic commitment to aid China against a retaliatory Soviet attack before Huang made any substantial remark about the situation.[26] In the event, Washington received news the day after the meeting that Chinese troops were moving toward the Indian border. While he acknowledged that the movement must have been planned before the U.S. offer, Kissinger

---

[22] Kissinger's talking points for this meeting, however, suggest that there would have been considerable limits to what intelligence information the United States could provide, as the next relevant satellite information would not be available until the end of December or the beginning of January, when, as it turned out, the crisis had already passed. See NSC, "Talking Points South Asia," n.d., NSA Doc. 229, p. 7.

[23] Kissinger, *White House Years*, p. 906.

[24] Memcon, 10 December 1971, Box 330, Lord Files.

[25] Bundy, *Tangled Web*, pp. 279–80, note 99.

[26] Kissinger wrote, "Had things developed as we anticipated, we would have had no choice but to assist China in some manner against the probable opposition of much of the government, the media, and the Congress." *White House Years*, p. 911.

observed that his meeting with Huang would in any case help to "reinforce Chinese penchant for action."[27]

By Kissinger's own admission, the White House's inclination to believe that Beijing would take military action contributed significantly to a series of escalatory and potentially dangerous actions on 12 December. Washington was still attempting to pressure Moscow into influencing its Indian allies to accept the new ceasefire proposal when a message was received that Huang Hua had an urgent response to deliver from Beijing. Kissinger, Nixon, and Haig immediately assumed that Beijing had decided to come to the military assistance of Pakistan. Haig was instructed to reply that the United States "would not ignore Soviet intervention," and Nixon ordered the carrier task force to proceed conspicuously toward the Bay of Bengal.[28] In the event, the Chinese message turned out to be that China would support the U.S. proposal in the UN for a ceasefire in both East and West Pakistan followed by mutual troop withdrawals.[29]

This Chinese stance was in line with the analyses of other departments, which gauged Chinese intentions to be more cautious than was assumed by the White House. For instance, a CIA assessment concluded that the Chinese capability to provide timely and extensive military assistance to Pakistan would be constrained by delivery distances and difficult lines of communication. Furthermore, as late as 9 December there had been no indication that the Chinese intended to take diversionary action against India.[30] In political terms, INR agreed that the Chinese did not want to become too deeply involved in the South Asian situation. INR thought that Beijing viewed Pakistani weakness vis-à-vis India in a realistic manner and was already reconfiguring its South Asian policy in the direction of a more even-handed approach, since the crisis could be expected to leave a "defeated and isolated Pakistan [which would be] less useful as a counterweight to India and potentially a burden on the PRC." China would also want to improve relations with India in order directly to counter Soviet influence in New Delhi.[31]

---

[27] Kissinger, "My December 10 Meeting," p. 3. See also Burr, *Kissinger Transcripts*, pp. 46–8.

[28] Kissinger, *White House Years*, p. 910.

[29] Haig–Huang memcon, 12 December 1971, Box 330, Lord Files.

[30] Intelligence appraisal, "Communist China's Capability to Support Pakistan," 9 December 1971, Box 572, NSF, NPM.

[31] INR intelligence note, "PRC/Pakistan/India: China and the Indo-Pakistan War," 7 December 1971, "China Reports," Box 87, NSF/HAK, NPM.

The combination of crisis decision making and the extent to which policy formulation had become concentrated in the Oval Office meant that Nixon and Kissinger did not take into account these other analyses. While Kissinger's and Nixon's policy during the South Asian crisis was determined by a host of considerations other than the new relationship with China, their perception of the significance of the U.S. reaction to the situation was considerably affected by the ongoing reconstruction of the image of China as a friend and strategic partner whose legitimate national interests were appreciated and supported by Washington. Ultimately, this exacerbated Nixon's and Kissinger's penchant for strong action, which they also projected onto Beijing in their desire to prove U.S. friendship and strategic cooperation. The policy impact was that the foundations for the practice of strategic support of, and cooperation with, the PRC in the protection of its perceived legitimate national interests were laid by the Nixon administration. As discussed in Chapter 7, this was followed shortly by a renewed offer to share intelligence information about the disposition of Soviet forces on the Chinese border.

NEGOTIATING PRINCIPLES, POSTPONING RESOLUTION:
U.S. POLICY TOWARD TAIWAN

Zhou En-Lai: "... in the formulation of the Taiwan question we are going to work out, each side states its own position, but if one has profound understanding one can see that there is common ground between our two countries towards this question.... we must arrive at an agreement on this one matter.... the Taiwan question is the crucial question."
Richard Nixon: "...my goal is normalization....I realize that solving the Taiwan problem is indispensable to achieving that goal...[but]I must be able to go back to Washington and say that no secret deals have been made....I must...have...'running room'...which will not make Taiwan a big issue in the next...two or three months and next two, three, or four years." [32]

Taiwan, the issue that had been the key source of bilateral conflict between the United States and China for over twenty years, slid into a position of secondary importance during this period due to the greater emphasis on strategic issues on both sides. [33] Beijing and Washington agreed on significant minimum "principles" while postponing the actual resolution of the Taiwan affair. The issue was divided into three parts: the U.S.

[32] Memcon, 24 February 1972, Box 87, POF, NPM, pp. 9–10.
[33] See Ross, *Negotiating Cooperation*, pp. 1–54.

military presence on the island, the U.S.–ROC Mutual Defense Treaty, and the political status of Taiwan vis-à-vis the PRC. U.S. military bases on Taiwan were arguably not crucial to the U.S. force deployment strategy in Asia and therefore were negotiable. American troop withdrawals would provide the key symbolic gesture, serving to downgrade the Taiwan issue as a source of bilateral contention in the opening years of the rapprochement. The U.S. defense commitment to the GRC, however, was a separate matter. The treaty provided a de facto guarantee that the eventual settlement of the issue would be peaceful, and for reasons of domestic sentiment and international credibility the Nixon administration regarded it as non-negotiable as long as Taiwan's political future remained unresolved. Beijing, on the other hand, viewed the political principle that Taiwan was a part of China over which the PRC ought to exercise sovereignty as its own non-negotiable position. While this political element was the fundamental problem, it also presented the most room for maneuver and for reaching a temporary solution.

As a corollary to the recognition of China as a great power, Kissinger and Nixon had to treat seriously Beijing's claims of sovereignty and territorial integrity regarding Taiwan. For the July 1971 meetings, Kissinger's preparatory notes indicated that he would convey to Zhou the idea that the United States "underst[ood] fully that to the PRC, Taiwan is a part of China, and the US is interfering in the internal affairs of the PRC by maintaining relations with the ROC on Taiwan, including a mutual defense treaty." When they met, he agreed with Zhou about the historical legitimacy of the claim, particularly the claim that Taiwan was returned to China according to the Cairo Declaration after the Second World War. Kissinger also pointed out that U.S. involvement in Taiwan was the result of a previous administration's decision to link the future of Korea to the future of Taiwan, "partly because of domestic opinion at that time." On the other hand, Beijing had to realize that the United States, "as a great power," also had considerations of credibility – it could not be seen to be selling out its allies. The relationship with Taiwan was a longstanding one involving significant emotional and political considerations, and severing all ties with the ROC immediately would represent an act of "unconscionable betrayal."[34] However, the Nixon administration was prepared to begin by reducing its military presence on Taiwan.

[34] NSC, "Polo – Taiwan," 3 July 1971, Box 850, NSF, pp. 1–2; Kissinger–Zhou memcon, 9 July 1971, p. 11.

The U.S. Military Presence on Taiwan: Bargaining
for Peaceful Unification

China had insisted throughout the Warsaw talks in the 1960s that the
United States should end its "occupation" of Taiwan as a first step toward
ending Sino-American estrangement. By 1968–9, State had recommended
that Washington reduce its military presence on Taiwan in conjunction
with the winding down of the Vietnam War and in accordance with the
Nixon Doctrine. EA had argued that such force reductions would not
significantly affect the U.S. ability to help defend Taiwan and would constitute an important symbolic gesture of conciliation that would help to
downplay the actual defense commitment.[35] The Chinese themselves had,
first in semiofficial statements at the end of 1968 and then via the back
channel in December 1970, invited a presidential envoy to Beijing specifically to discuss the "vacation of . . . Taiwan."[36]

In its May 1971 guidelines for the Sino-American summit talks, the
Politburo's first condition was that "a deadline should be set for all US
armed forces and military installations to be withdrawn from Taiwan
and the Taiwan Straits area." This was the "key issue in restoring Sino-
American relations," and Nixon's visit might be postponed if an agreement in principle could not be reached beforehand.[37] When Zhou Enlai
delivered this demand to Kissinger at their first meeting in July 1971, the
latter emphasized that Washington could definitely deliver on this military
aspect of the issue: two-thirds of the forces on Taiwan, which were related
to the Vietnam War, would be removed within a specified period after the
end of the war, which Kissinger anticipated would be within Nixon's first
term, and the remaining forces would depart "as our relations improve."
However, he was candid about these being "symbolic steps" and acknowledged that military withdrawal alone was not the "principal point" that
Zhou sought on the issue.[38]

Here Kissinger differed from State on the function of offering troop
withdrawals. While agreeing that it was an important gesture of goodwill, State saw the gradual withdrawal of U.S. troops from Taiwan as a
key bargaining tool in negotiations with China. As David Osborn, the

---

[35] SoS to RN, "US Policy toward Peking and Instructions for the February 20 Warsaw
Meeting," ca. January 1969, Box 1973, CFPF(1967–9), RG59, NA, pp. 7, 9. This was
suggested in exchange for a Chinese agreement to renounce the use of force in the Taiwan
Straits.

[36] Zhou note, 9 December 1970, Box 1031, NSF, NPM.

[37] Gong, *Mao Zedong yu Meiguo*, p. 252.

[38] Memcon, 9 July 1971, pp. 10–14.

consul general in Hong Kong, put it to the secretary of state, a good quid pro quo was "something that can be given or withheld with little harm to one's own interests, provided only that the other side makes corresponding concessions...ideally...in graduated increments." Force reductions provided just such a set of bargaining counters.[39] Fundamentally, State calculated that even though Beijing wanted the United States to "'deliver' Taiwan, recognize the PRC on its own terms...[and] abandon our commitments to the ROC," the Chinese fear of the Soviet threat and a resurgent Japan would persuade them to "put off or moderate" longer-term goals regarding Taiwan. Thus, Rogers advised Nixon that they could issue a "statement of intent" to reduce forces on Taiwan as tensions in the area diminished, but only in return for a PRC commitment to resolve the Taiwan issue by peaceful means. A Chinese renunciation of force would leave both the U.S.–ROC mutual security treaty and Washington's commitment to a peaceful settlement intact.[40]

By contrast, a formal renunciation of force by the Chinese was not high on Kissinger's agenda when he went to Beijing. He brought up the subject tentatively, but was finessed by Zhou's response that this would be linked to "the Taiwan question and the question of China's internal affairs" – the implication being that China would not renounce its right to use force in the Taiwan Straits.[41] During his October trip, Kissinger told Zhou that "[W]e recognize that the [PRC] considers the subject of Taiwan an internal issue and we will not challenge that." Thus, he would not press for a formal renunciation of force, but asked instead that Beijing "on its own, in the exercise of its own sovereignty, declare willingness to settle [the Taiwan issue] by peaceful means." Such a declaration of intent would make it easier for the Nixon administration to explain its actions, he told Zhou. Significantly, however, Kissinger added that this was not vital, for regardless of whether the Chinese did make such a declaration of peaceful intent, "we will continue in the direction which I indicated" – that is, the reduction of the U.S. military presence on Taiwan and eventual normalization of relations.[42]

---

[39] Osborn to Green, "Bargaining with China," 11 November 1971, Box 2189, SNF(1970–3), RG59, NA.

[40] SoS to RN, "The Scope for Agreement in Peking," 9 February 1971, Box 184, Haldeman Files, NPM, pp. 3–4.

[41] Memcon, 11 July 1971, p. 8.

[42] Kissinger–Zhou conversation, 21 October 1971, in "Private Statements made by PRC Leaders to Secretary Kissinger or President Nixon regarding the Peaceful Liberation of Taiwan," ca. 1974, Box 373, Lord Files. This portion of the dialogue is not included in the declassified transcripts of the October 1971 trip that I have used, which were marked

During the February 1972 summit, Kissinger again asked Vice Foreign Minister Qiao Guanhua whether the Chinese side could state that they would assert sovereignty over Taiwan by peaceful, nonmilitary means. Qiao replied that this was "not possible" because it would constitute "a fundamental violation of our principle...that it is an internal affair."[43] In the resulting communiqué, Kissinger did manage to persuade the Chinese to agree to a mutual renunciation of force in settling international disputes.[44] However, since Taiwan was an internal dispute, Kissinger promised Qiao that the agreement did not apply to the Taiwan issue.[45] The eventual quid pro quo compromise on troop withdrawal and renunciation of force was an indirect reference to the U.S. section of the communiqué, which stated that "[the U.S. government] reaffirms its interest in the peaceful settlement of the Taiwan question by the Chinese themselves. With this prospect in mind, it affirms the ultimate objective of the withdrawal of all US forces and military installations from Taiwan. In the meantime, it will progressively reduce its forces and military installations on Taiwan as the tension in the area diminishes."

In addition, Nixon himself had secretly assured Zhou during the summit that "I do not believe a permanent American presence [on Taiwan]... is necessary for American security.... my goal is the withdrawal of... not just two thirds, but all forces" from Taiwan. He only added the caveat that because of public and congressional opinion he would have to extend this total withdrawal over a period of four years, and that he would have to deny having made this promise if asked in public.[46]

Yet the Nixon administration made these commitments only on the basis of a brief list of informal statements by Zhou on peaceful resolution. During Kissinger's preparatory visits, Zhou did not offer anything more than the assurance that "we are doing our best" and "will try to bring about a peaceful settlement."[47] During the summit, Nixon told

---

"For the President" – this is suggestive, given that Kissinger had his staff supply various versions of these transcripts to different people on a "need-to-know" basis.

[43] Memcon, 22 February 1972, Box 92, NSF, NPM, p. 10.

[44] "...the two sides agreed that countries, regardless of their social systems, should conduct their relations on the principles of respect for the sovereignty and territorial integrity of all states, non-aggression against other states, non-interference in the internal affairs of other states, equality and mutual benefit, and peaceful coexistence. International disputes should be settled on this basis, without resorting to the use or threat of force."

[45] Memcon, 24 February 1972, Box 92, NSF, NPM.

[46] Memcon, 24 February 1972, pp. 11–12.

[47] Memcon, 11 July 1971, p. 10; p. 16.

Zhou that the removal of the remaining third of U.S. forces on Taiwan would go forward "as progress is made on the peaceful resolution of the problem." In response, Zhou stated that "you want a peaceful liberation [for Taiwan]. . . . we will strive for peaceful liberation. . . . We want this." He added an indirect assurance that the PRC would not employ force, if only to avoid conflict with the United States: "While your armed forces are there our armed forces will not engage in military confrontation with your armed forces." However, there was a time limit attached, as Zhou added that "it would be good if the liberation of Taiwan could be realized in your next term of office"; "ten years . . . would be too long. . . . I can't wait ten years." But Zhou expressed "self-confidence" that the issue could be settled peacefully.[48]

Letting "History" Take Care of It: The U.S.–ROC Mutual Security Treaty

The U.S.–ROC mutual security treaty, which obliged the United States to come to Taiwan's aid if it were attacked by the PRC, was not mentioned in the Shanghai Communiqué. Instead, with Chinese agreement, Kissinger reiterated the commitment during a brief press conference after the release of the communiqué on the last day of the summit.[49] This treaty commitment was regarded by the U.S. side as separate from the American military presence on Taiwan; it was less negotiable because it acted as a guarantee of the island's peaceful transition toward its yet-undetermined political future and lay at the heart of Washington's concern with its credibility among allies. Beijing's official stance, on the other hand, was simply that a treaty signed with an entity it considered a province of China was "illegal."[50]

From the outset, there was an unspoken understanding that the U.S.–ROC treaty was inextricably tied up with the eventual resolution of the Taiwan question and thus was not up for immediate negotiation. Kissinger

---

[48] Memcon, 24 February 1972, pp. 6, 8. In its list of guidelines for the talks, the Politburo had included the principle that "China would try its best to liberate Taiwan by peaceful means and deal conscientiously with this issue" – Gong, *Mao Zedong yu Meiguo*, p. 253. This was not a dramatic departure from previous policy, for, as noted before, Mao had stated as early as 1963 that China would prefer not to use force against Taiwan. However, private reassurances were probably as far as the Chinese leaders were willing to go, since a public statement would adversely affect the credibility of Chinese claims of sovereignty over Taiwan.

[49] "Kissinger Press Briefing" (Shanghai), n.d., Box 49, Haig Files, NPM.

[50] Zhou to Kissinger, 9 July 1971, p. 10.

framed the issue clearly within the scenario of a future peaceful unification, telling Zhou that in this case, "it goes without question" that the
U.S.–ROC military relationship would be "re-examined."[51] Zhou wanted
to know if this applied to wider U.S. military assistance to Taiwan, but
Kissinger sidestepped the question, stating that "[w]e will not insist on
maintaining an American presence or military installations on Taiwan after unification of China by peaceful negotiation has been achieved. And
in those conditions we will be prepared to abrogate [the defense treaty]
formally. If there is no peaceful settlement . . . then it's easier for us to withdraw our military presence in stages . . . than to abrogate the Treaty."[52] His
meaning was more explicit in the talking points prepared for Nixon for
the summit, which added that "so long as peaceful conditions prevail" in
the Taiwan area, the defense treaty "would not be operative" and "we
could allow history to take care of this problem."[53] That is, the treaty
would be allowed to lapse if, over an unspecified length of time, China
did not use force against Taiwan.

Of course, a significant consideration behind Kissinger's and Nixon's
apparently "soft" position on the renunciation of force in the Taiwan
Straits was that China did not yet have the military capacity to invade
and take over Taiwan. Thus, the two sides could afford to buy some
time before such a crisis was likely to occur. Indeed, Kissinger found
it necessary to promise Zhou that the United States would not support
any attempt by the Nationalists to attack the mainland, and he agreed to
inform Beijing of any missions Taipei had planned against the mainland.[54]
Moreover, as Zhou himself pointed out, a continued U.S. military presence
and commitment to Taiwan also helped China to deter Japanese forces
from entering Taiwan.[55]

A Political Problem Awaiting a Political Solution: The Status of Taiwan

It was the political aspect of the Taiwan problem that dominated the
discussions for rapprochement. From his first meeting with Kissinger in

[51] Memcon, 21 October 1971, 10.30am–1.45pm, pp. 16–18.
[52] Kissinger–Zhou conversation, 21 October 1971.
[53] NSC, briefing papers for Nixon China Trip, "Taiwan," n.d., Box 847, NSF, NPM.
[54] Memcon, 10 July 1971, 11.20–11.50pm, pp. 1–2; on his next trip, Kissinger informed
    Zhou about some upcoming ROC reconnaissance flights on the Chinese coast – see
    memcon, 23 October 1971, p. 2.
[55] Memcon, 10 July 1971, 12.10–6pm, p. 19. These two assurances were reiterated as part
    of Nixon's confidential five-point commitments on the Taiwan issue during the summit –
    see RN–Zhou memcon, 22 February 1972, p. 5.

July 1971, Zhou emphasized that the key Chinese requirement was that the United States must "unreservedly" recognize the PRC as the sole legitimate government of all of China, including Taiwan, "an inalienable part of Chinese territory which must be restored to the motherland." Washington should give up its official position that the status of Taiwan was "undetermined," and it should not support the Taiwan Independence Movement.[56] Essentially, Beijing sought Washington's acceptance of Chinese sovereignty over Taiwan in terms of three principles: the legitimacy of the mainland's historical claim to territorial integrity with Taiwan; an acceptance that reunification was an internal affair in which Beijing had the right to use force; and the recognition that Beijing was the sole legitimate governing authority over all of China, including Taiwan.

The U.S. approach, by contrast, was to distinguish between the "military situation" on Taiwan and the "question of political evolution" between Taiwan and the PRC. Kissinger told Zhou that on the latter issue, the Nixon administration's dilemma lay in the gulf between "what we can say and what our policy is."[57] Kissinger pointed out that Nixon was the only president who could normalize relations with the PRC without a crippling backlash from the China lobby, because he had the support of the "center and right of center."[58] But, having said this, as Nixon himself later expressed to Zhou, he labored under considerable domestic constraint posed by the "very unholy alliance of the [pro-Taiwan] far right, the pro-Soviet left, and pro-Indian left," and also a pro-Japanese faction. In terms of policy advocacy, therefore, they had to be "clever enough" to find language in the communiqué that would meet Chinese needs and yet not stir up these "animals" in the United States so much that they ganged up to "torpedo" the China opening.[59]

In this regard, Washington's handling of the related issue of Chinese representation in the UN reflected the careful balancing act that the Nixon administration had to perform. After the 1970 General Assembly vote that saw a majority in favor of expelling the ROC and replacing it with the PRC, there had been a strong sense of foreboding in Washington that its traditional tactic of declaring the issue an "important question" requiring a two-thirds majority vote would not succeed much longer. After the Ping-Pong diplomacy of April 1971, and particularly after the 15 July

[56] Memcon, 9 July 1971, pp. 8–16; 10 July 1971, 12.10–6pm, p. 4.
[57] Memcon, 21 October 1971, 10.30am–1.45pm, p. 16.
[58] Memcon, 10 July 1971, 12.10–6pm, pp. 20–1.
[59] Memcon, 22 February 1972, p. 7.

announcement of Kissinger's secret trip to Beijing and the coming summit, there was a growing conviction that the battle would be lost that year, especially if the United States stuck to its present tactics.[60] In searching for a new solution, State was in favor of a formula seeking dual representation for the two Chinas based on the principle of universality of membership. However, the major problem was that this was obviously a gimmick in light of the common knowledge that the PRC would never enter the UN on those terms because of its commitment to the "one China" principle.[61]

Thus Kissinger and his NSC staff had argued in favor of an alternative tactic that would combine a proposal for dual representation with no prejudice to the ultimate settlement of the Taiwan issue, and a resolution making the expulsion of the ROC an "important question." This had the advantage of causing less offense to Beijing because of its explicit acceptance that it was only "temporarily one China, one Taiwan," as Kissinger told Zhou.[62] It was also more convincing as an effort to keep the ROC in the UN, thus demonstrating U.S. determination not to abandon its ally. However, Kissinger's proposal was underlain by the conviction that the PRC would have its way sooner rather than later. That Kissinger was actually in Beijing on his second, public trip when the General Assembly voted on the issue did not help the ROC.[63] In the event, the PRC did gain its UN seat in the 1971 vote – the General Assembly first voted that the Chinese representation issue was no longer an "important question," and then, by a simple majority, voted to replace the ROC with the PRC.[64]

In the wider rapprochement, the greater problem of the contradiction between soothing domestic opinion and satisfying Beijing's claims over Taiwan was eventually overcome by a combination of tactics: less specific public statements supplemented by clearer private assurances, and a reliance on symbolic gestures. The key section of the Shanghai

---

[60] As Marshall Green and Assistant Secretary for International Organizations Samuel De Palma told Rogers, "In the last analysis, even eventual defeat on the basis of dual representation seems preferable to imminent defeat on the basis of present policy." – "Talking Points for NSC Meeting on Chinese Representation in the UN," 23 March 1971, Box 3210, SNF (1970–3), RG59, NA.

[61] De Palma and Brown to Rogers, "Recommendations to the President on Chinese Representation," 26 May 1971, Box 3210; Yost to Rogers, 8 February 1971, Box 3209, SNF (1970–3), RG59, NA.

[62] Memcon, 11 July 1971, p. 12.

[63] Kissinger has claimed that this coincidence occurred because the vote was called earlier than usual that year. However, the White House had anticipated that this might happen, and Nixon and Kissinger decided to go ahead with the trip anyway. See Haldeman daily notes, 1 October 1971, 3 October 1971, Box 44, Haldeman Files, NPM.

[64] See Foot, *Practice of Power*, pp. 45–6.

Communiqué was the U.S. declaration on Taiwan, which read: "The United States acknowledges that all Chinese on either side of the Taiwan Strait maintain that there is one China and that Taiwan is a part of China. The United States Government does not challenge that position. It reaffirms its interest in a peaceful settlement of the Taiwan question by the Chinese themselves."

This paragraph was undoubtedly a success in terms of "clever" wording. The last sentence clearly indicated U.S. acceptance that the Taiwan issue was an internal Chinese affair, but offered the caveat that a resolution should be peaceful. The paragraph was clearer on the issue of territorial integrity: the Nixon administration did not dispute the Chinese position that Taiwan was part of China. This was consistent with, if more taciturn than, Kissinger's private statement to Zhou in July 1971 that "we are not advocating a 'two Chinas' solution or a 'one China, one Taiwan' solution." He had then added the personal prediction that Taiwan's political evolution was "likely to be in the direction which the Prime Minister indicated" – that is, unification rather than independence.[65]

At the summit, Nixon personally endorsed these private assurances, reiterating the principles that (a) "There is one China, and Taiwan is a part of China. There will be no more statements made – if I can control our bureaucracy – to the effect that the status of Taiwan is undetermined; (b) "We have not and will not support any Taiwan independence movement"; and (c) "We seek the normalization of relations with the PRC."[66] The greatest departure in this confidential agreement was its first point, which could be interpreted to mean a formal U.S. acceptance of Chinese sovereignty over Taiwan. However, in view of the Chinese leaders' professed patience over the issue, this would more likely be read as a statement of principle with only future implications. And yet Nixon's personal notes for the meeting suggest that he might have thought about it in more definite terms as a change in policy that had clear long-term implications for U.S. recognition of the PRC as the only legitimate Chinese government. He wrote that Taiwan's "*status is determined* – one China, Taiwan is part of China"; and that the U.S. "won't support Taiwan independence."[67]

---

[65] Memcon, 9 July 1971, pp. 8–16; 10 July 1971, 12.10–6pm, p. 4.

[66] RN to Zhou, memcon, 22 February 1972, p. 5; and RN–Zhou memcon, 24 February 1972, pp. 13–14.

[67] RN, 15 February 1972, 21 February 1972, China Notes folder, Box 7, PPF, NPM. Emphases mine. It is possible that we have read too much into what was essentially the shorthand manner in which Nixon wrote his personal notes. However, there is a substantial difference between not making statements that the status of Taiwan was undetermined and stating that Taiwan's status was determined, as well as between not supporting the

The longer-term policy implications of Nixon's private assurances to Zhou were well rehearsed at State, which had urged that, if pushed, Washington ought to adhere to the line that the status of Taiwan was undetermined. Fundamentally, State saw that part of the American obligation to its ally was to keep open the option of future independence for Taiwan – as Marshall Green put it, the future status of Taiwan was "not negotiable" in Beijing.[68] Indeed, those arguing for a change in China policy in the later 1960s had consistently argued, or at least implied, the need to shift to a clearer "two Chinas" policy. Similarly, State's legal adviser now cautioned against giving the PRC assurances that the United States was not supporting or encouraging Taiwanese independence elements. This would put Washington in a position of some direct responsibility in the political evolution of the issue, and could too readily be invoked against the United States should the political situation on Taiwan develop in the direction of independence.[69]

The issue provoked some contention within State, though, in the run-up to the summit. INR analysts reminded Rogers that if the "one basic US interest" was to "promote the peaceful resolution of the Chinese civil war," this would best be served by avoiding actions that overtly indicated that Washington was "working to preserve Taiwan's independence." INR judged that the ROC desk had assigned "too much hope to flexibility on the PRC side" – there was no indication that Beijing was "tiring in its quest for the return of Taiwan," and a pro-independence position might induce higher tensions in the Taiwan Straits.[70] There was also the question of whether the United States would be willing to bear the consequences of Taipei's declaring independence, for fundamentally, as Osborn put it, it was not in the U.S. interest to have an independent state of Taiwan that owed its existence to U.S. military protection.[71] This was

---

TIM, which was a loose collection of political pressure groups, and not supporting the general principle of independence for Taiwan. These differences are not likely to have escaped Nixon's legally trained mind.

[68] Green to Rogers, "President's Visit to China – Scope Paper," 25 September 1971, Box 2696, SNF(1970–3), RG59, NA, p. 4. The Taiwan desk, predictably, made the same argument. See Leo Moser to Winthrop Brown, "The Future of Taiwan," 15 November 1971, Box 8, LOT#5412, RG59, NA.

[69] Starr to Green, "EA's January 4, 1972 Paper on the Future of Taiwan," 18 January 1972, Box 1697, SNF(1970–3), RG59, NA.

[70] Popple to Brown, "The Future of Taiwan," 23 December 1971, Box 9, LOT#5412, RG59, NA.

[71] Grant to Brown, "The Future of Taiwan," 21 December 1971, Box 9, LOT#5412; Osborn to Green, "Bargaining with China," 11 November 1971, Box 2189, SNF(1970–3), RG59, NA.

clearly Kissinger's and Nixon's rationale as well – given their desire to improve relations with Beijing, their emphasis on great-power relations, and Nixon's doctrine of drawing down U.S. military commitments abroad.

In all, though, Nixon's private promises to Zhou were relatively circumspect and did not affect the most sensitive issue of the U.S. defense commitment to Taiwan and thus the *means* of the eventual resolution of the problem. The U.S. declaration regarding Taiwan in the Shanghai Communiqué had carefully protected the legality of the U.S.–ROC defense treaty. An important legal basis for the defense treaty was the argument that the status of China was "unsettled"; therefore, if Washington recognized Taiwan as a province of China or conceded that the PRC exercised sovereignty over Taiwan, this would render any U.S. action to defend Taiwan against China intervention in a civil war and thus inadmissible, according to the UN Charter.[72] However, as State's legal adviser assured the secretary, legally, a declaration that Washington "does not challenge" the position of one China "is not necessarily the same as USG acceptance of that position." Furthermore, the legal basis of the treaty was not affected as long as the U.S. continued to recognize the GRC as legitimately occupying and exercising jurisdiction over Taiwan independently of the PRC. Accordingly, in the communiqué, the term "China" was not clearly defined, and the document did not indicate whether Washington regarded one or both of the two governments as the official government of China. But the reference to "all Chinese on either side of the Taiwan Strait" did implicitly acknowledge that there were two contending Chinese authorities and so was consistent with the ROC's continuing to occupy and exercise jurisdiction over Taiwan.[73]

It would appear from the legalistic point of view that Beijing did not make much headway in its demand for formal recognition as the sole legitimate government of all China. In policy terms, this would have amounted to the United States establishing diplomatic relations with the PRC while de-recognizing the GRC. However, it was recognized by both sides from the beginning that this was the end point of the "normalization" process. Zhou had stated in July 1971 that recognition was not a prerequisite to Nixon's visit. For his part, Kissinger emphasized that diplomatic relations were obviously Washington's eventual aim in the opening to the

---

[72] Stevenson to Green, "Legal Aspects of Normalization of Relations with China," 12 November 1971, Box 2189, SNF(1970–3); DoS, "NSSM 106: US China Policy," 16 February 1971, Box 3, LOT 72D504, RG59, NA, p. 40.

[73] Starr to Brown, "US Legal Position on the Status of Taiwan and the 1954 US-ROC Mutual Defense Treaty," 2 March 1972, Box 1698, SNF(1970–3), RG59, NA.

PRC. He pointed out that the key value of the summit was symbolic; it would "make clear that normal relations were inevitable," that the "direction is obvious."[74] Indeed, the intention was made clear in the Shanghai Communiqué, which stated no less than three times that "normalization of relations" was the aim both parties were committed to work toward. Kissinger and Nixon did, however, privately add a time frame to this declaration of intent. As early as July 1971, Kissinger informed Zhou that the Nixon administration could be expected to move formally toward recognition within the "earlier part" of Nixon's second term.[75]

DISCURSIVE RECONSTRUCTIONS AND POLICY OUTCOMES

Any attempt to evaluate the extent of the change in the U.S. position on Taiwan under the Nixon administration will yield a mixed picture. Initially, with its new stance on Chinese representation at the UN and the opening to the PRC, Washington seemed to have headed toward a "two Chinas" policy. However, the Shanghai Communiqué and private undertakings demonstrated that Nixon was firmly moving in the direction of normalization of relations with the PRC and acceptance of eventual unification of Taiwan with the mainland – a clear "one China" policy. In both Washington's reaction to the 1971 South Asian crisis and its reconsideration of the Taiwan issue, we see that the process of constructing a new identity of and relationship with the PRC, which attended the rapprochement, carried concrete policy implications. As Kissinger and Nixon re-represented China and the Chinese leaders as friends and strategic partners and tried to construct new norms of partnership with Beijing, their new discourse warranted new "commonsense" policy choices that accorded with the desired relationship. In this way, discursive transitions were already determining important new policy outcomes at this early stage of the new U.S.–PRC relationship.

In the case of the Taiwan issue, Kissinger and Nixon acted from the basic belief that the Chinese leaders were realists and were thus ready to be more flexible on Taiwan owing to more pressing security concerns vis-à-vis the Soviet Union. However, Kissinger and Nixon sought less bargaining advantage from this issue than one might have expected. To some extent, this was because the Chinese themselves privileged the political aspects of the Taiwan problem and proved to be hard negotiators. On

[74] Memcon, 9 July 1971, p. 14; 10 July 1971, 12.10–6pm, pp. 5, 16.
[75] Memcon, 9 July 1971, pp. 14–15.

the other hand, Kissinger and Nixon also seemed primarily concerned with obtaining Chinese acquiescence on postponing the resolution of the conflict. In the meantime, they were content to use the Taiwan issue as an important policy opportunity to demonstrate their trust in Zhou's and Mao's "principled" nature. Thus, they were content to make informal commitments, to accept Zhou's word, and to agree on general "basic principles," while constructing ambivalent formal agreements that would not compromise the most basic security guarantee to Taiwan and that would minimize domestic opposition. At the same time, the various norms that were negotiated on this fundamental issue reflected Washington's new perception of China as a major power with legitimate claims of sovereignty and territorial integrity. The two sides agreed to focus immediate action on U.S. troop withdrawals from Taiwan, which served to diminish the military aspect of their disagreement. However, Nixon and Kissinger also acquiesced to the principle of "one China" and to Beijing's claims to sovereignty over Taiwan, and they accepted Beijing's informal assurances of peaceful transition.

Overall, as Ross has argued, this yielded a postponement of the contentious Taiwan issue, which allowed the U.S.–PRC relationship to develop based upon more immediate strategic concerns. However, the agreements and norms that were established were open-ended enough to ensure that the Taiwan issue remained intimately linked to the wider development of bilateral relations between the United States and China. On the positive side, Kissinger and Nixon managed to keep the United States involved in the process of resolving the issue and thus retained Washington's commitment to the ROC. This formed the basis for their efforts over the following years to persuade Beijing that it was to its advantage to resolve the issue peacefully, and to let the United States help it to do so by retaining its relationship with Taipei. On the negative side, Taiwan would remain an intractable issue due to the significant domestic concerns and strong demands on both sides, and it would resurface as a longer-term unresolved thorn in the side of the relationship when strategic concerns changed.

9

"Selling" the Rapprochement

The Nixon Administration's Justification of the New China Policy

As a consummate politician, Nixon was keenly aware of the imperatives of policy advocacy and the need to present his policies in a way that was palatable to his key constituencies. Indeed, in contrast to the Democratic administrations that preceded it, the Nixon administration was remarkably proactive and firmly led public opinion on China policy. As discussed in Chapter 4, Nixon was forthcoming about his approach to China in public statements and policy gestures, and he paid particular attention to locating his moves toward China within the context of a "grand strategy" of peace through strength and negotiation. All of these moves were undertaken before it was clear that public opinion had moved decisively in favor of China.[1] Once actual policy changes had been made and the Chinese began to respond, the White House moved assiduously toward a carefully managed campaign to convince various domestic and international audiences of the rationality of Nixon's departures in China policy. This was necessary because public distrust of China was deeply entrenched: for example, even after the announcement of Kissinger's secret trip to Beijing in July 1971, a 56 percent majority of the public still regarded China as the world's most dangerous country.[2] Thus the Nixon administration worked to disseminate the new image of China as a "Former Enemy," with an emphasis on the potential areas for constructive dialogue between the United States and China. Notably, however, different elements

---

[1] For instance, it was only after "Ping-Pong diplomacy" in April 1971 that the American public registered for the first time their preference for PRC membership in the UN – Kusnitz, *Public Opinion and Foreign Policy*, pp. 133–5.
[2] Ibid., p. 138.

of the overall argument were presented to different constituencies; in this more orthodox aspect of policy advocacy, the Nixon administration consciously exploited the distinctions within its discourse of reconciliation with China.

The Nixon administration faced three main episodes of policy advocacy in the opening to China. The first was in March and April of 1971, when, as part of the process of signaling their interest in establishing direct communications, Beijing initiated "Ping-Pong diplomacy," and Nixon responded by significantly easing the restrictions on travel and trade with the PRC. The second and most important occasion was in the wake of the announcement on 15 July 1971 that Kissinger had returned from a secret trip to Beijing and that Nixon himself would be visiting the Chinese capital. The final bout of policy briefings and clarification occurred around the February 1972 summit itself.

"REALIST RESURGENT POWER": EXPLAINING THE FORMER ENEMY

The administration faced two key groups of audiences. The first was made up of sections of the general public that might loosely be termed the "liberals" and the "left," and U.S. allies such as Britain and – perhaps surprisingly – Japan, South Korea, and the ROC. This was regarded by the White House as a group that required less convincing, either because they were already in favor of a change in China policy or because they were perceived to have little option but to fall in line with U.S. policy. With this group, the administration's key aim was to establish an understanding of the opening to China sufficient to preempt charges of being duplicitous or overly simplistic.

Essentially, a satisfactory rationale for the dramatic reversal of China policy in 1971 had to be grounded in an explanation of how Communist China had changed in a way that warranted different treatment. To this first group, the White House and State Department provided an extension of Nixon's prior arguments based on a modified "Resurgent Power" argument, placing the rapprochement within his broad strategy of reducing tensions between the United States and its adversaries and maintaining peace in the international system.

A Resurgent Power Crucial to International Peace

Nixon's 15 July special television address announcing that he would visit China is well known. In it, Nixon repeated his claim that "there can be no stable and endurable peace without the participation of the PRC and its 750 million people," and he matter-of-factly presented Kissinger's trip as a logical extension of the initiatives over the previous year to open up more normal relations with China.[3] To the White House staff, Nixon elaborated by rehearsing his 1967 *Foreign Affairs* argument that China constituted "one-fourth of the world's population" and would be a "decisive" military force "25 years from now." Thus, it would now be "very dangerous" if the United States did not do what it could to end China's isolation. Even a "total détente" with the Soviets would mean "nothing" in terms of international peace, Nixon warned, if China, that crucial "third power," remained quarantined. Hence he sought "dialogue" with Beijing in order to "make the world . . . safer."[4] To the American people, Nixon intoned: "I have taken this action because of my profound conviction that all nations will gain from a reduction of tensions and a better relationship between the US and the PRC. . . . in this spirit . . . I will undertake what I deeply hope will become a journey of peace."[5]

The China opening was relatively well received by the American public. Opinion polls showed a mood of "cautious optimism," with 82 percent of those polled agreeing that the move took "a lot of courage." Moreover, significant pluralities downplayed the potential negative impacts of the move: while 27 percent of those polled felt that it was wrong to "sell out" the GRC, 50 percent disagreed; and 44 percent (against 29 percent) did not think that "other anti-communist nations [would] trust the US less in future" as a result. Overall, the Harris poll estimated that the move had visibly upset between a fourth and a third of the political coalition Nixon had put together in the 1968 election, but that the young and affluent sectors of the electorate had responded "overwhelmingly positively" to the move.[6] This gave Nixon's advisers cause for optimism; they generally felt that they had sufficient public opinion on their side to be able to afford to handle the key criticisms from the right wing.[7]

The good public reception was related in no small measure to the appeal of Nixon's apparent move to ensure a more peaceful world and to give hope to the Vietnam-weary nation. As Lou Harris, the polling

---

[3] *PPP:RN 1971*, p. 819.

[4] WH memo, "Briefing of the White House Staff on the July 15 Announcement of the President's Trip to Peking," 19 July 1971, Box 85, POF, NPM, pp. 2–3.

[5] *PPP:RN 1971*, p. 819.

[6] Press release, "Harris Public Opinion Analysis," 23 September 1971, Box 2, Scali Files, NPM.

[7] Colson to Nixon, "George Meany/China," 19 July 1971, Box 12, POF; Haldeman to McGregor, 28 July 1971, Box 85, Haldeman Files, NPM.

magnate, pointed out, "people have been hungering for something this dramatic, something bold." Nixon's trip to China provided welcome relief and excitement for the nation:

Millions of Americans, who must have had their own childhood fantasies of visiting far-off places, were perhaps starved for excitement in a world that by the early 1970s seemed to be closing in on them, a world where many foreigners no longer welcomed them, a world where they had been humiliated by a determined enemy in Vietnam. Millions of Americans wanted to believe that the China initiative was a grand adventure. And through television, they were able to feel part of it.[8]

Indeed, a Gallup poll showed that Nixon's trip registered the highest public awareness score for any event in history up until then, and that 98 percent of the respondents viewed the Chinese people in favorable terms.[9]

In domestic political terms, Harris enthused that the result of this positive public response to the China opening was to "put the President in total command of the international issue and the peace issue."[10] He had demonstrated that he would talk to the enemy and was not blindly committed to the use of force. Indeed, Nixon's left flank seemed safe. By and large, the Democrats – led by George McGovern, the only declared presidential aspirant at that point, Hubert Humphrey, Harold Hughes, and Mike Mansfield – could only praise the move, which was in line with their own policy, although they ascribed clear electioneering motives to Nixon.

However, having billed Beijing as a power that would help to ensure international peace, the administration now had to dampen congressional expectations linking the Sino-American summit to a peaceful settlement in Vietnam.[11] It would seem that this element was badly managed. After the summit, there was significant speculation about the implications for the Vietnam War, including allegations that a secret deal had been made in Beijing.[12] Kissinger could have reported the Chinese refusal to discuss the issue, but instead he flatly refused to comment. While this would

[8] Madsen, *China and the American Dream*, pp. 72–3. Madsen emphasizes that what made the visit such a "powerful collective experience, a spectacular fact" for Americans was the fact that it was the first major diplomatic event since the advent of global telecommunications, which allowed its televised coverage.

[9] See Kusnitz, *Public Opinion and Foreign Policy*, pp. 138–9.

[10] WH memcon, "Lou Harris' Comments on the President's China Initiative," 28 July 1971, Box 48, Colson Files, NPM.

[11] Mansfield and Javits, quoted in "Officials Tell of Secret Trip by Dr. Kissinger," *NYT*, 17 July 1971; Mansfield on *The Today Show*, quoted in "Further Reaction to President's Announcement on PRC," 16 July 1971, Box 149, Haldeman Files, NPM.

[12] See, e.g., Alsop in *Newsweek*, 7 March 1972.

have reflected the concrete lack of agreement with Beijing on the issue, Kissinger's public stance may have been calculated precisely to give the press some leeway to speculate about the biggest potential gain that the United States could have achieved in Beijing. Similarly, upon his return, Nixon ordered that all officials were to refrain from comment on future U.S. force levels on Taiwan or from statements that might imply linkage between Taiwan force levels and a possible Vietnam settlement[13] – an omission that, in the light of the U.S. statement in the Shanghai Communiqué that it would withdraw its forces on Taiwan "as tensions in the region diminish," could only fuel speculation.

Nixon's visit to China was less well received by America's key Asian allies, the ROC and Japan.[14] The Japanese government was seriously undermined by the move: Tokyo's efforts to establish greater economic ties with China had been dampened at U.S. insistence, and now the Sato government was under attack by opposition parties and powerful business interests for the "great failure in the history of Japanese diplomacy."[15] The greatest impact of the Sino-American rapprochement fell on the ROC, which received only a few hours' warning in advance of Nixon's 15 July broadcast. Taipei's palpable indignation and sense of having been betrayed were summed up in Ambassador James Shen's remark that "it is not the kind of thing a friend and ally should do . . . without prior consultation or without even sufficient notice."[16]

Kissinger repeatedly explained the lack of advance notification by recourse to the danger of leaks through allied governments, but Nixon's response was to emphasize the peace dividends, as it were, for these allies. He reiterated his main "imperative . . . to attempt to break down barriers of hostility and suspicion . . . [that] could threaten the peace of the world," and he assured President Chiang that "the people of free Asian nations should be the first to benefit from efforts to lower tensions in relations

---

[13] DoS memo, 7 March 1972, Box 1697, SNF(1970–3), RG59, NA.

[14] For a succinct discussion of the impact of the rapprochement on East Asia, see Michael Yahuda, *The International Politics of the Asia-Pacific, 1945–1995* (London, 1996), pp. 77–91. He argues that, in the Asia-Pacific region, the new tripolarity had more impact in changing China's position and relations than on altering the fundamental pattern of alliances affecting the United States and the USSR.

[15] "Nixon Visit Infuriates Formosa, Embarrasses Japan and Makes UN Changes Likely," *NYT*, 17 July 1971. For a good discussion of the impact of U.S.–PRC rapprochement on Japanese relations with China, see Sadako Ogata, *Normalization with China: A Comparative Study of US and Japanese Processes* (Berkeley, 1988).

[16] Selig Harrison, "Nixon Move Angers Taiwan; Japan Is Startled, Uncertain," *International Herald Tribune*, 17–18 July 1971.

between the US and the PRC."[17] When Marshall Green visited Taipei after the February 1972 summit, he tried to persuade Foreign Minister Chow Shu-Kai that the PRC was now a status quo power in important respects. Beijing had indicated its "acceptance of the status quo as regards the US presence in Asia and our relationship with the ROC, ROK, Japan and even Vietnam." That Beijing was willing to sign a communiqué that avoided denunciation of the U.S.–ROC security treaty and contained no reference to the immediate withdrawal of U.S. troops from Taiwan represented "remarkable concessions which would not have been possible a few years ago." Thus, the Nixon visit had in fact *"enhanced* the ROC's security." Furthermore, Green pointed out that while the PRC had not renounced the use of force in the Taiwan Straits, its acceptance of the Nixon visit and the terms of the communiqué constituted "concrete evidence" of the priority it accorded to improving relations with the United States. This made it unlikely that Beijing would risk the use of force against Taiwan, which would jeopardize its more urgent policy objective vis-à-vis Washington.[18]

Under the circumstances, though, Taipei's reaction was surprisingly mild. Chiang and his advisers had apparently decided that creating an uproar might only further jeopardize U.S.–ROC relations, the GRC's increasingly precarious international status, and the Kuomintang regime's security.[19] The White House's efforts with Taipei reflected this. Publicly, in order to reassure allies and pro-ROC sentiment, Nixon was careful to emphasize the limits of what he sought from dialogue with Beijing. In his 15 July announcement, Nixon stated that his action in seeking a new relationship with the PRC would not be undertaken "at the expense of old friends."[20] He repeated this reassurance in personal letters to the heads of state of major allies, but ultimately it would seem that the White House was not overly concerned about the negative effects on Japan or the ROC.

---

[17] DoS to McConaughy, "Letter to President Chiang from President Nixon," 16 July 1971, Box 67, PPF, NPM.

[18] AmEmb Manila to DoS, "Green-Holdridge Call on FonMin Chow," 4 March 1972, Box 2691, SNF(1970–3), RG59, NA.

[19] Interviews with GRC officials by Robert A. Madsen, in "Chinese Chess: US China Policy and Taiwan, 1969–1979," unpublished D.Phil. thesis, Oxford University, 1998, pp. 49–52, 101–3. Taipei did "toy with" the options of a rapprochement with Moscow and, in the later 1970s, the development of nuclear weapons. More successful, however, were its stepped-up intelligence-gathering activities in the United States and a political campaign of stimulating opposition to U.S.–PRC relations. See Garver, *Sino-American Alliance*, pp. 277–81; Tucker, *Uncertain Friendships*, pp. 127, 130, 146–7.

[20] *PPP:RN 1971*, p. 820.

The extensive White House preparations for the China trip did not include any detailed plans of how to reassure Asian allies, and eventually it was Green who suggested that he should visit various Asian capitals after the trip to brief their leaders about the results of the summit.[21] At the same time, Kissinger somewhat ambiguously advised Taipei to remain calm and "sit tight," and to await the "upheaval" of the coming regime change on the mainland, which might be favorable to the Nationalists' hope of returning to the mainland.[22]

This reflected the White House's preoccupation with developing the great power triangle and its desire to downplay other bilateral problems with China. Indeed, Nixon and Kissinger evinced a certain sangfroid regarding the consequences for Taipei of the U.S.–PRC rapprochement, primarily because they were convinced that Beijing genuinely did not perceive Taiwan to be the most urgent or important issue and was content to let it rest for the time being. Besides, as discussed in Chapter 8, Nixon was acutely aware of the political stakes in not being perceived to have "sold out" Taiwan, domestically and also in terms of Washington's international credibility. More importantly, perhaps, he felt that the Shanghai Communiqué was a more than adequate safeguard in this respect.

A Realist Power Ready to Compromise

An important component of the Nixon administration's reassurance to the domestic audience about the consequences of the China opening was the idea that Washington had struck a good bargain. Hence, while Nixon initially emphasized the image of China as a resurgent power that was an important determinant of international stability, in the post-summit evaluation of what had been gained or lost from the negotiations, Kissinger stressed instead China's relatively weak geopolitical position in order to persuade his audiences that the United States had gained from important Chinese compromises.

Against potential criticisms that Nixon had "sold out" American allies, "gone soft" on the communists, or been "duped" by the Chinese leaders, Kissinger argued that Beijing's primary strategic security concerns had made it willing to make difficult compromises in order to establish a new

---

[21] And this was approved by the White House only days before the summit. Haig to Kissinger, 9 February 1972, Box 7, NSF/HAK, NPM.

[22] James Shen, *The US and Free China: How the US Sold Out Its Ally* (Washington, DC, 1983), pp. 97, 110.

relationship with Washington. It had made advances toward Washington and was opening up to the United States in an attempt to overcome this strategic weakness. After the announcement of the coming summit trip, Kissinger assured his staff and opinion leaders that "we have not paid anything in this China opening and . . . we will pay nothing in the future." The Chinese, on the other hand, had incurred a high domestic and international price in issuing the invitation – the decision was a "traumatic" one for Beijing and, once made, represented high stakes for the leadership. The nature of the Chinese turnaround and its dramatic opening to the United States could seriously undermine China's ideological and revolutionary leadership position, and Kissinger was particularly fond of repeating the metaphor of Beijing's having lost its "revolutionary virginity" by the very act of "simply inviting us in."[23]

However, the substantive results of the summit itself generated significant domestic debate about what the United States stood to gain from the China opening. The idea that, during the summit, China gave way on very little while Nixon made many concessions in his ardent wooing of Beijing was widely articulated. One of Nixon's fiercest critics, the conservative journalist William Buckley, described the trip with the phrase "*Veni, Vidi, Victus*" [we came, we saw, we were conquered].[24] Here the key focus was Taiwan, an issue that concerned both the political left and right. There was very little mainstream political support for giving up the U.S. defense treaty or diplomatic relations with Taiwan, because the ROC was regarded as a faithful ally and was represented by a well-connected and well-financed lobby within the United States. In particular, the relationship with Taipei was "a central, sacred, passionately held principle of the conservatives who provided Nixon with key political support."[25] Overall, the press contingent accompanying Nixon assessed that the United States had made five concessions to China. First, it had acknowledged formally that Taiwan was Chinese, ending the long-standing position that its status was undetermined. Second, it had pledged to reduce forces on Taiwan, an undertaking unmatched by a reciprocal gesture from Beijing, such as the renunciation of force in the Straits.[26] Third, the U.S. commitment

[23] WH memo, "Briefing of the White House Staff on the July 15 Announcement of the President's Trip to Peking," 19 July 1971, Box 85, POF, NPM, p. 6; memcon, Kissinger briefing to group of conservatives, 12 August 1971, pp. 5–6; memcon, Kissinger to Hoover Institution Overseers, 17 December 1971, Box 49, Haig Files, NPM, p. 9.

[24] *Evening Star*, 23 February 1972. Copy in Haldeman Files, Box 118, NPM.

[25] Madsen, *China and the American Dream*, pp. 62–3.

[26] *New York Times*, 28 February 1972.

to Taiwan was not affirmed in the communiqué – a glaring omission in view of the pledge to continue close ties with the ROK and Japan. Fourth, the United States had endorsed the five principles that China had insisted upon since 1955, including "sovereignty and territorial integrity," which could be seen as an oblique reference to "one China." Finally, the Nixon trip itself was seen as a suppplicatory gesture, and some questioned the need for the president to have made the trip at all.[27] In return, the United States obtained only some ambiguous gains. It had unquestionably opened up dialogue with Beijing, but the two major achievements – the broad understanding that both nations would oppose Soviet dominance in Asia, and the exchanges that the PRC had agreed to in principle – were of mutual benefit rather than gains for the United States per se.

Kissinger responded to these negative assessments by emphasizing the fact that these bilateral agreements would have been unthinkable a year earlier.[28] Mostly, though, he concentrated on arguing that the Nixon administration had not compromised its ally and old friend, stressing instead Chinese concessions on Taiwan. Along with some "old China hands," he pointed out that the blandness of the communiqué compared to past Chinese rhetoric was a dramatic indication of muted ideology.[29] Kissinger also drew press attention to the fact that Beijing had neither asked for the abrogation of the treaty nor reaffirmed its usual position that it was "null and void." Furthermore, it had acquiesced to the U.S. statement at a press conference in Shanghai a few hours after the communiqué had been issued, reaffirming the defense commitment to Taiwan.[30]

Kissinger insisted that, fundamentally, the Chinese did not get "a hell of a lot concrete on Taiwan" because the two sides had not come together in the first place for a deal on Taiwan. Instead, Beijing had been drawn to the United States because of its realist assessments of geopolitical needs: "They did it because necessity has brought them, not our brilliant

---

[27] Press conference, Kissinger and Green, Shanghai, 27 February 1972, Box 48, Colson Files, NPM.

[28] Ibid.

[29] Kissinger post-summit press briefing, n.d., Box 49, Haig Files, NPM; James Thomson, interview on ABC television special, 27 February 1972; A. Doak Barnett and Alexander Eckstein, quoted in the *Washington Post*, 28 February 1972.

[30] Kissinger post-summit press briefing; Kissinger–Green press conference. This was done in a painfully indirect manner: Kissinger told the assembled journalists that the U.S. position on the defense treaty as set out in the president's World Report remained unchanged and requested that no more be asked about the issue at that time. Rogers later made the same points to the ROC ambassador. DoS telegram, "ROC Ambassador Shen Calls on the Secretary," 3 March 1972, Box 2206, SNF(1970–3), RG59, NA.

policy.... our policy only took advantage of the opportunity.... necessity has shown them that they needed a parallelism with us on a number of policies." The Chinese leadership had to demonstrate that they could agree with the United States on something, and "this common statement of principles was a hell of a lot more crucial to them than these waffled phrases on Taiwan."[31] In other words, the Chinese were somewhat reluctant conciliators, driven by a strategic necessity that, fortunately, had been recognized by Nixon and Kissinger and turned effectively to U.S. advantage. According to this presentation, China, because of its strategic weakness, had become a reduced threat, and Chinese leaders were now people with whom American leaders could conduct serious dialogue. It also portrayed the United States as a realistic power, willing to open dialogue with the Chinese Communists in the pursuit of peace, but without compromising its allies and key interests.

CHINA AS "THE ENEMY OF MY ENEMY": *REALPOLITIK* FOR THE RIGHT

The group of constituents that occupied most White House attention consisted of the conservative end of the domestic political spectrum that might oppose Nixon's policy for anticommunist, pro-Taiwan, or commercial protectionist reasons. Nixon's aides expended considerable effort in identifying and cultivating Republicans who supported the China opening and in defending the policy change against right-wing opponents. Also included in this group were policy "insiders," particularly members of the White House staff, who had the potential to harm the opening in its earlier stages by leaks and innuendos. To this group, Kissinger deliberately stressed the practical geopolitical advantages of the China opening against the Soviet Union.

To the general public, Nixon and Kissinger admitted – however cryptically – the contributing factor of the Sino-Soviet dispute in the China opening, but they flatly denied exploiting the split. Instead, they portrayed it as a factor pushing Beijing to improve relations with the United States, providing an opportunity that Nixon had grasped for the purpose of furthering peace. Thus, Nixon's key caveat in explaining the China opening was that "It is not directed against any other nation. We seek friendly relations with all nations. Any nation can be our friend without being any other nation's enemy."[32]

---

[31] Kissinger post-summit press briefing.
[32] *PPP:RN 1971*, p. 819.

Yet, if it should seem that Nixon's remarks were meant as much to draw the attention of certain parties to the maxim that "the enemy of my enemy is my friend," the idea would not be off the mark. Nixon and Kissinger had hoped to play the "China card" in order to exert pressure on the Soviet Union to pursue détente, and they duly did so in imparting the news that Nixon was going to visit China. Kissinger spoke to Ambassador Dobrynin a few hours before the 15 July announcement and told him bluntly, "It is not directed at you." However, he also made clear that some of the negative impact of the China opening on the Soviet position was Moscow's own fault. Washington had given priority to a U.S.–USSR summit, but "your government's decision to delay the date for such a summit has forced us to proceed first with [the China announcement]." Thus, Kissinger's emphasis that the China opening was not aimed at Moscow carried a veiled warning that Washington nevertheless possessed this option. Therefore, he advised that they should now proceed on the course of détente rather than retreat to an "agonizing reappraisal" of U.S.–USSR relations.[33] Furthermore, Kissinger brandished the China card in order to goad Moscow into helping to end the Vietnam War. The war, he told Dobrynin, "introduced distortions" to China's status and power – the Soviets insisted that China was "very weak," but it was undeniable that Beijing was crucial to resolving regional issues. Thus, because of Vietnam and because of "the rather ungenerous reactions of the Soviet Union to our repeated efforts to bring about a fundamental change in [the Soviet–American] relationship," Washington had turned to China.[34]

The Nixon administration was most concerned about justifying the president's planned China trip and China policy to domestic conservatives, and Kissinger held numerous briefings with groups of Republicans and other influential conservative figures. To these audiences, Kissinger was most explicit about triangular politics. The geopolitical angle and balance of power logic were deployed because they lent the enterprise a crucial element of hard-headed necessity. In the face of conservative anti-communist sentiment, it was essential to emphasize that the turnabout on

---

[33] NSC, "Talking Points for Ambassador Dobrynin," ca. 15 July 1971, Box 1036, NSF, NPM; Dobrynin, *In Confidence*, pp. 226–7; Kissinger to Nixon, "My Conversation with Ambassador Dobrynin, July 19, 1971," 27 July 1971, Box 492, NSF, NPM. Indeed, the White House had made a final effort to get the Soviets to agree to a date for the summit just before Kissinger left for Pakistan and China, but the Soviets had not been forthcoming. Haig to RN, "Soviet Response," 6 July 1971, Box 1031, NSF, NPM.

[34] Memcon, 18 November 1971, Box 492, NSF, NPM, pp. 6–7.

China policy had not occurred because Nixon had suddenly found virtue in communism; rather, it was an action taken for power political reasons, in consideration of strategic national interest.

In explaining the China opening to conservatives, therefore, Kissinger concentrated on justifying how and why Washington's perception of the PRC and of the kind of relations it would like to have with Beijing had been modified. The focus was shifted away from the identity of China per se; rather, the opening to China was portrayed as a means to the more important ends of the superpower competition with the Soviet Union and defending the domestic political position of the conservatives. That is, Kissinger's focus was more on building a particular political image of America – and of Nixon – than on representing China itself.[35]

Leverage against the Greater Adversary

Kissinger told his conservative audiences that while the Nixon administration understood that for them, the Chinese appeared to pose a "peculiarly devilish threat," the China opening was designed to afford Washington leverage against the Soviet Union, which was "a far more formidable threat than the Chinese." While Moscow possessed 1,500 intercontinental ballistic missiles, Beijing had none. Moreover, the Soviets had built up their forces on the Chinese border and had again revealed their hegemonic ambitions during the South Asian crisis. While Haig was telling Zhou this in Beijing, Kissinger explained to a group of Nixon administration supporters that they faced a situation "not unlike that in which the Germans attacked Russia, and Churchill commented that if Hitler invaded hell, he [Churchill] would make a pact with the Devil."[36] The Chinese might not be the most desirable of partners, but the rapprochement was necessary for the greater goal of "prevent[ing] the Eurasian land mass and its resources from ... falling exclusively under the control of the Russians."[37] To the White House staff, Kissinger acknowledged that the Chinese "don't wish us well," but in view of the greater Soviet pressure, "it is in our interest

---

[35] This is consistent with Schurmann's argument that the key objective of triangular politics was to regain a position of leadership and centrality for the United States in international politics. See Schurmann, *Foreign Politics of Richard Nixon*, p. 2.

[36] Churchill himself put it this way: "If Hitler invaded Hell I would make at least a favourable reference to the Devil in the House of Commons." Winston Churchill, *The Grand Alliance* (Boston, 1950), p. 370.

[37] Rodman to Haig, "Hawk Talkers – Peking Summit," 2 December 1971, Box 49, Haig Files; report of Kissinger remarks to a group of conservative administration supporters, 5 January 1972, Box 1026, NSF, NPM, p. 6.

to bring the Chinese in." From a realist balance-of-power viewpoint, "[w]ith two formidable opponents contesting against each other, it is not obvious that it is in our interest to side with the stronger one against the weaker one."[38]

Hence the main aim of Nixon's rapprochement with China was to ex- acerbate Soviet concerns about a possible U.S.–PRC alliance, and thus to encourage Moscow to engage more actively in negotiating détente with Washington and to exercise restraint in its involvement in other parts of the world. The implication, as the Nixon administration hastened to assure conservatives in particular, was that it had little interest in im- proving relations with China for its own sake. Thus, the statement that "Richard Nixon has no illusions about Chinese Communism" featured prominently in talking points for conservative groups. The Nixon admin- istration was not proceeding on the "naïve assumption" that the many bilateral differences – especially Taiwan – could be overcome quickly. There remained many fundamental differences in policy, and there were "no preconditions" to Nixon's trip, "no secret deals" resulting from it, and "absolutely no sell-out" of the ROC.[39]

China Policy and Domestic Conservative Politics

The Nixon administration was forced to be particularly attentive to its conservative supporters in view of the presidential election in late 1972. Predictably, Nixon came under attack from right-wing conservatives such as George Meany (an influential labor leader) and William Buckley, who led the opposition to Nixon within the Republican campaign. Two weeks after Nixon's announcement, a group of eleven prominent conservative leaders issued a public statement suspending their support for Nixon, mainly for "his failure to call public attention to the deteriorated [U.S.] military position in conventional and strategic arms," and in part be- cause of his "overtures to Red China, done in the absence of any public concessions by Red China to American and Western causes."[40]

While these attacks were relatively contained and confined to the more extreme elements of the right, the White House was conscientious in trying

---

[38] "Briefing of the White House Staff on the July 15 Announcement," p. 5.
[39] Holdridge to Kissinger, "Your Briefing on China for Billy Graham and Influential Con- servatives," 9 August 1971, FG 6–11–1 HAK folder, Box 15, WHCF, NPM; Rodman, "Hawk Talkers."
[40] Press release, "Prominent Conservative Leaders 'Suspend' Support of President Nixon," 29 July 1971, Box 149, Haldeman Files, NPM.

to forestall their spread within the conservative electorate. At his briefings to insiders and conservative leaders, Kissinger portrayed the China opening as being fully in line with conservative values and strategies, and as a shrewd political move by Nixon in the face of liberal opposition. Sketching a scenario of a domestic political siege on the administration, Kissinger told the White House staff, "The choice for us was this: to sit still, with our whole foreign policy under assault at home, and let ourselves be chopped up, or try to bring the Chinese into play."[41] Kissinger reiterated to leading conservatives that Nixon wanted to strengthen the United States' strategic capabilities vis-à-vis the Soviet Union, and he emphasized that the administration had come into office facing "an erosion of power" against the Soviets, compounded by Vietnam fatigue at home and an "irresponsible" Congress. Nixon's efforts at building up the defense arsenal had been attacked at every step by Congress, the bureaucracy, the intellectuals, and the newspapers, Kissinger railed. But Nixon had gone ahead with the ABM program as a means to pressure the Soviets into negotiating SALT, and had developed the MIRV programme as well as new fighter projects. Given this situation in which the administration's instruments for a "stick-and-carrot" approach to Soviet policy – military strength, military aid, economic aid – were being "hobbled by liberal assault" domestically, it needed new forms of leverage. In this context, the opening to China provided the vital "diplomatic maneuverability" against the Soviets.[42] Kissinger urged that Nixon needed the full spectrum of conservative support, complaining that "[t]his . . . is the loneliest administration imaginable" and pointing out that there was a "great need to develop a counterweight to the liberal consensus" within domestic politics.[43]

Overall, Nixon's China policy received significant support from many conservatives. There were some highly publicized critiques and breaks, but these were relatively contained within the extreme right wing. Among the conservative press generally, Nixon's staff reported responses that were more moderate than expected, and key conservatives such as Ronald Reagan and Barry Goldwater supported Nixon after July 1971.[44] For his part, Goldwater told Nixon: "Get me the forums and I'll speak anytime

[41] "Briefing of the White House Staff on the July 15 Announcement," p. 5.
[42] Kissinger briefing to group of conservatives, 12 August 1971, p. 2; Kissinger to conservative administration supporters, 5 January 1972, p. 5; Rodman, "Hawk Talkers."
[43] Kissinger briefing to group of conservatives, 12 August 1971, pp. 7–8.
[44] Klein to Nixon, 19 July 1971, Box 19, WHCF/CO; Warren to Haldeman, 22 July 1971, Box 273, Haldeman Files, NPM.

on your behalf." He seemed convinced by Nixon's line that "You know me . . . I am not going to sell us out."[45] The expulsion of the ROC from the UN in October 1971 presented a setback for this conservative support, as Republicans in the Senate, including Goldwater and Senator James Buckley, campaigned to reduce U.S. support for the UN.[46] As discussed earlier, some eleven prominent conservatives publicly broke with Nixon in part because of China policy. However, other high-profile conservatives continued to support Nixon, among them Ronald Reagan, who, convinced by the *realpolitik* explanation that Kissinger offered to him in a private briefing, agreed to act as Nixon's personal envoy, traveling to Taipei at the end of 1971 to reassure the GRC about the new China policy.[47] Ultimately, this conservative support probably stemmed in large part from the unique room for maneuver that Nixon enjoyed because of his background as a conservative and a staunch anticommunist. Also, the breakthrough and the summit – labeled "TV's biggest show since man-on-the-moon"[48] – were undeniably dramatic and reaped significant domestic political gains for the Republican Party, and for Nixon as the incumbent candidate, in an election year. In terms of results, too, the "China card" appeared to be effective, as Moscow accelerated negotiations over Berlin and SALT after July 1971 and agreed to the Moscow summit in June 1972.[49]

CONCLUSION

The Nixon administration was relatively successful in garnering support for the China opening. This was due in no small part to the altered domestic perception of China, which was tied up with the prominent changes in China policy discourse of the late 1960s and with Nixon's own process of policy relaxation beginning in 1969. It also stemmed from a strong desire for peace among a Vietnam-weary public. However, a crucial factor was the careful policy advocacy employed by the White House.

---

[45] WH memo, "The President's Meeting with Senator Barry Goldwater," 31 August 1971, Box 49, Haig Files, NPM.

[46] Bob Dole press release, "Setback for Reason"; UPI news telegram, 26 October 1971, Box 48, Colson Files, NPM.

[47] Holdridge, *Crossing the Divide*, p. 76; Tyler, *A Great Wall*, p. 109. In a speech in Taipei, Reagan pledged that the United States would "weaken no cherished associations and break no promises" – *NYT*, 12 October 1971, p. 40.

[48] *NYT*, 18 February 1972.

[49] See Dobrynin, *In Confidence*, pp. 228–35; Hyland, *Mortal Rivals*, pp. 24–5; Robert Gates, *From the Shadows: The Ultimate Insider's Story of Five Presidents and How They Won the Cold War* (New York, 1996), pp. 44–50.

For the benefit of the "doves," the liberals, and the left, Nixon emphasized the themes of peace and negotiation and continued to present China as a resurgent major power with which the United States had to engage in order to maintain international peace. At the same time, in reiterating the practical and realistic aims of the Nixon administration in not compromising allies and old friends in its search for dialogue with the Chinese, Kissinger also found it expedient to argue that China was in a weak geopolitical position and therefore ready to compromise with the United States on important issues such as Taiwan. Strikingly, however, the White House's main concern was with its domestic, rather than allied, audience – the ROC had to be content with the same reasons that were being offered to the general public, as it was seen to be in a weakening position and increasingly dependent on the United States.

To the anticommunist conservatives, on the other hand, Kissinger flagged the *realpolitik*, anti-Soviet triangular politics rationale to demonstrate that Nixon remained true to his conservative credentials and acted in the best national interest. In this hard-headed discourse, China was in itself a diminished threat, primarily because it now clearly shared with the United States the greater adversary of the Soviet Union. Nixon and Kissinger, for their part, were unsentimental realist operators who were taking advantage of the Sino-Soviet split in order to turn the balance of power to U.S. advantage vis-à-vis its superpower rival. At the same time, Kissinger stressed the party political aspect of the challenges faced by the Nixon administration, arguing that the new China policy was an integral part of Nixon's attempts to rescue his strong and realistic foreign policy from the enemies of the Republicans and conservatives – the Democrats and liberals.

Thus, in spite of the prominence of the triangular politics rationale in Kissinger's memoir accounts, it was rather the "liberal" revisionist school of thought about the opening to China, which originated in the 1960s and was then modified by Nixon, that was emphasized for public and allied consumption. The *realpolitik* argument was articulated only on a "limited distribution" basis at the time, for instrumental reasons, principally to help to protect the administration's domestic right flank by arguing that Nixon was in fact driving a good bargain against the two communist adversaries. This strategy of selective reasoning was effective, and support for Nixon's China policy in the next year or so began to unravel seriously only with the Watergate crisis.

10

"Tacit Ally," June 1972 to 1974

Consolidating or Saving the U.S.–China Rapprochement

This chapter traces and offers some explanations for the transition, in practice, from a rapprochement relationship in which China was characterized as a "former enemy" – a fellow realist power with whom the United States cultivated a mutual distrust of the Soviet Union, and toward whom the United States "tilted" covertly while pursuing a superpower détente – to a relationship that encompassed more intimate diplomatic and military ties with a China represented as a "tacit ally." The latter contained a much more overt anti-Soviet focus, within which Kissinger emphasized offering strategic reassurance to the Chinese and the development of conceptual and domestic opinion bases for a closer security relationship, while bargaining for more favorable terms of diplomatic normalization.

After the Beijing summit, the negotiation of the U.S.–PRC rapprochement was closely influenced both by triangular politics and by domestic politics. At the same time, the sustained interaction between the two sides had a significant impact upon the development of the discursive context and resulting policy actions. Interestingly, this process was again characterized by competing discourses: this time, Kissinger's representation of the Soviet threat and U.S.–PRC relations versus that of the Chinese leaders. Kissinger portrayed the Chinese not just as former adversaries or friends but as tacit allies, whose strategic viewpoint increasingly coincided with that of the United States and who placed their priority on anti-Soviet aspects of the relationship rather than on bilateral issues. This contrasted with the Chinese discourse, which questioned U.S. sincerity and reliability as a friend based on disagreement with and suspicion about Washington's détente policy, and which denigrated the Soviet threat in order to reduce American leverage in U.S.–PRC normalization negotiations.

In this context, Kissinger tried further to construct the "tacit alliance" he envisaged, at first discursively in his presentation of the outcome of his dialogues, then by offering Beijing various means of strengthening bilateral military ties.

TRIANGULAR POLITICS, JUNE 1972 TO FEBRUARY 1973: FORMER ENEMY TO TACIT ALLY?

After Nixon's China trip, Kissinger traveled again to Beijing for talks in June 1972 and February 1973. Between those visits, Kissinger and his staff continued to meet frequently with Huang Hua, the PRC representative to the UN, in New York. According to Kissinger's reports to Nixon, this short one-year period following Nixon's summit trip was a "honeymoon" of sorts in the new U.S.–PRC relationship, during which their common interests were confirmed and the norms of the bilateral relationship further consolidated.

China as Kissinger's "Tacit Ally"

For Kissinger, the two sets of dialogues in Beijing in June 1972 and February 1973 provided definitive evidence of the vitality of the strategic basis for the developing relationship. The Chinese leaders were now more forthcoming in discussing the Soviet threat, and there was such an apparent convergence of Chinese and American strategic viewpoints that upon his return from Beijing in June 1972, Kissinger told Nixon that "the Chinese have moved . . . from an adversary posture to one which can only be described as tacit ally."[1] Eight months later, Kissinger reported "remarkable" progress: the two sides, which had come together in 1972 "despite different world outlooks," "have now become tacit allies." In fact, "we are now in the extraordinary situation that, with the exception of the United Kingdom, *the PRC might well be the closest to us in its global perceptions.*"[2]

There were two main elements to Kissinger's image of the PRC as "Tacit Ally." First, Beijing explicitly recognized the Soviet Union as a common adversary and shared Washington's strategic assessment of the

---

[1] Kissinger to RN, "My Trip to Peking, June 19–23, 1972," 27 June 1972, Box 851, NSF, NPM, p. 2.

[2] Kissinger to RN, "My Trip to China," 2 March 1973, Box 6, PPF, NPM, pp. 2–3 (italics in original). I am grateful to William Burr of the National Security Archive for sharing the unsanitized version of this document, which he obtained through an FOIA request.

global threat posed by the Soviets. While Mao and Zhou had been relatively reticent in their discussions of the Soviets in 1971 and at the summit, Beijing now clearly articulated the shared American and Chinese interest in containing the Soviet threat. As Kissinger put it, "the floodgates opened privately and publicly" – Mao and Zhou were "obsessed" with the Soviet Union, which "completely permeated" the talks, and they saw the Soviet hand at play in every region of the world.[3] The Chinese leaders asserted that Moscow harbored expansionist ambitions all over the world, competing with the United States for influence in the Middle East, expanding into the Mediterranean and South Asia, and continuing to threaten China. Zhou warned that Washington could not afford to react "too slowly and prudently" in these areas.[4]

Second, besides affirming Moscow's identity as a common adversary, Mao asserted that the United States and China should "work together to commonly deal with [the] bastard."[5] Kissinger's discourse of China as "Tacit Ally" drew from the way in which the Chinese leaders voiced support for U.S. policies of containment against the Soviet Union and for American involvement in various regions to counter the Soviet threat. To begin with, there now appeared to be an explicit recognition in Beijing that it was in the Chinese interest for the United States to maintain its power to counter Soviet pressure internationally.[6] At the June 1972 meetings, Zhou and Marshal Ye Jianying probed Kissinger on the American capacity for continued international containment of the Soviet Union, expressing concern about the likelihood of cuts in the U.S. defense budget in case the Democrat George McGovern was elected in the presidential elections, and openly praising Defense Secretary Melvin Laird's call for increasing military expenditure.[7]

Additionally, Kissinger and Mao and Zhou further developed a security dialogue, much like that between close allies – they had long discussions about the state of American alliances in Europe and Asia, and about U.S. containment strategy in South Asia and the Middle East. Mao urged that

---

[3] Kissinger to RN, "Atmospherics of My Trip to Peking," 2 March 1973, p. 2; Kissinger to RN, "My Asian Trip," 27 February 1973, Box 6, PPF, NPM, p. 6; "My Trip to China," p. 4.

[4] Zhou–Kissinger memcon, 15 February 1973, pp. 17–18. All memcons from Kissinger's February 1973 trip can be found in Box 98, NSF, NPM.

[5] Mao–Kissinger memcon, 17 February 1973, in Burr, *Kissinger Transcripts*, p. 88.

[6] This was noted by members of Kissinger's staff who accompanied him on the trip. See Howe to Kissinger, "China Trip," 24 June 1972, Box 97, NSF/HAK, NPM.

[7] Zhou–Kissinger memcon, 20 June 1972, pp. 15–16; 21 June 1972, p. 3. The memoranda of conversations from the June 1972 trip are found in Box 851, NSF, NPM.

Washington should work more closely with its allies, particularly in order to maintain NATO unity, and derided the European communist parties, favoring instead those that wanted stronger ties with Washington.[8] Beijing was itself expanding contacts with Western European leaders and urging resistance to Moscow, and Zhou discussed with Kissinger the hope that West Germany would develop as a balance to Soviet power.[9] In conjunction with this, Chinese attitudes toward the U.S.–Japan relationship were now clearly modified. From their previous insistence that Japan was a rising power that might help to carve up China, and their firm opposition to the U.S.–Japan treaty, the Chinese leaders moved toward the view of Japan as an "incipient ally...to counter Soviet and Indian designs."[10] Publicly, this change was evident in Sino-Japanese normalization; in private, Zhou had gone further, acknowledging that "we are not...in favour of a transition from [the]...Japan-US Security Treaty." Implying that China saw the treaty as a brake on Japanese militarism, he reminded Kissinger that the United States had a responsibility to restrain Tokyo and to prevent it from being "won over" by the Soviet Union.[11] Mao himself sent the same message: "rather than Japan having closer relations with the Soviet Union, we would rather they would better their relations with you."[12]

Generally, Mao urged the United States to create an anti-Soviet axis that would include Europe, Turkey, Iran, Pakistan, and Japan.[13] Washington ought to take more action to prevent the Soviets from spreading their influence in the Middle East, the Persian Gulf, the Near East, South Asia, and the Indian Ocean, he counseled. In South Asia, Beijing supported U.S. involvement and support of independent Pakistan as a balance to Soviet-supported India. The Near and Middle East were regions in which the Chinese leaders had professed little interest thus far, but Kissinger reported that they now "clearly looked with favor on our continuing presence in the Middle East to counter the Soviets."[14] Indeed, Chinese scholars note that during this time, "Mao in particular grew attached to

[8] Mao–Kissinger memcon, in Burr, *Kissinger Transcripts*, p. 89.
[9] Kissinger, "My Trip to Peking, June 1972," p. 10; Kissinger–Zhou memcon, 19 June 1973, pp. 21–5.
[10] Kissinger, "My Trip to China," p. 16.
[11] Zhou–Kissinger memcon, 18 February 1973, pp. 29–33.
[12] Mao–Kissinger memcon, in Burr, *Kissinger Transcripts*, pp. 91–2.
[13] Ibid., p. 94. Notably, Mao did not include China in this axis, an indication of the way in which Beijing seemed to regard itself more as a source of "moral support" than as a U.S. ally or recipient of U.S. military supplies or aid.
[14] Kissinger, "My Trip to China," p. 11. This was censored in the sanitized version.

the concept of 'a parallel', of the Chinese uniting with the Americans in the fight against the Soviet Union."[15]

This convergence of strategic assessments was accompanied by the further institutionalization of the U.S.–PRC relationship in the form of an agreement during Kissinger's February 1973 trip to set up liaison offices in each other's capitals. Not only did these offices – which would be "closely equivalent to Embassies in everything but name"[16] – represent a concrete advance toward normalization, but the simultaneous presence of a GRC embassy and a PRC liaison office in Washington would also signify Beijing's continued willingness to downplay the contentious issue of Taiwan. Kissinger explained to Nixon that this breakthrough was the result of four factors: the Vietnam peace agreement, which had removed the remaining stubborn disagreement between the two sides; "the growing Chinese preoccupation with the Soviet threat"; "the shadow of the advancing age of the PRC leaders"; and Chinese confidence in the Nixon administration.[17]

For all his triangular politicking, Kissinger was noticeably taciturn about the effect of the developing Soviet–American détente on Chinese calculations. Although the logic of "triangular politics" underlay both the American and Chinese moves toward rapprochement, the dynamics of the strategic triangle became fully functional only during 1972, when the U.S.–PRC and U.S.–USSR summit meetings were held within four months of each other. The Nixon White House devoted the months following the China summit to negotiations with the Soviet Union about Berlin, SALT, Vietnam, and the Soviet–American summit. Thus, Beijing's conviction that the United States and China should join in countering Soviet expansionism did not develop suddenly in mid-1972; as the momentum of triangular politics grew, so too did the Chinese leaders' desire for closer relations with the United States as a means to counteract U.S.–USSR ties. At the same time, Chinese disquiet and suspicions about Soviet–American collusion also increased, leading to a significant divergence in the Chinese leaders' representation of U.S. and Soviet intentions, which Kissinger played down in his reports to Nixon.

---

[15] Gong, "Chinese Decision Making," p. 356.

[16] Ibid., pp. 20–1.

[17] Ibid., p. 1. In fact, as far back as May 1971 the Chinese Politburo had recommended that during the interim period, while Beijing awaited the full realization of its conditions on Taiwan prior to normalization of relations with Washington, the two sides could set up liaison offices. – Zhang, "The Changing International Scene," p. 75.

The United States as a False Friend: Beijing Questions U.S. Intentions

The documentary record shows that – rhetorically, at least – Mao and Zhou did not share Kissinger's representation of the United States and PRC as tacit allies or partners. In their talks with Kissinger in June 1972 and February 1973, the Chinese leaders constructed a more ambivalent account of the developing U.S.–PRC relationship. While they agreed with the United States about the shared danger and scope of the Soviet threat, Mao and Zhou put forward a diverging assessment of Soviet intentions and strategy. As part of their critique of Washington's policy of détente with the Soviet Union, Mao in particular questioned U.S. sincerity and intentions in the rapprochement, portraying the United States as opportunistically exploiting the Sino-Soviet split in order to achieve its ultimate aim of defeating its superpower rival.

As the Chinese leaders began to make more explicit the anti-Soviet thrust of the Sino-American rapprochement from their point of view, so too Beijing articulated a stronger image of an aggressive and expansionist Soviet Union. In February 1973, Zhou warned Kissinger that the "new Czars" were "extremely sly," "extremely aggressive," and willing to "disregard all diplomatic promises," so that "as soon as you slack your steps [in any key region]... they will step in."[18] By contrast, Washington's policy of détente with Moscow was predicated on the assumption that the Soviet Union might choose the course of "changing its policy in a more peaceful direction." This was an option that the Nixon administration, through negotiations and agreements, was prepared to give Moscow "every incentive" to pursue.[19] Zhou's blunt retort was that the Soviets' "so-called détente is false. . . . they are engaged in expansion." But because Moscow was "afraid of fighting a nuclear war," it was trying to negotiate a nuclear nonaggression treaty with the United States while shifting its challenges to "remote areas" such as the Middle East.[20] This reasoning went to the heart of Chinese suspicions about the fallout of a European détente on themselves, which underlay the tension between the U.S. policies of détente and rapprochement.

[18] Zhou–Kissinger memcon, 15 February 1973, pp. 17–18. The Soviets also did not disguise their low opinion of the Chinese: Brezhnev told Nixon that they were "peculiar," "treacherous and spiteful," "extremely sly and perfidious," and "ruthless." RN–Brezhnev memcon, 23 June 1973, Box 75, NSF/HAK, NPM.

[19] Kissinger to Zhou, memcon, 20 June 1972, pp. 22–3.

[20] Zhou–Kissinger memcon, 17 February 1973, 10.22–11.10pm, pp. 4–6.

Beijing was particularly skeptical about Soviet-American negotiations regarding a nuclear nonaggression treaty during the second half of 1972, which eventually evolved into the Agreement on the Prevention of Nuclear War (PNW) signed in June 1973. The agreement, proposed by the Soviets, would have the two superpowers refrain from using nuclear weapons against each other and required that they consult each other in the event of conflicts that might involve nuclear weapons.[21] Beijing denounced the proposed agreement as "nakedly aimed at nuclear world hegemony" and thus in violation of the Shanghai Communiqué principle against collusion to divide the world into spheres.[22]

Kissinger responded to these concerns by constructing an even more menacing Soviet threat and arguing that détente was part of the U.S. strategy to aid China in containing the Soviet Union. He warned Huang that "there is a deliberate Soviet policy to isolate you": "the many agreements the Soviet Union has made in the last two years . . . in the West, can only be explained . . . in terms of aggressive intent in the East."[23] Washington had every intention of helping its Chinese friends to counter this threat, but it had to negotiate with Moscow as well, in order to "to play for time." The Nixon administration needed to get its domestic audience "used to" some "entirely new" propositions, such as the idea that Chinese security affected American interests. Ultimately, Kissinger assured the Chinese, the aim was to provide a firmer basis for resistance to Soviet hegemonic aspirations. Agreements such as the nuclear nonaggression treaty would "maneuver the Soviet Union into a position where it clearly [would be] the provocateur" if it acted aggressively, providing a moral and legal basis for U.S. military reaction.[24]

The Chinese leaders disputed Kissinger's representations of both Soviet and American intentions and strategy. In August 1972, Huang Hua declared frankly that the Chinese side was "not so worried about the

---

[21] The key aspects of the PNW agreement were: a declaration that the superpowers would refrain from the use of force against each other and against others, and an agreement to consult with each other to avert the risk of nuclear war in the event that relations between them or between either side and any third country appeared to involve the risk of nuclear war. See Garthoff, *Détente and Confrontation*, pp. 376–86.

[22] Kissinger–Huang memcon, 4 August 1972, Box 329, Lord Files, pp. 1–2; note from Zhou, in Huang–Kissinger memcon, 27 May 1973, Box 328, Lord Files, pp. 5–6. Chinese sources reveal that there was internal disagreement about the implications of the PNW within the Chinese leadership, but Mao prevailed in his view that it did not signify a true superpower cabal, as détente could only be temporary because Soviet–American "contradictions" were too entrenched. Gong, *Mao Zedong yu Meiguo*, pp. 358–9.

[23] Kissinger–Huang memcon, 4 August 1972, pp. 7–8.

[24] Kissinger–Zhou memcon, 16 February 1973, pp. 12–15.

Soviet attempt to isolate China." On the contrary, there were signs that Moscow was trying to create "through its anti-China propaganda a false sense of security in Europe."[25] In other words, Beijing believed that Moscow retained its primary designs on the West, and that the United States ought to reexamine its policy of détente.[26]

By February 1973, the suspicions expressed by the Chinese leaders about U.S. intentions shifted from an overt U.S.–USSR cabal against China toward the possibility of more subtle U.S. strategies to overcome its superpower rival by using the PRC. As their concern grew about developments in Europe – the establishment of the European Security Community, the Mutual and Balanced Force Reduction (MBFR) negotiations, and *Ostpolitik* in general[27] – Zhou and Mao, in the best elliptical Chinese fashion, suggested that the U.S. policy of détente in the West was really a tactic the Americans and Europeans were using to "push the ill waters of the Soviet Union ... eastward."[28] In other words, it was a policy of deliberate appeasement of the Soviet Union in the West, so as to channel Moscow's expansionist tendencies toward China, the Middle East, and the Indian subcontinent. Zhou pointed to "historical examples" of such (unsuccessful) appeasement by the Western Europeans in trying to push German aggressors eastward during World War I and World War II. Now they were trying to repeat the strategy with the Soviets.[29] In this Chinese representation, the United States was not a tacit ally but a false friend.[30]

---

[25] The success of the U.S.–China opening may have contributed to this state of affairs, for as a Foreign Policy Research Institute study had warned, too warm a Sino-American relationship would breed the notion in Europe and the United States that the Soviets were so concerned about the strengthened position of the PRC that it would be ready to negotiate détente in the West so as to concentrate on the East. – William Kintner, "The Impact of President Nixon's Visit to Peking on Global Relations and US Foreign Policy in the 1970s," 14 February 1972, Box 502, NSF, NPM, pp. 56–61.

[26] Huang–Howe memcon, 14 August 1972, Box 850, NSF, NPM, p. 2. On 10 July 1972, Mao himself had warned the French foreign minister about the danger of the Soviet "feint towards the East": "while they speak of attacking China, the reality is that they want to conquer Europe." – *Mao Zedong waijiao wenxuan*, p. 597.

[27] Kissinger, "My Trip to China," p. 6.

[28] Zhou–Kissinger memcon, 15 February 1973, p. 11; Mao–Kissinger memcon, 18 February 1973, *Kissinger Transcripts*, p. 89.

[29] Memcon, 17 February 1973, 10.22–11.10pm, pp. 2, 4.

[30] Indeed, Schurmann argues that Nixon's new "grand design" was effective precisely because he offered Moscow a redefinition of the superpower relationship that encompassed both détente and cooperation, as well as a continued rivalry that was relocated away from Europe toward the Third World periphery. See his *Foreign Politics of Richard Nixon*, pp. 5, 44.

Mao ascribed to the United States even more devious intentions, suggesting that Washington's strategy of appeasement in Europe was not only accompanied by the deliberate aim of encouraging Moscow to target the East, but also would be backed eventually by temporary collusion with Moscow there. The aim would be to let the Soviets "get bogged down in China," as the United States had been in Vietnam. Washington might even "help them in doing business, saying whatever you need we will help against China." The point of this would be to exhaust the USSR, and after a period of years to allow the United States to confront Moscow ("poke your finger at the Soviet back"), to "bring the Soviet Union down."[31] By sketching this extreme scenario, Mao reminded Kissinger that Beijing was well aware that the Nixon administration's China policy was a means toward the goal of ultimate victory in the U.S.–USSR superpower contest.

In the face of the Chinese image of the United States as an unscrupulous exploiter, Kissinger was forced to moderate his presentation of the Soviet threat and to emphasize the common threat faced by both West and East. The United States would "never knowingly cooperate in an attack on China" and had no desire for a stalemated Sino-Soviet war, he told Mao, as "this would dislocate the security of all other countries and will lead to our own isolation."[32] Indeed, the lesson of the two world wars was that "once a big war starts, its consequences are unpredictable"; thus, "we would consider aggression against China as involving our own national security."[33] He conceded that Moscow also had aggressive intentions in Europe, since the "intense effort of major military proportions going forward [there] . . . cannot be accounted for unless one assumes that the option of use is being prepared." Indeed, Kissinger now told Zhou that there were twice as many Soviet divisions in Europe as there were on the Chinese border, with far more air power. Thus, Europe and China were in equal peril, and, returning to the theme of the United States and China as strategic partners, it was important to try to prevent the Soviet Union from "breaking out in one direction or another."[34]

[31] Mao–Kissinger memcon, *Kissinger Transcripts*, p. 100. Both Zhou's and Mao's analyses of U.S. intentions of pushing the Soviets eastward were presented by the "Four Marshals" in their 1969 report – see "Our Views about the Current Situation," 17 September 1969, in *CWIHP Bulletin* 11 (Winter 1998), p. 167.

[32] Ibid., pp. 89, 99–100.

[33] "My Trip to China," p. 6. Much of Kissinger's response was censored in the sanitized version.

[34] Zhou–Kissinger memcon, 15 February 1973, pp. 11–12; 17 February 1973, 10.22–11.10pm, p. 3.

At one level, Mao's calculated probes were bargaining tactics aimed at exerting pressure on Washington to deliver on its promise of Sino-American normalization, as the ultimate means of cementing bilateral relations. At the same time, Mao's suggestion of an extreme form of U.S.–USSR collusion was designed to question the sincerity of Kissinger's assurances against the ill effects of détente for China's position and to indicate that Beijing disagreed with Washington about the means of dealing with their common adversary.[35] It was clear to Beijing that the American opening to China was motivated by its desire to play the "China card" in order to motivate the Soviet Union to negotiate détente with the United States. Beijing's fundamental concern, though, was that having successfully exploited the "China card," Washington would deemphasize its containment policy and might not perceive the urgency of fully normalizing relations with the PRC, or of doing so on terms favorable to Beijing. Hence Zhou's observation in February 1973 to Kissinger that "[y]ou want to reach out to the Soviet Union by standing on Chinese shoulders," and his warning that "[t]he more you do this, the more naughty the Soviet Union becomes."[36]

Essentially, Zhou's remark was the barest statement of the basic Chinese concern regarding the U.S. strategy of détente, as opposed to the preferred Chinese style of direct containment of the Soviet Union. Both the Chinese and American sides clearly perceived the link between Beijing's security concerns and the Nixon administration's grand strategy, but they envisaged different means and ends to the relationship. Nixon and Kissinger wanted to exploit Chinese worries about Soviet intentions in order to tie Beijing to a closer, more "normal" relationship with the United States, so that the "China card" could be played more effectively in persuading the Soviet Union to develop détente and restraint. Mao and Zhou,

[35] For a detailed analysis of the implicit ways in which Kissinger and the Chinese leaders communicated their interests, fears, intents, and commitments to each other during their 1973 dialogues, see Evelyn Goh and Gavan Duffy, "Playing the Soviet Card: Henry Kissinger's Reconstruction of 'Triangular Relations' in the Opening to China, 1971 to 1974," paper presented at the annual meeting of the International Studies Association, Chicago, February 2001; and Gavan Duffy and Evelyn Goh, "From Tacit to Secret Alliance: Pragmatic Analysis of Kissinger's 1973 Reconstruction of US-China Relations," paper presented at the European Consortium for Political Research Fourth Pan-European International Relations Conference, University of Kent, Canterbury, September 2001.

[36] Memcon, 15 February 1973, p. 18. Kissinger tried twice to forestall this Chinese worry by making attempts, somewhat embarrassing in their obvious transparency, to convince Zhou that the "speeding up" of U.S.–USSR relations in the wake of the China summit was "not a case that we particularly sought." Memcon, 20 June 1972, pp. 3, 22–3; memcon, 16 February 1973, p. 11.

on the other hand, saw Chinese security as bound up with the U.S. role as a strong countervailing force to the Soviet Union, and tried to use the new Sino-American relationship to influence Washington toward a firmer containment policy against the Soviet Union. In other words, Nixon and Kissinger prioritized a triangular balance of power (my Option 3), while the Chinese sought U.S. support against the Soviet Union (Option 4).[37] Moreover, as John Garver has argued, Beijing's opening to America in 1971 was not motivated primarily by the desire to deter a Soviet attack on China – there was an extensive leadership debate about this, and the Chinese decided to depend mainly on self-defense. Instead, Beijing's key aim was the longer-term one of preventing superpower collusion to contain China, which seemed increasingly likely as the Sino-American détente developed.[38] Thus, the détente that Nixon and Kissinger sought with the Soviets in parallel to rapprochement with China was anathema to Beijing.

Building the Tacit Alliance: Linking U.S. Strategy and Chinese Security

In response to the Chinese leaders' portrayal of the United States as an opportunistic superpower and a false friend, and in order to counter Beijing's divergent views on U.S. and Soviet intentions and strategies, Kissinger was obliged to reinforce his discourse of China as a crucial strategic partner of the United States by taking steps to demonstrate that American strategy was indeed one of developing closer relations with the PRC in order to contain Soviet power. Central to this exercise was the explanation of how maintaining China's national security was intrinsic to America's contest against its superpower rival, and how the policy of détente fitted into the shared goal of constraining the Soviet drive for hegemony.

Nixon and Kissinger had tried from the beginning to convince the Chinese leaders that Washington perceived itself as having a vital stake in China's national security, that "a strong, self-sufficient, independent China exercising control over its destiny is in our own interest."[39] As the Chinese leaders became more insistent regarding their doubts about U.S. intentions, Kissinger expressed this principle more clearly. In August 1972, he told Huang Hua that Washington wanted to establish "enough of a relationship with [the PRC] so that it is plausible that an attack on you

---

[37] Harding discusses this divergence in aims in *Fragile Relationship*, pp. 48–50.
[38] Garver, *Chinese Decision for Rapprochement*, Chapters 1–3.
[39] Kissinger to Zhou, 15 February 1973, p. 4.

involves a substantial American interest."[40] The Nixon administration would do this in three ways. To begin with, the growing convergence of Washington's and Beijing's strategic assessments must be accompanied by a strengthening of the bilateral relationship. This could be done most effectively by "speeding up the process of normalization and mak[ing] it more visible" in terms of trade, exchanges, and liaison offices.[41]

Second, Washington would continue to pursue détente with Moscow. In addition to buying time to prepare domestic opinion, Kissinger argued that the U.S.–USSR détente was a means to ease *Moscow's* suspicions. With U.S.–PRC rapprochement, in order to avoid giving the Soviet Union "the pretence of claiming they are being encircled," Washington had to "do enough with the Soviet Union to maintain a formal symmetry."[42] This allusion to a "formal symmetry" between U.S.–USSR relations and U.S.–PRC relations was a transparent attempt to elevate the status of the latter, since the superpower relationship clearly outweighed the Sino-American one in form as well as substance.[43]

Kissinger also provided a time line for this strategy: "the period of greatest danger" for China, he told Huang, would be 1974–6, when the USSR would have completed the "pacification" of the West through détente and disarmament, the shifting of its military forces, and the development of its offensive nuclear capabilities.[44] This time period, of course, coincided with that by which Nixon and Kissinger had promised the Chinese that they would achieve normalization.[45] Thus, the implication was that Beijing should prioritize U.S.–PRC normalization, and in the meantime trust that U.S. engagement with the Soviets through negotiations might help to temper some of the excesses of Soviet ambitions. In order to indicate their seriousness, Nixon and Kissinger sought other ways of sending this message to Beijing. At the end of May 1972, they met with French President Pompidou, who was shortly due to visit Zhou in Beijing. In discussing the PNW agreement, Kissinger was explicit in explaining

[40] Ibid., p. 8.
[41] Kissinger–Zhou memcon, 15 February 1973, Box 98, NSF/HAK, NPM, p. 7.
[42] Kissinger–Huang memcon, 4 August 1972, Box 329, Lord Files, pp. 7–9.
[43] Some authors have thus discounted China's importance in the strategic triangle on account of its relative weakness – see, for instance, Steven Levine, "China's Foreign Policy in the Strategic Triangle," in June Dreyer, ed., *Chinese Defense and Foreign Policy* (New York, 1988).
[44] Kissinger–Huang memcon, 4 August 1972, pp. 11–12.
[45] In February, Kissinger specifically told Zhou that the Nixon administration was working to achieve "full normalization and full diplomatic relations" with the PRC "before the middle of 1976." Memcon, 16 February 1973, p. 4.

that "our objective is to gain some years for the Chinese-American relationship to mature as a counterweight to Soviet power," and that part of
the reason for the nuclear agreement was to forestall "the possibility of
pre-emptive Soviet aggression to humiliate China." Kissinger reasserted
that there was "no sense in choosing the stronger against the weaker" and
that America's "deliberate policy" was to support China against the Soviet
Union. Indeed, it had "the intention to turn rapidly toward China in the
space of two or three years."[46] These loaded remarks – which could have
implied diplomatic or military relations – were probably made with the
expectation that Pompidou would "leak" them to the Chinese, and perhaps also the Soviets. In any case, Kissinger showed Huang the transcripts
of this meeting.[47]

Third, Washington would make certain commitments to the PRC as a
counterbalance to U.S.–USSR agreements. In the run-up to the U.S.–USSR
summit in June 1973, Kissinger reaffirmed to the Chinese that "anything
we are prepared to do with the Soviet Union, we are prepared to do with
the People's Republic." But in view of the impending PNW agreement,
he added, "we may be prepared to do things with the People's Republic
that we are not prepared to do with the Soviet Union."[48] Specifically, he
offered to consider "some joint declaration that neither of us will engage
in any negotiation against the other or that neither of us will join in any
agreement without consultation with the other." Furthermore, "we are
prepared to do it publicly."[49] Here Kissinger appears to have been somewhat carried away by the momentum of negotiating "watered down"
agreements, for it is difficult to see how the Nixon administration could
have justified such an agreement with a country with which it still had
no diplomatic relations. In the event, the Chinese declined the offer, and
Nixon contented himself with sending Zhou a formal note promising that
"in no case will the US participate in a joint move together with the Soviet
Union under [the PNW] agreement with respect to conflicts . . . where the
PRC is a party."[50] The Nixon administration also paid attention to material demonstrations of U.S. interest in strengthening the PRC. In response
to Chinese requests for Rolls Royce technology, the U.S. government,
which could not supply it due to existing trade restrictions on strategic

[46] Kissinger to RN, "Meeting with President Pompidou," n.d., Box 949, NSF, NPM;
    "Dr. Kissinger's Remarks to President Pompidou, May 1973," n.d., Box 328, Lord Files.
[47] Kissinger–Huang memcon, 14 June 1973, Box 95, NSF/HAK, NPM, p. 5.
[48] Kissinger to PRCLO chargé Han Xu, memcon, 15 May 1973, Box 238, Lord Files, p. 7.
[49] Kissinger to Huang Zhen, memcon, 29 May 1973, Box 328, Lord Files.
[50] RN to Zhou, 19 June 1973, Box 328, Lord Files.

goods, arranged for the British to provide the technology instead, thus circumventing U.S. regulations.[51]

It is worth noting that Kissinger's more earnest attempts to reassure the Chinese might have reflected a degree of genuine concern that Moscow was contemplating an attack on China. As he informed the Chinese, Brezhnev had suggested to Kissinger during his preparatory trip to the Soviet Union in May the possibility of taking "joint action against Chinese nuclear facilities."[52] In his report to Nixon after the visit, Kissinger had emphasized the "ominous overtones" of Brezhnev's remarks, which suggested that he was "obsessed" with the China problem. Kissinger surmised that China was a "major variable" in Soviet policy, one that might lead to a "major crisis" in the next twelve to eighteen months. Thus, there was a need to "look at our contingency planning for the event of Soviet military action against China."[53] In this connection, the Department of Defense was asked to examine the scenario of a Soviet attack on PRC nuclear facilities and to develop options for a U.S. nuclear response.[54]

The pressures on Washington of reconciling the policies of détente with the Soviet Union and rapprochement with the PRC had built up significantly by mid-1973. Chinese perspectives on détente diverged from American reasoning, and Kissinger reacted to Beijing's skepticism and questioning of U.S. sincerity by reinforcing his arguments about the U.S. interest in Chinese security. He tried subtly to remind the Chinese leaders that the United States might be the ultimate guarantor of Chinese security against a Soviet attack, and he urged that it was in Beijing's best interest to further improve relations with the United States. As Michael Yahuda has pointed out, even though China's international status was elevated by its inclusion in tripolar diplomacy, it was obvious that the dominant relationship in the international system remained that between the two superpowers.[55] Therefore, as a form of discursive compensation, Kissinger's explanation of United States strategy to the Chinese deliberately placed the PRC at the center of U.S. foreign policy and downgraded

---

[51] Kissinger to Huang Zhen, memcon, 6 July 1973, Box 328, Lord Files.

[52] Kissinger to RN, "Reports on Meetings with Brezhnev," 11 May 1973, Box 75, NSF/HAK, NPM, p. 7; Kissinger–Han memcon, 15 May 1973, pp. 5–6. The transcripts of this trip have not been declassified.

[53] Kissinger, "Reports on Meetings with Brezhnev," p. 7.

[54] Odeen to Kissinger, "NSSM 169 – Nuclear Policy," 8 June 1973, NSA Doc. 265.

[55] Yahuda, *International Politics of the Asia-Pacific*, p. 78. On the power asymmetry within the strategic triangle, and on China's essentially reactive participation, see Robert Ross, "Conclusion: Tripolarity and Policy Making," in Ross, ed., *China, the United States, and the Soviet Union: Tripolarity and Policy Making in the Cold War* (London, 1993).

the importance of the superpower détente. But Kissinger and Nixon also supplied Beijing with concrete commitments not to use U.S.–USSR agreements against China, much as they might have done for an undeclared ally. At the same time, they hinted that Washington would soon take significant steps toward consolidating the U.S.–PRC relationship, and they made gestures to increase the ease of supplying military technology to China. These steps were taken to develop the "tacit alliance" relationship Kissinger envisaged with Beijing, and to reassure the Chinese about U.S. strength and credibility against the Soviet threat. Kissinger's construction of this need is important here, because during this period, Chinese doubts about the United States need not necessarily have impinged seriously on the relationship, since fundamentally, Beijing had limited room to maneuver. "Triangular politics" was working against the Chinese, because the apparent success of the superpower détente left China in a position whereby it had worse relations with both of the superpowers than they did with each other. Beijing continued to need the U.S. relationship as a counterweight against Moscow, as evinced by the agreement to set up liaison offices and by Beijing's desire to work toward normalization.

MAINTAINING MOMENTUM IN U.S.–PRC RELATIONS, JULY–NOVEMBER 1973

From July 1973 onward, however, Washington's strong bargaining position began to fade as external and internal political pressures increased, challenging the détente policy and limiting the administration's flexibility regarding China policy. As Beijing's worry that U.S.–USSR relations would continue to improve began to fade, its bargaining position regarding normalization also became stronger. In the face of these pressures, Kissinger escalated along his preferred trajectory of maintaining the U.S.–PRC rapprochement through greater strategic assurance, but with less effectiveness.

Downturn?

The sour note struck in U.S.–PRC relations by Chinese suspicions about the U.S.–USSR détente and the June 1973 PNW agreement was soon followed by a further downturn in relations from July onward. First, there were delays in setting the date for Kissinger's next trip to Beijing. This was partly the fault of the White House, which tried to tie the Kissinger trip to Chinese assistance in seeking a ceasefire and peace talks in Cambodia.[56] In the event, Beijing, which had been offering to mediate the conflict since the end of 1972, declined to help as Congress voted to end the bombing campaign in Cambodia on 15 August, and as Prince Sihanouk refused to engage in talks.[57]

Signs of a downturn were also manifested in bilateral issues. In late August 1973, the Chinese government asked that the Marine Guards deployed at the U.S. liaison office (USLO) compound in Beijing be withdrawn, in spite of an earlier agreement. At the same time, little progress had been made in advancing exchanges and trade. The bilateral exchange program was still "flagging and erratic," and no final action had been taken after the agreement in principle in February to conclude the claims/assets issue so as to remove impediments to bilateral trade.[58]

Kissinger was enraged by the uncertainty over the arrangements for his coming trip to Beijing, and in line with his preoccupation with the strategic element of the U.S.-PRC rapprochement, he insisted that Beijing's actions must reflect "fundamental" Chinese doubts. He was worried about the state of "triangular relations" in the context of the unfolding Watergate crisis and congressional challenges to the war in Cambodia, U.S. force deployments in Europe, and the defense budget. Kissinger feared that the Chinese leaders now questioned the value of the relationship with the United States, since they saw "a paralyzed President unable to provide firm support in matters affecting their security." As he had often stressed before, the relationship depended upon U.S. strength, and "all this talk about 25 years of mutual estrangement was crap. What the Chinese wanted was support in a military contingency."[59]

Other China watchers, however, stressed a combination of domestic political factors and strategic considerations on the Chinese side. NSC

---

[56] Memcon, Scowcroft–Han, 11 July 1973, Box 5, LOT #5411, RG59; Arnold Isaacs, *Without Honor: Defeat in Vietnam and Cambodia* (Baltimore, 1983), pp. 234–5; Kissinger, *Years of Upheaval*, pp. 351–2.

[57] Qiao–Kissinger memcon, 13 November 1972, Box 329, Lord Files; Chinese note, 18 July 1973, quoted in "Cambodia – US-PRC Exchanges since February," ca. November 1973, Box 97, NSF, NPM.

[58] Solomon to Kissinger, "Your Meeting with PRC Liaison Office Chief Huang Chen, Saturday, September 29, 9am in the White House," 28 September 1973, Box 328, Lord Files; Bruce to Kissinger, 6 October 1973, Box 40, NSF, NPM.

[59] Memcon, Kissinger, Scowcroft, Eagleburger, Lord, Howe, Solomon, Rodman, 19 July 1973, Box 328, Lord Files.

China specialist Richard Solomon argued that in the run-up to a Chinese Communist Party Congress, Zhou and the moderates were under attack from hard-line factions and were "backing off from the recent high-profile posture of US-PRC normalization." Ambassador David Bruce, chief of the USLO in Beijing, agreed that this reflected temporary "domestic political maneuverings" rather than "an outright rejection of their policy toward us."[60] However, Bruce's deputies Al Jenkins and John Holdridge added that the Chinese might have felt that they could afford to "show pique" recently because "they no longer believe a Soviet attack to be at all likely, or at least imminent, though the hatred and mistrust thrive thumpingly."[61] EA agreed, noting that Zhou had privately claimed that the Soviets would not provoke a major war with China in the foreseeable future. This assessment can be attributed in part to the "mere passage of time during which the Soviets have not attacked," but also to the "the altered position of the US in the US-USSR-PRC strategic triangle."[62] In other words, in spite of Chinese misgivings about Soviet intent and the U.S.–USSR détente, and despite Kissinger's continued efforts to stoke the fires of Sino-Soviet antagonism, the very success of Nixon's and Kissinger's policy of trying to restrain Moscow by détente and by linking Chinese security to the U.S. interest had bred this situation.

Observations about this apparent slowdown in U.S.–PRC relations prompted the question of what Washington ought to do about it, particularly once the date for Kissinger's next trip to Beijing was finally set for 10–15 November. Kissinger's key aide, Winston Lord, wrote him a personal memorandum in which he identified a "watershed" in relations with the PRC: "the opening of institutional and personal contacts has about run its course," he warned, and they were now at an "ambiguous and fragile stage where if we do not go forward, we may go backwards." He reviewed the difficulties in reassuring Beijing about U.S. dealings with the USSR, but concluded that China basically did not have an alternative to balance Moscow, and that strengthening the relationship with the United States remained a priority. Additionally, given the twin pressures

---

[60] Solomon to Kissinger, "Mao and Chou Under Pressure? Some Recent Pieces in the Chinese Puzzle," 24 July 1973, Box 328, Lord Files; Bruce to Kissinger, 19 August 1973, Bruce to Kissinger, "My Meeting with Ch'iao Kuan-hua," 29 August 1973, p. 4, Box 95, NSF/HAK, NPM.

[61] Jenkins/Holdridge to Kissinger, 20 July 1973, Box 328, Lord Files, p. 2.

[62] DoS briefing paper, "Developments in PRC Foreign Policy," ca. July 1973, Box 2694, SNF(1970–3), RG59, NA.

of domestic politics and advanced age, Mao and Zhou would want to accelerate U.S.–PRC relations in order to "lock their country on a course that could not be lightly reversed in the successor struggle."[63] Thus, Lord urged that Kissinger, on his coming trip to Beijing, must seek a "major advance" in relations in order "to strengthen the policy hands of Mao/Chou." The time had arrived for the rapid turn toward China that Kissinger had discussed with Pompidou. As Lord saw it, Kissinger now had two options by which to produce significant momentum in U.S.–PRC relations: they could establish a "more concrete security understanding" with the Chinese, or they could seek significant progress in the normalization of bilateral relations.[64] Lord favored the latter; but Kissinger tried to do both.

Confirmed Tacit Allies versus Doubtful Strategic Partners

According to Kissinger, his November 1973 trip to Beijing resulted in a "confirmation and deepening" of the close identity between Chinese and American strategic perspectives. He told Nixon that they were more than ever "tacit allies" sharing similar views about Soviet strategy, the necessity of a strong American world role and defense capability, and the strategic importance of the Europe–Japan–Middle East–Near East–South Asia axis.[65]

Washington, he said, was "walking a delicate tightrope of public détente with Moscow and tacit alliance with Peking," but the "meticulous care and feeding of the Chinese on our Soviet policy" continued to pay off.[66] Indeed, he had been able to reinforce the justifications for the PNW agreement by citing the way in which Washington reacted to Soviet actions in the Middle Eastern crisis that developed after the Yom Kippur war in October. Kissinger told Zhou that the U.S. strategy of forcing the USSR into "a posture of provocation" had worked: when Brezhnev had sent Washington a message demanding that it join a Soviet-American expeditionary force to the Middle East, and declaring Moscow's intention to move unilaterally otherwise, Nixon had been able to justify putting U.S. forces on alert because a unilateral Soviet move would violate Article 2

---

[63] Lord to Kissinger, "Your Trip to China," 11 October 1973, Box 370, Lord Files, pp. 1–2.
[64] Ibid., p. 3.
[65] Kissinger to RN, "My Visit to China," 19 November 1973, Box 330, Lord Files, p. 1.
[66] Ibid., pp. 2–3.

of the PNW treaty.[67] Both Mao and Zhou welcomed Nixon's strong handling of the Middle Eastern crisis.[68]

Reflecting Kissinger's assessment of the deepening tacit alliance, the joint communiqué issued at the end of the trip broadened the implications of the Shanghai Communiqué by specifically extending the mutual agreement to refrain from and oppose hegemony beyond the Asia-Pacific region to "any other part of the world."[69]

Yet again, however, the transcripts of the dialogues reveal that the tenor of the Chinese leaders' discourse on U.S.–PRC relations was more ambivalent. In their central three-hour long interview, Mao expressed to Kissinger continuing suspicions about the Soviet–American détente. More significantly, he deliberately constructed a reduced Soviet threat to China itself, and he reminded Kissinger about the mutual dependency of American and Chinese interests in countering Soviet expansionist ambitions. These were obviously attempts to reduce Washington's perceived strategic leverage in the U.S.–PRC relationship and to improve Beijing's bargaining position with regard to conditions for normalization.

Mao denigrated the Soviet threat in two ways. First, he argued that Moscow had very little reason to want to attack China. When Kissinger again discussed the "realistic possibility" that Moscow would attack China, "above all . . . to destroy your nuclear capability," Mao declared that Chinese nuclear capability was "no bigger than a fly" and thus was not worth attacking. Kissinger qualified the assessment by saying that the Soviets were worried about China's nuclear capability "ten years from now," but Mao dismissed the argument on the basis that China would need thirty to fifty years to develop a nuclear capability significant enough to threaten the Soviet Union.[70]

Mao's second key theme was that the Soviets' "ambitions [were] contradictory with their capacity." Because they had to deal with "so many adversaries" around the world – in the Pacific, the Middle East, and

---

[67] Zhou–Kissinger memcon, 11 November 1973, Box 372, Lord Files, p. 12. Article 2 stated that the United States and the USSR would refrain from threat or use of force against third parties in circumstances that might endanger international peace and security.

[68] Ibid.; Mao to Kissinger, memcon, 12 November 1973, in Burr, *Kissinger Transcripts*, p. 188; Kissinger to Scowcroft for RN, Situation Message No. 42, 12 November 1973, Box 41, NSF, NPM. Nonetheless, as Kissinger's staff acknowledged, Moscow's initial threat to take unilateral action during the crisis showed that the PNW treaty itself failed to encourage restraint. NSC briefing paper, "US-Soviet Relations," n.d., Box 97, NSF/HAK, NPM.

[69] See Kissinger–Zhou memcon, 14 November 1973, Box 372, Lord Files, pp. 6–7.

[70] Mao–Kissinger memcon, 12 November 1973, in Burr, *Kissinger Transcripts*, p. 183.

Europe – Moscow's forces were thinly spread, making attempts at Soviet expansionism "pitiful."[71] In China's case, this overextension meant that only one million troops were spared for the Sino-Soviet border – "not enough even for the defense of [the Soviet eastern front] and still less for attack forces." Thus, the Soviet threat to China was greatly diminished, this time in conventional military terms.

Here Mao also took the opportunity to question again U.S. sincerity and intentions. He noted that the Soviet Union could not attack China "unless you let them in [by]...first giv[ing] them the Middle East and Europe so they are able to deploy troops eastward."[72] This reinforced Mao's probes in February and conveyed the enduring Chinese concern about: (a) at best, the possibly unintended consequences for the East of the superpower détente, or, (b) at worst, the possibility of deliberate U.S. collusion with the Soviets against China. In this regard, Mao broadly hinted at Beijing's conviction that Washington and Moscow had made secret deals at the Washington summit.[73] In order to stress the point that the U.S. ought to regard China as a coequal partner in containing the Soviet Union, rather than as a pawn in the game, Mao reminded Kissinger that China was "also holding down a portion of [Soviet] troops which is favourable to you in Europe and the Middle East." That is, just as the United States helped to prevent a Soviet attack on China by keeping the Soviets occupied in the Middle East and Europe, China's posture toward the Soviet Union served U.S. interests. Washington and Beijing were mutually dependent in strategic terms, and there was a need to pursue a "coordinated course" so that "nobody will be attacked."[74]

Against Mao's portrayal of the United States and the PRC as doubtful strategic partners, Kissinger exercised his option of offering Beijing a stronger security understanding in order to preserve the momentum in Sino-American relations. In his pre-trip memorandum, Lord had been openly skeptical of this option, which would indicate a change "from our currently balanced (evident) diplomacy to one that clearly favors Peking over Moscow." Lord had particularly warned against any secret commitments for "constitutional, legal and political" reasons, particularly in the wake of Vietnam and Watergate. Besides, he argued, secret commitments would be useless to Beijing as a deterrent against Soviet attack and thus

---

[71] Ibid., pp. 183, 180.
[72] Ibid., p. 184.
[73] Ibid., pp. 182–3.
[74] Ibid., p. 184.

would inevitably be leaked. More importantly, though, the Chinese leaders "don't expect, and probably wouldn't even want such a move"; in any case, they "would not necessarily believe such a commitment, or at least this President's ability to fulfill it."[75]

Against Lord's advice, Kissinger tried to bring about significant movement in the U.S.–PRC relationship by offering to consolidate the bilateral security dialogue with concrete measures. On the night of his arrival in Beijing, Kissinger told Zhou that the United States could aid China against Soviet attack in ways that were "very secret and not obvious." A "formal relationship" (that is, an alliance) was not desirable, but Washington could unilaterally provide help of a "technical nature" to lessen the vulnerability of Chinese forces and increase the warning time in the event of an attack. Specifically, they could set up a "hot line" arrangement that would allow Washington to provide Beijing with early-warning information about Soviet military action directed against China; and Washington could also sell to Beijing its superior high-resolution satellite images to heighten the accuracy of Chinese targeting of Soviet sites.[76] After his meeting with Mao, Kissinger brought up the subject again with Zhou. In the event of a Soviet attack on China, Kissinger stated that the United States could help in two additional ways: first, if the war should be prolonged, it could supply "equipment and other services." Second, it could also help with the improvement of communications between Beijing and the various Chinese bomber bases "under some guise," and it could provide the technology for "certain kinds of radars" that the Chinese could build.[77]

In sum, Kissinger offered to aid the PRC materially in the event of a war and to establish the beginnings of a military supply relationship between the two countries. Together, these steps indicated Washington's

---

[75] Lord to Kissinger, "Your Trip to China," p. 3.

[76] Kissinger–Zhou memcon, 10 November 1973, *Kissinger Transcripts*, pp. 171–2. These steps were proposed to Kissinger before his trip by Fred Iklé, director of the Arms Control and Disarmament Agency. See Iklé to Kissinger, "Your Trip to Peking: Arms Control Aspects," 22 October 1973; Solomon to Kissinger, "Director Iklé's Memorandum Suggesting Arms Control Issues for Possible Discussion in Peking," 1 November 1973, Box 370, Lord Files. The idea was also being mooted by RAND China scholar Michael Pillsbury, who submitted a study to the various government agencies in the autumn of 1973 suggesting that the United States might establish a military relationship with China. See Banning Garrett, "The 'China Card' and Its Origins: US Bureaucratic Politics and the Strategic Triangle," Ph.D. dissertation, Brandeis University, 1983; Mann, *About Face*, pp. 57–60; Michael Pillsbury, "US-Chinese Military Ties?," *Foreign Affairs* 20 (Fall 1975), pp. 50–64.

[77] Zhou–Kissinger memcon, 13 November 1973, NSA Doc. 283.

willingness to "lean toward" Beijing in a far more obvious and concrete way than hitherto acknowledged. Zhou's response was measured, but reasonably receptive. He commented that American cooperation with early warning would be "intelligence of great assistance," but this had to be done in a manner "so that no one feels we are allies," since "such a course of action... would have great impact internationally." Thus, "we would need to study it before we can consult you further."[78] Kissinger's proposal would be controversial and explosive, given the bitter Sino-Soviet rivalry and the internal dissent in the Chinese bureaucracy about Zhou's U.S. policy. However, given the decline in his position and his health, and because of Mao's personal opposition, Zhou never managed to steer the proposals through the decision-making channels, and there is no evidence thus far to show that any Chinese official responded to Kissinger's proposals.[79]

Normalization: China as a Realist or Nationalist Power?

Ultimately, though, concrete progress in Sino-American relations after rapprochement could be achieved only if advances were made regarding the modalities that would allow the establishment of diplomatic relations between the United States and the PRC. On this count, too, Kissinger reported success after his November 1973 trip, in the form of the statement in the joint communiqué: "The Chinese side reiterated that the normalization of relations... can be realized only on the basis of confirming the principle of one China." Kissinger told Nixon that this indicated that normalization would require "only the 'principle' of one China... as opposed to requiring the practice." It suggested that Beijing might be willing to settle for "considerable autonomy for Taiwan and continuing US ties [after U.S.–PRC normalization] so long as the nominal juridical framework reflects the one China approach."[80] According to Kissinger, therefore, a potential solution to the central obstacle to normalization was in sight; Washington could perhaps, after all, have its *mao tai* and drink it too. To him, this represented a "major concession" on Beijing's part, suggesting that China was still a realist power primarily motivated by its security concerns, and that it was willing to compromise on the Taiwan issue in order to maintain its leverage against the Soviets.

---

[78] Zhou–Kissinger memcon, 14 November 1973, NSA Doc. 284.
[79] Tyler, *A Great Wall*, p. 174.
[80] Kissinger, Situation Message No. 51; "My Visit to China," pp. 1–2, 4–5.

And yet, the ambiguity in the communiqué sentence on Taiwan should be noted. There is a hermeneutic difference between the two grammatical expressions: "*only* on the basis of confirming the principle of one China," and "on the basis of confirming *only* the principle of one China." The former leaves open the question of how the principle is to be confirmed, while the latter more clearly expresses the idea that it is the principle, rather than the practice or anything else, that matters. It was the former version which was used in the communiqué, while Kissinger's interpretation derived from the latter.

That the Chinese leaders might not have compromised to the extent that Kissinger indicated is also suggested by the transcripts of the dialogues. During his February 1973 trip, Kissinger had probed Zhou about the possibility of the United States retaining "some form of representation" on Taiwan even after establishing diplomatic relations with Beijing.[81] In November, he offered to speed up the process of normalization if, instead of the Japanese formula – which would involve severing all official ties between Washington and Taipei – the two sides could work out a "more flexible" formula.[82] In the course of a circuitous presentation, Kissinger suggested to Zhou that this formula – "along the lines of the Shanghai Communiqué" – would "make clear that that principle [of one China] is not being abandoned." In other words, Kissinger was asking for a declaration of principle in exchange for Chinese acquiescence to the continuation of some form of official U.S. relations with Taiwan while U.S.–PRC relations were being normalized.[83] Zhou's response to this was markedly evasive: he did not reply directly, but repeatedly referred to the interpreter, saying that she knew what Kissinger meant.[84]

Mao, on the other hand, conveyed a clearer message. He told Kissinger that "[s]o long as you sever diplomatic relations with Taiwan, then it is possible for our two countries to solve the issue of diplomatic relations...like we did with Japan." That is, the Japanese formula for

---

[81] Kissinger–Zhou memcon, 16 February 1973, p. 4.

[82] For a succinct summary of the six alternative normalization formulas considered by the Nixon and Carter administrations, see Yufan Hao, *Dilemma and Decision: An Organizational Perspective on American China Policy-Making* (Berkeley, 1997), pp. 61–6.

[83] Note that Kissinger was not retreating from Nixon's earlier positions that Taiwan was a part of China, that the United States would not support Taiwan independence movements, and that Washington would work toward normalization with Beijing. While these principles implied that the United States would move to de-recognize the ROC and extend diplomatic recognition to the PRC, Nixon never explicitly undertook to end all official ties with Taipei in the process.

[84] Zhou–Kissinger memcon, 3–5.30pm, 12 November 1973, Box 372, Lord Files, pp. 4–5.

normalization was the only acceptable one for Beijing. Moreover, Mao presented a harder line on the issue of the use of force, declaring, "I do not believe in a peaceful transition. . . . They [the Nationalists] are a bunch of counter-revolutionaries. How could they cooperate with us?" Nevertheless, he suggested that Beijing would wait upon the issue instead of employing force now: "we can do without Taiwan for the time being, and let it come after one hundred years."[85] When Kissinger alluded to the possibility of finding a formula to "demonstrate symbolically that our relationship is now normal in every aspect," Mao declared that there was no rush to normalize relations and that the issue was not important, unlike "the issue of the overall international situation [i.e., the Soviet threat] [which] is an important one."[86] The import of this part of the discussion was ambiguous. In effect, Mao refused to commit to peaceful reunification with Taiwan, and declined to discuss any formula other than the Japanese model for U.S.–PRC normalization. For the Chinese leaders, Taiwan clearly remained a central, nationalistic issue, and strategic cooperation with the United States against the Soviet threat, while important, was not sufficiently critical to induce Mao to compromise on Taiwan. Yet Mao seemed to suggest, to no avail, that the Soviet factor ought to be important enough to induce Washington to deliver on its promises for normalization with China.

By November 1973, therefore, it seemed that the U.S.–PRC relationship had washed indeterminately over a watershed. The principal interlocutors on both sides desired some forward movement in the relationship. For the Chinese side, in spite of Mao's rhetoric playing down the Soviet threat to China, closer ties with the United States remained an important means of countering Beijing's Soviet adversary. This was evident in Zhou's thoughtful – though cautious – reaction to Kissinger's offers of an intensified strategic relationship. On the other hand, the brewing power struggle in Beijing acted as a significant constraint on moderates like Zhou, who would forge closer relations with Washington rather than seek rapprochement with Moscow. As the factional challenges intensified, Zhou in particular had to tread a tightrope between maintaining

---

[85] Mao–Kissinger memcon, 12 November 1973, in Burr, *Kissinger Transcripts*, p. 187; Kissinger, "My Visit to China," p. 7. This would have been in line with Zhou's more direct statement in February that "I can assure you that we don't mean . . . to liberate it [Taiwan] by armed forces." Crucially, though, Zhou's remark also contained a degree of long-term ambiguity, since he added, "We have no such plan at the moment." See Kissinger–Zhou memcon, 16 February 1973, p. 4.

[86] Mao–Kissinger memcon, in Burr, *Kissinger Transcripts*, pp. 186–7.

the momentum in his policy of rapprochement with the United States while avoiding criticisms that he had leaned too far toward the American imperialist camp.[87] An important consequence was that, as Kissinger's staff had pointed out, Zhou now needed to produce results in terms of progress in regaining control over Taiwan in order to demonstrate that the policy of reconciliation with America was yielding results for China.[88] The November 1973 communiqué language on Taiwan reflected Zhou's need to give Kissinger reason to expect that some flexible resolution of America's Taiwan dilemma might be possible, while preserving sufficient ambiguity to defend against charges of having made a significant concession to Washington.

Similarly, the fact that Kissinger exercised both the strategic and normalization options bears testimony to the Nixon administration's need for movement, and preferably a breakthrough, in U.S.–PRC relations. The extent to which Kissinger was prepared to lean toward Beijing in order to achieve this was clearest in the strategic element. The eventual move toward a military relationship with China during the Carter administration is well known, and was seen as a way to strengthen the U.S. position vis-à-vis the Soviet Union with the collapse of détente.[89] But the foregoing analysis shows that the seeds had been planted by Kissinger five years earlier. Initially, at the height of détente, it was a means to reassure the Chinese and to keep them in play in the strategic triangle; in late 1973, it was employed as a strategic incentive to persuade Beijing to consider normalization of relations on U.S. terms. However, Kissinger's attempt was singularly unsuccessful. The strategic offers failed to sweeten the pill of U.S.–Taiwan relations, and they were never again mentioned during the rest of the Nixon administration. As Lord had warned, Taiwan and normalization remained key Chinese concerns, and the centrality of the

[87] On the increasing attacks on Zhou from the left in 1973, see Ross Terrill, *Mao: A Biography* (Sydney, 1995), Chapter 21; and Roderick MacFarquhar and John Fairbank, eds., *The Cambridge History of China Volume 15* (Cambridge, 1991), pp. 428–9.

[88] Ross argues that the factional succession struggle in Chinese domestic politics did not affect Beijing's willingness to normalize relations with the United States between 1973 and 1975, as Mao remained the clear authority, and that it was not until he fell critically ill in mid-1976 that the policy environment changed markedly. See his *Negotiating Cooperation*, pp. 60–77. Yet Ross also notes that in 1973, Zhou was attacked by Mao himself for being too liberal on the Taiwan issue. Hence, even though Mao still controlled foreign policy in 1973, it was evident that the Chinese political winds had begun to blow leftward, as they inevitably did in uncertain times, and Kissinger's interlocutors must certainly have felt the need to exercise caution.

[89] See Ross, *Negotiating Cooperation*, Chapters 4 and 5; and Zbigniew Brzezinski, *Power and Principle: Memoirs of the National Security Adviser, 1977–1981* (New York, 1983).

Taiwan issue was reinforced as domestic pressures increased on both sides, and as U.S. leverage was reduced with rising domestic challenges to the détente policy. During the last eight months of the Nixon administration, the sense of momentum toward normalization that Kissinger had lauded at the end of 1973 proved to be an illusion.

STALEMATE: U.S.–PRC RELATIONS IN 1974

Kissinger's active reconstruction of China from a former enemy to a tacit ally ground to an ignominious halt after his November 1973 trip to Beijing. In fact, for the first half of 1974, he did not pay much attention to China policy. Kissinger had promised to contact the Chinese regarding the new language on Taiwan and normalization in the joint communiqué within a month, but he did not do so. By late May of 1974, Kissinger's China advisers were obliged to write him a long memorandum outlining the "imperatives for planning and action" on the China issue. They pointed out that "our China policy is drifting without a clear sense of how we will move towards normalization, or indeed what the shape of a future normalized relationship with the PRC will look like – particularly as it affects Taiwan. We are in danger of losing a sense of momentum . . . and need a normalization strategy which will give coherence to . . . our China policy."[90]

If the November 1973 communiqué did indeed promise the breakthrough that Kissinger proclaimed it to, why did he put off considering this issue? The delay, according to Winston Lord and to Assistant Secretary of State for East Asia Arthur Hummel, was mainly keyed to the increasing signs of uncertainty on the Chinese domestic front. However, the domestic political crisis in Washington probably played a larger role – the question was not whether particular changes in Taiwan policy would be defensible domestically and to the PRC, but "whether the gain would be worth the risk and effort to an administration already up to its ears in problems."[91] The Watergate imbroglio was closing in on Nixon and his immediate circle of advisers, and the administration's policy of détente was coming under sustained attack in Congress. Thus, Kissinger was preoccupied not only with shuttle diplomacy in the Middle East, the oil crisis,

---

[90] Hummel/Lord/Solomon to Kissinger, "Imperatives for Planning and Action on the China Issue," 24 May 1974, NSA Doc. 300, p. 1.

[91] Osborn (ConGen/HK) to Lord, 14 December 1973, Box 380, Lord Files. See also Tyler, *A Great Wall*, pp. 185–6, 201–4.

and the U.S.–USSR relationship, but also with defending and maintaining the overall fabric of the administration's foreign policy in general.[92]

Against this backdrop, delay and confusion dogged China policy thinking in Washington. Having bought themselves "breathing space" on Taiwan in 1972, it seems that Kissinger and his advisers proceeded not to think very much about it after Nixon's trip to Beijing. Because of the exclusion of the State Department from the China policy process, Kissinger's staff did not seriously consider what shape the U.S.–Taiwan relationship would take when Washington and Beijing eventually normalized relations. The first detailed studies on the subject were produced only in January 1974, and they could only point out the same dilemmas that had been identified in 1971.[93]

On the other hand, it would seem that once they began to think about it, Kissinger and his advisers concluded that the administration's goal must be the maintenance of the "greatest possible links" with Taiwan as the normalization process with the PRC was carried to its diplomatic conclusion.[94] In this vein, Washington appointed a new ambassador to the embassy in Taipei, which had been headed by a chargé for over two years. Also, plans for the construction of a new U.S. embassy building in Taipei went forward, and the ROC was allowed to open a new consulate in New York. As a result of these moves, Kissinger's staff reported that Taipei was wont now to hope that a combination of Beijing's political problems and Nixon's domestic difficulties might save the U.S.–ROC relationship.[95]

Kissinger's failure to follow up on the normalization process during the first half of 1974 irked the Chinese. There were indications throughout this period that Chinese leaders were making an effort to heighten Washington's awareness of their concern for movement on the Taiwan issue and normalization. On 2 April, Vice Foreign Minister Qiao Guanhua called in Bruce to protest about developments in U.S. policy toward the ROC, and to warn that the United States "should not go too far" on the Taiwan issue, in directions not in the spirit of the Shanghai Communiqué. In May, Qiao and Vice Premier Li Xiannian stressed to a group

---

[92] Kissinger's account of this period during which the Nixon administration was under siege fills an entire volume of his memoirs – see his *Years of Upheaval*.

[93] Solomon to Kissinger, "'Confirming the Principle of One China': Next Steps in the Evolution of US-PRC-ROC Relations," 19 January 1974, Box 371; Hummel/Lord to Kissinger, "Normalization of Relations with the PRC and the Issue of Taiwan," 29 January 1974, Box 330, Lord Files.

[94] Hummel/Lord, "Normalization of Relations," p. 6.

[95] Hummel/Lord/Solomon, "Imperatives for Planning and Action," p. 2.

of American state governors visiting Beijing the need to settle the Taiwan issue, which was impeding further steps toward normalization.[96] From Beijing, Bruce warned of the "disappointment" among Chinese leaders that the United States had not fulfilled their "expectations" of the "fruitfulness" of the bilateral relationship. He identified four factors that contributed to their concern: (1) "latent fears" that the U.S.–USSR détente would be inimical to the PRC; (2) a suspicion that the United States would not within the next couple of years proceed to full diplomatic relations with the PRC and a corresponding break in ties with Taiwan; (3) impatience with alleged lack of U.S. interest in a decisive solution of the Cambodian problem; and (4) fears that U.S. concern with crises elsewhere and domestic problems would have repercussions on U.S. China policy. Despite claims of patience, Bruce reminded Washington, Mao and Zhou were "two old men in a hurry."[97] This was exacerbated by renewed leadership infighting in which Mao and Zhou's "soft" approach toward the United States had come under attack from the left. That the pro-U.S. section of the Chinese leadership was under pressure was evident in Beijing's "increasingly aloof" posture toward the United States in official bilateral contacts.[98] The direction of U.S. China policy during this time helped to weaken the moderate Chinese leaders.

Nixon resigned on 8 August 1974, whereupon Gerald Ford took over as president. He retained Kissinger as secretary of state and quickly confirmed with Beijing the validity of "all discussions, understandings, and commitments made with President Nixon as well as by [Kissinger]."[99] In the China briefing papers prepared for Ford, Kissinger stated that they now had to make clear that "we are not committed to delivering Taiwan to Peking rule, and that US public opinion would not allow us to make unilateral decisions about the future of 15 million people." Washington also had to make Beijing understand that the ROC had "substantial capabilities for actions that would make serious problems for both the PRC and the US (declaring independence, or going nuclear, or flirting with a

---

[96] NSC memo for Kissinger, "Indicators of PRC Internal Debate and Desire for Movement on the Taiwan Issue," 23 May 1974, Box 371, Lord Files.

[97] Bruce to SoS, "Present US-PRC Relationship," 24 May 1974, NSA Doc. 301, p. 1.

[98] Solomon to Kissinger, "The PRC's Domestic Political Situation and Foreign Policy as a Context for Your Meeting with Teng Hsiao-ping and Chiao Kuan-hua," 12 April 1974, Box 371, Lord Files.

[99] Huang–Kissinger memcon, "The Secretary's Reassurances to the PRC Upon Mr. Ford's Assumption of the Presidency," 9 August 1974, Box 376, Lord Files; White House to Bruce, 9 August 1974, NSA Doc. 306.

third country such as the USSR whose overtures it has so far rejected) and therefore a strict 'Japan formula' of no real US-Taiwan ties would not serve either PRC or US interests."[100] Thus, Kissinger had decided that Washington should dig in its heels on the Taiwan issue. Perhaps he calculated that the domestic political climate would not permit Ford to even try to normalize U.S.–PRC relations by severing ties with Taiwan. At the same time, Kissinger might still have believed that Washington retained the "Soviet card" leverage over Beijing, since, as he told Ford, while Taiwan was "a question of national destiny," the Soviet threat remained Beijing's "overwhelming national security problem."[101]

That was not Beijing's assessment. Kissinger's hardened position coincided with a parallel resolution on the Chinese side against further compromise. During Kissinger's next trip to Beijing in November, he duly emphasized to Vice Premier Deng Xiaoping the need for some Chinese undertaking for a peaceful settlement of the Taiwan issue as well as Washington's desire to retain liaison offices in Taipei after normalization.[102] But this was a doomed effort, given the hardening of Beijing's position all through 1974. The leadership succession was now under way, and with Zhou critically ill, Deng and Qiao Guanhua were the new American policy principals. Both made concerted attempts to flatten out the ambiguities in Mao's November 1973 comments and to emphasize only the hard-line elements. On the Taiwan issue, Qiao had asserted in April that "as Chairman Mao told you," normalization could proceed only on the Japanese model – "No other pattern is possible."[103] By November, Deng added that Beijing would brook no external interference in the reunification process and would not consider a renunciation of force.[104] As regards the Soviet threat, Deng repeated Mao's observation that there were only a few Soviet troops at the Chinese border, not enough for an attack, and that they were intended only to scare people with "weak nerves."[105] He also pointed out that the Soviet military strength in the East was not directed against China alone; it was also directed against Japan and "your Seventh

[100] Kissinger to Ford, briefing paper, "PRC," 14 August 1974, NSA Doc. 307, p. 11.

[101] Kissinger to Ford, "Commitments to the PRC," August 1974, Box 371, Lord Files, p. 1.

[102] Memcon, "Normalization," 26 November 1974, *Kissinger Transcripts*, pp. 295–8.

[103] Deng–Qiao–Kissinger memcon, 14 April 1974, *Kissinger Transcripts*, pp. 275–284. Qiao repeated the statement to a congressional delegation in Beijing a month later – see DoS reftel, "Governors' Delegation Meeting with Ch'iao Kuan-hua," 20 May 1974, Box 96, NSF, NPM.

[104] Memcon, "Sino-Soviet Relations; Europe," 27 November 1974, Box 372, Lord Files, pp. 21–2.

[105] Deng–Qiao–Kissinger memcon, 14 April 1974, *Kissinger Transcripts*, pp. 281–3.

Fleet, your air and naval forces."[106] Picking up Mao's earlier theme that Soviet attention was fixed equally on the West, Deng taunted, "the Polar bear is after you."[107]

From the start, Kissinger had privileged the strategic aspects of the U.S.–PRC rapprochement and emphasized Beijing's national security motivations. However, as triangular politics intensified and then began to break down in 1973 and 1974, Washington's leverage was seriously reduced. While yet another leadership crisis accounted to some extent for Beijing's harder line toward normalization, it was also the result of a perceived strengthening of China's position in the strategic triangle as a result of the U.S. domestic disarray and heightened U.S.–USSR tensions. Thus, Kissinger's continuing efforts progressively to construct the Soviet menace increasingly fell on deaf ears, as Beijing could afford to downplay the Soviet threat and to bargain harder with Washington on the terms of normalization.[108] For his part, serious domestic constraints aside, Kissinger appeared to retain considerable faith in the continuing overriding value of the shared Soviet threat in propelling Sino-American relations forward. It seemed that having pulled off the coup of the compromise on Taiwan in the Shanghai Communiqué, he believed that the Chinese would be indefinitely patient on the subject. Yet the fact that the Chinese ultimately measured the developing U.S.–China relationship by progress toward normalization and thus a resolution of Taiwan's status was made clear by the way in which low-level bilateral talks and exchanges were halted and USLO contacts in Beijing soured in 1974. At the same time, Kissinger's personal credibility declined in Beijing, and the Chinese leaders tried to cultivate more sympathetic interlocutors such as Secretary of Defense James Schlesinger, who was known to oppose the policy of détente.[109] In a situation where the Nixon administration's strategic

---

[106] Memcon, "Sino-Soviet Relations, Europe," pp. 4–6.

[107] Memcon, "Europe; Japan; Middle East; South Asia; Cambodia, Energy and Food; Normalization," 27 November 1974, pp. 1–2; Deng-Kissinger memcon, 28 November 1974, Box 372, Lord Files. For a good analysis of the Chinese leaders' increasing concern over Soviet-American relations after the June 1973 summit based on Bruce's memoirs and meetings with Chinese leaders, see Priscilla Roberts, ed., *Window on the Forbidden City: The Beijing Diaries of David Bruce, 1973–1974* (Hong Kong, 2001), pp. 28–30.

[108] For instance, when Kissinger informed Huang Zhen after the June 1974 Moscow summit that Washington would not consider Brezhnev's suggestion to Nixon of a treaty of mutual assistance if either were attacked by a third party – meaning China – Huang replied, "We don't care." Memcon, "The Secretary's Meeting with PRC Liaison Office Chief Huang Chen after the Moscow Summit," 15 July 1974, NSA Doc. 303.

[109] Author interview with Richard Solomon, 26 February 2001. In November 1974, Deng extended an invitation to Schlesinger to visit China, which was rapidly quashed by

option of closer clandestine military ties with China had been exercised and found wanting, while domestic constraints prevented the fulfillment of earlier understandings on Taiwan and normalization, a stalemate had developed by the time Nixon resigned, and had deepened by the end of 1974.

CONCLUSION: TRIANGULAR BALANCE OF POWER
TO TACIT ALLIANCE

This chapter has analyzed the way in which Nixon and Kissinger's *realpolitik* rapprochement discourse was reconstructed during the two years following the Sino-American summit in February 1972. In 1971 and early 1972, as discussed in Chapters 6 and 9, Kissinger and Nixon had indicated to selected audiences that the opening to China was part of a strategy of building a triangular balance of power in which the United States would enjoy better relations with Beijing and Moscow than they did with each other. In this way, Washington would act as the balancer between the two communist rivals, orchestrating a general reduction of tension and promoting equilibrium in the international system. This is what I have labeled Option 3 in the Introduction.

The analysis in Chapter 6 showed that Nixon's and Kissinger's immediate aim in seeking rapprochement with China in 1969 was to boost the momentum of détente with the Soviet Union; that is, it was conceived as leverage to *improve* relations with and seek cooperation from Moscow, not as a way to form a quasi-alliance to contain it.[110] However, the concepts of triangular balance of power (Option 3) and a de facto Sino-American alliance to contain the potential Soviet hegemon (Option 4) often coexisted. In 1969, the scenario of a large-scale Soviet attack on China was presented by the Nixon administration as the determining factor for choosing Option 4, although short of that, its key aim was Option 3. Chapters 7 and 8 revealed that in the process of constructing the bases for the new relationship with the Chinese, Kissinger played up the Soviet threat and the value of the U.S. relationship to China, thus

Kissinger – see Deng–Kissinger memcon, 27 November 1974, NSA Doc. 325. On Kissinger's and Schlesinger's divergent views on détente and China policy, see Banning Garrett and Bonnie Glaser, "From Nixon to Reagan: China's Changing Role in American Strategy," in Kenneth Oye et al., eds., *Eagle Resurgent: The Reagan Era in American Foreign Policy* (Boston, 1987), p. 291.
[110] Garrett, "Strategic Basis of Learning in US Policy toward China," p. 229; Mann, *About Face*, p. 56.

implicitly presenting Option 4 as U.S. policy. However, the continuing superpower détente, agreements, and summitry suggested that Option 3 was still Washington's priority. This chapter has argued that as pressure mounted on the détente policy and on U.S.–PRC normalization owing to the inherent tensions of triangular politics and to domestic pressures, Kissinger began to pursue Option 4 to a greater degree than before. He not only articulated China's identity as a "tacit ally," but actively tried to construct a tacit alliance relationship by means of bilateral security agreements and a new military relationship. This moved the tenor of U.S.–PRC relations much closer to neo-realist defensive balance-of-power behavior.

Kissinger would argue that this was part of the normal vagaries of triangular politics – there was a need to balance the U.S.–USSR détente with closer U.S.–PRC relations as part of maintaining better U.S. relations with each of the two communist powers while ensuring that their mutual relations remained acrimonious. And yet the extent to which Kissinger's propositions to the Chinese represented judicious balancing for equilibrium is arguable. He ran the risk of overcompensating for détente. This becomes evident if we consider the consequences should the Chinese have accepted the offers: the secret arrangements would almost certainly have been leaked, for, as Lord observed, they had no deterrence value if kept secret. Brezhnev had specifically warned against such a U.S.–PRC quasi-alliance in mid-1973, although the question of what he might have done in the event was an open one.[111] More importantly, though, Soviet worries about the apparently stagnating U.S.–China relationship had diminished from the end of 1973 onward, and leaks about Kissinger's proposals to Zhou might have rekindled Moscow's concerns with unpredictable consequences.[112] At the same time, the Nixon administration's actions in excluding the Soviet Union from the process of brokering a settlement in the Middle East crisis of 1973 left Moscow feeling disgruntled and posed problems for détente. Brezhnev was coming under pressure domestically, as doubts and debates about the wisdom of a policy of détente without a corresponding emphasis of defense, and about the expected economic

[111] Brezhnev–Nixon–Kissinger memcon, 23 June 1973, Box 75, NSF, NPM. During the June 1973 U.S.–USSR summit, Brezhnev speculated that Washington and Beijing might conclude "a military arrangement" that year, adding: "We do not intend to attack China but it will be different if China has a military arrangement with the United States. That will confuse the issue." He did not elaborate.

[112] See Sestanovich, "US Policy toward the Soviet Union," pp. 132–3.

benefits of détente, grew within some factions in the Soviet leadership.[113] These, in combination with the growing domestic political pressures faced by the White House, might have caused revelations of Kissinger's attempts at a secret alliance with the Chinese to have had further negative effects on the prospects for détente and the sustainability of the strategic triangle. Thus, even if Kissinger had intended the offers as a further demonstration to the Soviets that the United States had other options that could complicate Moscow's policies, this would have been a risky move.

So why did Kissinger try to advance along the "tacit alliance" trajectory in developing U.S.–PRC relations during the second half of 1973? There are two possible reasons. First, he miscalculated. Kissinger's own deliberate progressive construction of the Soviet threat to China, and his conviction that Beijing was motivated primarily by its security requirements, produced a "discursive entrapment" effect.[114] He overcompensated for détente because he had overperceived Beijing's need for reassurance, and had thus decided that the United States should more blatantly tilt toward the PRC rather than maintain equilibrium in the triangle. The alternative explanation is that Kissinger's offer of a closer strategic relationship with China was "cheap talk." On the one hand, it could have been aimed at unsettling Moscow at a time when détente was again slowing down. On the other hand, it could have been predicated upon Lord's argument that the Chinese neither wanted nor needed it, and so would not accept it, and thus was a deliberate gesture during increasingly trying times to demonstrate America's commitment to the U.S.–PRC relationship and to reassure Beijing that Washington understood its strategic concerns.

Kissinger's actions can probably be explained by a combination of both these factors. In any case, as domestic pressures in the United States and deepening Chinese intransigence prevented any movement on the Taiwan issue and normalization, he had little alternative in trying to maintain some momentum in the young U.S.–PRC relationship. The findings of this chapter will deepen the controversy about the impact of triangular politics.[115] Whether Kissinger harbored the intention of creating an

---

[113] Burr, *Kissinger Transcripts*, pp. 218–9; Garthoff, *Détente and Confrontation*, pp. 480–5.

[114] The term "discursive entrapment" was brought to my attention by Rosemary Foot.

[115] A good appraisal of the complexities of triangular politics can be found in Ross, ed., *China, the United States, and the Soviet Union*. See especially Stephen Sestanovich, "US Policy Toward the Soviet Union, 1970–1979: The Impact of China," which argues that improved U.S.–PRC relations had relatively little effect on U.S.–Soviet relations during the 1970s and in fact failed to restrain Moscow's adventurism, which culminated in the invasion of Afghanistan in 1979.

alliance with the Chinese in the first place – a question on which the available evidence allows only conjecture – may be the hinge on which an ultimate evaluation of the strategic triangle will turn. For now, the analysis here suggests that the inherent tensions within the logic of triangular relations, combined with domestic pressures and Kissinger's own discursive tenacity, led him to move toward a tacit alliance with the Chinese. The transition from "Former Enemy" to "Tacit Ally" under Nixon and Kissinger was a precursor to the debate about the nature of, and about how to use, the "China card" that would plague the later Carter and Reagan administrations.[116] In the event, U.S.–PRC relations would be sidetracked by domestic political considerations on both sides for the next four years, until Jimmy Carter and Deng Xiaoping managed to agree on the normalization of relations in 1979 under a different set of pressures, aided once again by a combination of discursive continuities and innovations.

[116] For a summary of the contending positions on China policy between Carter's Secretary of State Cyrus Vance and his National Security Adviser Zbigniew Brzezinski, and between Reagan's successive Secretaries of State Al Haig and George Shultz, see Robert Ross, "US Policy toward China: The Strategic Context and the Policy-Making Process," ibid., pp. 157–71.

II

Conclusion

Instead of asking, "Why did the U.S.-China rapprochement happen in 1972?," this study began by posing the broader question, "How did China, after having been America's most implacable enemy, become its friend and even tacit ally during the Nixon administration?" It sought the origins of the policy of bilateral rapprochement in American officials' ideas about reconciliation with China in the decade preceding Nixon's presidency, and it investigated the creation and implementation of rapprochement during the Nixon administration. At the heart of this attempt to situate the U.S.–China rapprochement within the wider discursive and policy-making context of the time is a skepticism about the orthodox realist balance-of-power explanation of events and its ability to account for the process of change. These doubts, in turn, reflect and build upon recent developments in two disciplinary fields – the increasing engagement with theory on the part of some diplomatic historians, and the rise of constructivist approaches in political science and international relations.

The last two decades have produced a greater awareness of the utility of theory within the discipline of history, so that there has developed a steady stream of historical works informed by various theoretical stances derived from the humanities and social sciences. Diplomatic historians have readily employed the political science concepts of bureaucratic politics, public opinion, and ideology and have more recently introduced into their works theories of corporatism, cognitive psychology, world-systems, and dependency.[1] Moreover, social historians have led the field

---

[1] For an earlier overview of these trends, see Michael Hogan and Thomas Paterson, eds., *Explaining the History of American Foreign Relations* (Cambridge, 1991).

into a deeper engagement with cultural studies, discourse analysis, and postcolonial studies.[2] With "their implicit understanding that knowledge and truth are situational" and "their attempts to get outside dominant foreign policy discourses in order to dissect them critically," the social historians in particular have helped to move the field beyond debates about historiographical details alone toward questions about who creates history and for what purposes, and about normative judgment, ethics, and the differential impacts of foreign policy on disparate groups.[3]

There remains, however, deep controversy about the utility of such theories within the discipline. Realist diplomatic historians still dominate the field of American foreign relations in general and the study of U.S.–China relations in particular. They emphasize the primacy of archival research, concentrate on issues of policy making within the state, and are less concerned with economic or cultural forces than with military power and traditional strategic categories such as "balance of power," "national interests," and "national security."[4] In this regard, the use of political-science-inspired methodology in this book to analyze a case that relates to interstate relations at the level of high politics with an emphasis on key foreign policy actors, suggests that there is room for refining method and theory even within the traditional realm of realist historical research.

The nexus between history and political science in the study of international relations, while small and contested, contains significant areas of mutual overlap and potential contribution. For instance, case study researchers in political science have favored using process-tracing methods to explain outcomes. These methods of "trac[ing] empirically the

[2] See, particularly, Rosenberg, *Spreading the American Dream*; Frank Costigliola, *France and the United States: The Cold Alliance since World War II* (New York, 1992); and Matthew Connelly, *A Diplomatic Revolution: Algeria's Fight for Independence and the Origins of the Post-Cold War Era* (Oxford, 2001).

[3] Emily Rosenberg, "Walking the Borders," in Hogan and Paterson, eds., *Explaining the History of American Foreign Relations*, p. 29; Frank Costigliola, "Reading for Meaning: Theory, Language and Metaphor," in Michael Hogan and Thomas Paterson, eds., *Explaining the History of American Foreign Relations*, 2nd ed. (Cambridge, 2003).

[4] See Michael Hunt, "The Long Crisis in Diplomatic History: Coming to Closure," in Michael Hogan, ed., *America in the World: The Historiography of American Foreign Relations since 1945* (Cambridge, 1995). Chapters 1–5 of Hogan's volume contain an exchange reflecting the controversy between realist and revisionist historians. Within the broader field of diplomatic history in general, however, there has been more fragmentation and theoretical eclecticism in recent years – see Michael Hogan, "The Next Big Thing: The Future of Diplomatic History in a Global Age" SHAFR (Society for Historians of American Foreign Relations) Presidential Address 2003, *Diplomatic History* 28(1) (January 2004), pp. 1–21.

temporal and possibly causal sequences of events within a case that intervene between independent variables and observed outcomes" mirror the sequential narrative that a historian undertakes as a matter of course, taking into account the decisions and actions of a variety of actors at a number of causal levels of analysis.[5] Such attention to process, in turn, reveals whether outcomes are sensitive to prior choices made by actors and helps to trace path dependence – that is, whether a temporal sequence of events enabled or foreclosed certain choices.

Political scientists who focus on case studies, employ process tracing, and give credence to path dependence would tend to challenge the notion, favored by structural realists, that states act in set patterns in accordance with structural conditions. But increasingly there are other approaches within political science that offer greater promise of bridging the gap between history and international relations. As this study demonstrates, the greatest potential may lie with the constructivists, who are specifically interested in explaining how past interactions shape future patterns of behavior among states.[6] Constructivist approaches are premised upon the acceptance and expectation that state identities and interests, and international structures, can and do change. Thus actors and their perceptions, representations, and actions are crucial, and international relations are historically contingent, because "alternative actors with alternative identities, practices, and sufficient material resources are theoretically capable of effecting change." This mind set coincides with the historian's concern with explaining what led to changes in international relations and what resulted from those changes.[7]

Yet constructivist approaches, as such, have so far been underemployed in historical research. Although discourse analysis has influenced some works on American foreign relations, and although there has been more emphasis on language and meaning in some historical analyses, these are

---

[5] Andrew Bennett and Alexander George, "Case Studies and Process Tracing in History and Political Science: Similar Strokes for Different Foci"; and Stephen Pelz, "Toward a New Diplomatic History: Two and a Half Cheers for International Relations Methods," both in Colin Elman and Miriam Fendius Elman, eds., *Bridges and Boundaries: Historians, Political Scientists, and the Study of International Relations* (Cambridge, MA, 2001), pp. 144, 101. The two groups tend to employ process tracing for different reasons, though – historians to explain particular outcomes, political scientists to develop and test generalizable theories.

[6] See Elman and Elman, eds., *Bridges and Boundaries*, pp. 33–5; John Lewis Gaddis, *The Landscape of History: How Historians Map the Past* (Oxford, 2002), pp. 61–2.

[7] Hopf, "The Promise of Constructivism," p. 180; Paul Schroeder, "History and International Relations Theory: Not Use or Abuse, but Fit or Misfit," *International Security* 22(1) (Summer 1997), p. 67.

exceptional and sometimes ad hoc applications.[8] The research design and findings of this book indicate that the promise of constructivist approaches for diplomatic history lies in three key areas.

First, they encourage the explicit revelation of the constructed nature of things by giving agency – in this case manifested in the form of discursive representations, but also conceivable by means of ideological frameworks or rhetorical strategies, for example – its due. A constructivist approach such as the one used here helps to strengthen historical research by providing theoretical and conceptual tools to analyze the connections between ideas and outcomes. For instance, discursive representations are important in shaping policy options and choices because, at the most basic level, ideas as presented in discourses affect policy by rendering some courses of action more reasonable than others based on a particular representation of subjects and the relations between them. Thus, if China is regarded as a Red Menace more dangerous and intransigent than the Soviet Union, then containment and isolation makes more sense than establishing bilateral contacts. In other words, path dependence may occur in the form of actions being shaped by particular representations and the related cognitive closures they engender.

Second, constructivist analyses of foreign policy actions have so far concentrated on demonstrating that discourses perform a constraining or enabling function with regard to state action.[9] Yet the constructivist emphasis on discursive representations also implies that external events may be interpreted in different ways by different groups of actors, depending on their existing discourses and ideational predilections. This in turn throws open the critical question of causal processes – how do these different ideas then translate into policy? This is a problem that is also faced by historians who have used ideational concepts to explain policies and events.[10] In the attempt to grapple with relating an effect to its cause, the scholar, rather than relying on the apparent congruence between outcomes and a theory's prediction, may discover a fruitful combination of historical and conceptual methods. This study posits some specific mechanisms by which discursive practice is translated into policy.

---

[8] For instance, Michael Hogan, *A Cross of Iron: Harry S. Truman and the Origins of the National Security State, 1945–1954* (Cambridge, 1998); and see Costigliola, "Reading for Meaning"; Michael Hunt, "Ideology," in Hogan and Paterson, eds., *Explaining the History of American Foreign Relations*, 2nd ed.

[9] Political scientists who do such work include Doty, "Foreign Policy as Social Construction"; Jutta Weldes and Diana Saco, "Making State Action Possible."

[10] For instance, Michael Hunt, *Ideology and US Foreign Policy* (New Haven, 1987).

Far from exerting an "automatic" impulse in a specific policy direction, significant material changes give rise to contending perceptions of the situation, resulting in a condition in which there exists a "salad" of "competing ideas." Eventually, one particular discourse "wins" because it is successfully propagated or "captured," either by particularly powerful or adept bureaucrats or interest groups, by the weight of external events, or by skillful rhetoric and appeal to domestic sentiment. It is important to note that discursive representations are important tools of diplomacy and politics – constructions of another country and of the international situation are more often than not deliberate and instrumental to supporting particular policy predilections and to persuading policy audiences. At the same time, a focus on discourse provides a conceptual handle that can be used to trace the evolution of ideas rather than of personalities per se. The latter approach is traditionally preferred by diplomatic historians, but it is perhaps less useful in tracing policy evolution, since policy discourses are seldom formulated by single officials alone, and since ideas tend to have a longer life span than their originators within an institutional context. Individuals may also have multiple and sometimes contradictory ideas that may change over time.

In instances where an individual may exercise disproportionate effects on policy formulation, the mechanisms by which the actor's actions may be influenced by his or her discursive representations can be more complex. In this study, the concept of discursive entrapment is used to explain how Kissinger apparently experienced the self-reinforcing effect of making subsequent policy choices based primarily upon a strong prior representation of the situation, rather than on a continual reassessment of the changing intersubjective context. Other ways of relating an actor's ideational inclinations, conceptual limitations, or reactions to social conditions to their actions may be drawn from the fields of cognitive psychology and sociology.[11] The aim would be to question the logic and path dependence of an actor's actions over time and to proffer some possible explanations.

Third and ultimately, a stronger engagement between constructivist and historical approaches carries implications for the basic issue of causality, which continues to be a source of contention between historians and political scientists. Historians tend to be more comfortable with positing multiple and contingent causes for events, and while they may rank

[11] See, for instance, Deborah Welch Larson, *The Origins of Containment: A Psychological Explanation* (Princeton, 1985); and Wendt, *Social Theory of International Politics*.

the significance of causes, they are not in the habit of isolating single independent variables.[12] In contrast to rationalist political science, constructivist approaches adopt a standpoint more akin to that of historians. In this view, there is no one *causal* variable; instead there are *constitutive* relationships between ideational and material factors that shape policy outcomes. This stance involves a more complex understanding of the relation between structure and agency and makes possible a more nuanced understanding of causality. As this study begins to demonstrate, the explanatory potential of this constitutive relationship can be helpful: ideas and representations shape the interpretation of, and response to, changes in the international power structure, but the resulting actions and ideas in turn contribute to creating new material or discursive conditions that then condition further responses. For instance, Kissinger believed that Sino-Soviet hostility would provide lasting motivation for China to seek reconciliation with the United States. However, Beijing's fear of the Soviet threat had decreased by mid-1973 precisely because the American discourse of reassurance associated with the Sino-American rapprochement changed the psychological and material balance of power and therefore reduced the likelihood of a Soviet attack on China. In part because of this, the Chinese leadership became more critical and demanding about the conditions for the normalization of relations with Washington, leading Kissinger to believe that the United States had to take greater steps to maintain the rapprochement.

Ultimately, the test of the efficacy of the use of theory in explaining history lies in how much our understanding of the historical event in question is enhanced by the new treatment. The foregoing chapters have employed the rubric of discursive representations in explaining the Sino-American rapprochement in three ways. First, they identified the key subdiscourses of reconciliation with China and explored their individual rationales, achievements, and limitations. Second, they analyzed how these separate discursive strands related to each other: in the case of conflicting discourses, how one eventually became dominant; and in other cases, how one subdiscourse evolved into another, with what continuities and innovations. This included an examination of the "mechanics" of transition – in particular, the structural or external factors that influenced the efficacy of a particular discourse; the bureaucratic politics that

[12] As John Gaddis puts it, historians do not accept "the doctrine of immaculate causation" – "In Defense of Particular Generalization: Rewriting Cold War History, Rethinking International Relations Theory," in Elman and Elman, eds., *Bridges and Boundaries*.

determined the effectiveness of internal policy advocacy; and the methods of persuasion and negotiation that were employed, such as the deliberate representation of particular subjects. Third, these discourses were then related to policy choices and outcomes, since policy action is the ultimate means by which discursive change is consolidated.

The resulting analysis finds that China evolved from America's mortal foe to its friend and ally in the drive to rapprochement as the result of a gathering understanding by American officials of Communist China's weakness, but also of its growing international influence and potential strength. The change in perception and policy also derived from an increasing preoccupation with the way in which America's interests and international position could be buttressed by adopting more moderate attitudes toward the PRC. By investigating the contested process of identity and interest construction prior to the definitive systemic changes emphasized by the realist account, the approach taken in this book helps to explain the resulting policy choices. By "nesting" the realist account within discourse analysis, it is able to specify the impact of systemic forces on the timing and nature of the rapprochement, as well as to differentiate between policy outcomes.[13] Thus, this study demonstrates that realism is neither an automatic nor an independent cause of policy, and that realist practice is rooted in the preparatory soil of foregoing discourses and subject to the dynamics of ensuing ones. The narrative of this book contributes to the historiography of U.S. relations with China in three key ways.

1. Discourses of Reconciliation Prior to the Nixon Administration

The analysis in Part I demonstrated that official discourses of reconciliation with China preceded the Nixon administration. These discourses, based on socioeconomic ideals and political (but not *realpolitik*) calculations, came to dominate in official circles from 1966 onward as a result of a combination of factors. These factors were, in particular: the force of events in China, which reinforced its image as an internally troubled and weakened power; Washington's increasing recognition that it had to reassure Beijing that it had no intention to extend the war in Indochina

---

[13] This is an attempt to flesh out, in an empirical case, the relations of complementarity that may be obtained between constructivist and rationalist lines of theorizing. The idea is summarized, but not developed, in Ronald Jepperson, Alexander Wendt, and Peter Katzenstein, "Norms, Identity and Culture in National Security," in Katzenstein, ed., *Culture of National Security*.

into China; and the gathering domestic consensus on the need to improve relations with China. Before Nixon entered office, the "winning" revisionist discourse found expression in internal documents and high-level public statements about a policy of "containment but not isolation."

However, these revisionist discourses of reconciliation had limited impact in the sense that they certainly did not bring about a U.S.–China rapprochement. For much of the 1960s, this lack of progress was due to the absence of a bureaucratic consensus on the need for reconciliation with China, but the key reason, particularly after the onset of the Cultural Revolution in 1966, was Beijing's continuing intransigence toward the United States, which rendered the American conduct of the Vietnam War and "occupation" of Taiwan insurmountable obstacles to the improvement of relations. Moreover, there were also fundamental limitations within the revisionist discourse itself. The arguments for relaxing China policy were aimed primarily at reducing America's rising international isolation. As a result, their policy influence was heavily circumscribed by a discourse that mainly warranted policy changes that shifted the onus for the inflexible U.S. policy onto Beijing, rather than proposing a basic change in bilateral relations. Furthermore, revisionist officials did not really expect Communist China to change its behavior in the near future. Thus, Kissinger was correct in his claim that the "moralistic" or "liberal" arguments for improving relations with China in the 1960s did not go very far, but he was wrong in his assumption that they disregarded national interest and power considerations. It was precisely the self-interested motivation of buying Washington more room for maneuver and regaining credibility in order to exercise power more effectively in the international arena that fundamentally limited the policy impacts of the 1960s discourse of reconciliation.

Realists contend that the systemic changes in the balance of power were not significant enough during the 1960s to cause a significant alteration in U.S.–China relations. But while American officials were well aware of the deepening Sino-Soviet dispute throughout the 1960s, balance-of-power politics did not feature prominently in the consideration of China policy then, because these officials either regarded China as a more troublesome threat to be contained and persuaded to turn inwards, or argued that Washington would in fact help to heal the Sino-Soviet rift if it attempted to exploit it in some way.

Be that as it may, the 1960s revisionist discourse constituted an important legacy for the Nixon administration's eventual rapprochement with China. Its proponents produced extensive internal documents setting out the rationale for, and specific policy steps toward, reconciliation with China, and they helped to forge a significant internal official consensus on, and to prepare public opinion for, the need to improve relations with China. Equally importantly, the 1960s revisionist discourse formed the basis for Nixon's public justification of the rapprochement with China. As an ex–vice president seeking the presidency, Nixon himself had contributed to the development of the consensus on the need to improve relations with China during the latter part of the 1960s. Nixon's public arguments in favor of better relations with the PRC borrowed from the twin ideas of China as a "Troubled Modernizer" and a "Resurgent Power." However, his discourse of reconciliation differed from that of the Johnson administration in its more coherent combination of the ideas of China's temporary weakness and eventual resurgence, thereby distinguishing between short- and long-term policies. Also, Nixon placed greater emphasis on the need for continued strong containment of China in his "tough coexistence" approach, which carefully represented China as a potential dialogue partner like the Soviet Union. In this respect, he presented the policy of reconciliation as one pursued out of national interest and not out of fear or duress, thus making it more acceptable to conservatives.

The most important departure in U.S.–China relations during the Nixon administration was Beijing's new readiness to respond to U.S. overtures. In this sense, the realist motivations associated with the escalating Sino-Soviet conflict that prompted the change in China's priorities are clear. However, far from inducing an automatic response in kind from Washington, the changing international balance of power led to differing strategic calculations within the U.S. foreign policy bureaucracy because of variations in perceptions of Chinese identity and intentions.

2. How Policy Change Was Effected

Delving into the process of how the China policy reversal was in fact brought about during the Nixon years illuminates the indeterminacy of realist power-balancing logic as applied to this apparently clear-cut case. In response to the Sino-Soviet war of 1969, the Nixon administration had four policy options, all of which would have been consistent with realist reasoning. It could have (1) done nothing and allowed the two communist rivals to weaken each other; (2) supported the Soviet Union against China; (3) improved relations with both Beijing and Moscow; or (4) supported the Chinese against the Soviets. As shown in earlier chapters, all four options were discussed and advocated by various U.S. officials in 1969.

In Washington, there was general appreciation of the systemic changes and the *realpolitik* impetus for Beijing's interest in improving relations with the United States. The real debate was that between the State Department and the White House based on their different assessments of the likelihood of a major Sino-Soviet war and of basic Chinese intentions toward the United States. The State Department, confined by the limits of the gradualist 1960s discourse of reconciliation, argued that Beijing aimed to play the "U.S. card" as a way to gain temporary leverage against Moscow rather than to seek a concrete improvement in bilateral relations. Kissinger, on the other hand, believed that the Chinese leaders could be persuaded by their urgent strategic need to turn more definitely toward the United States and to some make significant concessions over bilateral issues in the process. The White House triumphed because of bureaucratic politics and personal predilection – Nixon and Kissinger soon centralized China policy making in the White House, using "back channels," and so isolated State from the policy process.

In terms of policy justification, though, far from constituting a drastic departure, Nixon and Kissinger's *realpolitik* discourse of reconciliation with China built upon the prevailing reconciliation discourse, while making some important innovations. Most notably, they reconstructed China's identity as a major power, from a potential "Resurgent Power" to a "Threatened Major Power" vulnerable to Soviet attack, whose national security was essential to maintaining international peace and the power equilibrium. At the same time, a modified version of the non-*realpolitik* discourse of reconciliation based on the "Resurgent Power" image remained relevant to the process by which the Nixon administration advocated the new China policy. It was employed in order to justify the change in policy to the general public and to some American allies, while the *realpolitik* rationale was used only to convince domestic conservatives who might otherwise have accused Nixon of "selling out" to the communists.

3. Kissinger's Construction of a "Tacit Alliance" in the Course of Carrying Out the Policy of Rapprochement

The most notable instance of ideas affecting policy choice in this study is the way in which Kissinger eventually opted for the policy of supporting China against the Soviet Union in the course of constructing the rapprochement with Beijing. Newly declassified transcripts of Kissinger's dialogues with Zhou Enlai and Mao Zedong in Beijing during the Nixon administration reveal that in 1973, Kissinger offered the Chinese leaders a variety of bilateral agreements and covert American military assistance that would have amounted to the creation of a tacit or secret alliance between the two countries. These developments signified a substantive shift from one variant of realist policy aimed at improving U.S. relations with both Moscow and Beijing in order to increase U.S. leverage over both, to a different policy of aligning with China against the Soviet Union.

Analyzing the implementation of Nixon's policy of rapprochement with China reveals the various layers of advocacy involved in constructing and developing the new relationship from 1971 onward. Most striking is the finding that Nixon and Kissinger paid considerable attention to "selling" reconciliation to the Chinese themselves. This process of negotiating the terms of rapprochement involved a conscientious effort at reconstructing China's identity in the direction of a "Principled Realist Power," which could be a friend and security dialogue partner of the United States by virtue of its great power status and the two countries' shared interest in countering hegemony. The construction of the new U.S.–China relationship was largely discursive, but it was also backed up by some policy action, such as the U.S. reaction to the South Asian crisis at the end of 1971 and Nixon's adoption of the "one China" policy regarding the Taiwan issue.

The focus on discourse reveals that while the two sides were brought together by the perception of potential mutual strategic benefits, the coincidence of interests was not as obvious as some have suggested. As Kissinger has claimed, the process of signaling and dialogue, in which he played a crucial part, was vital. Beyond that, however, over a period of three years Kissinger felt compelled deliberately to construct a growing Soviet threat to China in order to reinforce the Chinese leaders' security concerns and to persuade them of the value of closer U.S.–PRC relations as a counterweight. So acute was this perceived need that even as domestic and international political circumstances altered during the latter part of the Nixon administration, Kissinger intensified his discursive and policy activity along this same trajectory, despite the fact that it had become less effective.

From mid-1973 onward, the U.S.–China relationship was threatened with stagnation as Nixon and Kissinger's strategy of parallel détente with the two communist powers appeared to falter. The Chinese were opposed to, and suspicious of, the U.S.–USSR détente, and they increasingly disputed Kissinger's discourse on the Soviet threat while applying pressure on Washington for the resolution of the Taiwan issue and normalization. On the other hand, domestic pressures in the form of the

Watergate crisis and congressional attacks on the administration's conduct of the war in Indochina and its détente policy called into question
the Nixon administration's credibility, making it impossible to effect any
controversial changes to Taiwan policy. In this situation, Kissinger chose
to continue emphasizing China's requirement for U.S. support against
the Soviet threat, not only in symbolic but also in increasingly material terms. He used offers of a closer military-strategic relationship with
China to try to maintain a sense of momentum in the relationship even
though the scenario of a large-scale Sino-Soviet war was not imminent.
He acted in response to a combination of domestic political pressures and
because of discursive entrapment. The latter is salient especially when
we consider that the Chinese wanted normalization but not a covert military relationship with the United States, and that Kissinger's offers, if
made public, might have further jeopardized the superpower détente.
In sum, Kissinger opted for a more extreme policy than circumstances
warranted. Even if he did so as a calculated form of "cheap talk," the
fact remains significant, because in doing so, Kissinger set China policy in the direction of a military alliance much earlier than is commonly
thought.

The Nixon administration's construction and conduct of China policy
was remarkable on two additional counts. The first relates to the concentration of power that is often ascribed to the executive branch of government in general. In the case of China, Nixon's thinking about the policy
change predated Kissinger's, and in the run-up to and around the February
1972 visit to China, the president exerted as much control over policy as
his national security adviser did. From 1973 onward, however, it seems
from the available record that Kissinger exercised more independent initiative over the subsequent development of the bilateral relationship. For
instance, unlike the situation in 1971 and early 1972, there is little written record of Nixon's making suggestions or offering comments on China
policy. Moreover, while Kissinger kept Nixon well briefed, his written
reports to the president did not refer to his proposals of strategic aid to
China in November 1973. Kissinger's relatively free hand in determining
China policy from 1973 onward may have reinforced his confidence in
the effectiveness of his negotiating strategy and tactics. A second point
of note is the relationship between the Nixon administration's approach
toward China and that of the Kennedy and Johnson administrations. The
focus on discursive representations rather than policy outcomes per se
has highlighted continuities where others have previously identified departures, while allowing us to recognize that Nixon and Kissinger must be

credited for the style with which they effected change and the substantial
ways in which they developed previous policy recommendations. Future
work on the Ford and Carter administrations may well reveal further
continuities in the way in which triangular relations were debated and
developed, how the tacit U.S.–China strategic partnership was brought
about, and the eventual negotiation of diplomatic normalization.

For now, we may observe that the Sino-American rapprochement was
neither an automatic reaction to structural change nor the result of the
genius of great men; rather, it was a process of evolution of a crucial set
of new ideas in postwar U.S. foreign policy toward China. Nixon and
Kissinger effected a dramatic fruition of the Sino-American rapprochement in 1972, a fulfilment and an extraordinary culmination of a process
of discursive reconstruction, policy debate, and reappraisal that can be
traced back to 1961. Even as this account moderates the drastic nature
of the policy change in 1972, it also reveals that the real innovation in
Nixon's and Kissinger's opening to China lay in the way in which they subsequently developed the policy of rapprochement toward a closer strategic partnership than many had previously realized. This increased understanding of the initial drive to Sino-American reconciliation from the
Kennedy to the Nixon administration will also contribute to our understanding of the later process of normalizing U.S.–PRC relations. It has
revealed the origins and early development not only of ideas of reconciliation, but also of the interim discursive and policy actions taken to
facilitate the rapprochement. In this way, it aids our understanding of the
nature of key problems such as the Taiwan issue and sheds light on the
conditions that made normalization possible in 1979. More broadly, this
study demonstrates the importance of discursive representations in shaping policy options and choices, and provides pertinent food for thought
in the ongoing debate about whether Washington should perceive and
treat Beijing as a "strategic partner," a "competitor," or even as a "rogue
state" in the "Pacific century" to come.

Bibliography

Archival Sources

Association for Diplomatic Studies and Training [ADST], Foreign Affairs Oral History Collection, Lauinger Library, Georgetown University, Washington, DC

John F. Kennedy Presidential Library [JFKL], Boston, MA
  President's Office Files [POF]
  National Security Files [NSF]
  White House Central Subject Files [WHSF]
  Papers of Roger Hilsman
  Papers of James Thomson
  Papers of Arthur Schlesinger
  Oral History Interview Transcripts

Lyndon Baines Johnson Presidential Library [LBJL], Austin, TX
  National Security Files [NSF]
  Vice Presidential Papers [VPP]
  White House Central Files [WHCF]
  White House Confidential Files [CF]
  Papers of George W. Ball
  Papers of William P. Bundy
  Oral History Interview Transcripts

National Archives II [NA], College Park, MD
  Decimal Central Files for 1961, 1962
  Record Group 59, General Records of the Department of State [RG59]
  Central Foreign Policy Files [CFPF], 1963, 1964–6, 1967–9
  Top Secret Files [TSF], 1955–63, 1964–6
  Subject-Numeric Files [SNF], 1970–3
  LOT Files 77D112 & 77D114: Files of the Director of Policy Planning, 1973–7 [Lord Files]
  Record Group 273, Records of the National Security Council

National Archives Pacific Region [NA-PR], Laguna Niguel, CA
   Richard M. Nixon Pre-Presidential Papers
National Security Archives [NSA], George Washington University, Washington,
   DC
   Special Collections Series, Microfiche Collection, *China and the United States:
   From Hostility to Engagement, 1960–1998*
Nixon Presidential Materials Staff [NPM], National Archives II, College Park,
   MD
   President's Office Files [POF]
   President's Personal Files [PPF]
   National Security Files [NSF]
   White House Subject Files: Confidential Files [WHCF]
   White House Subject Files: Top Secret Files [TSF]
   White House Subject Files: Staff Member Office Files: Special
   Staff Files
   George Bush Files
   Dwight Chapin Files
   John Ehrlichman Files
   Leonard Garment Files
   Alexander Haig Files
   Bob Haldeman Files
   Ronald Ziegler Files
Richard Nixon Library and Birthplace Foundation [RNL], Yorba
   Linda, CA
   Pre-Presidential Papers

Published Documentary Sources

Congressional Record [CR]. Washington, DC: U.S. Government Printing Office.
Iriye, Akira, ed. *US Policy toward China: Testimony Taken from the
   Senate Foreign Relations Committee Hearings – 1966.* Boston: Little, Brown,
   1968.
Nixon, Richard. *United States Foreign Policy for the 1970s: A New Strategy for
   Peace* (a report to the Congress, 18 February 1970). Washington, DC: U.S.
   Government Printing Office, 1970.
The Pentagon Papers (as published by the *New York Times*). London: Routledge
   and Kegan Paul, 1971.
Public Papers of the Presidents: John F. Kennedy [PPP:JFK]. Washington, DC: U.S.
   Government Printing Office, 1961–3.
Public Papers of the Presidents: Lyndon B. Johnson [PPP:LBJ]. Washington, DC: U.S.
   Government Printing Office, 1963–8.
Public Papers of the Presidents: Richard Nixon [PPP:RN]. Washington, DC: U.S.
   Government Printing Office, 1969–72.
U.S. Department of State. *American Foreign Policy: Current Documents* [AFP].
   Washington, DC: U.S. Government Printing Office, 1961–68.
U.S. Department of State. *Department of State Bulletin* [DSB]. Washington, DC:
   U.S. Government Printing Office, 1961–68.

U.S. Department of State. *Foreign Relations of the United States* [FRUS]. Washington, DC: U.S. Government Printing Office.
1952–4, vol. XIV, *China and Japan* (1985)
1955–7, vol. II, *China* (1986)
1955–7, vol. III, *China* (1986)
1958–60, vol. XIX, *China* (1996)
1961–3, vol. VII, *Arms Control and Disarmament* (1995)
1961–3, vol. VIII, *National Security Policy* (1996)
1961–3, vol. XXII, *Northeast Asia* (1996)
1961–3, vol. XIX, *South Asia* (1996)
1964–8, vol. I, *Vietnam, 1964* (1992)
1964–8, vol. II, *Vietnam, January-June 1965* (1996)
1964–8, vol. III, *Vietnam, July-December 1965* (1996)
1964–8, vol. IV, *Vietnam, 1966* (1998)
1964–8, vol. XI, *Arms Control and Disarmament* (1997)
1964–8, vol. XXX, *China* (1998)
U.S. Department of State. *United States Policy toward Communist China.* Statement by Secretary Rusk made before the Subcommittee on the Far East and the Pacific of the House Committee on Foreign Affairs, 16 March 1966. Washington, DC: U.S. Government Printing Office, 1966.
U.S. Senate Committee on Foreign Relations. *China, Vietnam and the United States: Highlights of the Hearings of the Senate Foreign Relations Committee.* Washington, D.C.: Public Affairs Press, 1966.
U.S. Senate Committee on Foreign Relations. *The Vietnam Hearings.* New York: Random House, 1966.
Mao Zedong waijiao wenxuan [Selected diplomatic papers of Mao Zedong]. Beijing: Zhongyang wenxian, 1994.
Zhou Enlai waijiao wenxuan [Selected diplomatic papers of Zhou Enlai]. Beijing: Zhongyang wenxian, 1989.

Secondary Sources

Accinelli, Robert. *Crisis and Commitment: United States Policy toward Taiwan, 1950–1955.* Chapel Hill: University of North Carolina Press, 1996.
Acharya, Amitav. *Constructing a Security Community in Southeast Asia: ASEAN and the Problem of Regional Order.* London: Routledge, 2001.
Adler, Emmanuel. "Seizing the Middle Ground: Constructivism in World Politics." *European Journal of International Relations* 3(3) (1997), pp. 319–63.
Aitken, Jonathan. *Nixon: A Life.* London: Weidenfield and Nicolson, 1993.
Ambrose, Stephen E. *Nixon: The Triumph of a Politician, 1962–1972.* London: Simon and Schuster, 1989.
Nixon: The Education of a Politician, 1913–1962. London: Simon and Schuster, 1987.
Ang Cheng Guan. *Ending the Vietnam War: The Vietnamese Communists' Perspective.* London: RoutledgeCurzon, 2004.
Armstrong, J. David. *Revolutionary Diplomacy: Chinese Foreign Policy and the United Front Doctrine.* Berkeley: University of California Press, 1977.

Bachrack, Stanley D. *The Committee of One Million: 'China Lobby' Politics 1953–1971*. New York: Columbia University Press, 1976.

Barnett, A. Doak. *Communist China and Asia: Challenge to American Policy*. Oxford: Oxford University Press, 1960.

Bassett, Lawrence J., and Stephen E. Pelz. "The Failed Search for Victory." In Thomas G. Paterson, ed., *Kennedy's Quest for Victory: American Foreign Policy, 1961–1963*. New York: Oxford University Press, 1989, pp. 223–52.

Becker, Jasper. *Hungry Ghosts: China's Secret Famine*. London: John Murray, 1996.

Bennett, Andrew, and Alexander L. George. "Case Studies and Process Tracing in History and Political Science: Similar Strokes for Different Foci." In Colin Elman and Miriam Fendius Elman, eds., *Bridges and Boundaries: Historians, Political Scientists, and the Study of International Relations*. Cambridge, MA: MIT Press, 2001, pp. 137–66.

Blaufarb, Douglas. *The Counterinsurgency Era: US Doctrine and Performance*. New York: Free Press, 1977.

Blum, Robert M. *Drawing the Line: The Origin of the American Containment Policy in East Asia*. New York: Norton, 1982.

Boulding, Kenneth E. *The Image*. Ann Arbor: University of Michigan Press, 1956.

Bowie, Robert R., and Richard H. Immerman. *Waging Peace: How Eisenhower Shaped an Enduring Cold War Strategy*. Oxford: Oxford University Press, 1998.

Bowles, Chester. *Promises to Keep: My Years in Public Life, 1941–1969*. New York: Harper and Row, 1971.

    "The 'China Problem' Reconsidered." *Foreign Affairs* 38(3) (April 1960), pp. 476–86.

Bundy, William P. *A Tangled Web: The Making of Foreign Policy in the Nixon Presidency*. New York: Hill and Wang, 1998.

Burr, William. "Sino-American Relations, 1969: The Sino-Soviet Border War and Steps towards Rapprochement." *Cold War History* 1(3) (April 2001), pp. 73–112.

    The Kissinger Transcripts: The Top Secret Talks with Beijing and Moscow. New York: Norton, 1999.

Burr, William, and Richelson, Jeffrey T. "Whether to 'Strangle the Baby in the Cradle': The United States and the Chinese Nuclear Program, 1960–64." *International Security* 25(3) (Winter 2000/1), pp. 54–99.

Brzezinski, Zbigniew. *Power and Principle: Memoirs of the National Security Adviser, 1977–1981*. New York: Farrar, Straus and Giroux, 1983.

Chang, Gordon H. *Friends and Enemies: The United States, China and the Soviet Union, 1948–1972*. Stanford, CA: Stanford University Press, 1990.

Checkel, Jeffrey T. "The Constructivist Turn in International Relations Theory." *World Politics* 50 (January 1998), pp. 324–48.

Chen Jian. *Mao's China and the Cold War*. Chapel Hill: University of North Carolina Press, 2001.

    China's Road to the Korean War: The Making of the Sino-American Confrontation. New York: Columbia University Press, 1994.

Chen Jian and James Hershberg. "Informing the Enemy: Sino-American 'Signalling' and the Vietnam War, 1965." Paper presented at Cold War International History Project workshop, New Evidence on China, Southeast

Asia, and the Vietnam War, January 2000, Hong Kong University, Hong Kong.

Chen Jian and David L. Wilson. "'All under the Heaven Is Great Chaos': Beijing, the Sino-Soviet Border Clashes and the Turn towards Sino-American Rapprochement, 1968–9." *Cold War International History Project Bulletin* 11 (Winter 1998), pp. 155–75.

Christensen, Thomas J. *Useful Adversaries: Grand Strategy, Domestic Mobilization, and Sino-American Conflict, 1947–1958.* Princeton, NJ: Princeton University Press, 1996.

Churchill, Winston. *The Grand Alliance.* Boston: Houghton Mifflin, 1950.

Clark, Mark. *From the Danube to the Yalu.* New York: Harper, 1954.

Cohen, Warren I. *America's Response to China: A History of Sino-American Relations,* 4th ed. New York: Columbia University Press, 2000.

Dean Rusk. Totowa, NJ: Cooper Square, 1980.

Cold War International History Project Bulletin. Issues 6–7, "The Cold War in Asia" (Winter 1995/6).

Congressional Quarterly. *China: US Policy Since 1945.* Washington: DC: Congressional Quarterly, 1980.

Conlon Associates Ltd. *United States Foreign Policy: Asia.* Washington, DC: U.S. Government Printing Office, 1959.

Connelly, Matthew James. *A Diplomatic Revolution: Algeria's Fight for Independence and the Origins of the Post–Cold War Era.* Oxford: Oxford University Press, 2001.

Costigliola, Frank. "Reading for Meaning: Theory, Language and Metaphor." In Michael J. Hogan and Thomas G. Paterson, eds., *Explaining the History of American Foreign Relations,* 2nd ed. Cambridge: Cambridge University Press, 2003, pp. 279–303.

France and the United States: The Cold Alliance since World War II. New York: Twayne, 1992.

Dittmer, Lowell. *Sino-Soviet Normalization and Its International Implications, 1945–1990.* (Seattle: University of Washington Press, 1992).

"The Strategic Triangle: An Elementary Game-Theoretical Analysis." *World Politics* 33(4) (July 1981), pp. 485–515.

Dobrynin, Anatoly. *In Confidence: Moscow's Ambassador to America's Six Cold War Presidents, 1962–1986.* New York: Times Books, 1995.

Doty, Roxanne Lynn. "Foreign Policy as Social Construction: A Post-positivist Analysis of US Counter-Insurgency Policy in the Philippines." *International Studies Quarterly* 37(3) (1993), pp. 297–320.

Duffy, Gavan, and Evelyn Goh. "From Tacit to Secret Alliance: Pragmatic Analysis of Kissinger's 1973 Reconstruction of US-China Relations." Paper presented at the European Consortium for Political Research Fourth Pan-European International Relations Conference, University of Kent, Canterbury, September 2001.

Duiker, William. *China and Vietnam: The Roots of Conflict.* Berkeley: Institute of East Asian Studies, University of California, 1986.

Ellison, Herbert J., ed. *The Sino-Soviet Conflict: A Global Perspective.* Seattle: University of Washington Press, 1981.

Elman, Colin, and Miriam Fendius Elman, eds. *Bridges and Boundaries: Historians, Political Scientists, and the Study of International Relations.* Cambridge, MA: MIT Press, 2001.

Fairbank, John King. *China Watch.* Cambridge, MA: Harvard University Press, 1987.

Fejtö, François. "France and China: The Intersection of Two Grand Designs." In A. M. Halpern, ed., *Policies toward China: Views from Six Continents.* New York: McGraw-Hill, 1965, pp. 42–76.

Fetzer, James. "Clinging to Containment: China Policy." In Thomas G. Paterson, ed., *Kennedy's Quest for Victory: American Foreign Policy, 1961–1963.* Oxford: Oxford University Press, 1989, pp. 178–97.

Fiebig-von Hase, Ragnhild, and Ursula Lehmkuhl, eds. *Enemy Images in American History.* Providence, RI: Berghahn Books, 1997.

Finnemore, Martha. *National Interests in International Society.* Ithaca: NY: Cornell University Press, 1996.

Foot, Rosemary. "Redefinitions: The Domestic Context and America's China Policy in the 1960s." In Robert S. Ross and Jiang Changbin, eds., *Re-examining the Cold War: US-China Diplomacy, 1954–1973.* Cambridge, MA: Harvard University Press, 2001, pp. 261–87.

"The Study of China's International Behaviour: International Relations Approaches." In Ngaire Woods, ed., *Explaining International Relations Since 1945.* Oxford: Oxford University Press, 1996, pp. 259–79.

The Practice of Power: US Relations with China since 1949. Oxford: Clarendon Press, 1995.

The Wrong War: American Policy and the Dimensions of the Korean Conflict, 1950–1953. Ithaca, NY: Cornell University Press, 1985.

Foucault, Michel. *The Archaeology of Knowledge.* London: Tavistock, 1972.

Franck, Thomas. *The Power of Legitimacy among Nations.* New York: Oxford University Press, 1990.

Freedman, Lawrence. *Kennedy's Wars: Berlin, Cuba, Laos and Vietnam.* Oxford: Oxford University Press, 2000.

Gaddis, John Lewis. *The Landscape of History: How Historians Map the Past.* Oxford: Oxford University Press, 2002.

"In Defence of Particular Generalization: Rewriting Cold War History, Rethinking International Relations Theory." In Colin Elman and Miriam Fendius Elman, eds., *Bridges and Boundaries: Historians, Political Scientists, and the Study of International Relations.* Cambridge, MA: MIT Press, 2001, pp. 301–26.

"The American 'Wedge Strategy', 1949–1958." In Harry Harding and Yuan Ming, eds., *Sino-American Relations 1945–1955: A Joint Assessment of a Critical Decade.* Wilmington, DE: Scholarly Resources, 1989, pp.157–82.

Strategies of Containment: A Critical Appraisal of Postwar American National Security Policy. Oxford: Oxford University Press, 1982.

Gallicchio, Marc S. "The Best Defense Is Good Offense: The Evolution of American Strategy in East Asia, 1953–1960." In Warren I. Cohen and Akira Iriye, eds., *The Great Powers in East Asia, 1953–1960.* New York: Columbia University Press, 1990, pp. 63–85.

Garthoff, Raymond L. *Détente and Confrontation: American-Soviet Relations from Nixon to Reagan*, rev. ed. Washington, DC: Brookings Institution, 1994.

Garrett, Banning N. "The Strategic Basis of Learning in US Policy toward China, 1948–1988." In George W. Breslauer and Philip Tetlock, eds., *Learning in US and Soviet Foreign Policy*. Boulder, CO: Westview, 1991, pp. 208–63.

"The 'China Card' and Its Origins: US Bureaucratic Politics and the Strategic Triangle." Unpublished Ph.D. dissertation, Brandeis University, 1983.

Garrett, Banning N., and Bonnie S. Glaser. "From Nixon to Reagan: China's Changing Role in American Strategy." In Kenneth A. Oye, Robert J. Lieber, and Donald Rothchild, eds., *Eagle Resurgent: The Reagan Era in American Foreign Policy*. Boston: Little, Brown, 1987, pp. 256–63.

Garver, John W. "Food for Thought: Reflections on Food Aid and the Idea of Another Lost Chance in Sino-American Relations." *Journal of American-East Asian Relations* 7(1–2) (Spring/Summer 1998), pp. 101–6.

Sino-American Alliance: Nationalist China and American Cold War Strategy in Asia. London: M. E. Sharpe, 1997.

China's Decision for Rapprochement with the United States, 1968–1971. Boulder, CO: Westview Press, 1982.

Gates, Robert M. *From the Shadows: The Ultimate Insider's Story of Five Presidents and How They Won the Cold War*. New York: Simon and Schuster, 1996.

Gellman, Irwin F. *The Contender, Richard Nixon: The Congress Years, 1946–1952*. New York: Free Press, 1999.

George, Alexander L. "The 'Operational Code': A Neglected Approach to the Study of Political Leaders and Decision-Making." *International Studies Quarterly* 13 (1969), pp. 190–222.

George, Jim. *Discourses of Global Politics: A Critical (Re)Introduction to International Relations*. Boulder, CO: Lynne Rienner, 1994.

Gobarev, Viktor M. "Soviet Policy toward China: Developing Nuclear Weapons 1949–1969." *The Journal of Slavic Military Studies* 12(4) (1999), pp. 37–47.

Goh, Evelyn, and Gavan Duffy. "Playing the Soviet Card: Henry Kissinger's Reconstruction of 'Triangular Relations' in the Opening to China, 1971 to 1974." Paper presented at the annual meeting of the International Studies Association, Chicago, February 2001.

Goldstein, Judith, and Robert O. Keohane, eds. *Ideas and Foreign Policy: Beliefs, Institutions, and Political Change*. Ithaca: Cornell University Press, 1993.

Goldstein, Steven M. "Dialogue of the Deaf? The Sino-American Ambassadorial-level Talks, 1955–1970." In Robert S. Ross and Jiang Changbin, eds., *Re-examining the Cold War: US-China Diplomacy, 1954–1973*. Cambridge, MA: Harvard University Press, 2001, pp. 200–37.

"Nationalism and Internationalism: Sino-Soviet Relations." In Thomas W. Robinson and David Shambaugh, eds., *Chinese Foreign Policy: Theory and Practice*. Oxford: Clarendon Press, 1994, pp. 224–65.

Goncharov, Sergei V., John W. Lewis, and Xue Litai. *Uncertain Partners: Stalin, Mao and the Korean War*. Stanford, CA: Stanford University Press, 1993.

Gong Li. "Chinese Decision Making and the Thawing of Sino-US Relations." In Robert S. Ross and Jiang Changbin, eds., *Re-examining the Cold War: US-China Diplomacy, 1954–1973*. Cambridge, MA: Harvard University Press, 2001, pp. 141–72.

L

Mao Zedong yu Meiguo [Mao Zedong and America]. Beijing: Shijie Zhishi Chubanshe, 1998.

Green, Marshall. "Omens of Change." In Marshall Green, John H. Holdridge, and William N. Stokes, *War and Peace in China: First-Hand Experiences in the Foreign Service of the United States*. Bethesda, MD: DACOR Press, 1994, pp. 83–95.

Hagen, James N., and Vernon W. Ruttan. "Development Policy under Eisenhower and Kennedy." *Journal of Developing Areas* 23 (October 1988), pp. 1–30.

Haldeman, H. R. *The Haldeman Diaries: Inside the Nixon White House*. New York: Putnam, 1994.

Haldeman, H. R., and Joseph DiMona. *The Ends of Power*. New York: Times Books, 1978.

Handel, Michael. *The Diplomacy of Surprise: Hitler, Nixon and Sadat*. Cambridge, MA: Harvard University Press, 1981.

Hao Yufan. *Dilemma and Decision: An Organizational Perspective on American China Policy-Making*. Berkeley: Institute of East Asian Studies, University of California, 1997.

Harding, Harry. *A Fragile Relationship: The United States and China since 1972*. Washington, DC: Brookings Institution, 1992.

"From China, with Disdain: New Trends in the Study of China." *Asian Survey* 22(10) (October 1982), pp. 934–58.

He Di. "The Most Respected Enemy: Mao Zedong's Perception of the United States." *China Quarterly* 137 (March 1994), pp. 145–58.

Hersh, Seymour M. *The Price of Power: Kissinger in the Nixon White House*. New York: Summit Books, 1983.

Hoffman, Stanley. *Primacy or World Order: American Foreign Policy since the Cold War*. New York: McGraw-Hill, 1978.

Hogan, Michael J. "The Next Big Thing: The Future of Diplomatic History in a Global Age." SHAFR (Society for Historians of American Foreign Relations) Presidential Address 2003. *Diplomatic History* 28(1) (January 2004), pp. 1–21.

A Cross of Iron: Harry S. Truman and the Origins of the National Security State, 1945–1954. Cambridge: Cambridge University Press, 1998.

Hogan, Michael J., ed. *America in the World: The Historiography of American Foreign Relations since 1945*. Cambridge: Cambridge University Press, 1995.

Hogan, Michael J., and Thomas G. Paterson, eds. *Explaining the History of American Foreign Relations*. Cambridge: Cambridge University Press, 1991.

Holdridge, John H. *Crossing the Divide: An Insider's Account of Normalization of US-China Relations*. Lanham, MD: Rowman and Littlefield, 1997.

Hollis, Martin, and Steve Smith. *Explaining and Understanding International Relations*. Oxford: Oxford University Press, 1990.

Hong Zhaohui. "The Role of Individuals in US-China Relations, 1949–1972." In Li Hongshan and Hong Zhaohui, eds., *Image, Perception, and the Making of US-China Relations*. Lanham, MD: University Press of America, 1998, pp. 345–64.

Hood, Stephen J. *Dragons Entangled: Indochina and the China-Vietnam War*. Armonk, NY: M. E. Sharpe.

Hopf, Ted. "The Promise of Constructivism in International Relations Theory." *International Security* 23(1) (1998), pp. 171–200.

Hunt, Michael H. "Ideology." In Michael J. Hogan and Thomas G. Paterson, eds., *Explaining the History of American Foreign Relations*, 2nd ed. Cambridge: Cambridge University Press, 2003, pp. 221–40.

Ideology and US Foreign Policy. New Haven, CT: Yale University Press, 1987.

The Making of a Special Relationship: The United States and China to 1914. New York: Columbia University Press, 1983.

Hyland, William G. *Mortal Rivals: Superpower Relations from Nixon to Reagan.* New York: Random House, 1987.

Iriye, Akira, ed. *Mutual Images: Essays in American-Japanese Relations.* Cambridge, MA: Harvard University Press, 1975.

Isaacs, Arnold R. *Without Honor: Defeat in Vietnam and Cambodia.* Baltimore: Johns Hopkins University Press, 1983.

Isaacs, Harold R. *Images of Asia: American Views on China and India.* New York: Harper and Row, 1968.

Jepperson, Ronald J., Alexander Wendt, and Peter J. Katzenstein. "Norms, Identity and Culture in National Security." In Peter J. Katzenstein, ed., *The Culture of National Security: Norms and Identity in World Politics.* New York: Columbia University Press, 1996, pp. 33–75.

Jervis, Robert. "A Political Science Perspective on the Balance of Power and the Concert." *American Historical Review* 97(3) (1992), pp. 716–24.

Perception and Misperception in International Politics. Princeton, NJ: Princeton University Press, 1976.

The Logic of Images in International Relations. Princeton, NJ: Princeton University Press, 1970.

Johnston, Alastair I. "Cultural Realism and Strategy in Maoist China." In Peter J. Katzenstein, ed., *The Culture of National Security: Norms and Identity in World Politics.* New York: Columbia University Press, 1996, pp. 216–68.

Kaiser, David. "Men and Policies: 1961–69." In Diane B. Kunz, ed., *The Diplomacy of the Crucial Decade: American Foreign Relations during the 1960s.* New York: Columbia University Press, 1994.

Kalb, Marvin, and Bernard Kalb. *Kissinger.* London: Hutchinson, 1974.

Kalicki, J. H. *The Pattern of Sino-American Crises: Political-Military Interactions in the 1950s.* Cambridge: Cambridge University Press, 1975.

Kang, Jean S. "Food for Communist China: A US Policy Dilemma, 1961–1963." *Journal of American-East Asian Relations* 7(1–2) (Spring/Summer 1998), pp. 39–72.

Katzenstein, Peter J., ed. *The Culture of National Security: Norms and Identity in World Politics.* New York: Columbia University Press, 1996.

Kaufman, Victor S. *Confronting Communism: US and British Policies toward China.* Columbia: University of Missouri Press, 2001.

"A Response to Chaos: The United States, the Great Leap Forward, and the Cultural Revolution, 1961–1968." *Journal of American-East Asian Relations* 7(1–2) (Spring/Summer 1998), pp. 73–92.

Keith, Ronald C. *The Diplomacy of Zhou Enlai.* London: Macmillan, 1989.

Kennedy, John F. "If India Falls." *The Progressive* 22 (January 1958), pp. 8–11.

Khong Yuen Foong. *Analogies at War: Korea, Munich, Dien Bien Phu, and the Vietnam Decisions of 1965.* Princeton, NJ: Princeton University Press, 1992.

Kimball, Jeffrey. *Nixon's Vietnam War.* Lawrence: University Press of Kansas, 1998.

Kissinger, Henry A. *Diplomacy.* New York: Simon and Schuster, 1994.

Years of Upheaval. London: Weidenfeld and Nicolson, 1982.

White House Years. Boston: Little, Brown, 1979.

Kochavi, Noam. *A Conflict Perpetuated: China Policy during the Kennedy Years.* Westport, CT: Praeger, 2002.

"Kennedy, China, and the Tragedy of No Chance." *Journal of American-East Asian Relations* 7(1–2) (Spring/Summer 1998), pp. 107–16.

"Mist across the Bamboo Curtain: China's Internal Crisis and the American Intelligence Process, 1961–1962." *Journal of American-East Asian Relations* 5(2) (Summer 1996), pp. 135–55.

Kratochwil, Friedrich V. *Rules, Norms, and Decisions: On the Conditions of Practical and Legal Reasoning in International Relations and Domestic Affairs.* Cambridge: Cambridge University Press, 1989.

Kubálková, Vendulka, Nicholas G. Onuf, and Paul Kowert, eds. *International Relations in a Constructed World.* London: M. E. Sharpe, 1998.

Kusnitz, Leonard A. *Public Opinion and Foreign Policy: America's China Policy, 1949–1979.* Westport, CT: Greenwood Press, 1984.

Kux, Dennis. *Estranged Democracies: India and the United States, 1941–1991.* London: Sage, 1994.

Larsen, Henrik. *Foreign Policy and Discourse Analysis: France, Britain and Europe.* London: Routledge, 1997.

Larson, Deborah Welch. *The Origins of Containment: A Psychological Explanation.* Princeton, NJ: Princeton University Press, 1985.

Levine, Steven I. "China's Foreign Policy in the Strategic Triangle." In June Dreyer, ed., *Chinese Defense and Foreign Policy.* New York: Paragon, 1988.

Lewis, John Wilson, and Xue Litai. *China Builds the Bomb.* Stanford, CA: Stanford University Press, 1988.

Li Jie. "Changes in China's Domestic Situation in the 1960s and Sino-US Relations." In Robert S. Ross and Jiang Changbin, eds., *Re-examining the Cold War: US-China Diplomacy, 1954–1973.* Cambridge, MA: Harvard University Press, 2001.

Litfin, Karen T. *Ozone Discourses: Science and Politics in Global Environmental Cooperation.* New York: Columbia University Press, 1994.

Litwak, Robert S. *Détente and the Nixon Doctrine: American Foreign Policy and the Pursuit of Stability, 1969–1976.* Cambridge: Cambridge University Press, 1984.

MacFarlane, Robert C. (with Zofia Smardz). *Special Trust.* New York: Cadell and Davies, 1994.

MacFarquhar, Roderick. *The Origins of the Cultural Revolution,* vols. 1–3. New York: Columbia University Press, 1974, 1983, 1997.

MacFarquhar, Roderick, and John King Fairbank, eds. *The Cambridge History of China Volume 15: The People's Republic Part 2: Revolutions within the Chinese Revolution 1966–1982.* Cambridge: Cambridge University Press, 1991.

Madsen, Richard. *China and the American Dream: A Moral Inquiry.* Stanford, CA: Stanford University Press, 1995.

Madsen, Robert A. "Chinese Chess: US China Policy and Taiwan, 1969–1979." Unpublished D.Phil. thesis, Oxford University, 1998.

Manac'h, Etienne. *Memoires d'Extreme Asie: La Face Cachée du Monde*. Paris: Fayd, 1977.

Mandelbaum, Michael. *The Ideas That Conquered the World: Peace, Democracy and Free Markets in the Twenty-first Century*. New York: Public Affairs, 2002.

Mann, James H. *About Face: A History of America's Curious Relationship with China, from Nixon to Clinton*. New York: Vintage, 1998.

Mao Tse-tung. *Selected Works of Mao Tse-tung*. Peking: Foreign Language Press, 1961.

Marshall, S. L. A. *The River and the Gauntlet*. New York: Harper, 1953.

Mayers, David Allan. "Eisenhower and Communism: Later Findings." In Richard Melanson and David Mayers, eds., *Reevaluating Eisenhower: American Foreign Policy in the 1950s*. Urbana: University of Illinois Press, 1987, pp. 88–119.

Mazo, Earl, and Stephen Hess. *Nixon: A Political Portrait*. New York: Harper and Row, 1968.

McMahon, Robert J. *The Cold War on the Periphery: The United States, India, and Pakistan*. New York: Columbia University Press, 1994.

Milliken, Jennifer. "The Study of Discourse in International Relations: A Critique of Research and Methods." *European Journal of International Relations* 5(2) (June 1999), pp. 225–54.

Morgenthau, Hans. *Politics among Nations*. New York: Knopf, 1948.

Nagai, Yonosuke, and Akira Iriye, eds. *The Origins of the Cold War in Asia*. New York: Columbia University Press, 1977.

Nixon, Richard M. *Leaders*. New York: Warner Books, 1982.

  RN: The Memoirs of Richard Nixon. London: Sidgwick and Jackson, 1978.

  "Asia after Vietnam." *Foreign Affairs* 46(1) (1967), pp. 111–25.

  "Needed in Vietnam: The Will to Win." *Reader's Digest*, August 1964.

Nye, Joseph S., Jr. *Bound to Lead: The Changing Nature of American Power*. New York: Basic Books, 1991.

Ogata, Sadako. *Normalization with China: A Comparative Study of US and Japanese Processes*. Berkeley: University of California Press, 1988.

Onuf, Nicholas G. "Constructivism: A User's Manual." In Vendulka Kubálková, Nicholas G. Onuf, and Paul Kowert, eds. *International Relations in a Constructed World*. London: M. E. Sharpe, 1998, pp. 58–78.

  World of Our Making: Rules and Rule in Social Theory and International Relations. Columbia, SC: University of South Carolina Press, 1989.

Ostermann, Christian, ed. "East German Documents on the Border Conflict." *Cold War International History Project Bulletin* 6–7 (1995/96), pp. 186–93.

Parmet, Herbert S. *Richard Nixon and His America*. Boston: Little, Brown, 1990.

Paterson, Thomas. *Meeting the Communist Threat*. Oxford: Oxford University Press, 1988.

Pearce, Kimber Charles. *Rostow, Kennedy, and the Rhetoric of Foreign Aid*. East Lansing: Michigan State University Press, 2001.

Pelz, Stephen. "Toward a New Diplomatic History: Two and a Half Cheers for International Relations Methods." In Colin Elman and Miriam Fendius

Elman, eds., *Bridges and Boundaries: Historians, Political Scientists, and the Study of International Relations*. Cambridge, MA: MIT Press, 2001, pp. 85–110.

Pettman, Ralph. *Commonsense Constructivism, or the Making of World Affairs*. New York: M. E. Sharpe, 2000.

Pillsbury, Michael. "US-Chinese Military Ties?" *Foreign Affairs* 20 (Fall 1975), pp. 50–64.

Prados, John. *Keeper of the Keys: A History of the National Security Council from Truman to Bush*. New York: Morrow, 1991.

Qing Simei. "The Eisenhower Administration and Changes in Western Embargo Policy against China, 1954–1958." In Warren I. Cohen and Akira Iriye, eds., *The Great Powers in East Asia, 1953–1960*. New York: Columbia University Press, 1990, pp. 121–42.

Roberts, Priscilla, ed. *Window on the Forbidden City: The Beijing Diaries of David Bruce, 1973–1974*. Hong Kong: University of Hong Kong Centre of Asian Studies (Monograph No. 145), 2001.

Robinson, Thomas. "The Sino-Soviet Border Conflict." In Stephen S. Kaplan et al., *Diplomacy of Power: Soviet Armed Forces as a Political Instrument*. Washington, DC: Brookings Institution, 1981, pp. 265–313.

Rosenberg, Emily S. *Spreading the American Dream: American Economic and Cultural Expansion, 1890–1945*. New York: Hill and Wang, 1982.

Ross, Robert S. *Negotiating Cooperation: The United States and China, 1969–1989*. Stanford, CA: Stanford University Press, 1995.

———. "US Policy toward China: The Strategic Context and the Policy-Making Process." In Robert S. Ross, ed., *China, the United States, and the Soviet Union: Tripolarity and Policy Making in the Cold War*. London: M. E. Sharpe, 1993, pp. 149–77.

———. "Conclusion: Tripolarity and Policy Making." In Robert S. Ross, ed., *China, the United States, and the Soviet Union: Tripolarity and Policy Making in the Cold War*. London: M. E. Sharpe, 1993, pp. 179–95.

Ross, Robert S., ed. *China, the United States, and the Soviet Union: Tripolarity and Policy Making in the Cold War*. London: M. E. Sharpe, 1993.

Rostow, Walt Whitman. *The Diffusion of Power: An Essay in Recent History*. New York: Macmillan, 1972.

———. *The Stages of Economic Growth: A Non-Communist Manifesto*. Cambridge: Cambridge University Press, 1960.

Rusk, Dean. *As I Saw It: A Secretary of State's Memoirs* (as told to Richard Rusk). London: I. B. Tauris, 1991.

Safire, William. *Before the Fall: An Inside View of the Pre-Watergate White House*. New York: Doubleday, 1975.

Schaller, Michael. "Détente and the Strategic Triangle: or, 'Drinking Your Mao Tai and Having Your Vodka, Too.'" In Robert S. Ross and Jiang Changbin, eds., *Re-examining the Cold War: US-China Diplomacy, 1954–1973*. Cambridge, MA: Harvard University Press, 2001, pp. 361–89.

Schlesinger, Arthur M., Jr. *A Thousand Days: John F. Kennedy in the White House*. London: Andre Deutsch, 1965.

Schoenbaum, Thomas J. *Waging Peace and War: Dean Rusk in the Truman, Kennedy and Johnson Years*. New York: Simon and Schuster, 1988.

Schroeder, Paul W. "The Nineteenth Century System: Balance of Power or Political Equilibrium?" *Review of International Studies* 15(2) (1987), pp. 135–53.
"History and International Relations Theory: Not Use or Abuse, but Fit or Misfit." *International Security* 22(1), (Summer 1997), pp. 64–74.
Schulzinger, Robert D. "The Johnson Administration, China, and the Vietnam War." In Robert S. Ross and Jiang Changbin, eds., *Re-examining the Cold War: US-China Diplomacy, 1954–1973.* Cambridge, MA: Harvard University Press, 2001, pp. 238–61.
Schurmann, Franz. *The Foreign Politics of Richard Nixon: The Grand Design.* Berkeley: Institute of East Asian Studies, University of California, 1987.
The Logic of World Power: An Inquiry into the Origins, Currents, and Contradictions of World Politics. New York: Pantheon, 1974.
See, Jennifer W. "An Uneasy Truce: John F. Kennedy and Soviet-American Détente, 1963." *Cold War History* 2(2) (January 2002), pp. 161–94.
Sestanovich, Stephen. "US Policy toward the Soviet Union, 1970–1979: The Impact of China." In Robert S. Ross, ed., *China, the United States, and the Soviet Union: Tripolarity and Policy Making in the Cold War.* London: M. E. Sharpe, 1993, pp. 125–47.
Shen, James C. H. (with Robert Myers). *The US and Free China: How the US Sold Out Its Ally.* Washington, DC: Acropolis Books, 1983.
Solomon, Richard H. *Chinese Negotiating Behavior: Pursuing Interests through 'Old Friends.'* Washington, DC: United States Institute of Peace, 1999.
Sorensen, Theodore C. *Kennedy.* London: Hodder and Stoughton, 1965.
Speer, Glenn. "Richard Nixon's Position on Communist China, 1949–1960: The Evolution of a Pacific Strategy." Unpublished Ph.D. dissertation, City University of New York, 1992.
Steele, A. T. *The American People and China.* New York: McGraw-Hill for the Council on Foreign Relations, 1966.
Stevenson, Adlai E. "Putting First Things First: A Democratic View." *Foreign Affairs* 38(1) (January 1960), pp. 191–208.
Sullivan, William M. *Reconstructing Public Philosophy.* Berkeley: University of California Press, 1982.
Sutter, Robert. *China Watch: Toward Sino-American Reconciliation.* Baltimore: Johns Hopkins University Press, 1978.
Tang Tsou. *America's Failure in China, 1941–50.* Chicago: University of Chicago Press, 1963.
Terrill, Ross. *Mao: A Biography.* Sydney: Hale and Iremonger, 1995.
Thomson, James C., Jr., Peter W. Stanley, and John Curtis Perry. *Sentimental Imperialists: The American Experience in East Asia.* New York: Harper and Row, 1981.
"On the Making of China Policy, 1961–9: A Study in Bureaucratic Politics." *China Quarterly* 50 (1972), pp. 220–43.
Tuathail, Gearoid O., and John Agnew. "Geopolitics and Discourse: Practical Geopolitical Reasoning in American Foreign Policy." *Political Geography* 11(2) (1992), pp. 192–3.
Tucker, Nancy Bernkopf. *China Confidential: American Diplomats and Sino-American Relations, 1945–1996.* New York: Columbia University Press, 2001.

Taiwan, Hong Kong, and the United States, 1945–1992. New York: Twayne, 1994.
"Threats, Opportunities and Frustrations in East Asia." In Warren I. Cohen
and Nancy Bernkopf Tucker, eds., *Lyndon Johnson Confronts the World.*
Cambridge: Cambridge University Press, 1994, pp. 99–134.
"John Foster Dulles and the Taiwan Roots of the 'Two Chinas' Policy." In
Richard H. Immerman, ed., *John Foster Dulles and the Diplomacy of the Cold
War.* Princeton, NJ: Princeton University Press, 1990, pp. 235–62.
*Patterns in the Dust: Chinese-American Relations and the Recognition Controversy,
1949–1950.* New York: Columbia University Press, 1983.
Tyler, Patrick. *A Great Wall: Six Presidents and China.* New York: Public Affairs,
1999.
Van Hollen, Christopher. "The Tilt Policy Revisited: Nixon-Kissinger Geopolitics
and South Asia." *Asian Survey* 20 (April 1980), pp. 339–61.
Van Ness, Peter. *Revolution and Chinese Foreign Policy: Peking's Support for Wars of
National Liberation.* Berkeley: University of California Press, 1970.
Waldron, Arthur. "From Nonexistent to Almost Normal: US-China Relations in
the 1960s." In Diane B. Kunz, ed., *The Diplomacy of the Crucial Decade:
American Foreign Relations during the 1960s.* New York: Columbia University
Press, 1994, pp. 219–50.
Walt, Stephen S. *The Origins of Alliances.* Ithaca, NY: Cornell University Press,
1986.
Walters, Vernon A. *Silent Missions.* New York: Doubleday, 1978.
Waltz, Kenneth N. *Theory of International Politics.* New York: McGraw-Hill, 1979.
Wang Bingnan. *Zhongmei Huitan Jiunian Huigu* [Nine Years of Sino-American
Dialogue in Retrospect]. Beijing: Shijie Zhishi Chubanshe, 1985.
Wang Junyan. *Da Waijiaojia Zhou Enlai* [Zhou Enlai: The Great Diplomat]. Beijing:
Jingji Ribao Chubanshe, 1998.
Wedeman, Andrew. *The East Wind Subsides: Chinese Foreign Policy and the Origins of
the Cultural Revolution.* Washington, DC: Washington Institute Press, 1987.
Weldes, Jutta. "Constructing National Interests." *European Journal of International
Relations* 2(3) (1996), pp. 275–318.
Weldes, Jutta, and Diana Saco. "Making State Action Possible: The US and the
Discursive Construction of 'The Cuban Problem', 1960–1994." *Millennium*
25(2) (1996), pp. 361–96.
Wendt, Alexander. *Social Theory of International Politics.* Cambridge: Cambridge
University Press, 1999.
"Anarchy Is What States Make of It: The Social Construction of Power Politics."
International Organization 46(2) (Spring 1992), pp. 391–425.
Westad, Odd Arne, ed. *Brothers in Arms: The Rise and Fall of the Sino-Soviet Al-
liance 1945–1963.* Stanford, CA: Stanford University Press / Washington, DC:
Woodrow Wilson Center Press, 1998.
Westad, Odd Arne, et al., eds. "77 Conversations between Chinese and Foreign
Leaders on the Wars in Indochina, 1964–77" (Cold War International His-
tory Project Working Paper No. 22). Washington, DC: Woodrow Wilson
International Center for Scholars, 1998.
White, Theodore H. *The Making of the President 1968.* London: Jonathan Cape,
1969.

Whiting, Allen S. "Sino-American Détente." *China Quarterly* 82 (1980), pp. 334–41.
   The Chinese Calculus of Deterrence: India and Indochina. Ann Arbor: University of Michigan Press, 1975.
   China Crosses the Yalu: The Decision to Enter the Korean War. Stanford, CA: Stanford University Press, 1960.
Wilson, Dick. *Chou: The Story of Zhou Enlai.* London: Hutchinson, 1984.
Woods, Ngaire, ed. *Explaining International Relations Since 1945.* Oxford: Oxford University Press, 1996.
Yahuda, Michael. *The International Politics of the Asia-Pacific, 1945–1995.* London: Routledge, 1996.
Yang Kuisong. "The Sino-Soviet Border Clash of 1969: From Zhenbao Island to Sino-American Rapprochement." *Cold War History* 1(1) (2000), pp. 21–52.
   "Changes in Mao Zedong's Attitude toward the Indochina War, 1949–1973." Cold War International History Project Working Paper No. 34. Washington, DC: Woodrow Wilson International Center for Scholars, n.d.
Yergin, Daniel. *Shattered Peace: The Origins of the Cold War and the National Security State.* London: Andre Deutsch, 1978.
Young, Kenneth T. *Negotiating with the Chinese Communists: The United States Experience, 1953–1967.* New York: McGraw-Hill, 1968.
Zhai Qiang. *China and the Vietnam Wars, 1950–1975.* Chapel Hill: University of North Carolina Press, 2000.
   "China and America: A Troubled Relationship." *Journal of American-East Asian Relations* 7(1–2) (Spring/Summer 1998), pp. 93–100.
Zhang Baijia. "The Changing International Scene and Chinese Policy towards the United States, 1965–1970." In Robert S. Ross and Jiang Changbin, eds., *Reexamining the Cold War: US-China Diplomacy, 1954–1973.* Cambridge, MA: Harvard University Press, 2001, pp. 46–76.
Zhang Baijia and Jia Qingguo. "Steering Wheel, Shock Absorber, and Diplomatic Probe in Confrontation: Sino American Ambassadorial Talks Seen from the Chinese Perspective." In Robert S. Ross and Jiang Changbin, eds., *Reexamining the Cold War: US-China Diplomacy, 1954–1973.* Cambridge, MA: Harvard University Press, 2001, pp. 173–99.
Zhang Shu Guang. *Deterrence and Strategic Culture: Chinese-American Confrontations, 1949–1958.* Ithaca, NY: Cornell University Press, 1992.
   Economic Cold War: America's Embargo against China and the Sino-Soviet Alliance, 1949–1963. Washington, DC: Woodrow Wilson Center Press and Stanford, CA: Stanford University Press, 2001.

Dramatis Personae

Aldrich, George H.
1969–1977: Deputy Legal Adviser, Department of State

Armstrong, Oscar Vance
October 1969–May 1971: Deputy Chief of Mission, Taipei

Ball, George W.
February–December 1961: Undersecretary of State for Economic Affairs
January 1962–September 1966: Undersecretary of State
June–September 1968: Representative to the United Nations

Barnett, Robert W.
February 1963–May 1970: Deputy Assistant Secretary for Far Eastern Economic Affairs, Bureau of East Asian and Pacific Affairs

Beam, Jacob D.
January–November 1961: Ambassador to Poland and U.S. representative at ambassadorial talks with PRC
March 1969–January 1973: Ambassador to the Soviet Union

Bowles, Chester A.
January–December 1961: Undersecretary of State
December 1961–June 1963: President's Special Representative and Adviser on African, Asian, and Latin American Affairs and Ambassador-at-Large
July 1963–April 1969: Ambassador to India

Brown, Winthrop G.
May 1968–April 1972: Deputy Assistant Secretary of State for East Asian and Pacific Affairs

Bruce, David K. E.
February 1961–March 1969: Ambassador to the United Kingdom
May 1973–August 1974: Chief of Liaison Office, Beijing

Bundy, McGeorge
January 1961–February 1966: Special Assistant to the President for National Security Affairs
June–August 1967: Executive Secretary of the Special Committee of the National Security Council

Bundy, William P.
January 1961–November 1963: Deputy Assistant Secretary of Defense for International Security Affairs
December 1963–February 1964: Assistant Secretary of Defense for International Security Affairs
March 1964–May 1969: Assistant Secretary of State for East Asian and Pacific Affairs

Bush, George H. W.
February 1971–January 1973: Representative to the United Nations
October 1974–November 1975: Chief of Liaison Office, Beijing

Cabot, John M.
March 1962–September 1965: Ambassador to Poland and U.S. representative at ambassadorial talks with PRC

Ceaușescu, Nicolae
1967–1989: President of Romania

Chapin, Dwight
1969–1971: Special Assistant to the President
1971–1973: Deputy Assistant to the President

Chen Yi (Marshal)
1958–1972: Foreign Minister, PRC

Chiang Ching-kuo
1965–1969: Minister of Defense, ROC
1969–1972: Vice Premier of the Executive Yuan, ROC
1972-January 1978: Premier, ROC
1978–1988: President, ROC

Chiang Kai-shek
March 1950–April 1975: President, ROC

Cleveland, J. Harlan
February 1961–September 1965: Assistant Secretary of State for International Organization Affairs

Cline, Ray S.
July 1962–January 1966: Deputy Director for Intelligence, Central Intelligence Agency
October 1969–November 1973: Director, Office of Intelligence and Research

de Gaulle, Charles
January 1959–April 1969: President of France

Deng Xiaoping
1973–1976: Vice Premier, PRC

Denney, George C., Jr.
April 1963–November 1973: Deputy Director, INR

De Palma, Samuel
February 1969–June 1973: Assistant Secretary of State for International Organizational Affairs

Dobrynin, Anatoly Fedorovich
1962–1986: Soviet Ambassador to the United States

Ehrlichman, John D.
January–November 1969: Counsel to the President
November 1969–May 1973: Assistant to the President for Domestic Affairs

Eliot, Theodore L., Jr.
August 1969–September 1973: Special Assistant to the Secretary and Executive Secretary of the Department of State

Freeman, Charles W., Jr.
June 1971–July 1973: Office of Asian Communist Affairs, EA

Ford, Gerald R.
1965–1973: House Minority Leader
October 1973–August 1974: Vice President
8 August 1974–20 January 1977: President

Fulbright, J. William
1959–1974: Chairman of the Senate Foreign Relations Committee

Galbraith, John Kenneth
April 1961–July 1963: Ambassador to India

Gandhi, Indira
1966–1977: Prime Minister of India

Gleysteen, William H., Jr.
September 1969–June 1971: Director, Office of Research and Analysis for East Asia and the Pacific, INR
June 1971–1974: Deputy Chief of Mission, Taipei

Goldberg, Arthur J.
July 1965–June 1968: Ambassador to the United Nations

Grant, Lindsey
February 1969–August 1970: Bureau of East Asian and Pacific Affairs, detailed to NSC

Green, Marshall
December 1961–September 1963: Consul General, Hong Kong
October 1963–June 1965: Deputy Assistant Secretary of State for East Asian and Pacific Affairs
May 1969–May 1973: Assistant Secretary of State for East Asian and Pacific Affairs

Gronouski, John A.
December 1965–May 1968: Ambassador to Poland

Haig, Alexander Meigs, Jr. (Colonel)
June 1969–June 1970: Senior Military Assistant to the President's Assistant for National Security Affairs
June 1970–January 1973: Deputy Assistant to the President for National Security Affairs
August 1973–August 1974: Assistant to the President and Chief of Staff

Haldeman, H. R.
January 1969–April 1973: Assistant to the President and Chief of Staff

Harlow, Bryce N.
1969–1970: Assistant to the President for Congressional Relations
1970–1974: Counselor to the President

Harriman, W. Averell
February–November 1961: Ambassador-at-Large
December 1961–April 1963: Assistant Secretary of State for Far Eastern Affairs
May 1963–March 1965: Assistant Secretary of State for Political Affairs
April 1965–1968: Ambassador-at-Large

Heath, Edward
June 1970–March 1974: British Prime Minister

Helms, Richard M.
June 1966–February 1973: Director of Central Intelligence

Hilsman, Roger, Jr.
February 1961–April 1963: Director of the Bureau of Intelligence and Research, Department of State
May 1963–March 1964: Assistant Secretary of State for Far Eastern Affairs

Holdridge, John H.
April 1968–July 1969: Director, Office of Research and Analysis for East Asia and the Pacific, INR
July 1969–April 1973: NSC staff member (East Asia)
May 1973–1974: Deputy Chief, Liaison Office, Beijing

Howe, Jonathan (Lt. Cmdr.)
1970–1972: NSC staff member

Huang Hua
November 1971–1975: Vice Chairman of the PRC delegation to the UNGA and Chief Delegate to the Security Council

Huang Zhen
April 1964–March 1973: Ambassador to France, PRC
May 1973–December 1977: Chief, PRC Liaison Office in New York

Hughes, Thomas L.
April 1963–August 1969: Director, INR

Hummel, Arthur W., Jr.
August 1965–November 1967: Deputy Chief of Mission, Taipei
February 1972–May 1973: Deputy Assistant Secretary of State for East Asian and Pacific Affairs
1973–1975: Acting Assistant Secretary of State for East Asian and Pacific Affairs

Humphrey, Hubert H.
January 1965–December 1968: Vice President

Hyland, William G.
1970–1072: NSC staff member (Europe)

Iklé, Fred
January 1973–1977: Director of U.S. Arms Control and Disarmament Agency

Jenkins, Alfred LeSesne
July 1966–1969: NSC staff member
July 1970–February 1973: Director, Office of Asian Communist Affairs, EA

Ji Pengfei
January 1955–April 1971: Vice Minister for Foreign Affairs, PRC
February 1972–November 1974: Foreign Minister, PRC

Johnson, Lyndon B.
January 1961–November 1963: Vice President
November 1963–December 1968: President

Johnson, U. Alexis
April 1961–July 1964, November 1965–October 1966: Deputy
Undersecretary of State for Political Affairs
November 1966–1968: Ambassador to Japan
February 1969–February 1973: Undersecretary of State for Political
Affairs

Judd, Walter
1943–1963: Republican Congressman from Minnesota

Katzenbach, Nicholas deB.
October 1966–December 1968: Undersecretary of State

Kennedy, John F.
January 1961–22 November 1963: President

Khan, Agha Muhammad Yahya
March 1969–December 1971: President of Pakistan

Kissinger, Henry A.
January 1969–November 1975: Assistant to the President for National
Security Affairs
September 1973–January 1977: Secretary of State

Klein, Herbert G.
January 1969–July 1973: White House Director of Communications

Komer, Robert W.
January 1961–September 1965: NSC staff member
October 1965–March 1966: Deputy Special Assistant to the President for
National Security Affairs
March 1966–May 1967: Special Assistant to the President
June 1967–December 1968: Special Assistant to the President for Peaceful
Reconstruction in Vietnam

Kreisberg, Paul H.
March 1969–July 1971: Director, Asia Communist Affairs, EA

Laird, Melvin R.
January 1969–January 1973: Secretary of Defense

Lord, Winston
1967–1969: Office of International Security Affairs, Department of Defense
1969–April 1973: NSC staff member
October 1973–1977: Director, Policy Planning Council

Mansfield, Michael
1961–1976: Senate Majority Leader

Mao Zedong
1949–1976: Chairman of the Central Committee of the Chinese Communist Party

McConaughy, Walter, P., Jr.
June 1966–April 1974: Ambassador to the ROC

McCone, John A.
November 1961–April 1965: Director of Central Intelligence

McNamara, Robert S.
January 1961–February 1968: Secretary of Defense

Meany, George
1955–1979: President of the American Federation of Labor–Congress of Industrial Organizations (AFL-CIO)

Moser, Leo J.
June 1967–August 1971: Political Officer, Taipei
August 1971–June 1973: Country Director for ROC, EA

Moyers, Bill D.
1964–1967: Special Assistant to the President

Nixon, Richard M.
January 1969–8 August 1974: President

Osborn, David Lawrence
August 1970–March 1974: Consul General, Hong Kong

Pompidou, Georges
June 1969–April 1974: President of France

Popple, Paul M.
June 1962–July 1964: Officer in Charge of ROC Affairs, EA

Qiao Guanhua
April 1964–November 1974: Vice Foreign Minister, PRC

Reischauer, Edwin O.
April 1961–September 1966: Ambassador to Japan

Rice, Edward E.
1961: staff member, Policy Planning Council
January 1962–December 1963: Deputy Assistant Secretary of State for Far Eastern Affairs
January 1964–September 1967: Consul General in Hong Kong and Macau

Richardson, Elliot L.
January 1969–June 1970: Undersecretary of State

Rodman, Peter W.
1970–1972: NSC staff member

Rogers, William P.
January 1969–September 1973: Secretary of State

Rostow, Walt W.
January–December 1961: Deputy Special Assistant to the President for National Security Affairs
January 1962–March 1966: Counselor of the Department of State and Chairman of the Policy Planning Council
April 1966–December 1968: Special Assistant to the President

Rusk, Dean
January 1961–January 1969: Secretary of State

Sato, Eisaku
November 1964–July 1972: Prime Minister of Japan

Scali, John
1971–1973: Special Consultant to the President

Schlesinger, Arthur M.
January 1961–1963: Special Assistant to the President

Schlesinger, James R.
February–July 1973: Director of Central Intelligence
July 1973–November 1975: Secretary of Defense

Scowcroft, Brent (Lt. Gen.)
1972–1973: Military Assistant to the President
1973–1975: Deputy Assistant to the President for National Security Affairs

Shen, James C. H.
May 1971–January 1979: ROC Ambassador to the United States

Shoesmith, Thomas P.
October 1967–August 1971: Country Director for ROC, EA

Sihanouk, Prince Norodom
1960–1970: Head of State of Cambodia
1970–1975: Leader of government-in-exile in Beijing

Sisco, Joseph J.
September 1965–February 1969: Assistant Secretary of State for International Organizational Affairs
February 1969–February 1974: Assistant Secretary of State for Near Eastern and South Asian Affairs

Solomon, Richard H.
1971–1976: NSC staff member (East Asia)

Sonnenfeldt, Helmut
1969–1974: NSC staff member (Europe)

Stevenson, Adlai E.
January 1961–July 1965: Ambassador to the United Nations

Stevenson, John R.
July 1969–January 1973: Legal Adviser, Department of State

Stoessel, Walter J.
July 1968–August 1972: Ambassador to Poland and U.S. representative at ambassadorial talks with PRC

Thant, U
1961–1971: Secretary-General of the UN

Thompson, Llewellyn E.
October 1962–December 1966: Ambassador-at-Large

Thomson, James C., Jr.
April–December 1961: Special Assistant to the Undersecretary of State
December 1961–June 1963: Special Assistant to the President's Special Representative and Adviser on African, Asian, and Latin American Affairs
August 1963–July 1964: Special Assistant to the Assistant Secretary of State for Far Eastern Affairs
July 1964–September 1966: NSC staff member

Unger, Leonard
July 1974–1979: Ambassador to the ROC

Valenti, Jack
January 1964–May 1966: Special Assistant to the President

Walters, Vernon A. (Lt. Gen.)
August 1967–March 1972: Military Attaché to Paris
May 1972–July 1976: Deputy Director of Central Intelligence

Ye Jianying (Marshal)
1969–1986: Vice Chairman, Military Council of the CCP Central
Committee
1966–76: Member of Central Committee and Politburo

Yost, Charles W.
January 1969–February 1971: Representative to the United Nations

Zhou Enlai
October 1949–January 1976: Premier, PRC

Index

Lightning Source UK Ltd.
Milton Keynes UK
UKOW02f0733231116
288249UK00001B/106/P